The Human Services Internship Experience

For Phil and Clyde

The Human Services Internship Experience

Helping Students Find Their Way

Marianne Woodside
The University of Tennessee

Los Angeles | London | New Delhi
Singapore | Washington DC | Melbourne

FOR INFORMATION:

SAGE Publications, Inc.
2455 Teller Road
Thousand Oaks, California 91320
E-mail: order@sagepub.com

SAGE Publications Ltd.
1 Oliver's Yard
55 City Road
London, EC1Y 1SP
United Kingdom

SAGE Publications India Pvt. Ltd.
B 1/I 1 Mohan Cooperative Industrial Area
Mathura Road, New Delhi 110 044
India

SAGE Publications Asia-Pacific Pte. Ltd.
3 Church Street
#10-04 Samsung Hub
Singapore 049483

Acquisitions Editor: Nathan Davidson
Editorial Assistant: Carrie Montoya
eLearning Editor: Lucy Berbeo
Production Editor: Kelly DeRosa
Copy Editor: Maggie McGurk-Kramer
Typesetter: Hurix Systems Pvt. Ltd.
Proofreader: Dennis Webb
Indexer: Mary Mortensen
Cover Designer: Michael Dubowe
Marketing Manager: Shari Countryman

Printed in the United States of America.

Library of Congress Cataloging-in-Publication Data

Names: Woodside, Marianne, author.

Title: The human services internship experience : helping students find their way / Marianne Woodside, The University of Tennessee.

Description: Los Angeles : SAGE, 2016. | Includes bibliographical references and index.

Identifiers: LCCN 2015040088 | ISBN 9781483377841 (pbk. : alk. paper)

Subjects: LCSH: Social work education. | Internship programs. | Social workers—Training of.

Classification: LCC HV11 .W7175 2016 | DDC 361.0071/55—dc23 LC record available at http://lccn.loc.gov/2015040088

This book is printed on acid-free paper.

16 17 18 19 20 10 9 8 7 6 5 4 3 2 1

Brief Contents

Detailed Contents

List of Exercises, Boxes, Tables, and Figures

Exercises

Boxes

Preface

The purpose of this textbook is to help you, the human service student enrolled in internship, bridge the theories and knowledge of human service delivery with its actual practice. Hopefully, the text will assist faculty as they guide their students through the internship process. And we believe that students will benefit from and feel supported by the text as they engage in their internship experiences. To meet these goals, we present this text, *The Human Service Internship Experience: Helping Students Find Their Way*. It is intended to be both a text and a workbook. This hybrid approach to learning during internship is guided by our teaching philosophy, that of striking a balance between an academic approach to learning with experience in a human service setting and self-reflection.

The inspiration for the text comes from over 40 years of experience teaching internship in human services and counseling. The content and approach illustrate what my students and I, over some 40 years, have learned from each other about internship. The text is filled with voices of students at differing stages of the internship process and from various parts of the country. It also includes messages from practicing professionals: a human service faculty member, a site supervisor, and a human service professional. Each of these speak to you to both share their experiences and support you during internship.

We know that an internship as a field-based experience is a powerful learning tool in human services, as in many other professions. This text assumes that internship is both a time students can fully apply their academic work in a real-world setting. It is also a time when students can confirm and expand their identity as human service professionals.

Internship is a time when various dichotomies pervade the lives of interns. For example, prior to and at the beginning of internship, interns feel anxiety as they anticipate working with clients and contributing to an agency. This anxiety is in direct contrast to their growing excitement about being able to actually practice their knowledge and skills in helping others. A second example has to do with how interns view clients. Early in the internship, interns may see their clients in simple ways and develop small interventions. Later, as their confidence grows and their skills increase, the issues may appear more complex than first thought, while the interventions may have contributed to small change, if any. A third dichotomy in their experience may appear during supervision. Effective supervision requires feedback, both positive and critical. While positive feedback confirms the intern's skill and progress, critical feedback is often less easy to receive and can shake an intern's confidence, if only initially.

We present you with these three example dichotomies of the highs and lows of internship as a way of emphasizing the importance of the approach to learning that we take in this text. We hope to create a supportive environment in which you can develop your skills as a human service professional. Internship is both exciting and challenging. And, in this text, we are with you during this experience! We developed the goals of this text to meet your own needs as an intern, as well as the needs of your faculty supervisor and your site supervisor.

GOALS

This text focuses on your internship experience. We provide a text to support you in your journey to become a competent and successful human service professional. Because we view this journey as a developmental process, our overall goal is to guide you through it. Further, we support the growth of your identity as a human service professional. Also, we help you integrate academic work with your real-world experience at your internship site. Part of this process involves your own self-reflection as you work with clients and your colleagues in your internship site. Lastly, we provide testimonies and accounts of experiences of several kinds of human service students and providers as they remember and reflect on their on professional development.

This text is divided into four parts so you can gain a clearer understanding of the developmental nature of your own professional growth. The 11 chapters of the text directly describe what you need to consider during each stage of your development.

Part One, *Introduction to the Internship Experience*, includes four chapters. Each chapter is intended to provide you insights about the internship experience and how you can successfully plan for and begin it effectively. In Chapter One, we introduce you to various aspects of the internship experience, by defining relevant terms, describing professional definitions of internships, and helping you locate and understand the ways in which your own program defines and understands what an internship is supposed to be. We emphasize the concept of collaboration as of special significance. In Chapter Two, we help you assess your readiness for internship. We introduce the core characteristics of the internship experience and ask you to reflect on your readiness to engage these. We also introduce you to a developmental model of professional growth that will help understand your own professional development. Chapter Three focuses on setting up your internship. It suggests practical guidelines for developing an internship site and describes essential steps such as filling out an internship application and preparing for and making your initial visit to your internship site. Finally, in Chapter Four you learn about the expectations of your first week or two at the internship site.

Part Two, *Involving Yourself in Human Service Work*, addresses various aspects of the work that you will encounter in internship. For example, in Chapters Five and Six, you explore the nature of ethical practice, develop a model of ethical decision making, and consider various issues that may arise while you are an intern. At the conclusion of these two chapters, we hope that you will be able to identify ethical issues that occur and, with consultation, address them by using professional codes of ethics, legal statutes, agency rules and regulations, and a model of ethical decision making. Chapter Seven introduces the concept of a multicultural perspective for your internship work with your clients and in your agency. We help you understand the principles and circumstances that underlie the need for a multicultural perspective. We help you identify the nature of your own culture, the culture of your clients and their environments. In Chapter Eight, we introduce and describe in detail the two important relationships you must establish and sustain during your internship, those with your site supervisor and your faculty supervisor. We define supervision and describe its purposes. After introducing a model of the supervisory relationship, we discuss the evaluation process in internship and then present an Intern Bill of Rights. The Bill of Rights details both the expectations you should have for supervision as well as the responsibilities you are expected to assume.

By the time you begin Part Three, *Expanding Your Skills*, we help you further develop your professional knowledge and skills. By the middle of your internship, you are already building on the basic helping skills you learned in your academic program and have been using during the first part of internship. During your study of Chapter Nine, "Working With Clients," we introduce you to the concept and practice of culture-centered helping. We illustrate the ways that you can use culture-centered helping within the framework of the helping process. An understanding of culture-centered helping builds on the focus of the concept of a multicultural perspective described in Chapter Seven. Then we ask you to consider integrating a strengths approach in your work with clients. In Chapter Ten, in order to help you view your clients in more complex ways, we introduce you to the concept of case conceptualization and then provide a guide for constructing a case conceptualization. We also help you construct a case study of a client. Finally, in this chapter, we provide tips for documentation and report writing.

The final part, Part Four, is *Concluding Your Internship*. Chapter Eleven of the same name helps you end your internship experience in a positive way. We help you plan ending your work at your internship site, with your site supervisor, other site staff, and clients, and with your academic program. We stress the importance of planning your leave-taking, both for your personal and professional growth. In this chapter, we also introduce two activities directly linked to internship that will support you as you look for employment in the human service sector. We help you begin or continue building a professional portfolio and then provide guidelines for asking for references.

FEATURES

This text, *The Human Service Internship Experience: Helping Students Find Their Way* includes many features designed to provide support for you in your internship work, challenge you to grow professionally, and develop new insights about yourself, your clients, and others with whom your work. We want these features to help you link what you learned and are learning in your academic work to your work in the real-world. Finally, we hope these features help you find ways you can support and challenge yourself well beyond the internship experience.

The Internship as a Developmental Process—We believe that learning to be a human service professional is a developmental process, one that ideally never ends. We organized the text around the four stages of professional development that occur during internship. These stages include beginning the internship, participating in human service work, expanding your knowledge and skills, and concluding your internship. Adding to your knowledge of professional development, we also introduce the Integrated Developmental Model (IDM) in Chapter Two. This model helps you understand your own development in terms of autonomy, motivation, and self- and other-awareness.

Deepening Your Knowledge—This final section of each chapter adds the voices of human service interns, faculty and site supervisors, and a human service professional to your internship experience.

The Presence of Student Voices—At the conclusion of each chapter Alicia, Lucas, and Tamika, all three human service interns, describe their experiences during internship, recount some of the challenges they encounter, and discuss their personal and professional growth and development. Hearing from these three students provides you with insight into internship experiences beyond your own. We hope that the three human service students can serve as a guide for you and help normalize your work at you internship site.

The Presence of Supervisor Voices—Dr. Claude Bianca, a faculty supervisor, and Ms. Bellewa, a site supervisor, write about their supervision experiences. These two individuals provide you with a perspective that differs from an intern's view of internship. We hope seeing these two alternate viewpoints can expand your understanding of both your academic program and site supervision, especially as they relate to internship.

The Presence of a Human Service Professional Voice—Gwen, a human service professional provides practical insights into the work of human service delivery. She covers timely topics such as how to collaborate at the work site, use social media in a work setting, develop a professional identity, and work with clients using culture-centered helping.

A Focus on Self-Reflection and Application—There are numerous exercises in each chapter that help you engage in the text material and integrate it with your actual day-to-day experiences. In some instances, the exercises ask you to make plans, indicate how you would use guidelines suggested, use the models presented in this text to develop a clearer understanding of a specific aspect of your internship, or to develop materials to share with your supervisors or peers. In each chapter, there are exercises entitled "Writing Your Own Story". The 32 entries of "Writing Your Own Story" are targeted opportunities for you to record or journal about your experiences.

Vignettes and Case Examples—Each chapter includes multiple vignettes and case examples to illustrate the concepts introduced. We introduce several students who give critical accounts of their experiences. Sue, a human service intern from Oklahoma, works in a homeless shelter. Tomas, also a human service intern, works in a drug and alcohol treatment facility in New York City. A small section titled "What Students Say" includes various thoughts and reflections by Steve, Maria, Al, and Shasha about topics that range from ethics and supervision to helping and culture.

<u>An Emphasis on Ethical and Multicultural Perspectives of Helping</u>— We include three chapters that emphasize integrating both ethical and multicultural perspectives during internship. Chapters Five and Six present you, as an intern, with background information about developing an ethical perspective and then addressing ethical issues specifically related to your work as an intern. Chapter Seven confirms the importance of developing a multicultural perspective working with clients and working in an agency setting. In addition, Chapter Nine introduces a model of culture-centered helping that integrates the multicultural focus with the helping process. As with all chapters, there are vignettes, case examples, illustrations, and exercises that hopefully help you become aware of even more ways to work with clients and agency staff.

<u>An Emphasis on Illustrations</u>—Throughout the text are boxes, figures, and tables that help illustrate the concepts presented and provide structure for thinking through the concepts and applying them to the internship experience.

<u>Intern Learning Support</u>—Each chapter focuses on another dimension or aspect of human service work and practice. Chapters begin with a list of learning goals. The readers will find exercises throughout suggesting ways to apply the knowledge presented in the text to the internship experience. At the conclusion of each chapter, there are a list of terms to remember and a reference list of helpful sources.

CONCLUSION

We developed *The Human Service Internship Experience: Helping Students Find Their Way* as a way to empower faculty and interns alike during the internship. Participating in a human service internship is an exciting and challenging endeavor. As you read the text and engage in the workbook components of the text, we hope you can enhance your growth and development as a human service professional. Our aim is for your experience with the text to help you transition from an intern to a human service professional.

Acknowledgments

My husband, Phil, served as a daily sounding board and editor for the text. His philosophy training and his unending curiosity provided me with both expertise and support through the writing of the text.

Numerous people supported the work on this book. My students, Allie Rhinehardt, Jorge Roman, Brittany Pollard, Dareen Basma, and Gwen Ruttencutter all spent countless hours sharing their wisdom and experience in the section "Deepening Your Understanding". These sections, in every chapter, allow you to see clearer the realities of human service internships. I thank them for their time, energy, and insights. Gwen Ruttencutter also created most of the figures for the text. Several of my friends from elementary school, Betty, Suzie, Sarah, and Stacey shared insights about the workplace, especially when transitioning to a new setting.

Special inspiration came from my spring 2014 and 2015 classes of interns! These interns were amazing. As they traversed the internship journey, they shared their experiences, readily asked for help, and accepted supervision and guidance. Finally, they gave me confidence in the book's content and approach. SAGE Publications and the author would like to thank the following reviewers for their contributions:

Barbara Carl, Pennsylvania State University, Capital College

Michael D. Collins, William Penn University

Michael D. Reiter, Nova Southeastern University

Susan Eidson Claxton, Georgia Highlands College

Chris M. Lucas, Bradley University

DeAnna Henderson, Alabama State University

Fred L. Hall, Mississippi College

Mary Olufunmilayo Adekson, St. Bonaventure University

Richard S. Takacs, Carlow University

Ronica Arnold Branson, Jackson State University

Terence Patterson, University of San Francisco

Wendy Eckenrod-Green, Radford University

Karen Roberts, Kansas State University

Mary Handley, Cazenovia College

Patricia A. Joseph, Lincoln University

About the Author

Marianne Woodside has been a faculty member in human services and counseling programs for over 40 years. As a human service educator, she has taught a variety of courses including Introduction to Human Services, Methods and Service Delivery, Case Management, Mental Health Across the Lifespan, and Assessment and Planning. She has also taught courses related to teaching and supervising in the helping professions. Her favorite area of focus is always working with students in practicum and internships. As coordinator of field-based experiences she has experience establishing placements, supervising site supervisors and students, and providing support to interns in class as well as in the field. Marianne also has coauthored nine texts in the human services and published over 50 research and applied journal articles. Working with students is always a highlight.

Marianne is married to Phil and has three adult children, Michael, Cathy, and Donna Lee, six grandchildren, and one small dog. She loves the outdoors and celebrates it through hiking and photography. She also seeks ways to play music and spend time with her family and friends.

PART I

Introduction to the Internship Experience

1

Defining the Internship

Reading this chapter will help you do the following:

- List the purposes of this textbook, *The Human Service Internship Experience: Helping Students Find Their Way*.
- Describe the primary participants in the human service internship experience.
- Define the terms that relate to the internship.
- Describe the context of the internship from the perspectives of three human service-focused professional organizations.
- Describe the internship experience for the human service academic program's description, program handbook and course description, and faculty-developed syllabus.
- Define the term *collaboration*.

- Outline the ways collaboration enhances professional growth and development.
- Learn about the motivations of *Alicia, Lucas,* and *Tamika,* to study human services.
- Learn about the faculty and site supervisors' perspectives about human service internship experiences.
- Describe the tips that Gwen provides for collaboration in human service professional practice.

Welcome and Introduction

Welcome to the world of human services and, specifically, the **internship experience!** Preparing for and beginning this experience marks an important point in your journey toward becoming a human service professional. By now, you have completed much of your coursework and you are ready to assume, under **supervision,** responsibilities within a human service organization or agency setting. This textbook assists you as an **intern** to (a) develop a strong professional identity; (b) work within an agency environment; (c) use ethical and multicultural perspectives in human service delivery; (d) use supervision effectively; (e) develop your knowledge, skills, and values to effectively perform the multiple roles of the human service professional; (f) successfully conclude your internship; and (g) transition from intern to human service professional.

The primary purpose of this chapter, Chapter 1, helps you understand the internship and your place in it. We begin this chapter with a brief introduction to three of your peers, Alicia, Lucas, and Tamika. These three students are studying to become human service professionals, and more important, they are getting ready to begin their internship experiences. Throughout this text, they will serve as one of the many guides you will have during internship. After your brief introduction to Alicia, Lucas, and Tamika, we present to you the primary perspectives in the internship experience. First, we introduce the participants in the internship, and then we define the common terms you will encounter as an intern. Next, we provide other perspectives of the internship, including how professional organization and human service programs describe it. In addition we look at academic program documents such as the human services program handbook or the **internship handbook,** the **course description,** and a course syllabus that detail what the specific intern experience should be. Each of these sources of information helps you identify the goals and functions of the internship. We then explore the collaborative nature of human services and the internship learning environment. As we discuss the importance of **collaboration,** we also introduce Sue, an internship student, and describe her experiences related to collaboration.

At the conclusion of the chapter, you meet Alicia, Lucas, and Tamika again. They share with you thoughts about their motivation to study human services and their personal readiness for the experience. You also meet Dr. Bianca, a human service faculty member, and Ms. Bellewa, a **site supervisor.** We end the chapter by introducing Gwen, a human service professional who will share with you tips on how to collaborate in your internship setting.

Now let's meet Alicia, Lucas, and Tamika.

Meeting Alicia, Lucas, and Tamika

As we stated earlier, Alicia, Lucas, and Tamika are also human service students beginning their internship experiences. We asked them to briefly introduce themselves by providing information about their family backgrounds.

©iStockphoto.com/Sylverarts

Alicia

Hello! My name is Alicia, and I am the single mother of a little boy called Thomas. I am excited to share my story with you. I am going to begin with a brief introduction and then later in the chapter, I will tell you more about myself, and my motivation to study human services. I was born and raised in a small town in Colorado, called Glenwood Springs. My family is of English and German descent. I was raised in a rather large family. My family is core of who I am and how I relate to the world; they are foundational to many of my choices and experiences and have influenced the way I come to view and understand life.

I was raised by my mother and stepfather, who married when I was very young. I am the youngest of five siblings. Both my parents worked long and hard hours in order to support my siblings and me, providing us with everything we needed. Although my stepbrother and stepsister primarily lived with their mother, they were regularly included in the family life my brother, sister, and I experienced. My parents raised my siblings and me with values that were woven into our everyday lives.

Written by Allie Rhinehart and Dareen Basma, 2015. Used with permission.

©iStockphoto.com/Sylverarts

Lucas

Hello! I hope you are having a blessed day! My name is Lucas, and I want to give you an overview of who I am and a little of my background such as where I came from. I am a Hispanic male, or to be more specific, I am a Puerto Rican. I have an older stepbrother and stepsister and a younger brother. In my family system, I am a first-generation college student because my parents and siblings neither attended a university nor obtained a degree beyond high school. Even though my parents lacked an advanced education, they taught my siblings and me the principles of Christian beliefs as a method of teaching and education.

Written by Jorge Roman, 2015. Used with permission.

©iStockphoto.com/Sylverarts

Tamika

Hi there! It's nice to meet you! My name is Tamika, and I would like to take this opportunity to introduce myself. I am African American and come from a very small family; I am an only child and my parents divorced when I was 9 years old. I come from an interesting family system; my parents remained best friends after splitting up, and so my nuclear family is still intact in its own unique way. I am extremely close to both of my parents, and they have been among my greatest supporters!

I have lived in several places throughout my life, which I think has contributed to my value of independence and my desire to experience new cultures. Here in the U.S., I have lived in Illinois, Arkansas, Michigan, New York, and now Tennessee. For several months during my junior year of college, I studied abroad in London, which was a fabulous multicultural experience! I spent most of my childhood in a small town in western Michigan, which is where I call home. My family lived about 15 minutes from Lake Michigan, which was great in the summer, but not so pleasant in the winter!

As I mentioned, I have a great relationship with each of my parents and have been close to them all of my life. I think that, as an only child, I spent more time with my parents than most kids do, and I grew up valuing their opinions above those of most other people I encountered. As a result, I was probably somewhat sheltered, but I also think it contributed greatly to my ability to withstand peer pressure. I never felt much of a need to conform to my peers or to base my self-worth on their opinions, which has allowed me to maintain a fairly healthy self-image (most of the time, anyway; I am still human, after all).

Written by Brittany Pollard, 2015. Used with permission.

Alicia, Lucas, and Tamika shared information about their families; this is an important consideration for how we think about others and how we help them. It is also one of the reasons that the human service internship is a different experience for each student enrolled. In this text, you will write a story about your internship that is uniquely yours. In Exercise 1.1, you can begin this story by writing about yourself, a brief summary of who you are. You can use the summaries written by Alicia, Lucas, and Tamika as models.

Exercise 1.1 A Brief Description of You: Writing Your Own Story, Entry 1

You just read short summaries about Alicia, Lucas, and Tamika. Now it is your turn!

Step 1

Provide basic information about yourself, including your name, age, gender, nationality, and ethnicity and family.

Step 2

Begin to describe how each of these demographics helps define who you are.

Now it is time to think about the world of the human service internship. We begin by describing the primary perspectives of the internship. Box 1.1 describes the organizational framework of this next section.

Box 1.1 Studying the Text: Primary Perspectives of the Internship

Studying the Text: The following outline will help you read and study the text material in this next section.

Primary Perspectives of the Internship

1. Participants in internship
2. Important terms and definitions
   a. Internship experience
   b. Intern
   c. Placement or internship site
   d. Faculty supervisor
   e. Site supervisor
   f. Supervision
   g. Midterm evaluation
   h. Final evaluation
3. Defining the internship
   a. Perspectives of professional organizations
   b. Human service program descriptions
   c. Course description
   d. Internship syllabus

Primary Perspectives of the Internship Experience

The perspectives of the internship experience reflect its many participants: students, faculty, agencies or site supervisors, and clients. First, from the student perspective, the internship affords an opportunity to learn about various human service settings and populations and to identify or confirm natural helping strengths and values, to hone skills, and to develop and assess fitness and commitment for this type of professional work (Diambra, Cole-Zakrzewski, & Zakrzewski, 2004). Second, from the faculty perspective, the purpose of a field-based experience for students is to help them integrate classroom knowledge with real world professional experience. In addition, the internship allows faculty to assess intern readiness to assume professional responsibilities and to promote continued professional growth. During this time, faculty also identify any deficiencies that the interns need to address prior to successfully completing their internship. Finally, faculty responsibility includes gatekeeping. Simply stated, this means evaluating intern performance (satisfactory or unsatisfactory) that allows them to advance or not to the next level of education or employment.

Figure 1.1   Multiple Perspectives of the Internship

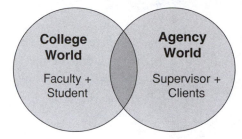

Source: Created by Gwen Ruttencutter, 2015. Used with permission.

From the third perspective, the site supervisor, a seasoned professional, introduces interns to the world of service delivery. Site supervisors structure the internship, making available learning opportunities, providing critical feedback, and overseeing the welfare of the clients the intern serves. Supervisors indicate they appreciate having an "extra pair of hands" to help with the agency work. They also learn from their interns about the latest trends and advances in the field. Finally, clients represent the fourth perspective. Clients often respond well to interns. In some instances, interns provide more time and attention and bring an enthusiasm and eagerness to help. Interns listen with a fresh perspective and a "can do" attitude. Of course, interns do not always have a complete understanding of agency policy or available resources; clients must wait until the intern searches for answers to their questions or seeks resources to meet their needs. Figure 1.1 illustrates these primary perspectives of the internship and the two worlds represented, the college or academic world and the organization or agency world.

Now that you understand the primary perspectives of the human service internship experience, let's look at important terms and their definitions. Knowledge of these terms helps you understand more fully this experience.

Important Terms and Definitions

As you read your text and begin to understand your internship, you will become familiar with the eight terms defined below. Each of these terms represents an important aspect of the experience.

Internship Experience

In many human service programs, students assume the roles and responsibilities of a human service professional under the supervision of a seasoned professional. Most often, this experience occurs in an organization, agency, or school setting. Internship students work in various settings, serving children, youth, adults, and families. This experience may also be described as *practicum* experience.

Intern

This is the term used to describe the student enrolled in and participating in the internship. The **intern** assumes a variety of roles and responsibilities, usually defined by both the educational institution setting up the internship experience and the agency in which the intern works.

Placement or Internship Site

This term describes the location of the internship experience. Educational institutions work with organizations and agencies in the community to develop placements for their interns. When organizations or agencies agree to be a **placement site**, they provide interns with an orientation to, and overview of, the agency, supervision, an increasing amount of responsibility over time, and feedback and evaluation. Interns usually assume a client load and perform other administrative and outreach tasks.

Faculty Supervisor

When students participate in the internship, they have responsibilities to the educational institution and to their placement site. Most often, interns maintain a regular schedule at their placement and attend an internship seminar on campus. The **faculty supervisor** teaches this seminar. The faculty supervisor's responsibilities may include developing a syllabus for the internship, meeting the weekly seminar, helping interns negotiate their placement site, facilitating the supervision process, and evaluating intern performance.

Site Supervisor

This individual assumes the responsibility for the intern's performance at the placement site. Typically, the site supervisor is an experienced human service professional with an established career in human services and experience working at the placement site. The **site supervisor** helps the intern define his or her role as an intern, meets the obligations of the placement to the intern, structures the placement, meets regularly with the intern to answer questions and provide feedback, and assesses the intern's performance. The site supervisor communicates during the term with the faculty supervisor.

Supervision

Both faculty and site supervisors provide observation, education, and support to the intern during the internship experience. This more experienced professional serves as a mentor to a less experienced intern. Responsibilities of **supervision** include helping the intern grow and develop as a professional, assuming responsibility for the care of clients the intern serves, and providing direct and honest feedback about intern's performance.

Midterm Evaluation

Feedback and evaluation are important to the intern. During the first few weeks of the internship, faculty and site supervisors regularly share comments about how the intern performs his or her responsibilities. At times, these comments are supportive and sometimes they are critical. Many views shared during supervision represent an informal assessment. Usually the **midterm evaluation,** occurring midway during the term, is the first formal evaluation conducted with the intern. It is a time when the intern and supervisors reflect on the growth and development of the intern. The mid-term evaluation usually concludes with areas of growth and areas of focus for the remainder of the term.

Final Evaluation

At the conclusion of the internship, faculty and site supervisors conduct a formal **final evaluation**. This evaluation becomes an important factor in the final assessment of internship performance and grade. A final evaluation of the intern includes specific personal dispositions (e.g., self-awareness, commitment), skills (e.g., attending behavior, goal setting), and professional behaviors (e.g., punctuality, maturity). The intern and the supervisors suggest specific examples to illustrate each specific area assessed. A final evaluation ends with a professional development plan that guides future intern responsibility and professional growth.

Exercise 1.2 Assessing Your Current Knowledge About Your Internship

If you are reading this chapter, you are preparing to begin your human service internship.

Step 1

As a way to assess your current knowledge of the experience, describe what you know about each of the terms as they relate to your own human service program.

1. Internship experience

   _____

2. Intern

   _____

3. Placement or internship site

   _____

4. Faculty supervisor

   _____

5. Site supervisor

   _____

6. Supervision

   _____

7. Midterm evaluation

   _____

8. Final evaluation

   _____

Defining the Internship Experience

As you begin to build your definition of the internship experience, it is important to seek various sources of information (see Figure 1.2). Each of these sources reflects the various aspects of your identity as a human service professional, specifically from the professional or work-related context. They provide **organizational definitions** from professional organizations and regulatory bodies, academic programs, and faculty syllabi.

A first approach is to see how professional organizations and regulatory bodies describe the nature, structure, and requirements of an internship in human services. A second is to learn how human service programs describe it. These programs usually have program handbooks, internship handbooks, and course descriptions available to the public, prospective students, and current students; each of these three documents relates the academic program experience to the internship. A third directly relates to your own student experience. Each faculty member directing the human service internship provides students a syllabus or road map that describes course requirements and course content. This syllabus becomes a key to defining the context of the internship.

Perspectives of Professional Organizations and Regulatory Bodies

As stated earlier, professional organizations and regulatory bodies describe the nature, structure, and requirements of an internship in human services. This is the first context in which you can consider the internship. The **National Organization for Human Services** and the **Council for Standards in Human Service Education** suggest standards for academic programs that educate students for the helping professions. In addition, the *Community Support Skill Standards* (Taylor, Bradley, & Warren, n.d.) delineate the roles performed and skills required for human service work and the **Human Services-Board Certified Practitioner credential** offers individuals a certification that establishes their professional status.

Figure 1.2   Defining the Internship

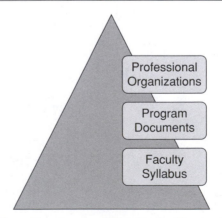

Source: Created by Gwen Ruttencutter, 2015. Used with permission.

National Organization for Human Services

The **National Organization for Human Services** (NOHS) (formerly known as National Organization for Human Service Educators) describes the purpose of human services as fourfold (NOHS, n.d.; Woodside & McClam, 2013). The first commitment is to assess and address human needs. The second is to meet human needs using quality interventions. A third commitment is to make services more accessible and accountable. Finally, a fourth commitment suggests that human service professionals are to treat those in need from a holistic perspective. This requires a coordination of the human service delivery system to address multiple needs.

NOHS provides human service professionals with a definition of human service practice. Relevant to our topic, the human service internship, NOHS outlines the knowledge, skills, and values of human service work (NOHS, n.d.). Most relevant to you as an intern are four NOHS statements listed in Box 1.2. They focus on behaviors and skills you will need to complete your internship effectively.

Box 1.2 NOHS Statements Relevant to the Human Service Internship

NOHS Statements Relevant to the Human Service Internship

We list the four NOHS statements most relevant to you as an intern.

- *Skill in identifying and selecting interventions which promote growth and goal attainment . . .*
- *Skill in planning, implementing, and evaluating interventions . . .*
- *Consistent behavior in selecting interventions which are congruent with the values . . .*
- *Process skills which are required to plan and implement services . . .* (NOHS, n.d.)

Council for Standards in Human Service Education

The **Council for Standards in Human Service Education** (CSHSE) provides guidance and consultation to human service programs in the United States and internationally. Established in 1979, this organization oversees human service program accreditation and quality improvement. Through the accreditation process, CSHSE offers a vision for human service programs in its *Member Handbook* (2012). Relevant to our discussion of the internship is the "Section III: The Self Study Process." Within that section, the members of CSHSE describe curricula and standards for human service accredited programs. More specifically a curriculum divided into two components represents the academic and field learning. The academic focus incorporates history, human systems, human service delivery systems, planning and evaluation, information management, interventions, interpersonal communication, administrative, client-related values, and self-development.

The field learning represents the second component. CSHSE presents both associate and baccalaureate national standards for the field component (CSHSE, 2013a, 2013b). Those standards for the associate degree follow in Box 1.3. **Bold type** indicates additional requirements for field experience for CSHSE-accredited baccalaureate degree programs.

Box 1.3 CSHSE Curriculum Standards Related to the Human Service Internship

CSHSE Curriculum Standards Related to the Human Service Internship

B. Field Experience
   Context: Field experience such as a practicum or internship occurs in a human services setting. Fieldwork provides an environment . . . to integrate the knowledge, theory, skills, and professional behaviors . . .
   Standard Number 20 (21): The program shall provide field experience that is integrated with the curriculum.

Source: CSHSE, 2013a, 2013b.

Community Support Skill Standards

Another source of information about human service practice is the **Community Support Skill Standards.** The Human Service Research Institute (Taylor et al., n.d.) developed these standards in 1993 to reflect community practice in the human services. Using a national occupational analysis of human service delivery, the researchers articulated 12 occupational functions or tasks performed by human service professionals. These include "Participant Empowerment; Communication; Assessment; Community and Service Networking; Facilitation of Services; Community Living Skills and Support; Education, Training and Self Development; Advocacy; Vocational, Educational and Career Support; Crisis Intervention; Organizational Participation; and Documentation" (Taylor et al., n.d.). These skills and knowledge reflect the field-based nature of human service practice.

Human Services-Board Certified Practitioner

The **Human Services-Board Certified Practitioner** (HSBCP) **certification** is a relatively new way in which human service students assume their place in the profession and advance their standing. Under the auspices of the Center for Credentialing and Education (CCE, 2015), human service students and practitioners may apply for this credential. Criteria for application include educational experience, professional work, and successful outcome on a national examination. The following areas represent the examination content: "assessment, treatment planning, and evaluation; theoretical orientation/interventions; case management, professional practice and ethics; administration, program development/evaluation and supervision" (CCE, 2015). The case study format used in this examination allows applicants to demonstrate skills, especially those working with clients. Since the case study is, in essence, field based, student work in internship allows students to prepare for the examination on a day-to-day basis. The following areas covered on the examination demonstrate the tie between the internship and the HSBCP credentialing.

The application handbook describes the areas that are covered by the examination:

- Ethics in helping relationships
- Interviewing and intervention skills
- Group work
- Case management
- Human development
- Social and cultural issues
- Social problems
- Assessment/treatment planning
- Intervention models/theories
- Human behavior
- Social welfare and public policy
- Research, program evaluation, and supervision (CCE, 2015)

As you look at the knowledge and skills listed here, you can see their relevance to the internship. Students will engage in this type of direct client's service.

The Human Service Program Documents

We now look at materials much more familiar to you, those of your own human service program. Before we discuss these materials in more detail, let's look at the many ways human services students just like you view these documents. Their comments provide a snapshot into the experiences of exploring what the human service internship is all about as shown in Box 1.4.

Box 1.4 Students Reflect on Finding Out About the Internship Experience

What do you know about your program's internship?

Steve: Help!!! Students who are currently in internships keep talking to me about their experiences. I feel lost whenever I hear them talk.

Maria: You might call me a nervous wreck. I am supposed to begin my internship next term. I looked on the program website and read through the current syllabus. It looks like a lot of work. I am not sure that I can get in all of the hours the syllabus describes.

Al: I work full-time and go to school full-time. I figure I can go to the orientation at the end of this term and find out all I need to know. I am just not worried about it. When I applied for the program, it was the internship that sold me on the program.

Shasha: At our school we had a 3-week preinternship orientation. I think that I am set. We looked at the internship handbook and my faculty supervisor answered my questions.

As you can see by reading these brief statements from the human service students, their experiences vary related to what they know about the internship. To help you gain information about the internship, each academic program provides various sources of information. Each academic program has its own **program description**, internship handbook, and course description. These provide a public view of the program and how the internship fits into the academic experience.

Human Services Program Description

All academic programs, including those in the human services, provide public **program descriptions** of "the mission and objectives of the instructional program that includes the instructional activity or innovation being evaluated or assessed, a statement of need, the expected effects, available resources, the program's stage of development, and the instructional context" (University of Texas, n.d.). First, we describe some of the commonalities that we found across human service program descriptions. These descriptions are usually available in an academic catalog and on the program website.

Common Goals of Human Service Programs

Most students enroll in the human service internship as a part of their education and training to work as a human service professional. Although human services programs vary in degrees offered (e.g., associate, baccalaureate, master's, and doctoral) and specific areas of focus (e.g., criminal justice, children and youth, health, mental health), commonalities abound. Let's look at several of the commonalities (knowledge, skills and experience, and professional values and behavior) within these programs (Bismarck State College—Human Services AAS, 2013; CSHSE, 2012; Woodside & McClam, 2013).

Knowledge

- Integrate knowledge from the social sciences, humanities, sciences, and the helping professions
- Understand various human service settings
- Appreciate the relevance of the history of human services
- Gain a theoretical understanding from the systems, families, and individual perspectives applied to the process of helping

Skills and Experience

- Work with individuals, families, groups, and communities
- Develop programming and intervention based on client, family, and community needs
- Develop assistance to clients using basic helping skills and an understanding of the helping process (planning, delivering, and evaluating)
- Use a multicultural perspective to deliver direct and indirect services to those in need
- Provide case management, needs assessment, advocacy, service delivery, crisis intervention, as well as program planning
- Work in a complex service delivery system (includes various sectors such as public, private, not-for-profit, and for-profit)

Professional Values and Behavior

- Understand and identify legal and ethical dimensions of helping
- Integrate theory into professional practice
- Focus on self-development (includes openness, commitment, responsibility, integrity, and self-reflection)

Human service program descriptions also provide details of a program's academic focus and its relationship to field-based learning. Because the internship experience is a critical component of human service education, many handbooks illustrate the connections between the internship and other aspects of the program. Sometimes they provide an introduction or information about the internship.

Exercise 1.3 Locating Your Human Services Program Description

Step 1

As you prepare for your human service internship experience, locate your human service program description on the Internet or in the curriculum catalog at your educational institution.

Step 2

1. Read through the program description and answer the following questions:

    a. What is the mission of your program?

    b. What are the goals of your program?

    c. Does the program description distinguish between educational and field-based experiences? If it does, how does it do so?

    d. What did you learn from this exercise?

    e. How does this new learning relate to the internship experience?

The internship becomes a way that students integrate their classroom experiences into a human service setting. Students move from an academic focus that may include activities and skills-based learning to a more applied focus. In an effort to help students better understand their educational experiences, human service programs develop support materials for their students. The next section introduces two important texts that guide your educational experience, the internship handbook and course description.

Written documents prepared by faculty and approved by the academic institution guide program development and academic practice. An **internship** handbook helps human service students better understand the field-based learning and its requirements. In addition, faculty write descriptions for each of their course offerings.

Internship Handbook

Most human service programs provide their students with a handbook to guide the internship experience. These internship handbooks may include topics related to (a) definitions and goals, (b) requirements and eligibility,

(c) responsibilities and expectations, (d) policies and procedures, (e) assignments and evaluations, and (f) professional development. Details of the content in these handbooks follow.

Definitions and Goals

- Description of the internship experience
- List of goals of the internship experience

Requirements and Eligibility

- Prerequisites or corequisites
- Eligibility for the internship experience

Responsibilities and Expectations

- Requirements of the internship experience
- Personal and professional dispositions
- Work-related obligations and responsibilities
- Ethical obligations and behaviors

Policies and Procedures

- Policies and procedures
- Establishing the internship
- Determining an internship work schedule

Assignments and Evaluations

- Internship class requirements and assignments
- Internship evaluations
- Terminating an internship
- Policies for student evaluation, retention, remediation, and dismissal
- College policies regarding academic honesty and academic appeal

Professional Development

- Endorsement policy for certification or licensure
- Letters of recommendation
- Professional organizations
- Continuing education

Exercise 1.4 Reviewing the Internship Handbook

Reviewing the internship handbook will help you gather information about your own program's internship experience.

Step 1

Locate your human service program's internship handbook. Read it carefully.

Step 2

Make a list of the information you believe is most important for you to know to begin your internship experience.

Course Description

Educational institutions approve course offerings and course descriptions for each of their programs and majors. The purpose of a **course description** is to summarize relevant information about a specific course. This includes a course prefix, number, title, brief description, number of credit hours, grading options, and prerequisites or corequisites. A human service internship course description provides us a brief and distinctive perspective of this field-based learning opportunity. Each institution's course description differs and reflects the way in which the institution and the human service program view the role of the internship course. For example, several institutions refer to the integrated experience as *practicum*, while others refer to the experience as the *field* or *internship*. Commonalities of the examples presented include the focus of the experience, number of hours in the field required, classroom hour requirements, and references to supervision.

The Internship Syllabus

The final document we review, the **internship syllabus**, establishes the context of the internship. Faculty prepare a syllabus to explain in detail the focus of a course, its goals and objectives, assignments, evaluation, calendar of topics, and due dates. In most cases, faculty use the internship handbook as a foundation for the contents. Because of the academic freedom involved with course construction, many syllabi integrate standard guidelines, policies, and procedures from the program handbook, the internship handbook, and the course description with individual faculty teaching styles and preferences.

The following syllabus outline suggests the components interns find in the internship syllabus:

Course information (number, prefix, name, semester, meeting time and location)

Instructor information (name, rank, department, contact information)

University policies (civility, honor code, academic policies, appeals, services)

Program dispositions (values and behavioral expectations)

Text and readings

Course (catalog) description and goals

Course outcomes (often linked to competencies)

Grades and evaluations

Assignments

Course calendar (course content by date, topic, and assignment)

Exercise 1.5 Reviewing Your Internship Course Description and Internship Syllabus

As a way of learning more about your program's internship experience, review its course description and internship syllabus.

Step 1

Look up the internship course description and describe the information below.

_____
_____
_____

Step 2

Obtain the syllabus for your internship and read it thoroughly.

Step 3

1. Describe what in the syllabus you consider the most important elements.

    _____
    _____
    _____

2. What new information did you gain?

    _____
    _____
    _____

3. What questions remain for you about the internship?

    _____
    _____
    _____

This section reviewed ways to define the internship, by reviewing professional organizations, human service program documents, and the internship syllabus. We now describe the concept and activity of collaboration that supports the internship experience in Box 1.5.

Box 1.5 Collaboration: A Model of Human Service Practice

Collaboration: A Model for Human Service Practice

1. Definition
2. Introducing Sue

3. Aspects of collaboration

    a. Learning new ideas

    b. Creating knowledge together

    c. Providing support

    d. Encouraging feedback

4. Dimensions of collaboration

    a. Formal settings

    b. Informal settings

Collaboration: A Model of Human Service Practice

As you are no doubt aware by your study of human services, the nature of work in human services is substantially collaborative. The simple definition of **collaboration** is "working jointly with others" ("Collaboration," 2015). First, in the process of human service delivery, working with others includes interacting with clients and others in the client network (such as family and friends) to address the problems in living that these clients experience. Second, collaboration occurs as professionals work side by side with colleagues in their own agency or organization or in the broader world of human service delivery. Third, if you are a student in a human service program, you also collaborate in the learning environment. Student collaboration includes working with faculty, supervisors, student peers, and clients, especially during the internship experience. All three collaboration efforts are important to participating in a positive and growth producing internship. To examine collaborative efforts in internship, let's read about Sue, an internship student who works at a homeless shelter.

Introducing Sue

The following account describes the experiences of Sue, a human service internship student, and the variety of kinds of collaborations she encounters:

Carmello Jones: Director of the homeless shelter

Maria Rodriguez: Site supervisor and case manager

George Stephenson: Volunteer and former case manager at the homeless shelter

Dr. Diacon: Faculty supervisor

Gorgia Nijul: One of Sue's peers also enrolled in the internship experience

By the beginning of the fourth week in her internship experience, Sue is providing case management services for seven adults receiving services at a homeless shelter in southeastern Oklahoma. The shelter uses a strengths assessment for case planning and providing interventions. Together, Sue and her clients fill out initial intake forms. Afterward, they develop goals and implementation plans. Sue and her clients include family, friends, and other community members in their planning. Sue believes she is gaining as much from her clients as they are gaining from her.

In addition, as she is working as a case manager, Sue attends the client staffing every Thursday morning. Five case managers, the program director, the shelter director, the outreach coordinator, and Sue meet to discuss client progress. Sue gains support and feedback during the staffing. During these meetings, Sue learns that not everyone working with clients focuses on client strengths. In fact, Sue wonders about shelter director Carmello Jones's attitude toward providing services. His approach is concrete—period! "Here are the services we provide—take them or leave them. He doesn't appear to have much empathy for the clients."

Sue has run into difficulties when she is working with other human service professionals in the community. One staff member at the local clothing bank told her, "I need to be careful how many clients from the shelter that I serve. If we shared clothing with everyone who is homeless in this city, we would have little left to share with other individuals who need our help." Sue was not sure how to respond.

On the other hand, individuals who belong to the County Homeless Coalition attend a meeting every 2 weeks in a downtown hotel. Committed to helping the homeless, these coalition members form a network of individuals and agencies that can help Sue's clients. All of the staff dress formally for these meetings. To her this means the members of the network take their membership in the coalition seriously. Also, Sue runs into members of the coalition from time to time in other parts of the community, the grocery store, a doctor's office, or the local mall. In those settings, these individuals greet her warmly and talk about their work together.

Sue encounters various forms of supervision during her internship experience. In her agency, she has two site supervisors, Carmello Jones, the agency director, and Maria, one of the five case managers. Carmello, while supportive, has little time to meet with her. When they do meet, Carmello is pleasant and supportive and talks to Sue about her future goals but not about her clients and the services she is trying to provide.

During a supervision session, Carmello helped her understand the appropriate dress for working at the shelter. During her first week, Sue wore a dress, boots, and hoop earrings. In their second meeting, he recommended that Sue dress in slacks, comfortable shoes, and smaller jewelry. Carmello indicated the more functional dress might help her relate to her clients more quickly. Sue had received different feedback from her faculty supervisor at the beginning of the semester about dress. He suggested that all interns dress up to distinguish themselves from the clients. Sue decided to follow Carmello's advice.

Sue's site supervisor, Maria Rodriguez, is a case manager, and although Maria has never supervised before, she is willing to talk with Sue every day if necessary about her work in internship. She helps Sue with the myriad of details about working with clients and completing the paperwork.

Also at her agency, Sue found a mentor, George Stephenson, who serves as a volunteer after working for the agency for 20 years prior to his retirement. She talks with him frequently when she encounters him in the hallway or the staff lounge. These conversations provide her with ideas and new insights about her clients and her work as a case manager. Sometimes she talks with him about some new projects she has in mind. For example, in her human services methods class, Sue learned about the "wellness" model, and she thinks she might be able to use that model to structure some of her interventions.

Figure 1.3   Aspects of Collaboration

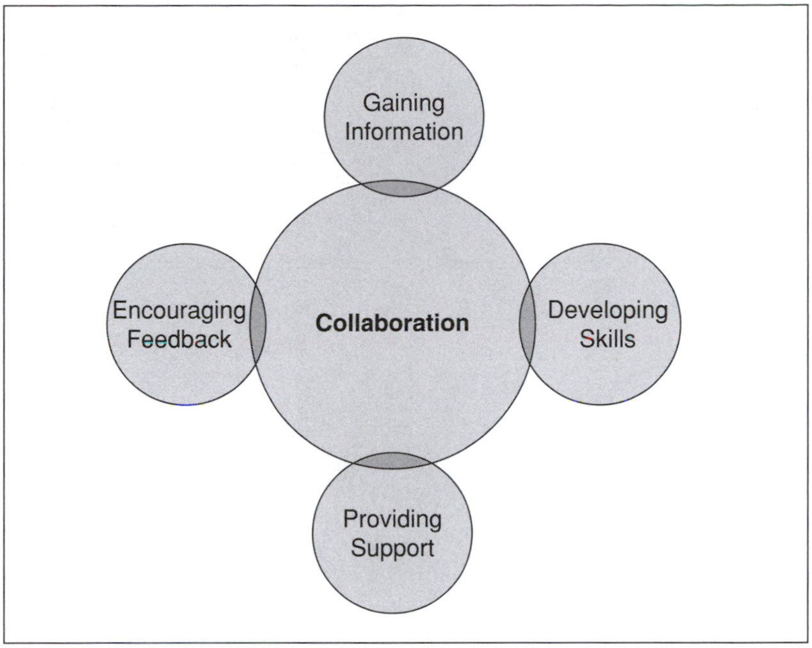

Source: Created by Gwen Ruttencutter, 2015. Used with permission.

Every Monday, Sue attends an internship class. This is an important time for her; she loves hearing about the experiences of her classmates. She is frustrated at times because she thinks her classmates don't understand the complexities of her case management responsibilities. None of them have responsibilities as a case manager, although several work in agencies that provide case management services. But they do understand what it is like to be an intern in an agency setting.

Sue remembers one internship class that was particularly helpful. During the second week of the internship, Sue texted her faculty supervisor, Dr. Diacon, and asked for supervision during her class meeting. While in class, Sue explained the difficulty she was having using the shelter's data management system to record how she spends her time. Another classmate, Gorgia, shared with Sue a personal log form she uses. Gorgia uses the form that she developed, and then she transfers the information to the agency system. The class spent 10 minutes helping Sue create a form to help her track her time.

Many of Sue's early experiences in her internship experience involve multiple opportunities to collaborate. In the following sections, we examine *aspects* of collaboration such as professional growth and *dimensions* of collaboration such as type of setting.

Aspects of Collaboration

Collaboration provides the foundation for how we learn to be human service professionals. In other words, collaboration encourages professional growth and development. Specifically, collaboration during the internship experience assumes a critical role in four areas as shown in Figure 1.3:

- Gaining information
- Developing skills

- Providing support
- Encouraging feedback

By rereading the personal account about Sue's experiences and the ways collaboration occurs in her internship placement, we see how others help Sue to develop professionally. Note that in Sue's collaboration with her clients, she is helping them and she is learning from them. Exercise 1.6 helps you consider collaboration in more depth.

Exercise 1.6 Assessing How Collaboration Contributes to Sue's Professional Growth

Step 1

Take a minute to describe Sue's experiences of collaboration. Indicate the person or agency with whom she collaborates, the nature of collaboration, the strengths and limitations of that collaboration, and the outcomes for Sue.

Step 2

Decide for each instance of collaboration you identify if or how it represents (a) gaining information, (b) developing skills, (c) providing support, or (d) encouraging feedback.

Gaining Information

- Partner/collaborator _____
- Focus of the collaboration _____
- Strengths and limitations of the collaboration _____
  _____
- Outcomes of collaboration for Sue's professional growth _____
  _____
  _____

Developing Skills

- Partner/collaborator _____
- Focus of the collaboration _____
- Strengths and limitations of the collaboration _____
  _____
- Outcomes of collaboration for Sue's professional growth _____
  _____
  _____

Providing Support

- Partner/collaborator _____
- Focus of the collaboration _____
- Strengths and limitations of the collaboration _____
  _____
- Outcomes of collaboration for Sue's professional growth _____
  _____
  _____

Encouraging Feedback

- Partner/collaborator _____
- Focus of the collaboration _____
- Strengths and limitations of the collaboration _____
  _____
- Outcomes of collaboration for Sue's professional growth _____
  _____
  _____

Characteristics of Collaboration

Collaboration can look very different, depending on whether it is structured or unstructured. And in the internship, you will experience both types of collaboration. Each shapes how, when, what, and why it occurs as individuals work together during an internship experience. Because **structured and unstructured collaboration** also offer different types of assistance and support, let's look at each in more detail (see Table 1.1).

Structured Collaboration

Your own experiences already include a variety of structured collaborations. Many of these occur in formal settings. One such formal setting is the university or college you currently attend. In the internship experience, you enter another formal setting, the agency or organization. In both of these formal settings, there exists a teacher or leader (manager, supervisor) who controls the many aspects of the collaborative experience. This manager

Table 1.1   Characteristics of Collaborative Learning

Characteristics of Collaborative Learning	Examples of Collaborative Materials, Tasks, and Activities in Internship Experience
Structured/more formal	<ul><li>Class syllabus</li><li>Internship contract</li><li>Class agenda</li><li>Assigned reflections</li><li>Case notes</li><li>Case presentation</li><li>Taping</li><li>Midterm evaluation</li><li>Final evaluation</li></ul>
Unstructured/more informal	<ul><li>In-the-moment consultation</li><li>Change of contract or assignment</li><li>Special request from clients</li><li>Special requests from site supervisor</li><li>Emerging needs or issues of internship site</li><li>Casual conversation with peers, faculty, site supervisor</li><li>Participation in discussion board, blog or social media</li></ul>

or supervisor, as an authority or expert, provides structure by establishing the goals of the collaborative interaction, developing a plan or agenda, and providing critical feedback. Thus, in Sue's internship experience/internship, structured collaboration includes both the homeless shelter weekly staffing and Sue's weekly internship class. In addition, internship class assignments such as case notes or case studies represent tasks that contribute additional structure. Sue's reports about her clients at the agency staffing also help her frame and document her work. A scheduled meeting with a site supervisor also suggests a more formal orientation to learning, especially as the supervision is a requirement for the internship experience.

When you reviewed Sue's collaborative experiences described earlier in this chapter in Exercise 1.6, you found multiple ways Sue works with others. For instance, as discussed earlier, Sue attends homeless shelter staff meetings and internship classes weekly. These two meetings represent formal, planned, and structured collaborative events, each with unique strengths and limitations. Regular meetings provide opportunities to work with others. Experts in charge of these meetings or classes bring a specific agenda to help each member of the group prepare for the meeting. A structured meeting focuses on the topics and issues addressed. There are several possible limitations of formal collaboration. Members of a staff or class may encounter issues for which they need immediate help, or salient topics not on the agenda may be brought up. However, a structured meeting may not provide time for brainstorming or a full discussion of topics or issues.

Unstructured Collaboration

Collaboration that is relatively unstructured or informal "refers to the experiences of everyday living from which we learn something" (Merriam, Baumgartner, & Cafarella, 2006, p. 24). One important aspect of the unstructured collaboration is that it can originate with the internship student rather than with the supervisor or the faculty. For example, if an intern encounters a client diagnosed with ADHD, and the intern understands little about the diagnosis, the intern may ask others to help her understand this diagnosis. The intern, within the unstructured framework, seeks someone who cares and is willing to help rather than only seeking "the individual in charge." Sources of informal collaboration may include internship peers, friends, electronic sources, and media to name a few. Informal collaboration also can include consulting with teachers, administrators, and experts in a less official way with less emphasis on evaluation or critical review.

Another characteristic of this more informal collaboration is that it can occur spontaneously. Examples in the human service internship experience may include a quick call or text with peers about issues and challenges, conversations with staff in the internship experience setting, and searching online for ideas about how to address specific client needs. (Note that searching online and reading textbooks and journal articles represent a different type of collaborative conversation. During your reading, the conversation occurs between you and the writer. It is a collaborative conversation nonetheless.)

Let's review Sue's collaborative experiences described in Exercise 1.6 again, this time looking for times when more unstructured and informal collaboration occurred. Informal collaboration appears to sustain some of Sue's work. For example, members of the County Homeless Coalition provide Sue support outside her agency internship environment. These professionals greet her if they encounter her in the community and provide her whatever support they can. She comes to the coalition meeting with her own agenda and members of the coalition respond in a helpful matter. A volunteer for the homeless shelter also provides guidance for Sue whenever she asks. He does not evaluate Sue or structure her work. Often, their collaboration is spontaneous and unstructured. Finally, Sue's peer, Gorgia, provides her with a way to address her data management tasks. Although Gorgia does this within the framework of a formal class, this collaboration between the two students is not part of the class agenda. Sue determines her specific need, and Gorgia offers a solution. This is a sharing among peers in which there is no expert and no evaluation.

We will return to the concept of collaboration and how it occurs in your own internship later in the term. For now, we think it is important that you note its importance and consider ways you might collaborate with others.

We end this chapter with a section titled "Deepening Your Understanding." See Box 1.6 to better understand the organization of this section.

Box 1.6 Studying the Text: Deepening Your Understanding

Studying the text: The following outline will help you read and study the text material in this next section.

1. Peer-to-peer dialogue
   a. Alicia: Motivation for studying human services
   b. Lucas: Motivation for studying human services
   c. Tamika: Motivation for studying human services
2. Faculty and site supervisor dialogue
   a. Dr. Bianca: Introduction
   b. Ms. Bellewa: Introduction
3. The professional voice and tips for success: Gwen: Collaboration
4. Terms to remember
5. References

Deepening Your Understanding

In this section you will hear more about Alicia, Lucas, and Tamika and their motivations for studying human services. In addition Dr. Bianca and Ms. Bellewa share their faculty and site supervisor backgrounds. Gwen, in the Professional Voice and Tips for Success section, introduces ways collaboration can occur in the **internship site**. We also include Terms to Remember and References to support your learning.

Peer-to-Peer Dialogue: Alicia, Lucas, and Tamika

We asked Alicia, Lucas, and Tamika to talk about the motivation and context of their internship experiences. Their perspectives can help broaden your understanding of the beginning of this experience.

Alicia

I am going to continue to talk about myself and describe why I decided to become a human service professional. Earlier I talked about my family. I pick up my story in a dramatic way.

When I was a senior in high school, a boy who was also in my grade raped me. That resulted in my being pregnant with Thomas. That period of my life was one that was filled with anger, pain, and struggle. I could not understand why it had happened to me and felt that my life, my future, and my goals had all come to a screeching halt. I could not look my family in the eyes because I was so ashamed of what had happened. My mother tried to reach out to me, but I kept pushing her away. I remember waking up on so many mornings hoping it was all just a nightmare, a reality that I never had to face. I considered running away from home because it all became so overwhelming. It wasn't until my first visit to the doctor, when I heard my baby's heartbeat that I realized life was not just about me anymore.

The journey to where I am today was, and still is, difficult. I told myself, "You need to keep going" because Thomas became my priority. I was raised to believe that love and support was at the foundation of a family, and I wanted Thomas to have that too. My mother tried to reach out to me again, and we worked on our feelings of anger and pain together. She became my rock and biggest support, and I know how grateful I am to have her in my life; I also knew this wasn't easy for her either. The relationship I had with my stepfather became strained; he had a difficult time understanding and accepting what had happened to me. At times, it was easier for him to blame me for the rape. I never talked to him about it because I, too, believed it was my fault.

I started meeting with the school counselor, who referred me to people who could help me. I attended parenting classes, and I made plans for a visiting teacher to come to my house when I couldn't attend school. At the time, I just wanted to get through the high school year and focus on everything I needed to do to make sure my baby was going to be okay. I thought about going to college but I knew I had to put it on hold for at least a year or two. But I also knew exactly what I wanted to study when I finally did get there. Two years after Thomas was born, my mother volunteered to keep Thomas in the mornings, if I wanted to start college. I started as a part-time student, majoring in human services. I went to school in the morning, and I worked a part-time job as a receptionist in the early afternoon. While I appreciated my mother's support, I did not want to be completely dependent on her.

I'm not going to lie—everyday is a struggle. Everyday I want to call my mother and ask for help. Everyday I ask myself if I can keep doing this, and everyday I remind myself that it is not only about me. Thomas needs me and I cannot let him down. My understanding of how I see the world has shifted a lot in the past few years. I don't think that life will ever be easy but my own goals are clear. I want to take care of Thomas. I want to work with victims of sexual assault. I don't know if things happen for a reason. I don't think I'm that optimistic. I do know what I have been through, and I want to help other women get through it as well. I look forward to sharing more of my experience, especially as it relates to the field of human services and the journey you are preparing to start.

Written by Allie Rhinehart and Dareen Basma, 2015. Used with permission.

Lucas

At the beginning of the chapter, I talked about my family. Now I want to talk about the two realities where I was raised. Both influenced me. I was born in Berks County, Pennsylvania, an urbanized city, and raised in a rural community in Lancaster County, Pennsylvania. I tell people that growing up I had the opportunity to experience two realities that shaped my beliefs and values. I will briefly explain these two realties to give you an understanding of where I came from. When I was born into this world, my first reality was Berks County. There was high cultural diversity, working-poor families, high drug and violence rates, and a poor educational system. In this reality, street life influenced me with eccentric languages, mannerisms, and beliefs different from dominate societal norms. I learned to try to beat the system. I heard from members of my family and friends in Berks County that "You must do what you have to do to survive."

When my parents realized the negative effects city life had on our development, due to the prevalence of drugs and violence in our community, they moved my little brother and me to Lancaster County. In my second reality, there was **no** *cultural diversity, affluent families, and high educational standards. I was a black dot on a white wall. During this reality, I was behind my peers in terms of reading and writing. My behaviors in class were different. And I had to work hard to catch up with my peers. The expectations in this reality consisted of a high grade point average, college ambition, and an aristocratic lifestyle. As a result, the beliefs and values in this system were the importance of education, power, and recognition.*

As you can imagine, I had to juggle the expectations from my family culture, inspired by the urban and city life, with the culture of a rural community that was predominantly White, upper-middle-socioeconomic level with different values and beliefs. In order to survive in this new world, I had to conform to its cultural norms and set aside my own beliefs. During these times, I experienced extreme anxiety and stress, due to the opposing beliefs and values from these two realities. However, I developed two skills growing up that helped me figure out ways to survive and cope with adversity: observation and self-reflection. These skills helped me identify who I was, what I needed to do to survive, and the expectations my new culture had for me. More important, I developed the social skills to fit in and to take advantage of the opportunities for personal advancement.

Throughout my life, I have seen people fall victim to the system, due to the lack of mental skills to cope with stress, to overcome adversity, and the lack of self-efficacy to better their lives. These personal experiences inspired me to pursue a degree in the helping profession to give others a chance to survive and thrive. In class we call this developing a sense of well-being and becoming self-actualized.

Written by Jorge Roman, 2015. Used with permission.

Tamika

As you can tell from the way I began my story, my parents had a major influence. They still do today. I want to tell you more about them and my earlier life with them.

My parents are both college educated and work in social services. My mom is the admissions director of a prominent nursing home in my hometown, and my dad works for the state's child welfare department in Michigan's capital. My parents were quite strict and a bit overprotective. They instilled in me strong values of self-respect and respect for others; and they also raised me to seek achievement at the highest level possible. My parents taught me the value of education at an early age and instilled in me the significance of helping those around me—principles that are still important to me and have shaped my decision to enter the helping profession.

Living as part of the lower middle class in my community, my parents chose to make sacrifices to ensure that I could take advantage of any educational or extracurricular opportunity available to me. Growing up, I competed in several sports, played flute and piccolo in the band, danced, and maintained involvement in several clubs and organizations. We lived in a small apartment for most of my childhood. I never had the most expensive clothes. But I do remember that my family provided me with what I needed for my academic work or for my extracurricular interests. And both of my parents attended my games, concerts, performances, and ceremonies. This provided a level of support that I always knew I was lucky to have. I never doubted that my parents loved me and wanted the best for me.

My mother also involved me in volunteer work from a very early age. Together, we have worked in soup kitchens, packaged Christmas presents at the Salvation Army, taught English to Spanish-speaking immigrants, and spent time reading to nursing home residents. I have always admired my mother's heart for giving to others, which is probably my primary motivation for entering the helping field.

Another motivation came from my lack of relationships with extended family. After leaving Illinois, where my parents both grew up, we were quite isolated from my aunts, uncles, cousins, and grandparents. Growing up, I felt as if something significant was missing from my life, and I can distinctly remember feeling jealous of those friends who enjoyed large family get-togethers. I especially missed not having a relationship with my maternal grandmother, as I was particularly distant from my mother's side of the family. As a result, I am interested in family and group dynamics, and in the ways relationships (or the lack, thereof) can impact a person's life. I have spent a great deal of time reflecting on my own life experiences. I credit my parents for the inspiration to pursue my passion of helping others to live the best lives that they can. I enjoy working with a variety of populations and have had interesting and unique experiences. Thank you for allowing me to introduce myself. I am looking forward to sharing more of my personal, academic, and professional endeavors with you along the way!

Written by Brittany Pollard, 2015. Used with permission.

Exercise 1.7 Writing Your Own Story, Entry 2

You just read short summaries of the personal development of Alicia, Lucas, and Tamika. In Exercise 1.1 you wrote Writing Your Own Story, Entry 1 and began a description of you and your family. Now it is your turn to write more about yourself.

Step 1

Use the questions below to expand your initial entry.

- Think about your own life and the people, events, and environments that contributed to your decision to help others.
- Provide basic information about yourself, including your name, age, gender, nationality, and ethnicity. Describe how each of these demographics helps define who you are. Provide information about how each of these demographics may influence your work as a human service intern.
- Describe your family and any ways you believe that your family influences your decision to study human services. Include the influences of your parents, siblings, and other family members.
- List five basic values and beliefs that shape who you are and guide your actions. Explain why you think you hold these values. How do you believe these values will shape your work in human services?

Step 2

- Tell the story of "coming" to or choosing the human services as your profession.

Faculty and Site Supervisor Dialogue: Dr. Bianca and Ms. Bellewa

In addition to meeting Alicia, Lucas, and Tamika, we asked Dr. Bianca, a human service faculty member, and Ms. Bellewa, a human service site supervisor, to introduce themselves. The goal in the summaries that follow is for you to get to know both of them in a personal way.

©iStockphoto.com/Sylverarts

Dr. Claude Bianca

Hi! My name is Claude Bianca. Marianne asked me to tell you about myself and how I became a faculty member in human services. I will begin with a brief introduction in this personal entry. Later, I can talk with you about my current work. First, I was born in Canada, and my parents moved to the United States when I was 6 years old. In Canada, we lived in the same town with my grandparents, aunts and uncles, and cousins. The move was very difficult for me. One of the things that made that move easier was the Boys and Girls Club just down the street from my house. We lived in a town on the edge of Tucson, Arizona. At the Boys and Girls Club, we had a wonderful time after school. I can remember the college students who volunteered at the club. They taught us how to play ball, how to draw, how to play games, and there was always time to read. When I was eight, I asked one of the volunteers who read to us each day if I could read to the younger children. I think my teaching career was launched at that point. I had so much fun, and this reading time soon became one of my favorite activities. Looking back on the experience, I think I was a natural teacher. My family says that I have the teaching gene just like my grandmother. The journey was long from that Boys and Girls Club to today and my job as a faculty member in human services. When I think about what I want you to understand most, it is that I want to "teach" you about how to thrive in your internship experience. Marianne asks that throughout this text, I provide you an inside look at how faculty think about internship and why faculty set up this experience as they do. So that is exactly what I will do. I also hope to learn from you during this time. See you in the next chapter.

©iStockphoto.com/Sylverarts

Ms. Zu Bellewa

My name is Zu Bellewa. I am very happy to meet you. I am honored to meet you and to talk to you about my work. Dr. Woodside asked me to write an informal paper about my life. I am not sure that I can offer the informal tone she suggested. In my family and in my culture, we show respect in formal ways. I respect you since you are learning. It is my humble hope that I can help you.

I moved to the United States about 7 years ago from Niger. In Niger, I worked in an NGO [nongovernmental agency] whose mission was to educate children. We operated an on-the-street program [outreach] for children who did not attend school. We were a team of three in our agency. We worked in a very large urban area. Unemployment was 40%. Only 10% of children had access to education. Our small contribution was to find 50 children living on the streets and bring them to our agency each day. We had a standard curriculum (today the program uses tablets to deliver instruction) and fed children breakfast, lunch, and dinner.

Today, I live in the Northeast. My first home was in New York City. Now I live and work in Syracuse, New York, with my husband and my two sons. My extended family remains in Niger.

Written by Dareen Basma.

The Professional Voice and Tips for Practice: Gwen

Gwen Ruttencutter has a long-time association with the human service profession. She has experience as a domestic violence counselor and as an executive director of a nonprofit affordable housing organization. In this chapter and each that follows, Gwen offers insights she gained while working in the human service delivery system. She is kind enough to share those ideas and "tips for success" with us.

Gwen

In this chapter, Marianne writes extensively about collaboration, which is defined as "working jointly with others" ("Collaboration," 2015). And while we can understand what collaboration is, and how it benefits us in human services, let's see what collaboration looks like in action. In other words, what are the behaviors that create collaboration? Below is an introduction to Seven Aspects of Reflective Practice, developed by John Peters (2011), who researches, writes, and teaches extensively about reflective practice as a means to working and thinking collaboratively:

Climate building: Creating an environment in which there is a sense of safety and respect, supportive of a collaborative relationship among all participants.

Questioning: Asking questions that help identify assumptions, clarify thoughts, and develop fair and balanced questions.

Listening: Skillful listening to others' mental models, wants, assumptions, and values.

Focusing: Seeing and hearing what each other say and how they say it, moment to moment, individually and jointly.

Thinking: Identifying and suspending one's own frames, assumptions, values, and biases, in order to understand one's own and others' viewpoints and behaviors.

Acting: Taking the next steps based on critical reflection of one's own and others' thoughts, feelings, and actions.

Facilitating: Enabling conditions that create and sustain dialogue by participants.

(Peters, 2011).

After reading and thinking about the behaviors and skills that create a collaborative environment, consider what behaviors and skills you already use in your school and personal life. How will these help you in your internship experience? And last, what are the behaviors and skills that are new to you? How might you develop and grow new collaborative behaviors and skills?

Collaboration is not only a key to success in your internship experience; collaboration is a key to success in all aspects of life. By developing the skills discussed above, and learning to implement them in your interactions with others, you are on your way to creating a collaborative way of being.

Written by Gwen Ruttencutter. Used with permission.

Terms to Remember

Collaboration

Community support skill standards

Council for Standards in Human Service Education

Course description

Faculty supervisor

Final evaluation

Human Services-Board Certified Practitioner

Intern

Internship experience

Internship handbook

Internship syllabus

Midterm evaluation

National Organization for Human Services

Organizational definitions

Placement or internship site

Program description

Site supervisor

Structured collaboration

Supervision

Unstructured collaboration

References

Bismarck State College—Human Services AAS. (2013). *Academics: Human Services Degree Plans*. Retrieved from http://www.bismarckstate.edu/academics/ programsfi/human/curriculum/

Center for Credentialing and Education. (2015). *Human Services-Board Certified Practitioner*. Retrieved from http://www.cce-global.org/hsbcp

Collaboration. (2015). In *Merriam-Webster dictionary* (11th ed.). Retrieved from http://www.merriam-webster.com/dictionary/collaborate

Council for Standards in Human Service Education. (2012). *Member handbook: Accreditation & self-study guide*. Retrieved from http://cshse.org/documents/ MemberHandbookSelfStudyGuide.pdf

Council for Standards in Human Service Education. (2013a). *CSHSE, national standards associate degree in human services, 2013 revised*. Retrieved from http://www.cshse.org/pdfs/Standards-Associate.pdf

Council for Standards in Human Service Education. (2013b). *CSHSE national standards for baccalaureate degree in human services*. Retrieved from http:// www.cshse.org/pdfs/Standards-Baccalaureate.pdf

Diambra, J. F., Cole-Zakrzewski, K. G., & Zakrzewski, R. F. (2004). Key lessons learned during the internship: Student perspectives. *Human Service Education*, 24(1), 5–18.

Merriam, S. B., Baumgartner, L. M., & Caffarella, R. S. (2006). *Learning in adulthood: A comprehensive guide* (3rd ed.). San Francisco: Jossey-Bass.

National Organization for Human Services. (n.d.). *What is human services?* Retrieved from http://www.nationalhumanservices.org/what-is-human-services

Peters, J. (2011, February). *The art of thinking together: Reflective practice for mediator and client communications*. Presented at the Annual Conference of Tennessee Association of Professional Mediators, Nashville, TN.

Taylor, M., Bradley, V., & Warren, R. (n.d.). *The community support skill standards: Tools for managing change and achieving outcomes*. Human Service Research Institute. Retrieved from http://www.hsri.org/publication/ community-support-skill-standards

University of Texas. (n.d.). *Instructional assessment resources: Glossary: Program description*. Retrieved from https://learningsciences.utexas.edu/sites/default/ files/iar_glossary.pdf

Woodside, M., & McClam, T. (2013). *Generalist case management* (4th ed.). Belmont, CA : Brooks/Cole, Cengage Learning.

2

Assessing Your Readiness for Internship

Reading this chapter will help you do the following:

- Define core characteristics of the human service internship and relate these to your own experiences.
- Describe the Integrated Developmental Model, including the levels of competence and the overarching structures.
- Assess your own levels of competence for self- and other awareness, motivation, and autonomy relative to the Integrated Developmental Model.
- Learn about how *Alicia, Lucas, Tamika,* and *Tomas* engaged in the human service internship.

- Learn about the faculty and site supervisors' perspectives related to the human service internship experiences.
- Describe the tips that Gwen provides for developing a human service professional identity.

In Chapter 1, you learned about the various perspectives of the human service experience and how to define the experience. You learned about the importance of collaboration in internship work and how collaboration looks. In this chapter, Chapter 2, we help you begin to assess your own **personal readiness** for the internship experience. The assessment of your readiness requires self-reflection. To organize your self-reflections, we introduce you to core characteristics that human service scholars have identified as important. You will also use these characteristics to examine your own preparation for the internship.

We also introduce a model of professional growth, called the **Integrated Developmental Model (IDM)** (Stoltenberg & McNeil, 2009; Stoltenberg, McNeill, & Delworth, 1998). Using this model, you can begin to predict your growth and development in internship. You will also learn about the **professional identity** of a human service practitioner. At the conclusion of the chapter, you meet Alicia, Lucas, and Tamika again. They describe their **internship context** and share with you thoughts about their own personal readiness. You also hear from Dr. Bianca, a human service faculty member, and Ms. Bellewa, a site supervisor. We conclude the chapter with Gwen's ideas for developing your professional identity as a human service professional.

Let's look at the characteristics of the human service internship experience and assess your personal readiness for that experience.

The human service internship experience represents a rich and complex field-based learning opportunity for interns. No two experiences are the same. Scholars agree that the human service internship experience represents an important learning opportunity for human service students (Kiser, 2009; Sweitzer & King, 2014). We suggest these scholars articulate similar core characteristics of the human service internship experience (Chaiferi & Griffin, 1997; Kiser, 2009; Sweitzer & King, 2014). Across disciplines (human services, counseling, social work, criminal justice, addictions, and health care) and human service-related academic programs, we identified five core characteristics: the **journey**, the **influence of time, expectations and anxieties, highs and lows**, and **changes and stages** that describe the internship experience.

To illustrate each of the core characteristics, four human service students provide you with brief reflections about each. Also, Tomas, a human service student beginning his field experience, shares his perspective on beginning the field experience. In addition, for each of these core aspects, you will assess your own personal readiness for your internship experience. Box 2.1 describes how we organize this section.

Box 2.1 Studying the Text: Core Characteristics of the Human Service Internship Experience

Core characteristics of the human service internship experience

1. A brief look at the core characteristics: The student's perspective
2. The journey
3. The influence of time
4. Expectations and anxieties
5. Highs and lows
6. Changes and stages
   a. Changes
   b. Stages

The Core Characteristics of the Human Services Internship Experience

We asked human service students across the country about their perceptions of each of the following five core characteristics of their learning experience. In this box you can read about some of their responses.

Box 2.2 Students Reflect on the Core Characteristics of the Human Service Internship Experience

The Journey

Steve: I think it is more like a roller coaster at the fair. I know some of my friends talk about their journey. I just take things as they come. I am not even sure I am on the road or any road.

Maria: A calling—that has been my journey since I was a small child. I always had a heart for others.

Al: I can't believe how quickly my coursework has gone. It seems like yesterday that I began the community health program.

Shasha: My dad taught me to always have a plan. My plan is going according to schedule. I can't wait for the next step.

The Influence of Time

Steve: I have been so busy since I began school. I am studying, working, and taking care of my family too. I have to be very organized.

(Continued)

(Continued)

Maria: I worry that I will not be able to control the amount of time I spend with my clients. My roommate is in the field experience now and she works until 7 pm every night just so she can complete all of her paperwork.

Al: I know I will like the work. Everyone talks about the unpredictability of it. You know, they say things like, "You can plan your day, and then you go with what happens." I like that. I won't be bored.

Shasha: Lists. Lists and more lists. I am a list maker. I always have made lists and then I check off items when I complete the tasks. I suspect I will have lots of list making to do in my field experience.

Expectations and Anxieties

Steve: Do you mean, what do I worry about? I worry that my supervisor won't like me.

Maria: When I think about being in the field experience, I hope that I can help my clients.

Al: I am not going to be working with my favorite population, teenagers. My first placement is with adults. I worry they will think that I am too young to help them.

Shasha: I try not to make things too complex. When that happens, then I get overwhelmed. As long as I can handle my assignments and responsibilities, I will be OK.

Highs and Lows

Steve: One day I am excited about the internship. Then by the end of the day, I start worrying about all the things that can go wrong.

Maria: I am totally psyched about the field experience. This is the work I was born for. And I absolutely love my placement.

Al: I have been having a difficult time lately with mood issues. This happened to me once before when I was in high school. I was on medication for a time for depression. Maybe I should tell my instructor about my troubles.

Shasha: I am pretty steady. I am not saying I will not have highs and lows, but usually I am rock solid.

Changes and Stages

Steve: I really can see myself changing everyday. I am more confident in my skills and my choice of a career than I was when I started my studies. I am relieved since I can't really afford to make mistakes and still support my family.

Maria: I hope that I can help others in a good way.

Al: I expect to be surprised by what I learn during my internship. Every time I think about it, I know I can't even guess what it will be like. I had this experience when I was in the service too.

Shasha: I don't like change. And I really don't like transitions. I will have to just hang on until I gain some stability once I start my fieldwork.

The Journey

The metaphor of the internship as a journey provides a useful way of capturing its dynamic nature (Sweitzer & King, 2014; Woodside, Mynatt, Hughes, Morgan, & Ramey, 2013). For those learning to be a human service professional, the internship presents a final segment of a long educational process. After you read about Alicia, Lucas, and Tamika in Chapter 1 and wrote your own story about becoming a helper, you realized that the internship experience becomes a special part of that story.

Why does the metaphor of the journey resonate so well for us as we consider the internship experience? Perhaps the notion of a journey emphasizes the dynamic nature of field-based learning and illustrates the definition of a journey as "something suggesting passage from one place to another" ("Journey," 2015). Even before you begin your internship, you hope this is the time you move from *studying* human services to *providing* human services. Let's look deeper into the idea of the journey of learning to be a human service professional. First, by reading about Tomas's experiences as he thinks about his upcoming internship and then by completing Exercise 2.1.

In 2 weeks Tomas begins his field experience. Tomas immigrated from Puerto Rico at age 9 with his father. Now, at age 25, most of his immediate family lives in Brooklyn. Attending his local community college was a dream that Tomas had even while he was in drug and alcohol rehabilitation. By the end of his rehabilitation experience, Tomas committed himself to helping other youth succeed in treatment. He enrolled in a local community college, applied to the human service program, and began classes. And now, Tomas stands on the edge of the internship experience. At least that is what it feels like to him.

Exercise 2.1 Describing the Beginning of the Journey

Step 1

Summarize the beginning of Tomas's journey to become a human service professional.

_____

_____

_____

Exercise 2.2 Describing the Beginning of the Journey—Assessing Your Own Readiness: Writing Your Own Story, Entry 3

Step 1

From Chapter 1, reread your written response to **Exercises 1.1 and 1.7: Writing Your Own Story, Entries 1 and 2.** Add to this story by discussing your experiences of becoming a human service professional in

(Continued)

(Continued)

terms of a journey. Identify any aspects of the journey that you believe will strengthen your own internship experience.

Step 2

Identify any aspects of the journey that you believe will make your own internship experience difficult or challenging.

The Influence of Time

A second core characteristic of the internship journey also relates to time (Woodside, McClam, Diambra, & Varga, 2012). First, as with any trip, there is a beginning, middle, and an end. As an intern, you will participate in these markers of the experience. A **pre-internship seminar or orientation** may mark the start of your field-based work. A visit to the agency in which you will intern, an interview with your new supervisor, and an agency-based orientation indicate a beginning. The first few weeks working in your internship setting will provide you with opportunities to learn more about the agency, the clients, work expectations, and your own role. By the middle of the experience, you will increase your involvement in agency meetings, service delivery, paperwork, and supervision. You will feel less like an intern and more like a member of the agency staff. During the final weeks of the internship experience and as you conclude your work at the agency, you will take account of the contributions you made and the skills you learned. Also you will focus on the next phase of your professional life: finding employment in human services.

Interns are continually reminded of the influence of time in their work. Time is a dimension in both their personal and professional behaviors and feelings. It provides meaning, such as recognizing limits and treasuring the moment. It introduces pressures such as wanting to help more clients than time allows. At first, interns try to manage or control their time. They speak of "mastering" it. They use calendars, planners, clocks, and alarms to structure their work and their interactions (Woodside & McClam, 2013).

In time, interns become aware of the pace in which they work (Woodside et al., 2012). Pace reflects the never-ending tempo of the intern experience. Even before their internship begins, pre-internship students hear from other interns about the demands of being in school and in an agency simultaneously. Specifically, the demands of the work, its constancy, and overwhelming client needs all foster this sense of a fast-paced life combined with the continual demands of school work (Woodside et al., 2012). Interns feel there is the constant pressure—day in, day out; hour after hour; minute by minute—as they move through their experience. The demands never let up. And at the same time, they also talk about taking time and being patient. Interns wait for the client to share important aspects of his or her life, they respond to crises (even when it interrupts their day), and they accept that their work occurs often on the clients' terms, not their own. Tomas tells us about time and his internship experience.

When Tomas entered the human service program he felt like he entered a new world. Sure he remained in Brooklyn, but the community college campus, its glass and chrome buildings, the book-filled library, and the computers all made it feel like an alternative reality. He wondered early on how this setting, so unlike his own neighborhood and his recent "home" at the halfway house, could actually prepare him for work in rehabilitation. Tomas noted other differences in this new life he was leading. In rehab, his time was regimented. He was busy but always had a routine. Others set his schedule for him. Now he feels the pressure of time seemingly every moment. Since he is going to school full-time and working full-time, he begins his days at 6 a.m. His first class meets at 7:50 a.m. He rides the subway to work midday and then returns for evening classes two nights a week. He volunteers at a local boys and girls club on Saturdays and Sundays; there, the children constantly demand his attention. When he arrives at 10 a.m. Saturday morning, a set of triplets are standing at the door waiting for him. By the time he leaves at 5 p.m., he has a trail of children waving good-bye. When Tomas thought about beginning his internship, he had difficulty imaging how he would manage all of his commitments. He has to keep his job. He wants to continue working at the boys and girls club. Adding to his responsibilities, he will still be enrolled in classes and involved in the field experience.

Exercise 2.3 The Influence of Time

Step 1

Summarize how time influences Tomas's experiences of becoming a human service professional.

_____

_____

_____

_____

Exercise 2.4 The Influence of Time: Assessing Your Own Readiness— Writing Your Own Story, Entry 4

Step 1

Return to **Writing Your Own Story**. You last responded to **Exercise 2.2: Entry 3**. Add to this story by discussing your experiences of becoming a human service professional in terms of the influence of time.

Step 2

Describe your thoughts and feelings about (a) the beginning of your internship experience, (b) how as an intern you will manage your time, and (c) how you believe you will respond to the pace, demands, and pressures of the internship experience, especially as you integrate into your other life demands.

Expectations and Anxieties

Emotions play a prominent role in the intern experience. Many of these emotions relate to the experience of time and the newness of the experience (Woodside et al., 2012; Woodside et al., 2013). This includes excitement about experiencing novel events and **anxiety** about the unknown. The central concern tends to reflect the uncertainty of the internship and an anticipation of the positives and negatives of the experience. As a beginning intern, you may be thinking something like the following:

- "I am going to love my internship in human services." Or "I will learn this is not the right career for me."
- "I don't have the knowledge and skills to help my clients." Or "I can't wait to practice all that I learned in class thus far."
- "It will be great to have a supervisor to help me." Or "I won't measure up to my supervisor's expectations."
- "If I have questions, there are plenty of people to help me learn." Or "If I ask too many questions, my colleagues will think I am incompetent."

Implicit in all of these statements is uncertainty about what *might* happen. The future contains both the familiar and the unknown. Interns draw comfort from their knowledge and experience that they have gained in the human services thus far. Having confidence in your abilities and being willing to take risks emerge from this comfort. Anxiety produces responses that can hinder your ability to learn during your internship experience. Negative consequences of anxiety might be experienced by behaviors such as coming late to the agency, avoiding responsibility, and declining to ask for feedback. In addition, anxiety can influence your "ability to learn, ability to demonstrate already present skills, and manner of responding to the supervisor" (Bernard & Goodyear, 2013, p. 178).

Tomas provides us some insights into his own expectations and anxiety.

Tomas

I can't decide if I am too excited to wait for my internship to begin or too nervous to begin. It seems to me like yesterday that I was a client rather than an intern. I really don't think I have had enough education to be ready to work in the field. Now I don't worry much about relating to the clients; I figure I will recognize them and they will look a lot like me—although I do wonder how I will work with female teens. Women always seem to like me, but that doesn't really apply to clients, does it? My best friend, Jon, told me to keep emotionally distance from the young women. I walked by my internship site yesterday just so I could find it easily when I go to my interview with my site supervisor. I guess I will have to wait and see how it goes.

Exercise 2.5 Expectations and Anxieties—Assessing Your Own Readiness: Writing Your Own Story, Entry 5

Step 1

In order to understand how expectations and anxieties might influence your own internship experience, respond to the questions that follow:

1. Describe the expectations and anxieties that Tomas experiences prior to his internship experience.

2. When you picture yourself in the first week of your internship experience, what stands out for you?

3. Describe your expectations and excitement about your internship.

4. What do you most worry about?

5. Who can you talk to about these feelings? Who can you ask for help?

Highs and Lows

Scholars in human services report that field internship experience represents both emotional and professional highs and lows for the intern (Bernard & Goodyear, 2013; Diambra, Cole-Zakrzewski, & Booher, 2004; Woodside et al., 2013). Difficult emotions included feeling lonely, scared, nervous, worried, insecure, uncomfortable, frustrated, "freaking out, vulnerable, and uncertain" (Woodside et al., 2013, p. 17). The emotions range from negative emotions such as "fear of incompetence," "fear of hurting clients or not meeting their needs," and "feeling lonely" to more positive ones such as "pride in skill development," "happiness in helping clients succeed," and "joy in belonging" (Woodside et al., 2013, p. 17). For instance, difficulties early in the internship include orientation and learning about the site, the supervisor, and the policies and procedures. These can elicit stress and anxiety (Diambra, Cole-Zakrzewski, & Zakrzewski, 2004). Furthermore, in the middle of the internship, students can experience stress related to "working too much" and confronting client difficulties. Interns struggle with the realities of their work, especially as it relates to their high expectations.

Internship remains a positive experience as students gain a comfort level in their sites, work successfully with their supervisors, and experience success with their work with clients. They express positive feelings associated with good relationships with clients, positive feedback from supervisors, and increased responsibilities (Diambra, Cole-Zakrzewski, & Booher, 2004; Kiser, 2009). Three keys to these positive feelings about the internship appear to be making a difference in clients' lives, establishing a bond with their supervisors, and being treated as "more than an intern" (Woodside, Paulus, & Ziegler, 2009; Woodside et al., 2012).

Changes and Stages

Changes

We also associate journeys with the possibility and the power to change or be transformed. Many times a major goal for the intern is to help clients change and make a difference in their lives. At the same time, by the end of the internship, interns also may marvel at their own changes and growth (Woodside et al., 2012). Many times, the differences mark a subtle shift in confidence or attitudes. For example, as described in Chapter 1, Sue, the human service intern working in a homeless shelter in Oklahoma, learns more about how and when to dress more formally and less formally. But on more occasions there will be a dramatic evidence of change. Returning to Sue, one clearly noticeable change is her growing understanding of the realities of the context of human services. For example, a professional such as Maria, Sue's supervisor, is a committed professional ready to help Sue at any time during the day with Sue's work with clients. On the other hand, Carmello Jones, the shelter's director, provides a very different type of supervision. He is less direct about how she should conduct herself day after day; rather, he focuses on a broader understanding of the agency.

Interns capture changes in their internship stories in terms of now and then, as they describe what the experience is like for them now in contrast to how it was in the past (Woodside et al., 2012). For instance, the phrases such as "before internship," "in my first week at my site," and "when I saw my first client," to describe the beginning of their internship. As the weeks pass and the stories change, they note differences. For example, during the middle of the internship, one intern recalls her first client, using the phrase "then and now" to structure and describe her experience.

"I remember the first time I saw Susie. She was my first client. I was so nervous and I was not even sure I could begin a conversation with her. Today I see her for the eighth time. I can't wait to hear about her week."

Another intern shares his insight about his supervisor, using *then* and *now* to express the changes occurring related to his familiarity of his supervisor and of the agency structure and procedures.

"I wasn't sure I would ever be able to feel comfortable at my placement. It is very structured with lots of rules, and we follow a set protocol with each client who comes for help. We are primarily working with mothers in the welfare-to-work program. The state prescribes our approach and treatment. We literally have to use a script as we provide our services. My first job was to conduct intakes. I kept wanting to go off script and wanted to get to know my clients better in our first intake meeting. Now I have developed professional relationships with five women who joined our program 2 months ago. In spite of these very difficult intakes, I managed to get to know them so I could establish good relationships with them. I feel I can help them achieve their goals and ultimately help them find employment."

Specific events can become historical markers or turning points in the growth and development of interns and their clients. The language interns use points to changes in an agency, staff, or an agency event or trend. Sometimes interns refer to these changes as benchmarks in their own learning. For instance, interns note the day "my supervisor was absent," "my client got arrested," "we held our career fair for the community," or "the week of the ice storm." Let's see how interns talk about these specific events in terms of their own growth.

"I remember clearly the first day my supervisor was absent. I had been at the agency for 2 weeks. My supervisor's baby daughter was in the hospital and she could not come in. I had to take her client load that day. We stayed in touch several times that day, especially when I had questions about the paperwork. I was nervous at first, but by the afternoon I was thinking, well I can do this job. Of course I was asking my co-workers questions all day."

"Oh my, this day was a crisis all around. I had a full day planned and was going to end the day at a professional development ethics workshop. But by the time I arrived at the office, the deputy sheriff's office had already called. My client, Tom, was arrested for following two young women on the street. I had to meet my supervisor at court. My supervisor asked me to handle the communication with the judge while she observed. I had been to court before but just to watch. I was so nervous. But I learned how to negotiate the court on behalf of my client."

"The day we held our career fair at the local community college, I had such a terrific time. What a way to watch all of our work come together. I was in charge of a local booth that reviewed resumes of the participants. It was so much fun. The career attendees who came to our booth were so nervous about sharing their resumes and so grateful to have the feedback. By the time they left the booth, they were singing our praises. The atmosphere was so upbeat. I knew then, 'I am in the right job.'"

"I thought I knew about hard work and helping maintain a steady and even environment in our rehabilitation center. But the day of the ice storm, the roof fell in. We had to evacuate all of our clients, find them somewhere to go for the night and then for the month. I will always remember that day and the days following. Nothing like a good crisis to make you forget you are intern. That day I became part of the team."

These quotes illustrate some of the intern stories and comments that others share. They provide models for you to use as you begin to record your own changes. Exercise 2.6 provides a way you can begin to monitor your own growth and change during your internship.

Exercise 2.6 Tracking Highs and Lows and the Process of Change— Assessing Your Own Readiness: Writing Your Own Story, Entry 6

Step 1

This exercise helps you describe your thoughts and feelings related to your experience in internship. You will be recording the highs and lows that you experience.

Step 2

In addition, you will note the changes that you experience. Use this table (see Table 2.1) throughout your internship to note your patterns of thoughts, feelings, and behaviors related to now and then and the specific events that shape your professional and emotional growth and development. Right now you can only begin to record some of your initial thoughts and experiences. Later you will have much more to share.

Table 2.1 Noting Your Growth and Development (Change) Through the Internship

Areas of Change	Beginning of Human Service Program	Beginning of the Internship Experience	End of the Internship Experience
Noting highs and lows Noting change Now and then			
Noting highs and lows Noting change Specific events			

Stages

Scholars in human services often describe growth and change in the internship in terms of professional development. Three assumptions undergird the developmental model. First is the assumption that changes occur over time. This means that during the internship you, as an intern, can expect to grow and develop throughout the entire process and well into your career as a helping professional. In fact, you continue to learn throughout your entire career as a helper.

A second assumption related to professional development is that it is multidimensional. For an intern, dimensions of development include aspects of personal development, an expanded knowledge base, the mastery of helping skills, and a better understanding of the human service delivery system. A third assumption, suggested by a developmental model, reflects the predictable stages that most interns will experience. Early in the internship experience, it is difficult for interns to know what to expect. In fact, the demands of internship are too novel for a deep understanding of the situation.

Using the IDM to Think About Your Internship

Using a model of development to think about your own internship will help you better understand your own internship experience. In this section we introduce the IDM (Stoltenberg & McNeill, 2009; Stoltenberg et al., 1998). As you use the IDM you will be able to reflect on your internship in these ways:

- Structure your thoughts about your internship experience.
- Predict your growth and development.
- Connect past learning with your field-based learning.
- Deepen your insights about your growth as a human service professional.
- Identify areas of strength and limitations, related skills, and professional behaviors.
- Understand what is typical for many interns who are learning to become helping professionals (Kiser, 2009; Sweitzer & King, 2014).

- See your experiences are similar to others in internship; reduce your sense of isolation.
- Increase your sense of community.

The IDM provides us with a fruitful way to think about professional growth and change during the internship experience (Stoltenberg & McNeill, 2009; Stoltenberg et al., 1998). The model uses three components to describe an intern's experience: (a) levels of competence, (b) overarching structures, and (c) specific domains. In this text, we will focus on the first two; levels of competence and overarching structures. As you read about the IDM, refer to Figure 2.1 to clarify how the components of the model work together.

Levels of competence: The IDM suggests that the work of students in the internship potentially represents three levels of competence, **Level 1**, **Level 2**, and **Level** 3 (Stoltenberg & McNeill, 2009) as shown in Figure 2.1. For each of the levels, Stoltenberg and McNeill offered three overarching structures to measure professional growth and development: (a) **self- and other awareness**, (b) **motivation**, (c) **autonomy**. For example, the authors look at the competence of Level 1 interns of individual self- and other awareness, motivation, and autonomy as a way to distinguish among professional performance among the levels. Return to Figure 2.1 to view how the overarching structures relate to the level of competence.

We introduce the IDM by providing descriptions of the three overarching structures listed in Box 2.3. Then, in the text, we describe professional development at Levels 1, 2, and 3 in terms of these three overarching structures.

Figure 2.1   Pictorial Representations of the Levels of Competence in the IDM

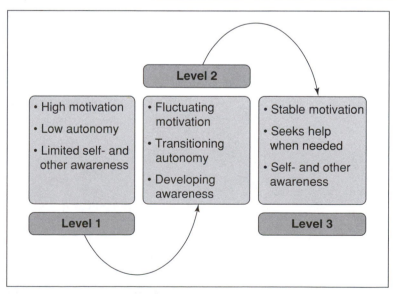

Source: Created by Gwen Ruttencutter, 2015. Used with permission. (Adapted from Stoltenberg & McNeill, 2009; Stoltenberg et al., 1998)

Box 2.3 Descriptions of IDM's Three Overarching Structures

Overarching structure: Self- and other awareness shifts according to the intern's level of competence. This awareness ranges from "self-preoccupation, awareness of the client's world, and enlightened self-awareness" (p. 23). There exist mental and emotional aspects of self- and other awareness.

Overarching structure: Motivation encompasses the intern's commitment to professional growth during the internship experience. Commitment represents an intentional desire and willingness on the part of interns to build their helping skills and learn about their clients. As interns engage in the learning process, this sense of purpose can translate into enthusiasm for the experience and concentrated attention and energy invested into the work. Motivation includes extrinsic (external) and intrinsic (internal) that changes throughout the levels of competence.

Overarching structure: Autonomy in the context of the internship experience represents the intern's willingness to act independently when assuming the roles and responsibilities at the internship site. Working in a new situation and assuming novel responsibilities can often result in a lack of confidence in one's abilities. Dependence upon supervisors and other colleagues often results. A growing sense of autonomy and independence may occur as an intern becomes more knowledgeable and comfortable working with clients.

Interns demonstrate their self- and other awareness, motivation, and autonomy differently, depending upon their levels of competence. Let's look at Levels 1, 2, and 3 in more depth and see how Stoltenberg and McNeill (2009) describe the three overarching structures as they change across the levels. The first two levels reflect the development internship students are most likely to experience. At the end of the description of these stages, we will ask you to assess your own self- and other awareness, motivation, and autonomy as related to your internship experience.

Level 1

According to Stoltenberg and McNeill (2009), many interns at Level 1 are beginning their internship experiences. They have completed recent classroom experiences focusing on the development of helping skills, but they lack any significant work-related helping experiences. The authors also suggested the overriding feature of interns functioning at Level 1 is their status as a novice helper. Even if the interns have prior experience in a human service setting, they may return to the novice state (or Level 1) when any of the following are encountered: They negotiate a new delivery system; they work with a new supervisor; they provide services for a different client population; they assume new roles and responsibilities; and they try new interventions. Reflecting the core characteristics described earlier in this chapter, at Level 1 interns are excited about their opportunities to practice their classroom learning and are anxious about their own abilities (Stoltenberg & McNeill, 2009).

With regard to *self- and other awareness* structure in Level 1, Stoltenberg and McNeil (2009) characterize this in the following ways:

- The intern remains focused on self, both from the thinking and feelings perspectives.
- The intern uses a cookbook or step-by-step approach to helping. They follow carefully what was taught in their academic program.
- The intern's primary focus is on what you do rather than on what the client needs or how the client responds.
- The intern has strong emotions, such as enthusiasm and anxiety that he or she must deal with. So much focus on the self may interfere with building a relationship with the client.

Motivation is high for most beginning interns according to Stoltenberg and McNeill (2009):

- The intern is excited to finally apply what he or she has been practicing in classes.
- The intern begins to acquire experience related to human service career goals.
- The intern is nervous about being evaluated by faculty, supervisors, clients, and peers related to the knowledge and skills.
- For the first time, the intern may begin to enjoy a feeling of competence.
- As the intern begins to master skills, confidence builds and motivation to learn may decrease.
- The intern may want to work where he or she feels confident. Hence the intern may be reluctant to work with new populations and learn new skills.

Autonomy expressed in Level 1 means a high dependence upon the faculty member and the supervisor for guidance and instruction (Stoltenberg & McNeill, 2009):

- Interns need and want structure. It makes sense that faculty ask supervisors to provide structure early in the internship experience.
- The intern needs an orientation to the internship site.
- The intern will want to shadow the site supervisor through the first couple of weeks of internship.
- Interns may look to the supervisor for "right" answers to questions relating to agency policy and protocol, for ways to establish relationships with clients, and for assurance about their professional promise.
- If the interns have positive experiences, they are more likely to move toward greater independence (Stoltenberg & McNeill, 2009).

Level 2

According to Stoltenberg and McNeill (2009), the characteristics of the Level 2 professional work represent considerable growth in (a) the interns' understanding and use of self in the helping process, (b) their motivations as helpers, as well as (c) their level of autonomy. Moving beyond the novice stance allows the interns to attend to more client needs and fewer of their own needs. While functioning on this level, confidence may vary as interns struggle with their sense of efficacy related to client change (Stoltenberg & McNeill, 2009). For example, while working at Level 2, interns become more aware of how clients receive the help that they provide. Hence, interns may move from a more cookbook or rigid intervention toward tailoring service delivery to meet individual client needs. The authors suggested that the fluctuation in confidence illustrates the core characteristic of highs and lows. As interns increase their understanding and skill level, their confidence grows. As they increase their awareness and self-reflection, frustrations also grow in relation to their work with clients. They begin to see more clearly the mixed results of their interventions and its influences on the complexities of their clients' lives. Stoltenberg and McNeill (2009) have described this stage as "turbulent" and "uncertain" (p. 37).

Stoltenberg and McNeill (2009) explain how self- and other awareness shifts for interns during Level 2:

- The intern feels more comfortable in the work with clients.
- The intern focuses less on self and more on the clients' perspectives and the clients' worlds.
- The intern's expanded view of the client and his or her world means seeing more of the complexities and ambiguities described earlier.
- The intern may begin to understand the limitations of previous interventions and return to a sense of inadequacy.
- The empathy the intern experiences for the client may increase.
- As the intern begins to understand more deeply clients' perspectives and reflect on clients' emotions, the intern may "take on" the emotions of their clients.
- As the intern internalizes the client's emotions, the intern may return to a state of self-focus.

Motivation during Level 2 becomes something like a roller coaster (Stoltenberg & McNeill, 2009). The interns experience a tug between the enthusiasm for helping and the complexities of helping. At this level, many interns ask the question, "Am I suitable for this work?" According to Stoltenberg and McNeill (2009), Level 2 becomes a time of assessment, as interns hone their skills and explore how their personalities can help and/or hinder their work as helpers.

Autonomy also fluctuates during Level 2. Interns may move from the initial sense of dependency on the supervisor to more independence:

- The intern experiences a greater sense of ability and more of a desire to work independently.
- The intern is challenged by the existence of the clients' multiple issues and ever changing environments.

- The intern bounces from a strong sense of independence to a need for supervisor support.
- The intern begins to feel the need for autonomy with support (this is a characteristic of Level 3).

Level 3

At the advanced Level 3, the mature professional engages in a more consistent and purposeful approach to the helping process. Most interns do not reach this advanced stage. At Level 3 the term *helper* or *professional* is a better description rather than the term *intern*. There are always interns who perform exceptionally well and, in some areas of development, who achieve higher levels of professional functioning.

In Level 3, although challenges and frustrations remain for a professional operating at this stage, there exist opportunities to develop patterns of understanding clients and determining effective interventions that fit both the professional's helping style and the client's needs.

Self- and other awareness in Level 3 is a point of stability as the helper's use of reflection about self and others. In Level 1, behaviors that illustrate the focus on self include saying the right words, performing the correct intervention, and struggling to feel confident in the moment. A helper's self-reflections within Level 3 manifest a more complex awareness of helping:

- The professional shifts awareness between what clients say and how clients behave.
- The professional shifts awareness between the multiple ways to interpret client behaviors.
- The professional can focus on clients and interact with clients while at the same time analyzing what is happening in the moment.
- The professional can focus on clients and interact with clients while at the same time developing possible alternative hypotheses and strategies for longer-range interventions.

Motivation becomes more stable at Level 3 as helpers rely more on internal rather than external rewards:

- For the professional, highs and lows still exist, but the frequency and range of these lessen.
- The professional still critiques his or her abilities and suitability for the work.
- This questioning relates to more fine-tuning of the work, rather than broad life-changing questions, such as vocational shifts that include leaving the helping profession.

Autonomy moves to the state of the conditional autonomy introduced in Level 2:

- The professional accepts and actively welcomes responsibility for his or her work.
- The professional continually integrates consultation with client care.

- Crisis events still demand for the professional conversations with others.
- The professional establishes regular opportunities to meet with colleagues and seek consultation with them about ethical issues.

Exercise 2.7 Stages: Making an IDM Work for You: Assessing Your Own Readiness: Writing Your Own Story, Entry 7

Step 1

As you are in a human service program, you are already involved in professional and personal change. Take a moment to identify three areas of growth that you have experienced since entering the human service program.

Step 2

Fill out the following chart so you can document your movement prior to entering the program and at the beginning of your internship experience; then project how you hope you will change by the end of the experience.

Step 3

Compare your responses in the columns Beginning of Human Service Program and Beginning of the Internship Experience with the IDM levels of competence. Indicate your levels of competence for self- and other awareness, motivation, and autonomy.

Areas of Competence	Beginning of Human Service Program	Beginning of the Internship Experience	Project: End of the Internship Experience
Self- and other awareness			
Motivation			
Autonomy			

One of the outcomes of assessing your personal readiness for internship is your developing sense of professional identity. In the next section, we introduce the concept of professional identity and how it relates to work in internship.

Professional Identity

Individuals involved in the world of work often refer to their **professional identity**. In fact, in the academic world, professional programs establish missions that include building the professional identity of their students. In this section, we define professional identity and then describe how internship plays a part in its development, especially in the human service profession. We also talk about the way that professional identity is acted out or practiced in the working world. Definitions and examples help clarify both of these terms and how they relate to your work as an intern.

Scholars suggest that professional identity is located both within the individual (e.g., personal beliefs, values, behaviors) and in a professional or work-related context (e.g., ethics, multicultural, knowledge, and skills) (Woodside & McClam, 2015). Professional identity is especially important to human service students and professionals engaged in learning about and delivering human services. In fact, while working within the human service context, individuals seek answers to two questions related to their professional activity: "Who am I?" and "What do I want to become?" (Beijaard, Paulien, & Verloop, 2004, p. 108). Both questions directly address and help define one's identity as a professional. Academic programs in human services strive to help their students answer both questions with the understanding that professional identity changes as individuals gain educational and career experiences.

Another way to begin to understand professional identity is to look at its many components or aspects. We present seven components that help clarify the concept and indicate whether the aspect is grounded in the individual context or professional or work-related context (Figure 2.2). We discuss each of these in more detail in the chapters that follow.

Individual Context

Personal beliefs are the foundations that guide personal and professional thoughts, feelings, and behaviors; this is sometimes known as the "use of self."

Wellness and self-care support a focus on positive lifestyle that maintains a balanced approach to health, family and relationships, work, and spirituality.

Professional or Work-Related Context

Professional knowledge and skills are an agreed-upon body of education that prepares individuals for professional practice.

Professional development and continuing education are ways that professionals extend their personal and professional development as lifelong learners.

Organizational definitions are how professional organizations and licensing bodies describe the professional work.

Professional values are principles and beliefs that help professionals determine how to conduct their work.

Ethical and multicultural practices are guidelines developed by professional organizations that establish standards for professional work.

In the chapters that follow, you will be able to see how professional identity relates to your own growth as a human service professional. By the end of internship, you will be able to articulate the two questions introduced earlier; "Who am I?" and "What do I want to become?" (Beijaard et al., 2004, p. 108).

As indicated earlier, professional identity is located both within the individual (personal beliefs, wellness and self-care) and with a professional

Figure 2.2   Aspects of Professional Identity

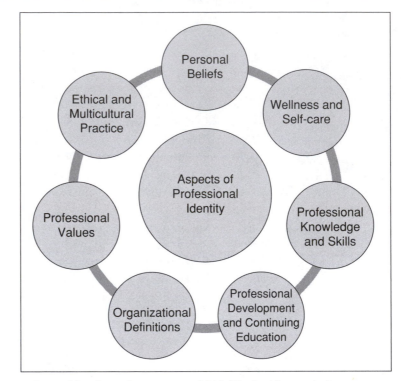

Source: Created by Gwen Ruttencutter, 2015. Used with permission.

or work-related context (**professional knowledge and skills, professional development and continuing education, organizational definitions, professional values, ethical and multicultural practice**). Although this identity, at times, seems fairly abstract, we can link behaviors in the workplace to it. These behaviors represent the way that professional identity is acted out or practiced in the working world. This includes thoughts, feelings, and behaviors labeled as professional activity. It occurs as helpers provide services to their clients, reflect and evaluate these services, and introduce new ideas and new approaches to their work (Cochran-Smith & Lytle, 2009). Your professional identity is dynamic: It is ever changing as you work in your internship and beyond.

Exercise 2.8 Professional Identity: Writing Your Own Story, Entry 8

Though it is early in your internship, it is a good time for you to begin to think about your professional identity as a human service professional.

Step 1

We ask you, in this exercise, to make notes about each of the aspects of professional identity and how you relate these to your current professional and personal development as an intern.

1. Personal beliefs _____

2. Wellness and self-care _____

3. Professional knowledge and skills _____

4. Professional development and continuing education _____

5. Organizational definitions _____

6. Professional values _____

7. Ethical and multicultural practice _____

Now that you understand the core characteristics of the internship experience, the IDM, and the concept of professional identity, especially as they relate to you and your internship, let's continue our efforts at deepening your understanding. See Box 2.4 to better understand the organization of this section.

Box 2.4 Studying the Text: Deepening Your Understanding

Studying the text: The following outline will help you read and study the text material in this next section.

1. Peer-to-peer dialogue

    a. Alicia: The journey to internship

    b. Lucas: The journey to internship

    c. Tamika: The journey to internship

2. Faculty and site supervisor dialogue

    a. Dr. Bianca: Finding internship placements

    b. Ms. Bellewa: Becoming a site supervisor

3. The professional voice and tips for practice: Gwen: Professional identity

4. Terms to remember

5. References

Deepening Your Understanding

In this section, you will hear more about Alicia, Lucas, and Tamika and their preparations for the beginning of their internships. In addition, Dr. Bianca and Ms. Bellewa continue to share their faculty and site supervisor perspectives. Gwen, in the section on professional voice and tips for practice, suggests ways you as an intern can enhance your professional identity. We also include terms to remember and references to support your learning.

Peer-to-Peer Dialogue: Alicia, Lucas, and Tamika

We asked Alicia, Lucas, and Tamika to talk about the context of their internship experiences. Their perspectives can help broaden your understanding of the beginning of this experience.

Alicia

Hello, again! I am excited to share more of my journey with you. I will be talking to you about my experience during the first two years of my undergraduate work. I started off at Colorado Mountain College, which is a community college that was in the town where I lived. I wanted to start at a community college for a few reasons. I wanted to ease my way back into school, and I knew a community college would help with the transition. It was also the closest campus to home; my son, Thomas, and I needed to be closer to my family because they provided a significant amount of support for us. Also, the community college was cheaper than a university and it would be slightly easier for me financially. I had originally known that I wanted to get into the human services field, but that specific degree wasn't offered at the college.

I had to set up a meeting with my adviser to discuss what classes I would need to take in order for me to be able to transfer to a university after 2 years and continue my degree. Luckily, my adviser, Dr. Stevens, was very knowledgeable and supportive throughout the whole process. He explained to me the different degrees that I may be interested in such as psychology, human services and social work. He suggested that I use my time at the community college to research the different fields until I find the best fit for me. Because the community college had limited offerings on the different fields and areas of study, I was limited to introductory courses in psychology.

My time at the community college had its ups and downs. While I did enjoy taking many of the classes, the workload alongside my job and taking care of my son was almost overwhelming. There were many times I would tell my mother that I didn't know if going back to school was a good decision. She constantly reminded me of the bigger picture and the goals that I wanted to accomplish. I kept telling myself, "You need to keep going."

I met with Dr. Stevens regularly to discuss any questions I had about the different fields of study. He suggested that I look into volunteering opportunities in different agencies and settings. I knew that would be a struggle because when I was not in class, I was either at work or taking care of Thomas. I was able to volunteer at a runaway youth shelter once a week, and I really enjoyed being with the kids there. As I started my second year of college, Dr. ns and I began discussing the different universities that I would want to apply to and possible scholarships or financial assistance that I could get. The closest university was around an hour away from my home, so I applied to that one. While I knew I had the good grades to apply to schools across the nation, I also knew it would be a bad decision for Thomas and myself.

Towards the end of my associate's degree at the community college, I received my acceptance to the University of Denver and was set on getting my bachelor's in human services. I was also excited to receive a scholarship that would cover my tuition for up to 2 years. In that moment, I remember feeling that maybe everything is beginning to fall into place. I knew that the next 2 years were going to be just as difficult, if not more so, but I just had to keep going.

Written by Allie Rhinehart and Dareen Basma, 2015. Used with permission.

Lucas

Hello, I hope everything is well with you, and I am excited to share with you my new journey at Tampa Bay Community College. I am currently in my second year in the Counseling and Human Services program at Tampa Bay Community College trying to obtain my AS degree. I still cannot believe I am almost done with my program. To be honest, I did not even think I would survive. I remember when I first visited my adviser, Dr. Franks, and her telling me about my requirements to graduate. When she said 65 credit hours to be completed in five semesters, I felt overwhelmed with the process to complete the degree. Not only did I feel overwhelmed, but the first two semesters, I was taking general education courses like math and English. These courses felt like a waste of time. I wanted to start my counseling and human services courses right away. I wanted to start learning how to work in community agencies to help people, but that was not the case. Dr. Franks told me that I had to take general education courses before I could take my major requirements and practicum, which was upsetting.

Just to give you a brief outlook of my first year, it was brief, lol. My first year went by so fast that I can hardly remember it. Every week I had to read material, do homework, and it felt like I had a project due every week. Therefore, I just reacted to what was due and focused on completing my next assignment. Overall, I can say my first year of college was overwhelming due to my lack of preparation. But it was satisfying as well because I developed a lot of positive relationships with friends and staff members, including my mentor Dr. Franks. Without Dr. Franks, I would not have survived my first year. I attribute all my success to her and thank her for being there for me when I wanted to give up.

Well, now I am in my second year, I am finishing up my major course requirements and getting ready for my practicum. Practicum is like an internship, and this is going to be my first experience in the field of human services. I just finished my practicum interview, and I will be at the Tampa Bay Justice Center working with victims of domestic violence. This has always been a passion of mine to help people who were physically and sexually abused, because growing up in the city this was a huge problem. Growing up I always wanted to make a difference in my community, so this is why I am pursuing a career in human services.

Now that I am finishing up my major course requirements and preparing for my field-based work, I am extremely nervous. To be honest, I am doubting myself. Will I be able to help my future clients at the Tampa Bay Justice Center? What counseling skills do I use? How do I build a therapeutic relationship? What happens if my clients get worse? All of these questions are popping in my head as I prepare for my first internship. However, I am lucky Dr. Franks is there to supervise me. Even though I am nervous, I am also excited to start practicing my counseling skills. I believe I am ready from an education standpoint, and all I need is to start applying what I have learned. This is also what my colleague James is telling me. He is in his final semester at Tampa Bay Community College. He told me that preparing for your first field-based experience is nerve-racking. He said that once you start sessions with clients and develop relationships at the internship site, then everything will slow down. Consequently, James is also helping me with the process to transition from coursework to field-based work and giving me pointers, which is really helpful.

Overall, I am excited for next semester to start my practicum and finally start helping people. I still cannot believe how fast the first year went. I have changed so much since I first entered the program. I was clueless about what helping looks like. I thought it was a simple conversation between you and another person, but it is more than that. I am very thankful for my coursework, because it is preparing me to help others.

Not only is my program educating me on what counseling skills to apply in human services, I have learned a lot about myself. It seems in every core counseling and human services course we are reflecting on ourselves, either by journaling or during advising. As a result, I know more about myself than I ever did, and I am thankful this program is helping me understand myself. Therefore, I matured in my first year, and without the demands of coursework and help from Dr. Franks and James, I would not have changed since the beginning of my program. I am more reflective and now I understand myself better.

Well, I hope you found my experience helpful as you pursue your dreams to help others. My advice to you is to be patient. Trust in the process and the outcomes will happen, as Dr. Franks tells me. Have a blessed day, and I look forward to talking with you soon!

Written by Jorge Roman, 2015. Used with permission.

Tamika

As I get ready to start my first internship placement, I want to take some time to tell you so far about my college experience. I chose to attend a school a few hours away from my hometown in Michigan so that I could stay somewhat close to my family but also get far enough away to be independent and start my own life. The school I chose to attend is a medium-sized, four-year university with a number of program options, which is great considering I started out with no clue of what I wanted to do!

After taking introductory psychology and sociology courses to figure out what subjects I liked best, I decided that I had a real interest in working with people who are incarcerated. This led to my decision to major in human services with a concentration in corrections work. The first two years of being here at college have been challenging and being away from home has been a real adjustment. But I really feel like I have found my calling now, and I am excited to start working in the field I have chosen.

My upcoming internship placement at a local justice center is going to provide me with my first real professional experience. During my first two years of college, I volunteered at a homeless shelter, where I got some great experience working with diverse populations. A lot of the people I encountered there had been in trouble with the law at some point. It gave me some great insight into legal issues that exist and the difficulties people experience once they are released from incarceration. I hope my upcoming internship will give me more insight into some of the issues these people face during incarceration. I really want to learn how to support their rehabilitation while they are in jail or prison, so that they can become productive citizens once they are released.

As I have prepared myself for this experience, I have felt a number of mixed emotions. I am very excited to actually begin working in the field, but I am also really nervous about the responsibilities that come along with such a challenging placement. As a woman, in particular, I feel like I might be a bit vulnerable in the corrections world, but I am hopeful that I will have good supervisors to help me feel comfortable and learn the ropes. Some of the students who interned at the justice center last year have shared their experiences with me, which has been tremendously helpful. They told me to be respectful of the inmates but remember to stay aware at all times for my own safety. That seems like sound advice to me, and I am grateful to know that I can continue to go to them when I have questions or concerns.

Since entering this program, I have seen a lot of changes within myself. I am certainly more mature than I was 2 years ago and have found a good sense of who I am and what I want to do with my life. My desire to connect with and help others is stronger than ever, and I am really looking forward to applying what I have learned in the classroom to working in the real world.

Written by Brittany Pollard, 2015. Used with permission.

Exercise 2.9 Addressing Your Personal Readiness

Step 1

Other human service students can help us learn about each other and ourselves. Make notes about what you learned from Alicia, Lucas, and Tamika.

Alicia: _____

_____

_____

_____

Lucas: _____

_____

_____

_____

Tamika: _____

_____

_____

_____

Step 2

Review the exercises in this chapter (Exercise 2.2–Exercise 2.8. Compare your experiences as they related to the core characteristics, your stage of development (according to the IDM), and your own personal identity with the experiences of Alicia, Lucas, and Tamika.

Similarities: _____

(Continued)

(Continued)

_____

_____

_____

Differences: _____

_____

_____

_____

Faculty and Site Supervisor Dialogue: Dr. Bianca and Ms. Bellewa

We asked Dr. Bianca and Ms. Bellewa to talk about the context of their work with student interns. Their perspectives can help broaden your understanding of the beginning of this experience from faculty and site supervisor perspectives.

Dr. Claude Bianca

I wanted to begin this dialogue by describing my faculty responsibilities. I assumed my current position as the field coordinator for the human services program 10 years ago. Although I teach other classes, the internship experience is my primary responsibility. When I started, the chair of our program asked me if I would revise and update our internship experience, develop a plan, and present it to other faculty in the program. With lots of consultation from the faculty and agencies in the community, I developed a new way of delivering our internship experience. First, I suggested ways that we could describe the internship experience in our program handbook and in our course description. Then I began to build structures to the experience so agencies and students would know what to expect. I developed an internship experience handbook and then shared it with faculty, agencies, and students. All of this effort took about 5 years. I decided this was enough change for a while. For the past 4 years, I coordinated the experience. I also kept notes about how to strengthen the program. The ideas came from the agency and site supervisors, faculty, students, and my own experience. Right now, I am consulting again about how to change the internship experience. Honestly, the best advice comes from students. Sometimes they can tell me directly what they need that we don't provide for them. One request they continually make is for a more comprehensive orientation to the internship experience. Other times, I can see what challenges students encounter in their first internship experience. There are many ways that I can support their internship work. In response, next semester I am offering an independent study that focuses on orientation to the internship experience. I hope to help students assess their readiness for the experience and help them feel more confident as they establish their placement and begin their agency work.

Ms. Zu Bellewa

Dr. Woodside asked me to write about my beginning involvement in human service education. This all starts with the values held deeply in my African culture. We believe that responsibility resides within the community to take care of others. In Western culture, especially in the human services, I hear people talking about advocacy and social justice. In our culture, we don't talk about it; we just do it. It felt perfectly natural to me to reach out to our local community college when our clients described their needs. Many of the clients immigrated to the United States, while others represent second-generation status. The range of needs included cultural support and community building on the one hand and needs related to food, housing, health, and education on the other.

As associate director my responsibility was to find or create programs that met client needs. My first response was to create a community-based team of interested professionals who were willing to assume a community-wide perspective and develop intraagency cooperation. My second was to explore the possibility of working with an intern to provide case management services to our most needy clients. Hence, that first contact began my association with the human service program and the internship experience.

Written by Dareen Basma, 2015. Used with permission.

The Professional Voice and Tips for Practice: Gwen

Here Gwen, a human service professional, provides insights into developing your professional identity and suggests practical ways you can demonstrate your development as a professional.

Gwen

In this chapter, you learned about the experiences of other students who are beginning their internships. Tomas describes his enthusiasm about his internship and also shares many of his worries. Alicia, Lucas, and Tamika share their thoughts about the beginning of the work. One idea that runs through all of these accounts is the beginning of a professional identity. Each student wants to be a human service professional; each student expresses concerns about being "professional" enough. I wanted to suggest to you several ways that you can develop your own professional identity.

Coming to Know Yourself

As you prepare for your internship experience, consider who you are. Ask yourself why you choose this profession, and who do you wish to become, as a human service professional. This type of self-reflection will allow you to see more clearly where you are today, the professional you want to become, and how to bridge the two.

Learning From Others

As you enter the human services arena, you have a wonderful opportunity to learn from the many other professionals you will meet. Some of these professionals will have logged countless hours as helping professionals, building deep wells of experiences and knowledge. When other professionals are willing to share their experiences, and their practical knowledge, listen. Listen with full attention and be willing to learn and benefit from their experiences.

Engaging in the Professional Arena

You may experience the beginning of your internship as daunting. But that is OK. It's natural to be timid in new situations. At the same time, don't allow that timidity to stop you from fully engaging in your environment. Share who you are with your colleagues, clients, and other helping professionals. You have unique gifts to contribute, so don't keep them all to yourself.

Seeking Help

A new environment is filled with the unknown. As you begin your internship experience, you may feel uneasy as you navigate your way in your new agency or organization. It's all right. If you don't understand how something works in your new workplace, ask. Ask for help. None of us is born knowing. We have to build that knowledge bank over time and through experience, and one way of doing that is to ask.

Recording Your Journey

Self-reflection is a powerful tool to help us come to understand ourselves and to understand how we interact with others in our world. One method of self-reflection is journaling. Journaling can capture your thoughts, reactions, hopes, fears, and ambitions. And according to Hiemstra (2001), journaling can provide "evolving insights" (p. 2). The "Writing Your Own Stories" exercises in this text are a good way to structure your journaling.

If you record events, and your feelings about those events, during your internship experience, a journal can illustrate to you your growing understanding of the field in general, and your growth as a professional (Hiemstra, 2001). In addition to seeing how you change, you also may discover that a journal aids in problem solving. Sometimes, once we write down a problem and review it later, how we frame and understand that problem changes, which opens the door for new ways of resolving it.

Written by Gwen Ruttencutter, 2015. Used with permission.

Terms to Remember

Anxiety

Autonomy

Ethical and multicultural practice

Highs and lows

Integrated Developmental Model (IDM)

Internship context

Journey

Level 1

Level 2

Level 3

Motivation

Organizational definitions

Personal beliefs

Personal readiness

Pre-internship seminar or orientation

Professional development and continuing education

Professional identity

Professional knowledge and skills

Professional values

Self- and other awareness

Wellness and self-care

References

Beijaard, D., Paulien, C. M., & Verloop, N. (2004). Reconsidering research on teachers' professional identity. *Teaching and Teacher Education, 20*, 107–128. Retrieved from https://openaccess.leidenuniv.nl/bitstream/handle/1887/11190/10_404_07.pdf?sequence=1

Bernard, J. M., & Goodyear, R. K. (2013). *Fundamentals of clinical supervision* (5th ed.). Boston, MA: Allyn and Bacon.

Chaiferi, R., & Griffin, M. (1997). *Developing fieldwork skills: A guide for human services, counseling, and social work students*. Belmont, CA: Brooks/Cole, Cengage Learning.

Cochran-Smith, M., & Lytle, S. L. (2009). *Inquiry as a stance: Practioner research for the next generation*. New York, NY: Teachers College Press.

Diambra, J. F., Cole-Zakrzewski, K. G., & Booher, J. (2004). A comparison of internship stage models: Evidence from intern experiences. *Journal of Experiential Education, 27*(2), 191–212.

Diambra, J. F., Cole-Zakrzewski, K. G., & Zakrzewski, R. F. (2004). Key lessons learned during the internship: Student perspectives. *Human Service Education, 24*(1), 5–18.

Hiemstra, R. (2001). Uses and benefits of journal writing. *New Directions for Adult and Continuing Education, 90*, 19–26.

Journey. (2015). In *Merriam-Webster dictionary*. (11th ed.). Retrieved from http://www.merriam-webster.com/dictionary/journey

Kiser, P. M. (2009). *The human service internship: Getting the most from your experience*. Belmont, CA: Brooks/Cole, Cengage Learning.

Stoltenberg, C. D., & McNeill, B. W. (2009). *IDM supervision: An integrative developmental model for supervising counselors and therapists* (3rd ed.). New York, NY: Brunner-Routledge.

Stoltenberg, C. D., McNeill, B. W., & Delworth, U. (1998). *IDM supervision: An integrated developmental model for supervising counselors and therapists*. San Francisco, CA: Jossey-Bass.

Sweitzer, H. F., & King, M. A. (2014). *The successful internship: Personal, professional, and civic development* (4th ed.). Belmont, CA: Brooks/Cole.

Woodside, M., & McClam, T. (2013). *Generalist case management* (4th ed.). Pacific Grove, CA: Brooks/Cole, Cengage Learning.

Woodside, M., & McClam, T. (2015). *Introduction to human services* (8th ed.). Pacific Grove, CA: Brooks/Cole, Cengage Learning.

Woodside, M., McClam, T., Diambra, J., & Varga, M. A. (2012). The meaning of time for human service professionals. *Human Service Education, 32*(1), 4–20.

Woodside, M., Mynatt, B., Hughes, A., Morgan, C., & Ramey, L. (2013, October). *Experience of supervision: A phenomenological study of mental health counseling interns.* Paper presented at 2013 Conference for Association for Counselor Education and Supervision, Denver, CO.

Woodside, M., Paulus, T., & Ziegler, M. (2009). The experience of school counseling internship through the lens of communities of practice. *Counselor Education and Supervision, 49*(1), 20–38.

3

Setting Up Your Human Service Internship

Reading this chapter will help you do the following:

- Describe the three worlds that comprise the human service internship.
- Describe the goals, expectations, roles, and tasks of the internship for the academic world and the internship site.
- List the components of the internship site agreement.
- Describe the process through which a student applies for the human service internship.
- Define the role of the academic program's pre-internship seminar/ brief orientation.

- List the ways that you can prepare for your initial visit to the internship site.
- Learn about the internship site (mission, goals, clients served, etc.).
- Generate a list of questions you have about the internship site.
- Describe what an initial visit to the agency might look like.
- List the issues discussed during the initial visit.
- Provide a rationale for being honest in your application for internship.
- Learn about how *Alicia, Lucas,* and *Tamika* chose their internship site and prepared for the initial visit.
- Learn about the faculty and site supervisors' perspectives related to the initial internship placement process.
- Describe the tips that Gwen provides for being honest in your internship application.

Introduction

Chapter 1 helped you understand the nature of the internship and your unique place in it. You also learned the collaborative nature of the internship site. In Chapter 2, you assessed your personal readiness for internship by learning about the core characteristics and the developmental nature of your professional growth. You also began to assess your identity as a human service professional. In Chapter 3, you will learn specific ways the three different worlds or perspectives (the academic program, the internship site, and the intern) interact during the human service internship. Each perspective is characterized by specific goals, roles, and tasks. Learning more about each of these perspectives will help you understand the expectations of both, the academic program and the internship site, and guide your work as a bridge between the two.

Background knowledge of the interface between an academic program and various internship sites provides a foundation for your entry into internship. A key task is to apply for your internship experience. Once you know the location of your internship, you will schedule and make your **initial visit** to the site. This chapter will help you prepare for it. Preparation includes gathering information about the site, developing a summary of program internship goals and requirements, preparing to talk about yourself, and formulating questions you have about the site and its programs. We discuss in depth how to prepare for and conduct the initial visit. We also introduce the concept of **orientation** and describe the type of orientation you might expect during your first encounter with the internship site. As with each chapter, we conclude with peer-to-peer, faculty, site supervisor, and human service professional dialogues; Alicia, Lucas, Tamika, Dr. Bianca, Ms. Bellewa, and Gwen will share their own experiences related to setting up the internship.

Box 3.1 describes the organizational framework of the next section, which details how the human service academic program, the internship site, and the intern's perspectives are related to the intern's experience.

Box 3.1 Studying the Text: Integrating Three Worlds: The Human Service Internship

Studying the text: The following outline will help you read and study the text material in this next section.

Integrating three worlds: The human service internship

1. The intern as a bridge between two worlds
2. The development of an internship site: Making university/ site agreements
3. The internship placement process
4. Pre-internship seminar or brief orientation

Integrating Three Worlds: The Human Service Internship

During an internship three very different worlds or perspectives, the human service academic program, the internship site, and the human service intern come together and interact. Before you begin your internship, we believe it is important for you to understand each perspective and their interactions with each other. A successful internship depends upon these **three worlds/ perspectives** working together in positive collaboration. Although in most internships, human service faculty and internship site staff establish ways to work together, it is you, the intern, who will negotiate between these worlds on a day-to-day basis. In other words, you are the bridge between the academic program and the internship site.

The Intern as a Bridge Between Two Worlds

To understand your role as a **bridge** between the academic program and the internship site, we begin with the definition of the term *bridge*. As a noun, *bridge* is a structure that "affords passage between two points" ("Bridge," 2015). As a verb, the term *bridge* represents joining together ("Bridge," 2015). In the case of the internship, bridge is a metaphor for the linking role the intern performs. In Chapter 1, Figure 1.1 provides a simple illustration of the world of the academic program and the world of the internship site. We know that these two worlds represent differing goals, definitions of supervision, and motivations for engaging in internship. In Table 3.1 we describe in more detail the two worlds.

While both the academic program and the internship sites have their own purposes and goals, it is the existence of the student internship, which makes possible the accomplishment of these goals and purposes. The interns learn the knowledge and acquire the skills which embody the

Table 3.1 Perspectives of the Academic Program and the Internship Site

Perspectives of the Experience	Academic Program (Training Institution)	Internship Site (Service Agency)
Aspects of the experience		
Major goal	Provide opportunity for students to develop knowledge and skills of a helping professional	Provide effective and efficient services to clients
Ideal supervision and motive	Establish a good relationship with an agreement on internship goals and tasks Motive: To help interns become helping professionals	Guarantee effective and efficient client care Motive: Monitor services provided by less experienced staff
Administrators (and students) and what they look for	Tasks and activities that engage student learning and interest (e.g., client population) Motive: Develop knowledge and skills	Students who have abilities to serve the clients Motive: Serve more clients
Supervisor (and students)	Supervisor who is accomplished in and committed to helping students of supervision	Student who demonstrates initiative and contributes quickly

provision of human services. At the same time, the service agency provides real-life settings and clients, where the interns can use their knowledge and practice their skills. Ultimately, as interns increase their knowledge and develop their skills, the clients they serve receive quality care and services. Exercise 3.1 will help you understand the internship experience from both the academic program and internship site perspectives. You will begin to define your place as the third perspective or world in internship, that of the bridge between the two worlds.

Exercise 3.1 Defining the Intern's Place in the Field-Based Experience: Writing Your Own Story, Entry 9

Step 1

As we stated earlier, the student as an intern represents a third perspective of the human service internship. Using the aspects of the internship experience described in Table 3.1, answer the following questions as a way to begin to articulate your own unique point of view as an intern.

1. As an intern, what is your major goal?

   _____

   _____

   _____

2. As an intern, what style of supervision works best for you? Why do you want this type of supervision?

_____

_____

_____

3. What do you look for in an internship? What do you hope to gain? What do you hope to give?

_____

_____

_____

Step 2

We use Figure 3.1 to suggest our own view of the perspectives or worlds of the human service academic program, the internship site, and the intern and how these three perspectives can be combined to form the internship experience.

Review Figure 3.1 and see how the ideas about interns and their roles compare with your own responses in Exercise 3.1. What responses are the same? Which are different? What should be added to our model to better represent the intern point of view as you describe it?

As we indicated earlier, to better understand your place in the internship, it is helpful to learn about the development of an internship site and begin to understand how faculty make decisions about internship placements. This background information provides valuable insights into the academic program and internship site perspectives.

Figure 3.1 The Three Perspectives/Worlds of the Human Service Internship Experience

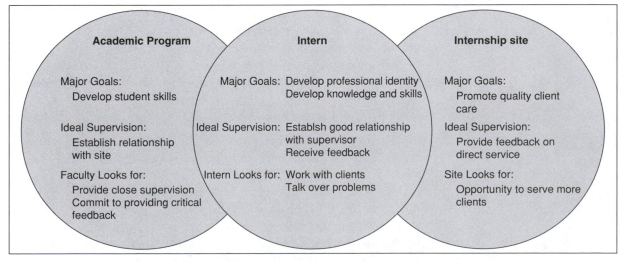

Source: Created by Gwen Ruttencutter, 2015. Used with permission.

The Development of an Internship Site

In Chapter 1, we described the internship as the culminating experience of the study of human services. Within the context of your own human service program, the internship process has a history and tradition all of its own. So the internship you participate in today reflects contributions of past faculty, internship site supervisors, as well as those currently involved in internships. In most instances, internships exist within two contexts, the human service academic program and the internship site. Once there is a commitment on the part of a human service agency to become an internship site, there is often a written **university/site agreement** between the academic program and the agency.

In Box 3.2, you can review the aspects of such an agreement.

Box 3.2 Off-Campus Site Agreement

Off-Campus Internship Site Agreement

Department of Human Services and Health Sciences

Requirements Agreed Upon by the Site, Student, and Campus

The academic program requires that the site supervisor provide an hour of supervision for each academic term. This is a minimum supervision time. In addition, if the supervisor is not available for any reason, there must be another supervisor designee to support the intern. Each supervisor must have served as a human service professional for 2 years, must have a bachelor's degree in a related human service field, and must have continuing education in supervision.

Audio and Video Taping of Client Work

One key aspect of the internship is reviewing work with clients. If an agency is to participate as an internship site, the intern must be able to audio or videotape work with clients. Permission for this taping must be gained from the client or, in the case of minors, from the parent or guardian. The site and faculty supervisors and other interns in individual and group supervision will review the tapes. Tapes will be erased no later than 3 weeks after the client session was recorded.

Working With Clients: Hours

The program asks that interns have direct contact with clients for at least 300 hours over a two-semester period. The interns may also assume responsibilities that are not directly related to client contact. The academic program, under the auspices of the faculty, will determine the number of hours the students must work at the site each academic term. There will be a faculty supervisor as a faculty of record. The site supervisor will participate in a midterm and final evaluation with the student. These evaluations will be one aspect in considering the intern's final evaluation in the course.

Broad Professional Experience

The program asks that the intern be involved in multiple aspects of agency work. This includes work with clients, projects, advocacy, record keeping, report writing, and other duties normally assumed by agency staff.

We Promise to Meet the Requirements Stated Above During the Intern's Experience at the Agency.

Signature of Intern and Date

Signature of Site Supervisor and Date

Signature of Site Director or Administrator and Date

Signature of Site Supervisor and Date

As you can imagine, establishing multiple internship sites is an ongoing process. In many cases, faculty or students continually develop new internship sites, and you may be the first intern working at a site. This may occur for a variety of reasons. At times, students present special requests for internships and the sites available cannot meet those requests, so a new site is developed. For instance, a human service student may want to work with special populations such as AIDS clients and their families, refugees and their families, or they may wish to work in an education-related setting. Students may also have special transportation needs, considerations related to language (English as a second language), or impairments related to hearing or vision.

In some circumstances, some programs ask their students to find their own internship sites. In these cases, students make the initial contact with an agency director or staff and then ask faculty to follow-up to explore and then confirm an agreement. Regardless of why you are engaging in an internship site as the first intern, you may encounter special opportunities and challenges.

Next we take a brief look at the decision making process of placing interns at an internship site. It is during the placement process that the three worlds (the human service program, the internship site, and the human service intern) come together for the first time.

The Internship Site Placement Process

What does the **internship placement process** entail? To answer this question, we describe the student application to the internship process. The internship placement process begins the semester prior to beginning the internship. Most academic programs ask students to submit an application to participate in the internship experience. The **internship application** asks students to provide much of the following information:

- Relevant student information (e.g., name, program, student ID)
- Basic contact information (e.g., e-mail address and mobile phone number)

- Record of academic coursework (e.g., list of courses completed, grades earned, grade point average [GPA])
- Description of prior human service-related work and volunteer experiences
- List of client populations with whom they would like to work

In addition, many applications ask students to supply information they believe faculty should know prior to making the internship placement:

- Expected difficulties working with specific client groups
- Information about learning style
- Transportation issues
- Preferred geographic location of site
- Assessment of helping skill strengths and limitations

Finally, students may submit a current resume and an up-to-date academic history with their internship application. Usually there is a deadline for applying for the internship. It is important to meet all deadlines. Box 3.3 provides a sample of the application for internship.

Box 3.3 Application for Internship

Application

Human Service Internship Site Placement

Deadline for submission of application

Fall term: June 15 **Spring term**: October 15

Name: _____

Address: _____

Cell number: _____

E-mail: _____ Alternate e-mail: _____

Faculty adviser: _____

Credit hours completed: _____ Overall GPA: _____

List courses you have taken in the program and the grade of record.

Course	Instructor	Semester	Grade

List and then discuss any human service work you have completed previously. Include any volunteer work in human services. Describe the place, responsibilities, and time spent.

As you consider your preferences in site placement, please indicate client populations with whom you would like to work. List at least three in order of preference.

Please indicate any special circumstances that might influence your placement (e.g., transportation, knowledge of skill limitations).

Is there anything else that faculty should know about you, relevant to internship prior to placement?

Have you ever been convicted of a felony: Yes _____ No _____ (If yes, please describe the adjudication: _____)

With this application, please attach the following materials:

Resume
• Consent of background check
• Consent of drug screening
• Consent for fingerprinting

Reminder: Please observe the due date for your application and accompanying materials.

OFFICE USE ONLY:

Date received: _____ Received by: _____

Program Standing and Eligibility for Internship

One issue related to **eligibility for internship** is linked to student performance or standing in the academic program. In human service programs, student performance usually reflects academic standing (GPA or course grades) and/or performance related to personal beliefs and values. (We discuss these personal beliefs and values in greater detail in Chapter 5). Good standing in an academic program usually means maintaining a quality GPA, fulfilling program requirements and responsibilities, and demonstrating personal beliefs and values that reflect professional promise. In many programs, only students in good standing are accepted as interns. When students are not in good standing, it is often because academic work (GPA) falls below established standards or behavior fails to reflect personal beliefs and values the program deems important. In most cases, these students must achieve good standing before they receive internship site placements. In addition, prior felony convictions or felonies currently being adjudicated are important to record.

If a student has a felony conviction, there may be restrictions related to an internship site. Some agencies may not allow students with these convictions to work or may require the students to have special supervision. It is important that each student inform the faculty, if he or she has a felony conviction, prior to admission to the program. If the student is involved in the adjudication of a felony while in the program, the student should inform the faculty of the charge and its status in the legal system.

As a way to better understand the application to your internship program, complete Exercise 3.2.

Exercise 3.2 Applying for Your Internship Placement

1. You may be getting ready to apply for your internship placement or have already done so.

2. Take some time to review the form your human service program uses. Review your form and fill it out, if you have not already done so. If there is additional information you believe faculty need about you include that in the material you submit (e.g., professional resume).

3. Once you have program or faculty approval, you are eligible for the internship.

4. Eligibility requirements can include successful completion of appropriate course work (prerequisites or corequisites), GPA, membership(s) in professional organizations, legal requirements (e.g., fingerprinting, background checks), to name a few.

5. Faculty will either place you at an internship site, or you will find your own site.

There are several reasons that an agency might take an intern. These include, a strong desire for an intern, a long association with the human service program, a clear sense of agency mission and how it fits with academic program goals, a match between the population the agency serves and program preparation, and a commitment to training new professionals.

Exercise 3.3 Thinking About Your Internship Site

Step 1

Whether faculty will place you at your internship site or you will find your own internship, you will soon have an internship placement. This exercise will help you think about the factors involved in determining the site. You can also think about what factors you think will influence the quality of the internship site and your chances of success.

Describe what you think would be the ideal site.

_____

_____

_____

Step 2

Look at the list from Step 1 and circle the top three priorities for you.

Step 3

Communicate this list and your priorities to your site supervisor. If you are looking for your own site, use this list and the established priorities in your search process.

It is important to remember that no internship placement is perfect. Your needs, as an intern, will change throughout the semester. Return to this list of determinants from time to time to reassess what your needs are and what your site supervisor can provide.

Preinternship Seminar or Brief Orientation

Prior to beginning your internship, you will participate in an orientation sponsored by your academic program. This orientation may take several forms: a semester-long seminar orientation class, a short 3- to 4-week introduction to the internship, or a 3- to 4-hour workshop focused on the upcoming internship. Regardless of the format, the purpose of these experiences is to prepare you for your internship experience. Topics covered in the semester-long seminar or the shorter workshop may include (a) general description of the internship experience, (b) goals of the internship experience, (c) faculty expectations, (d) site and site supervisor expectations, (e) professional behaviors, (f) assignments, (g) evaluation process, (h) ethical and legal issues, (i) handling crises, and (j) troubleshooting. In a preinternship seminar, you may cover these topics and others in more depth. During a brief orientation, faculty may introduce topics in a more cursory manner. At the conclusion of this preinternship orientation experience, you will learn the location of your placement site and the name of your site supervisor. The next step to securing the internship placement resides with you.

One of the first tasks is to contact the director of the agency or the site supervisor and schedule a time to visit the site. Here, we discuss this initial visit in detail. Both site supervisor and student assume the placement is secure. The focus for both parties is gathering and providing information and beginning to establish a positive relationship. Rather than an initial visit, you may be asked to participate in an interview before the placement site accepts you as an intern. This type of interview is similar to a job interview. The next section addresses the initial experience with the placement site.

In this section, first, we discuss ways you can prepare for this initial visit. Second, we explore how you can structure your initial visit so that it provides the agency personnel ways to know you better and helps you gather pertinent information about the site. Finally, we focus on the initial visit as a beginning orientation experience. Box 3.4 describes the contents of the section.

Box 3.4 Studying the Text: Your Initial Experience With the Placement Site

Studying the text: The following outline will help you read and study the text material in this next section.

(Continued)

(Continued)

Your initial experience with the placement site:

1. Preparing for the initial visit

   a. Considering student reflections

   b. Understanding basic program requirement of internship

   c. Gathering information about placement site

   d. Preparing questions about the placement site

   e. Preparing to talk about yourself

   f. Planning the next steps

2. The initial visit

   a. The site supervisor's introduction

   b. The beginning of orientation

Your Initial Experience With the Placement Site

In this section, we help you prepare for your initial experience with the placement site. This includes your **initial visit** and any **orientation** prior to beginning your internship. Both are important aspects of the internship experience.

As indicated earlier, this first visit resembles an initial interview. In fact, for some agencies that like to confirm a placement before offering it, the initial interview is indeed a job interview. We recommend you treat your first encounter with the placement as seriously as an interview for a job. Your goals for the initial visit are to demonstrate your readiness for the internship, begin to establish a relationship with those with whom you will work, and gather information about the internship site. A successful first visit helps your transition from student to intern and supports your internship work in your first week or two.

Preparing for the Initial Visit

In Chapter 2, we described the excitement and anxieties associated with the internship, especially at the beginning of the experience. You will experience both excitement and anxiety as you think about and prepare for your initial visit to the agency. In most instances the purpose of this initial visit is introductory. Often, site supervisors begin with an orientation to the agency. As mentioned earlier, there are exceptions to this when an academic program or agency requires an interview before the student is accepted as an intern. Regardless of the purpose of the initial visit, we suggest that preparing for the first visit to the agency will enhance your excitement and relieve your anxiety. Five ways you can increase your enthusiasm and allay some of your fears include (a) increasing your understanding of the academic requirements of internship, (b) gathering information about the placement site, (c) determining your agenda for the visit (ways you can share information about yourself), (d) preparing questions you have about the placement site, and (e) outlining what you need to know to begin the internship experience. We will review each of these aspects of preparation. But first let's hear from the students we met in Chapter 1 and Chapter 2 as they provide brief comments about their initial visits to their placements as shown in Box 3.5.

Box 3.5 Students Reflect on the Initial Visit to Their Internship Site

Thoughts Prior to Contacting the Internship Site

Steve: I didn't know anything about my placement site, so I was curious. Had my site supervisor had an intern before? Would she, in this case, accommodate me and be glad I was coming to work with her. I thought a quick follow-up to our placement meeting was important. I wanted to allow time for phone tag.

Maria: I get nervous when meeting someone like a site supervisor. I think I know what I want to do and what I want to learn at the agency—but I am not sure if the site supervisor has the same ideas in mind.

Al: I tried to figure out the best time to call and the best time to come for a visit. I had all of my times written down so I would not have to look at my calendar. I also wasn't sure all of the information I should give during the first conversation, so I jotted down some notes. I wondered if the placement would be a good fit for me.

Shasha: I knew I needed to know what I was going to say when my site supervisor answered the phone. And I already had a checklist in my mind of all that I needed to do. You know like knowing how to drive to the placement and knowing what I should wear.

Feelings Prior to the Contact?

Steve: I must admit I was nervous about my placement. Meeting my supervisor, I was not anxious a bit. Well I did worry if my new supervisor and I would get along.

Maria: I was so very excited. All I could think about was what a wonderful opportunity this was to network in the human service field and to find out how others deliver quality services.

Al: I was somewhat anxious when I thought about making this initial contact with my supervisor. I was also thrilled to work with the population I had requested.

Shasha: I was really nervous about making the contact and then visiting for the first time. I am a first-day jitters gal. This means I get nervous about doing anything for the first time. But I kept remembering that I had looked forward to being in my placement ever since I came to school. I have been preparing for this work.

(Continued)

(Continued)

Preparations for the Initial Meeting

Steve: This might sound funny for a guy, but I wanted to make sure that I looked the part of a professional. I thought the meeting would be quick. I anticipated that we would talk about a start date and then maybe I would get to see the facilities and the programs. I did write down a few questions to ask.

Maria: I spent quite a bit of time getting ready; most of my reading was on the web. I found the website and the page about services. There was also information about my site supervisor and I read her bio. I was trying to understand her goals for her work and for her clients. My faculty supervisor gave us a summary sheet about internship, so I read through that. I thought I would take it to the meeting too.

Al: I made sure that I took my calendar so we could talk about specifics of the semester including orientation, when I would start, my class schedule, and the like. I also had a list of questions that I wanted to ask my site supervisor.

Shasha: I got ready for my meeting using a method I have used before. I made a list of what I can control and what I cannot control. Since I am usually anxious about the unknown, I planned what I would wear (professional look but not too dressy), looked up directions to the site, and planned when I would leave so I could arrive early. And then I talked with some friends of mine who are also in the internship class. We worked together on questions we could ask site supervisors at that first meeting. I also feel funny just sitting and waiting so I brought a book to read while I was waiting.

Feelings After the Meeting

Steve: I was so excited and couldn't wait to begin. This was my second supervisor and my second internship. Both supervisors are very energetic, and they want to teach me so much.

Maria: It was great. I learned so much about my site supervisor and she told me about the mission and goals of the agency. After the first meeting I felt a great relief. I don't think I realized how nervous I was. Also, I was confident after the meeting that my site supervisor will help me work on my own goals. I want to be prepared for my first job. That is my priority.

Al: I know I was nervous at first, but my site supervisor made me feel so comfortable. She was so professional and yet so kind and welcoming. Now, rather than being nervous, I can't wait for the semester to begin. It helps that the faculty support me too.

Shasha: I talked with my friends and we were all nervous. But I wanted my supervisor to know a little bit about me and I wanted to know some about him. You know I am just starting so I wanted to appear competent even though I have a lot to learn. Really, I didn't want to appear stupid. Well the meeting went so well. I think that supervisors are happy to have interns. My supervisor just wanted to get to know me and tell me a little bit about the placement. We also worked out a lot of the details—knowing when I will go to work for the first time; that makes me feel steady.

What I Learned

Steve: I learned that I am welcome at the site. That is a really big thing for me. I also confirmed that my site supervisor is very friendly and flexible, especially about my schedule. And I learned a lot about the little things that help you begin your day in a positive way—I know where to park and how to find my new office. That will make a difference for me.

Maria: Honestly all went well. I liked my site supervisor, and I found out a lot about the school.

Al: From that first visit I accomplished quite a bit. My site supervisor was able to answer my questions. I met lots of the staff and I had my picture made. I will have an ID like the rest of the staff. And I applied for a parking pass. These may seem like small things but they make me feel I belong. I think I am confident that I can relate to the folks as I work with them.

Shasha: You know counselors are very social, and my site supervisor was no exception. We spent some of the time with the details of the internship. But we also told stories and started getting to know each other a little better. It went great! When I left I didn't feel like a stranger.

Understanding Basic Internship Requirements

In Chapter 2, we reviewed information that students find helpful prior to beginning the internship experience. Three documents, in particular, provide key information: (a) the description of the internship in the internship handbook, (b) the internship course description, and (c) requirements described in the internship syllabus. As part of your preparation for the initial visit to your internship site, you will want to review these documents for information that is important to share with your site supervisor. Exercise 3.4 helps you prepare a half- to full-page document for your agency director and/or site supervisor about the human service internship experience. The summary also helps you organize how you describe the internship to your site supervisor.

Perhaps human service faculty have developed such a summary for site supervisors. If not, Exercise 3.4 provides a guide for preparing one.

Exercise 3.4 Preparing for the Initial Internship Visit

Step 1

Review the description of the internship in the internship handbook, the internship course description, and the internship syllabus and then highlight answers to the following questions:

a. Describe the course: number, name, and course description.

_____

b. List the goals of internship.

_____

_____

c. Outline parameters of the internship experience (number of hours, nature of experiences).

_____

_____

d. List the various elements of the supervision supplied by the site supervisor and the faculty supervisor.

_____

_____

e. Detail the specific internship course requirements (professional disclosure, permission to tape, contract, weekly log, case notes, case study, etc.).

_____

_____

f. Describe the evaluation content and process.

_____

_____

Gathering Information About the Placement Site

You will also want to gather information about your placement site. There are several sources of this information such as written and website materials. Other sources include human service faculty, other interns, and human service professionals working in the community.

Agency websites offer a vast amount of information. Specifically related to the online presence, most agencies have broad categories in their main menu list and then more specific information related to each category. Expect to see websites that include the following:

- Name of agency, mission and goals, and board of director reports
- Contact information (address, e-mail, phone, fax, online chat)

- Programs available (various program descriptions, self-help materials, applications)
- Case studies (descriptions of clients who benefitted from the programs)
- Volunteers and donations (welcome, needs, applications, description of training, ways to make financial contributions)

In addition, Facebook sites and other social media sites provide information about an agency placement.

Another source of information about the placement site is the faculty members or site supervisors initiating the placement. Faculty may provide information about the agency and details about past internship placements. They also may have insights about the site supervisor and the clients served. Another way to learn about the site is to talk with past interns about their firsthand work at the placement site. This can help you learn about agency culture regarding interns including expectations and collaborations.

Finally, if you know other human service professionals, they may be a source of information about a placement site. Across agencies, professionals know each other professionally and personally. Often, there is a referral network among colleagues. Other contacts include asking for consultations, belonging to the same professional and service-related organizations, and participating in professional development.

Exercise 3.5 Describing Your Internship Site

In Exercise 3.5 we provide a way of developing a holistic picture of the agency using a variety of resources. This information gathering provides an initial view of your internship site.

Step 1

Fill out the form presented here after gathering information from the web, faculty, peers, and other human service professionals.

Areas of Focus	What I Learned	Source (e.g., Web Site, Facebook, Faculty, Peers, Professionals)	My Notes
Name of agency, mission and goals, and board of director's reports			
Contact information (address, e-mail, phone, fax, online chat)			
Programs			
Educational and other support materials			

(Continued)

(Continued)

Areas of Focus	What I Learned	Source (e.g., Web Site, Facebook, Faculty, Peers, Professionals)	My Notes
Case studies (descriptions of clients who benefitted from the programs)			
Funding and reports			
Volunteers and donations (how to make a contribution to the agency)			
Internship responsibilities			
Available support			
Other observations			

Preparing Questions About the Placement Site

As you learn more about your internship site, you may also develop a list of questions you have about it. Site supervisors will expect you to come to the initial visit with questions. In fact, they consider it an indication that you value the time you will spend at the agency if you take time to prepare for this visit. You make an even better impression if you bring your questions in writing. You could bring two copies or use your written copy to guide your discussion with the site supervisor. What questions should you ask? We think of the questions in terms of three categories: information about the agency, information about the site supervisor, and information about the internship. At times these categories overlap, but the categories themselves will help you refine your questions to suit your placement site. Examples of questions in each category follow. Since the initial visit is meant to be a give and take between site supervisor and intern, we only list a few potential questions in each category (Donohue, n.d.; Mahuron, 2014).

Information About the Agency

Many of these questions follow what you learned from the agency website or represent the materials you gathered in your search for information about the agency. As you ask your questions, you can use leads such as, "According to the information on the website . . ." or "I read about several programs you offer that I am interested in . . . ." These leads allow the site supervisor a glimpse of your preparation for the initial visit. Here are some areas that help you better understand the agency.

- What are the mission and goals of the agency?
- Who are the clients the agency serves?
- What is the range of programs the agency offers?
- What are the roles of the agency staff?
- What is a typical day in the agency like for you?
- Why is this agency a good place to work?

Information About the Site Supervisor

The site supervisor is the primary key to your entry into the agency. Although getting to know a site supervisor takes time, the following questions can help you understand your site supervisor and indicate to him or her that you want to establish a relationship.

- How do you define your role in light of the agency mission and goals?
- What is your educational and professional background and experience?
- What is your favorite part of your job?

Information About the Internship

It is also important for you to begin to understand how your site supervisor sees both his or her role as a supervisor and your role as an intern. The following questions will help expand your understanding of these two aspects of your future internship work.

- What do you see as the role of the intern?
- What goals would you have for me?
- How do you orient interns?
- What does supervision of my work entail?
- What will be my working conditions/space?
- What do we need to accomplish this first visit?
- What steps will we take for me to work with clients?

Exercise 3.6 Preparing Questions About Your Placement Site

Your initial visit to your placement site is the excellent time to begin to ask questions about your site. This exercise helps you construct a list of questions that you wish to ask about the agency, your site supervisor, and your internship. You may not have the opportunity to ask all of the questions listed.

Step 1

Re-read the questions in this section and highlight the questions that seem most important to you. Consult with faculty and peers, if you wish, when you make your choices. Remember, these questions reflect the beginning of what you will learn at the placement site. You will have time throughout the semester to ask questions and receive the help you need.

(Continued)

(Continued)

Step 2

Write the questions you will ask during your initial interview.

1. _____

2. _____

3 _____

4. _____

Preparing to Talk About Yourself

During the initial visit you will also want to talk about yourself. One way you can prepare for this type of disclosure is to anticipate questions your site supervisor may ask you and decide the information you might want to provide. The information you share may focus on your personal beliefs and values, your previous experience, and how you think about helping others. What might be some of these questions and prompts?

Please tell me about yourself. Site supervisors often begin the initial visit by asking you to talk about yourself (Parcells, 2015; Westerkamp, 2014). You can prepare a short statement that helps the site supervisor get to know you better. Here you want to talk about four aspects of your life: (a) your background, (b) your educational experiences, (c) your previous volunteer and work experiences, and (d) why you want to work in the human services field. You want this response to be brief, precise, and warm.

What do you do well? Begin with a description of what you do well. Be sure to provide specific examples of when and where you demonstrated your strengths. You can also cite positive feedback that you have received from others. In response to this question, it is also appropriate to follow up with areas where you hope to grow. Using the phrase "areas where I hope to grow" presents a positive focus on your own personal and professional development.

Describe program goals and your goals for the internship. This is a good time for you to review with your site supervisor the goals described by the academic program. In addition, you want to share any specific goals that you have in mind. Have two or three goals to discuss. This can include career goals. This information helps your site supervisor begin to plan how to help you with these goals.

You can anticipate that this discussion about you will be a dialogue and not a monologue or a strict question and answer session (where supervisor asks and you answer). During the time you talk about yourself, the site supervisor may also be disclosing about his or her life, experience, and work in the agency. You are free to ask questions of the site supervisor, but make sure there is a balance in the flow of information.

Jenny Westerkamp (2014), the cofounder of All Access Internships, suggests a helpful format for answering questions during an internship interview. We believe these apply to an initial visit too. We adapted the Westerkamp format to help guide you during your first conversation with your site supervisor.

Once the site supervisor asks a question, you will follow these steps as shown in Figure 3.2.

> **Step 1:** Listen intently to the question and then restate it in your own words.
>
> **Step 2:** Ask if your restatement captures the main point of the question.
>
> **Step 3:** Provide a short response and offer a specific experience or use an example to illustrate the point that you wish to make. Be brief and stay on the topic.
>
> **Step 4:** Ask a follow-up question to affirm you provided necessary information. One such question may be, "Are there areas where you would like more details?" or statement such as "I am happy to provide you additional information about . . . if you wish." Both invite the site supervisor to ask for more detail if he or she wishes.

Figure 3.2   Responding to Site Supervisor Questions or Prompts

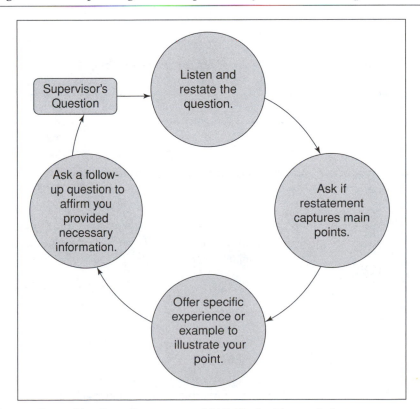

Source: Created by Gwen Ruttencutter, 2015. Used with permission.

You can use these steps to prepare and practice your responses. Keep them in mind as you form impromptu answers in the dialogue with the site supervisor.

Exercise 3.7 helps you prepare to talk about yourself.

Exercise 3.7 Preparing to Talk About Yourself

Step 1

Completing this exercise not only prepares you for your initial visit to your placement site, it also builds your confidence. And feeling confident reduces your anxiety. Answering these questions in writing allows you to construct thoughtful, coherent responses. You will communicate more clearly. Once you write your responses, practice delivering them in front of the mirror three or four times. Then ask a trusted friend to prompt you for a response.

Please tell me about yourself.

_____

_____

_____

What do you do well?

_____

_____

_____

Describe program goals and your goals for the internship.

_____

_____

_____

Now that you are prepared for your initial visit, what can you expect? In the next section you will learn what to expect from this first visit to your placement site.

The Initial Visit

Visiting your site placement for the first time is exciting! It is a moment in time you will remember. For many of you, walking into the building represents a moment you have been waiting for since you entered the human service program, the beginning of the internship experience. Earlier, we introduced ways you might prepare for this initial visit. Here is what you might expect.

Your Site Supervisor's Introduction

Your site supervisor may have a plan for the visit. The site supervisor, in all probability, has four goals for this initial visit: (a) getting to know you, (b) sharing information about the placement, (c) learning about your expectations, and (d) sharing site expectations. First, the site supervisor wants to get to know you. You can expect the site supervisor to greet you when you walk into the office and lead you to an office where you can sit and talk in a relatively quiet atmosphere. Trained in the helping professions, most site supervisors know how to greet you warmly, use an icebreaker to put you at ease, and share a few facts about themselves (personal and professional). Your site supervisor may then ask an open-ended question such as "tell me about yourself" to encourage you to join the conversation. This sounds familiar, doesn't it? We discussed this question earlier and helped you prepare an answer to it (refer to Exercise 3.7). You have already prepared a short answer to the prompt, "Tell me about yourself." Of course you don't need to read your script or respond in a wooden way. But you are ready for the prompt or question. Also, this is the type of greeting you learned about in your helping skills class—focused on how to begin an initial interview or encounter with a client.

Second, your site supervisor will want to share information about the placement site. This information may include, but is not limited to, the mission and goals of the agency, the clients they serve, and a broad general description of the services provided. Then the site supervisor may talk about how he or she fits into the agency structure. This is the perfect time to begin to ask the questions you have about the agency and about your site supervisor's responsibilities. Again, your preparation will help you during this discussion since you have some knowledge about the agency. Your curiosity can guide you as your site supervisor expands your knowledge about the site. Prompts from you, such as "Can you tell me more about that?" or "Is there an example you could share that helps illustrate that?" will signal to the site supervisor that you are paying attention and interested in the site. During this time, you can also indicate what you read on the agency web site and compare it to what the site supervisor shares and what you have learned about similar agencies. In this way you indicate to the site supervisor that you prepared for the visit.

Third, the site supervisor will want to know about your expectations for the placement site and the internship. He or she may ask questions about program expectations and specific details about what is expected in terms of supervision. It is here that you can review the expectations of your academic program as you understand them and compare these with the site supervisor's understanding. This is a time to ask the site supervisor any questions you may have, if there are things that require clarification. This is also a time for you to talk about what you want to gain from your internship. Although human services programs have specific goals for your experiences, you may have additional goals you would like to add. These you will have prepared ahead of time (refer to Exercise 3.4). It is also possible that you have added to your goals as you talked with your site supervisor and learned more about the agency. This is a great time to begin a list of ideas that you have for your internship work.

Fourth, many site supervisors view this initial visit as a time to conduct what we term business-related aspects of working in an agency. In many ways sharing this information represents the beginning of your **orientation** to the agency. In the next section we discuss specific aspects of the initial visit that comprise the orientation. In Chapter 4, we provide a more detailed description and your place in the orientation process.

The Beginning of Orientation

As one way to begin to orient you to the agency, your site supervisor will start the planning necessary for you to work in the agency as an intern. Sometimes the steps are similar to an orientation for volunteers and other times this resembles an orientation for employees. There may exist a checklist to ensure coverage of all of the necessary items. This checklist might include several or even all of the following:

- Reviewing any paperwork required by the agency for you to begin your internship
- Determining parking, name badges, keys, or other building-related tasks
- Viewing the work space, available equipment, and resources
- Reviewing any drug screening, fingerprinting, or other legal requirements
- Outlining next steps for orientation
- Touring the facilities
- Introducing you to other supervisors and colleagues
- Planning start and end dates
- Determining weekly schedule (daily arrival and departure)
- Describing any training related to employee policies and procedures specific to the agency
- Describing any training that focuses on client interventions

Many of the more practical issues discussed such as office space, identity badges, and parking are addressed in the first visit. These are one part of your orientation. Attention to necessary screenings may be as simple as providing verification from your academic program about drug testing or background checks. More in-depth training requires additional planning and may occur before your internship begins.

Exercise 3.8 focuses on your initial visit and its outcomes.

Exercise 3.8 Describing Your Initial Visit: Writing Your Own Story, Entry 10

When you visit your placement site for the first time, you can view this as a beginning of your orientation. Describe your initial visit, what happened during the visit, and your emotional reactions to the visit. At the end of the exercise, list the thoughts you have for your future work in your agency, the thoughts you have about supervision, and the questions about your agency and internship that remain for you.

What happened during the visit?

_____

_____

_____

What were your emotional reactions during the visit? After the visit?

_____

_____

_____

What are your thoughts about your future work at the agency?

_____

_____

_____

What are your thoughts about your site supervisor and supervision?

_____

_____

_____

What questions remain about the internship?

_____

_____

_____

Now that you are more aware of how internship site placements are determined and understand ways you can be more prepared, let's look at ways you can deepen your understanding by hearing from the experiences of others in Box 3.6.

Box 3.6 Studying the Text: Deepening Your Understanding

Studying the text: The following outline will help you read and study the text material in this next section.

1. Peer-to-peer dialogue
   a. Alicia: Setting up the internship
   b. Lucas: Setting up the internship
   c. Tamika: Setting up the internship
2. Faculty and site supervisor dialogue
   a. Dr. Bianca: Placing students
   b. Ms. Bellewa: Accepting an intern
3. The professional voice and tips for practice: Gwen
4. Terms to remember
5. References

Deepening Your Understanding: Consulting and Self-Reflection

In this section you will hear more about Alicia, Lucas, and Tamika and their preparations for the beginning of their internships. In addition Dr. Bianca and Ms. Bellewa share their faculty and site supervisor perspectives. Gwen, in the professional voice, describes tips for success related to honesty in the internship application. We also include terms to remember and references to support your learning.

Peer-to-Peer Dialogue: Alicia, Lucas, and Tamika

We asked Alicia, Lucas, and Tamika to talk about how they identified their choices for internship, how the placements were made, and their initial contact with their sites and supervisors. Their perspectives can help broaden your understanding of how internship begins.

Alicia

Hello again! I am happy to continue on this journey with you. As you prepare for your placement, I am going to share a portion of my internship preparation experience with you. When I started at the University of Denver, the first semester involved successfully completing prerequisites in order to enroll in the internship course and apply for placements. At our first internship meeting last week, Dr. Lynn discussed what we might expect from our placements and what they will expect from us. We also talked about how we were feeling about diving into the professional realm. Most of us have not had many professional experiences, so we could relate to one another about how little we knew. Two of the students had some experience and were able to calm our nerves a bit.

Dr. Lynn encouraged us to think about what would be a good fit for us in the human service profession. At that moment, I chose to focus on the excitement and accepted the apprehension as a normal part of the placement process. I requested to be placed in the Department of Human Services with the Foster Care and Adoption Department. After volunteering at the youth shelter, I knew I wanted to continue working with younger kids and adolescents. When I think about the upcoming internship, I am so glad to have the opportunity to dive in to the human service work and provide the help and support that many of those kids need.

Juggling taking care of Thomas, classes, internship, and a part-time job is going to be a struggle. I continue to have the support of my mother but I constantly feel guilty about asking more of her. I hope to have a strong, supportive relationship with my supervisor. I also hope my supervisor is someone who can be flexible, understands that I am new to this, and encourages me to grow. More specifically, I want to receive support and specific feedback on how I am doing and how I can improve.

At the time of this writing I have had two contacts with Dr. Davis. First, I called Dr. Davis at the Department of Human Services and set up a time for an interview. In my interview with Dr. Davis, I felt very comfortable and think I can go see him to seek guidance in my work. He gave me a brief tour of the site and then asked me to set up a longer initial visit, where I would shadow one of the case managers there. He also gave me some background information on the program, how it is run, how many foster care kids they are currently working with, and how many kids have been adopted this year. The high number of foster care kids and lower numbers of successful adoptions are painful to hear and made me realize the real struggle those kids go through.

My in-depth visit was a daylong process. I was paired up with Jarryn, a case manager who had been working in that department for a few years. She reviewed the description of the placement and the services that I would provide. Jarryn let me know that I will have to attend a few administrative trainings before I would be given a caseload. For now, I would be going on visits with her until I feel ready for my own cases. She seemed very nice, caring and supportive. I was glad to see that she continued to be passionate about her job in the department even after several years. She, too, was a single mother and we both discussed some of the struggles and rewards of parenthood. Overall, I knew she would be someone I can come to with any questions or issues.

Written by Allie Rhinehart and Dareen Basma, 2015. Used with permission.

Lucas

Hello! I hope you are doing well. As I mentioned before, I am doing my internship at the Tampa Bay Justice Center. I am really excited to start working with clients and practicing my clinical skills. I am extremely blessed that James, who is considered my peer mentor at my program, helped me with the process of signing up for my site. He also gave me pointers about what to expect from the initial visit. With the help James gave me, I figured I would pay it forward and help you, as you begin your internship process. I am going to share with you how I signed up for my internship and what the initial visit looked like.

The first part of the process was to meet with my faculty adviser, Dr. Franks, and Dr. Mike, the internship coordinator. In that meeting, we discussed my internship interests. My program is a small one so there were not many choices. The choices I had were the YWCA, Tampa Academy, Tampa Bay Justice Center, and North Star Community and Counseling Center. When I met with Dr. Franks, it seemed to me there was not a formal process to decide what internship site would work for me. To be honest, we started with the four placements available and then talked about the client populations I was interested in.

Here is how I hoped the process would work. First, I would meet with Dr. Franks for an initial discussion about the placement sites. Then I would visit each of the placements and meet potential supervisors and my faculty adviser and my internship coordinator would go with me to these meetings. I thought these visits would be the perfect way to learn about staff and clients. I felt discouraged because Dr. Franks and Dr. Mike told me they would not have enough time to make these visits with me. What they did recommend is that I would look at each site's websites and use that information to decide the site or sites I would prefer. So I did that, and after about a week of deliberating, I decided Tampa Bay Justice Center was the best site for me and my interests.

During the deliberation process, I focused on the pros and cons of each site. For example, the most important criteria for me were location, experience of the site supervisor, clients I will be working with, and how many staff members worked at the site. For instance, at the Tampa Bay Justice Center, I live 15 minutes from the site, my site supervisor is a licensed professional counselor, and there are currently two staff members there. I wanted more than one staff available to consult just in case my supervisor was not available or was absent from the building.

I recalled James telling me about a horrible experience at one of his internship sites. He was working with a suicidal client. He needed his supervisor to help with his client because this was his first encounter with a suicidal client. He only had one supervisor and she was out of the office. He did not know what to do, and he did not receive any support from people at his placement. Since James's story is seared on my brain, I wanted to have more than one staff member to help me. Two additional staff seemed adequate. I also wanted to have the opportunity to develop my own case load. At the Tampa Bay Justice Center, they depend upon interns to assume responsibility for a certain number of clients. So Tampa Bay Justice Center offered the caseload I wanted and the support I needed to help me during internship.

Before I visited my site, Dr. Franks and Dr. Mike provided a brief pre-internship seminar for me. Here is the sample of the outline of the seminar and the things I had to do in order to prepare for internship:

- *Contact site supervisor*
- *Visit site*
- *Site interview*

I will not go in-depth about the seminar, but I will talk about my follow-up. First, I called Dr. Kim, the individual assigned as my site supervisor. I introduced myself. She described briefly the mission of the Tampa Bay Justice Center and the population it serves. We set up a time for me to visit the site. Dr. Kim also provided me directions to the center and outlined the check-in procedure. I felt a sigh of relief because I was nervous about my internship site. After talking to Dr. Kim, I felt a little more confident that I had made the right choice about a placement site. The phone conversation reduced the anxiety I had about my site.

Before the initial visit, I reviewed the information I found about the Tampa Bay Justice Center on the Internet. I also found directions to the site. James, my peer mentor, told me to never show up late because you want to make a good first impression. I also tried to pick out an outfit to wear for the visit. During the preorientation seminar, my faculty adviser and internship coordinator preached the importance of being professional and dressing appropriately for your site, so I took their advice. When I left my house, I thought I was prepared and I felt confident. By the time I arrived at the site, I was extremely nervous. My head was spinning.

When I met with Dr. Kim, all the anxiety and nervousness went away. She greeted me, showed me around the facility, introduced me to all the staff members, and she even had lunch for me. During lunch, we got to know each other. She talked about her experiences in school and told me stories about her first internship experience. I asked her questions regarding clients and my roles and responsibilities. I didn't understand everything that she said, but I learned a good deal about the site. At the end of the visit, she asked another staff member to give me a tour around the facility. She wanted me to meet all of the staff and talk with them too.

Overall, visiting the site was a cool experience for me. I got to know my site supervisor better, toured the facility, met with staff members, and got my questions answered regarding clients and expectations from the site. Visiting the facility demystified my internship site and gave me an understanding of how it operates.

Well, I hope this helps you understand the process of choosing an internship site and what my experiences were like. When you are choosing your site, I strongly encourage you to find out as much information as you can about the different sites available. Even though I understand how difficult it would be for every intern to visit three or four sites, I still think that it might make a difference in how you make your choice. And James believes that organizational cultures are different. He says they determine what your life as an intern will be like.

Good luck! I look forward to sharing more of my experiences of internship with you. Have a blessed day!

Written by Jorge Roman, 2015. Used with permission.

Tamika

Wow, here I am already at the beginning of internship! I can't believe how quickly time has flown by but I feel great about the placement I've chosen. After signing up for internship credits this semester, I was required to attend a brief orientation about what the internship process would look like from start to finish. Some of my friends, at other schools, were just placed in the community by their faculty supervisors and weren't really given any indication about what to expect. Our process is a little bit more detailed, and I know that will be to my benefit as I transition into this new professional world. After our orientation, I had a good idea of what placements were available, what type of paperwork the school would require me to complete, and how the process of getting placed would unfold.

During orientation, my faculty supervisor had me review a list of possible placements and indicate my top three interests. I wasn't familiar with all of the locations listed, but I did my best to sort through them based on my work interests. My first choice was a local justice center, where inmates go to court, attend therapy, and check in for probation/parole. Although I wasn't sure exactly what I'd do there as an intern, I could tell I'd learn a lot just by being around all the action. My second and third choices both involved working in addictions treatment centers. Neither of these placements would allow me to work directly in the justice system, but I knew from learning about addictions that many of the clients would likely have legal issues. I also made sure to choose placements that I'd heard good things about from other students. For example, because I'm new to this work, it's important to me to have a supportive site supervisor. I've heard that all three supervisors at the sites I chose are tough but fair; they really encourage interns to learn by experience but also support them throughout the internship.

At the end of our orientation, our faculty supervisor told us that our placement preferences would be reviewed and we'd receive an e-mail within the week about where we would interview. The news that we would have to interview made me pretty nervous. It felt like the longest week ever, but I finally received an e-mail stating that I could interview at my first choice— the justice center. I'd heard through the grapevine that two of my classmates were also hoping to interview at this location, so I knew I had to be on top of my game. The e-mail gave me a contact person and phone number to call, which I did as soon as I finished reading the message. I wanted to be the first to show interest in any placement opportunity.

Fortunately, I got a hold of the contact person on the first try and we scheduled an interview for the following week. I wrote the date and time down in my planner to be sure I wouldn't forget and started preparing right away by researching the site online. I met with a senior student for coffee that weekend and tried to get some insight into what the interview would be like, how the site operated, and other important details I should know. He told me that the site supervisor I'd be interviewing with (Nancy) really likes good questions, so I made a list of questions about the site in general, clients served, what my role as an intern would entail, and what supervision would look like. I felt confident about the preparation work I had done and I made sure to get a good night's sleep the night before the interview.

I was really nervous walking into the interview but felt instantly at ease when I sat down in Nancy's office. She was very friendly and open and asked me mostly personal questions about why I wanted to do this type of work and what I hoped to learn as an intern. I thought I did a pretty good job of taking time to think about my answers before responding and really giving her a sense of who I am as a student, a person, and a new intern! I felt kind of nerdy pulling out my list of questions at the end of the interview. Nancy seemed pleasantly surprised that I had put so much thought into them and she answered every single question I had. I walked away from the interview feeling as though we would be a great match in terms of working together and really excited about all I had learned about the site and the internship work.

Three days later, as promised, Nancy called and offered me the internship position. I was thrilled and thanked her for the opportunity. She told me that my competition had been pretty stiff, but that my hard work in preparing for the interview had really put me at the top of her list. I readily agreed to the placement and contacted my faculty supervisor to let him know. I start the weeklong orientation process at the justice center next Monday. Right now I'm still a little nervous but also really excited to get started on this new adventure!

Written by Brittany Pollard, 2015. Used with permission.

Faculty and Site Supervisor Dialogue: Dr. Bianca and Ms. Bellewa

We asked Dr. Bianca and Ms. Bellewa to talk about their involvement in setting up internship sites. Their perspectives can help broaden your understanding of the beginning of this experience from faculty and site supervisor perspectives.

Dr. Claude Bianca

Boy, I had a rough day today. What started as an easy process this semester, that of placing practicum and internship students, turned out to be really a difficult one. And I am still not finished with the process. I will give you some background about how I was thinking about this semester. In our program I have 25 placements that I have established either formal agreements or working relationships. Some of the agreements have a "shelf life," which means that the agreements are for anywhere from 3 to 5 years. Then these agreements have to be renewed. The agency with working relationships, I am negotiating formal agreements, but either the lawyers at the agency or the legal staff here at our school are reviewing them. The agreement process is a long one. But I digress.

As of last Friday, I had applications for 10 students for practicum. This is a student's first agency placement. I try to be very careful about these placements. Some sites are better for practicum, others are better for more experienced students in internship. Some site supervisors provide more intense supervision while others are more hands off than hands on. I think students in practicum need close supervision. My other 15 students will be internship placements—unless I need to develop new placements or I place more than one student at a site, I am stretched to place everyone. That being said, I had the perfect matches in my mind before I sat down to make my list of students and their corresponding placements.

Here come the difficulties I told you about. I usually e-mail site supervisors asking them if they are willing to take a student(s) the following semester. I sent those e-mails last Friday. Today I received e-mails from 15 of the 25 site supervisors I contacted. Five of these cannot supervise this next semester. One will be on maternity leave by the middle of the semester, one promised another college an internship spot, one has just been offered a promotion, and two others say they just need a break from supervision. Of course, it is my responsibility to continue to develop new placements but I don't have much time to do so before students receive their placements.

By midmorning matters became even more complicated. Two students came by who wanted to enroll in the practicum. They hadn't filled out an application because they thought they were going to have to work full time next semester. But they figured out other options, so they want to apply late. Another student came by to say that he couldn't enroll in practicum this next semester because of some family issues. I had the perfect placement for him; it is a placement that almost nobody wants for various reasons. So my perfect plan unravels. Each semester the placement process is unpredictable. And I know that I will figure out the process, but the perfect match and the perfect fit—well that won't happen today.

Ms. Zu Bellewa

Dr. Claude Bianca called me at noon today to ask if I would be willing to take an internship student from the human service program this next semester. I had contacted him about a month ago because I wanted to be more involved in the human service program. He promised to call back and schedule a meeting to talk about establishing a site. Indicating that he had more internship sites available than students, he suggested we meet in a month or so. We were looking at establishing the site a semester or two down the line. Hence, I was surprised by his call. I invited him to come to our agency for our first meeting so he could see the site first hand and become familiar with the facilities and sources of support for a future intern. He said he would bring information with him about the program; he also sent a hard copy and indicated he would share the materials by e-mail.

I am reviewing these materials as I write this note to you. It is quite complicated, this internship. He also sent me information about practicum too. In my country, we didn't have training quite as formal and complex as these materials suggest. For example, we didn't make any distinctions between a student's first experience and the second experience. It was all internship. Also, we didn't have direct supervisors. Everyone in the agency became family to students and everyone in the agency became our supervisor. Of course there were directors and as students we didn't approach them much. But everyone else in the agency became our support. I don't mean to suggest that this is the perfect setting to learn, but all doors were open to us. Pretty much every day at the agency, each person, including interns, would come and we would divide up the work. I had to be flexible because each day I didn't know what I would be doing. As an intern, I would work wherever there was a need.

Of course my agency here in Syracuse is also more structured than in Niger. And I will have to talk to my director and our board of directors about having an intern. But I do have the materials I need to describe the internship process and how our agency could use an intern. There are several things that I want to do when I meet with Dr. Bianca and I have questions for him. There is also information about our agency I think he should have. And I want him to understand the strengths I think we could offer interns. But we also have limitations.

For instance, when we work with immigrants, we focus on helping meet their basic needs. This is not always easy because of the cultural differences—and that includes language. Also, because we are working with a dynamic population with very few services available, quite a bit of our work is advocacy and community based. I want to be sure that Dr. Bianca understands that interns would have face-to-face contact with clients but also would be performing advocacy work in the community. I noted that there is some discussion of direct and indirect hours. I think the distinction is when students are directly working face-to-face or ear-to-ear and when they are doing human service work but not with clients or colleagues. My understanding is that advocacy work, in the community, would be direct contact hours. But I need to ask if I understand correctly. A second concern or question that I have is, can students have more than one supervisor? Although our agency does not operate exactly like my agency in Niger, we collaborate quite a bit. I would like interns to feel the stability of my supervision combined with the freedom of what I guess I would term multiple person supervision.

Well Dr. Bianca comes on Wednesday to talk about establishing this partnership. I will let you know what happens after that!

Written by Dareen Basma, 2015. Used with permission.

The Professional Voice and Tips for Practice: Gwen

In this section, Gwen, a human service professional, discusses the importance of being honest in your internship applications. She provides guidelines for you to consider.

Gwen

What a wonderful place to be! You are beginning your internship. I thought about my own experiences when I started a class, internship or even a job. I always wanted to put my best foot forward. Yet I wondered if I was, at times, misrepresenting myself. One friend said to me, "Be careful how you present yourself; you want to be honest. You always want to ask, can I be the person I present?" The following tips for success focus on a difficult topic that may or may not be relevant to you, the felony conviction. If you find yourself in this type of situation, I hope the following discussion helps you decide how to move forward.

Honesty in Your Internship Application: If you have a felony conviction, entering a job interview can be challenging, as you anticipate how to answer the inevitable question regarding the conviction. While we understand your trepidation to talk about the past, it's important to focus on your future. After all, a perspective employer is looking to hire who you are now, not who you were. So the interview process provides you the valuable opportunity to show who you have become. Below is a four-step guide with an easy-to-remember acronym: S.T.E.P.

> *S ~ Speak honestly. Be honest about your conviction; however, monitor your air time so that you don't dwell on this aspect. Just state the facts of what happened and then move on.*
>
> *T ~ Take responsibility. After stating the facts of the conviction, take responsibility for your actions. Employers want to know that you acknowledge and accept the consequences of your actions.*
>
> *E ~ Express regret. State honestly your regret for your previous actions. Again, monitor your air time.*
>
> *P ~ Plan for the future. After stating factually the circumstances of the conviction, taking responsibility for your actions, and expressing regret, focus on and plan for the future. Use this time to share with the interviewer what you want to do with your life moving forward, in a new direction.*
>
> *As you move forward, just remember to take one S.T.E.P. at a time.*

Written by Gwen Ruttercutter, 2015. Used with permission.

Terms to Remember

Bridge

Eligibility for internship

Internship application

Internship placement process

Initial visit

Orientation

Three worlds/perspectives

University/site agreement

References

Bridge. (2015). In *Oxford English dictionary*. Retrieved from http://www.oed.com/view/Entry/23233?rskey=ZfhyNt&result=1#eid

Donohue, J. (n.d.). Strategies for successful interviewing. Retrieved from http://engineering.asu.edu/career/wp-content/uploads/sites/87/2012/04/prep_interview.pdf

Mahuron, S. (2015). Counseling internship interview questions. *Global Post*. Retrieved from http://everydaylife.globalpost.com/counseling-internship-interview-questions-16243.html

Parcells, N. (2015). The top 5 interview questions you should master. *Internship Guides*. Retrieved from http://www.internmatch.com/guides/internship-interview-questions-and-answers

Westerkamp, J. (2014). Interview questions. *All access internships*. Retrieved from http://www.allaccessinternships.com/articles/Article_Interview_Questions.pdf

4

Engaging in Internship During the First Week or Two

Reading this chapter will help you do the following:

- Prepare for the first day or week of internship.
- Learn practical tips about how to survive and thrive during the first day or week of internship.
- Describe your experiences of the different types of orientation to internship.
- Define dynamic orientation and describe its characteristics.
- Conduct an assessment of the knowledge and skills you will need to be a successful intern.
- Conduct an assessment of what you need to know about the placement site so you may have a successful internship experience.
- Define the concept of shadowing.

- Describe four characteristics that define your increasing responsibility in internship.
- Provide specific examples of how your site supervisor demonstrates human service roles and responsibilities.
- Describe the purposes of the professional disclosure statement and list the components of the statement.
- Outline the information you will need to complete a confidentiality statement and permission to tape.
- Work with your site and faculty supervisors to prepare an internship contract.
- Begin to maintain logs, notes, and weekly reflections about your internship.
- Learn about how *Alicia, Lucas, Tamika,* and *Tomas* describe their first two weeks in internship.
- Learn about the faculty and site supervisors' perspectives related to the first two weeks of internship.
- Describe the tips that Gwen provides for the use of social media and internship.

Chapters 1, 2, and 3 provide you with a basic understanding of the internship experience, your readiness of internship, and how to apply for and begin an internship. This chapter, Chapter 4, is the fourth and final chapter in Part I: Introduction to the Internship Experience. Chapter 4 focuses on how you will engage in the internship during the first week or two. First, we review how interns enter a field-based experience as a new member of the team and introduce ways they can orient themselves to internship work. Second, we look at specific tasks that help frame and structure the internship such as developing a professional disclosure statement, writing an internship contract, addressing issues of confidentiality, and gaining permission to tape from clients. Each of these activities helps interns develop their professional identity. Finally, in this chapter's peer-to-peer, faculty, site supervisor, and human service professional dialogues, Alicia, Lucas, Tamika, Dr. Bianca, Ms. Bellewa, and Gwen share their own experiences during the first two weeks of internship.

Box 4.1 describes the organizational framework of the first section of this chapter. This section helps you as an intern to enter the agency and structure your experiences there.

Box 4.1 Studying the Text: Entering the Internship Site

Studying the text: The following outline will help you read and study the text material in this next section.

Entering the internship site

1. Introduction

2. What you do the first few days

3. Dynamic orientation: Assessing what you know and what you need to know

Entering the Internship Site

Many of you will participate in an orientation before you begin to assume your responsibilities as an intern. Your orientation falls on a continuum that represents a range of experiences. For example, orientation may be as extensive as a 1-week orientation designed for all new employees such as intensive training related to the client interventions. Or it may be as limited as a 1-day training for all volunteers and interns. Orientation may only be the time you spend with your site supervisor during the initial visit. Regardless of the nature of the orientation, it represents the time when you first enter the internship site. You begin to learn about the site, the clients it serves, and its policies and procedures. The following section describes ways you might maximize your early experiences at your placement site.

What You Do the First Few Days

Similar to the initial visit, the first day in internship is both exciting and stressful. In Table 4.1 we provide some concrete suggestions collected from career experts that help you prepare for this first day (Bajic, 2013; McKay, 2014; Roos, 2014; Salpeter, 2014). In Table 4.2 and Table 4.3 we continue with strategies focused on practical and personal aspects of participating in internship for the first week or two. Following these suggestions provides a way to alleviate some of your sense of stress and helps you begin your internship in a productive way. Many of these guidelines build on what you learned on your initial visit to the internship site, while others relate to your status as the newest member of the agency team. All guidelines help you make a positive impression and assist you in building a bridge between your academic program and the internship site.

Table 4.1   Before the First Day or Week of Internship

Prepare for the First Day	Productive Steps
Learn more about your agency and the population it serves	Follow up your initial visit by gaining more information about your internship site. Begin to read about the clients with whom you will work.
Confirm route to the agency and travel time	You located the site of your agency while making your initial visit. Confirm the route and learn the traffic patterns related to your arrival time. Determine transportation time and arrive a few minutes early.
Create backup plans for travel to the site	Agencies and site supervisors understand that travel plans sometimes go awry. You want to minimize difficulties you encounter traveling to work by thinking ahead and developing backup plans for alternate transportation, alternate child care, and other travel routes.
Decide how to introduce yourself to agency staff and clients	During your first week you will be introducing yourself to members of the agency administrative staff and clients. Prepare a way to tell these individuals who you are and your place in the agency.
Plan appropriate dress	During your initial visit, you had an opportunity to observe the agency dress and ask your site supervisor about expectations. You may need to shop for a few pieces of clothing that allow you to dress as an intern rather than as a student.

In Table 4.2, we also provide some suggestions that will help you survive and thrive that first day and week of the internship. Again we follow the guidance of career experts (Bajic, 2013; McKay 2014; Roos 2014; Salpeter 2014) in making these suggestions. We believe these strategies help prepare you for the experience and reduce the awkwardness that you may feel as a *newcomer* to a setting.

Table 4.2   During the First Day or Week: Practical Aspects

Survive and Thrive	*Preparation Steps*
Know your schedule and be on time	An important professional behavior is to be on time. Prior to the first day, you and your site supervisor will have agreed upon the days and times you will work. Your supervisor expects to see you arrive on time or a little early to prepare for the day. *Call if you are going to be late.* On your first day confirm how to check in and out when you arrive and leave. Confirm your daily and weekly schedule.
Determine what supplies you need to bring to the placement site	Throughout your internship, you will be scheduling meetings, making notes, and making lists of things to accomplish. A small notebook or electric device is a tool you can use to jot down the names of individuals you meet, suggestions for reading, responsibilities or follow-up tasks you need to complete. Also in the category of *what to bring* is lunch. Since you might not know the agency culture around meals, it is a good idea to bring food to eat midday.
Plan how to use your electronic devices	You may be used to responding electronically 24/7, but in a work environment limit yourself to designated breaks in your schedule to check your messages and social media sites. Let your family and friends know you will not be available during the workday. Turn off your mobile phones or put them on vibrate. Don't check an incoming message or call during a meeting or when you are with clients. Don't use social media during working hours.
Be respectful but assertive in interactions	This first week is a time to learn about the agency. Balance listening and asking questions. Begin to identify questions you have and individuals who can help answer those questions. Ask questions and ask for help. Find a time to check in with site supervisor each day and schedule a time for a supervision meeting.
Create your own work space	This is the time to create a work space for yourself. Collect the supplies you need. Add small touches to make the space personal.
Stay until the end of the day	Don't leave early. Remain on task until your designated time to depart. Inform your supervisor when you leave.

Table 4.3   During the First Week or Two: Personal Aspects

Initiative and Commitment	Concrete Ways
Be positive and if asked, perform tasks	Be available to help. Perform tasks if asked. Ask questions if you cannot complete the tasks. Ask for feedback about your work.
Listen and observe	Watch for opportunities to contribute to the work, even on your first day. Observing and listening are the keys here to discover where you might be able to contribute.
Look for ways to help	During this time, look for ways that you might be able to contribute to the goals of the agency. You may identify ongoing projects where you can serve as part of a team or your may see a new project that helps the agency and matches your knowledge and skills sets. Find ways to help your site supervisor and others.
Ask about multicultural and ethical sensitivities	Each agency has a unique culture. You want to begin to learn about this culture, especially as it relates to multicultural and ethical issues. Ask your site supervisor about multicultural and ethical sensitivities particular to the agency and its clients.
Begin to develop a plan for acquiring new knowledge and skills	Build on initial orientation by maintaining a list of ways you could better understand the agency work.
Begin to plan what you want to learn	Think about what knowledge, skills, and experiences you want to have by the end of your internship experience. List these and begin to make a plan to gain them.

During the first two weeks, your personal orientation to work helps establish how others know you as a colleague. They learn about your attitude toward your internship and your approach to work. You want to establish a positive way of working in your agency. In Table 4.3 we suggest concrete ways you can demonstrate initiative and commitment to the internship experience. Again we integrate suggestions from a variety of experts writing about work and career (Bajic, 2013; McKay, 2014; Roos, 2014; Salpeter, 2014).

Exercise 4.1 Your First Two Weeks: Writing Your Own Story, Entry 11

Step 1

In this exercise, reflect on the first two weeks of internship. Describe the ways you prepared for the experience and what you learned about yourself and your internship.

Before the first day: Describe your concerns and the steps you took to address those concerns.

During the first day or two: Practical Aspects: Describe the ways you organize or manage the first day or two in the agency.

(Continued)

(Continued)

During the first day or two: Personal Aspects: Describe the ways you demonstrated initiative and commitment to your internship.

Now that you have prepared for the first two weeks of internship, let's look at how you continue to grow and develop beyond these initial experiences.

Dynamic Orientation: Assessing What You Know and What You Need to Know

The first two weeks of internship is the perfect time for you to begin to focus on your own growth and development. **Dynamic orientation** is the name we give to this attention to professional development. The word *orientation* suggests learning about the work required of you today, as well as in the future. The word *dynamic* indicates that an active and continuous assessment of both what you believe you know and what you think you need to know. In other words, dynamic orientation is the ongoing process of learning to be an effective human service intern. Here is one example of what dynamic orientation looks like.

In your internship site, there may be specific eligibility criteria individuals must meet before being accepted as clients. If you are learning to assess client eligibility, you must understand these criteria. Once accepted as clients, the human service care professionals use motivational interviewing as one aspect of their direct care. To work with clients, you would need to learn how to conduct a client session using motivational interviewing. Understanding what is required in an internship placement guides your dynamic orientation or professional development.

Approaching your professional development as a dynamic or continuous process helps you build on previous experiences such as the academic program's preinternship seminar or brief orientation, the initial visit to the internship site and the site-sponsored intern orientation.

Figure 4.1 illustrates how the four types of orientation work together to support the work of the intern at the internship site. This figure allows you to see how each orientation experience builds on the previous one.

Figure 4.1   The Orientation Experience

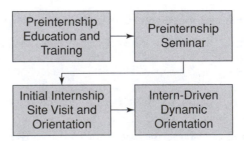

Source: Created by Gwen Ruttencutter, 2015. Used with permission.

There are several characteristics that distinguish dynamic orientation from these other three experiences. First, dynamic orientation is intern driven. In other words, interns, rather than site supervisors or faculty, make their own assessments of what they know and what they need to know. Second, once interns conduct this type of assessment, they seek out the education, information, training, and consultation to meet their unique needs. Third, as we discussed earlier, rather than orientation occurring at a specific point in time (e.g., midterm or end of term), this type of orientation is ongoing, hence the use of the term *dynamic*. We believe that this continuous evaluation of what one needs to know and the exploration of new perspectives and insights help convey an attitude of commitment to quality work and professional growth. Also dynamic orientation empowers the intern to identify what he or she needs to perform the required professional roles and responsibilities and meet client needs. This is an important quality that extends beyond internship and into human service professional practice.

How do interns begin to assess what they know and what else they need to know? This involves becoming familiar with your abilities in relation to the demands of the work. In Exercise 4.2, we suggest two different ways to assess your abilities. You may want to use one of these ways or combine the two. The first uses a set of questions to guide the assessment. The second uses a more structured way to guide an assessment of what you know and what you need to know. See Tables 4.4, 4.5, and 4.6.

Exercise 4.2 Focusing Your Dynamic Orientation

As you begin to think about your own dynamic orientation, we suggest you use both Assessment 1 and Assessment 2 to determine what you know and what you need to know. Using both allows you to discover the most helpful way to guide your professional development. You may also develop your own ways of focusing your orientation. Be creative in this process!

Step 1

Assessment Dynamic Orientation 1: Questions to Consider: Focus on Self and the Work

Answer the following questions about what you need to know about your internship work. Review these responses with your site supervisor.

1. What do I need to know about the day-to-day operations at the internship site?

   _____
   _____
   _____

2. How can I meet day-to-day expectations more effectively (content and skills) and more efficiently (organization and management)?

   _____
   _____
   _____

(Continued)

(Continued)

3. How can I improve the consistency of my work described in Question 2 above?

_____

_____

_____

4. How can I develop positive relationships with my site supervisor, peers, and clients?

_____

_____

_____

5. What are some of the common issues I am encountering? What might be effective responses to each of these challenges or issues?

_____

_____

_____

6. On what basis or according to what criteria will I be evaluated? What do I need to do to receive a positive evaluation?

_____

_____

_____

7. What are the materials that I need to reference quickly as I perform my responsibilities as an intern? Which of these do I understand? Which of these do I need help understanding?

_____

_____

_____

Step 2

As indicated earlier, another way of viewing dynamic orientation (or an assessment of what I know and what else I need to know) focuses on specific knowledge and skills interns need for their specific internship site's work. The following tables, 4.4, 4.5, and 4.6, help you consider specific information and skills about the (a) internship, (b) work with clients, and (c) your own helping skills.

Assessment Dynamic Orientation 2: Structured Rubric

Table 4.4   Dynamic Orientation Assessment: The Academic Program

Assessing What I Know and What Else I Need To Know

What I Know	Source of Education/Training	Benefits of Knowledge	What I Don't Know	Follow-Up If Needed
Academic Program				
• Purpose of internship				
• Documentation				
• Insurance				
• Professional disclosure				

What I Know	Source of Education/Training	Benefits of Knowledge	What I Don't Know	Follow-Up If Needed
• Contract				
• Confidentiality and Permission to Tape				
• Midterm evaluation				
• Final evaluation				
• Evaluation of site				
• Record of hours				
• Other written assignments				

Table 4.5   Dynamic Orientation Assessment: The Internship Site

Assessing What I Know and What I Need To Know

Internship Site			
Logistics			
• Badges or name tags			
• Keys			
• Orientation to building			
• Introduction to key personnel and staff			
• Parking			
Agency Structure			
• Mission and goals			
• Organizational structure			
• Services			
• Staffing			
• Funding			
• Role of intern			
Policies and Procedures			
• Program goals			
• Client services			
• Client records (types of records, documentation, policies)			
• Program evaluation			
• Quality management			

(Continued)

Table 4.5 (Continued)

• Physical plant and equipment				
• Policies related to the use of technology				
Client Rights				
• Client Bill of Rights				
• Addressing needs of clients with disabilities				
• Addressing cultural aspects of client needs				
• HIPPA				
• Informed consent				
• Grievance and due process				
Special Situations				
• Determination of suicide risk assessment				
• Determination of threat assessment				
• Agency response to crisis				
• Active shooter training and response				
Personnel Services				
• Agency personnel job descriptions				
• Agency personnel policies				
• Evaluations				
• Employee Bill of Rights and Responsibilities				

Table 4.6 Dynamic Orientation Assessment: Knowledge and Skills

Assessing What I Know and What I Need To Know

Knowledge related to				
• Client groups (incidence, history)				
• Client needs				
• Client culture				
• Client systems (family, neighborhood, wider locale)				
• Client developmental needs				
• Client barriers to service				

• Supportive services and institutions				
• Relationship to agency				
Basic Skills				
• Listening				
• Reflecting (restating)				
• Paraphrasing				
• Summarizing				
• Using questions appropriately				
• Using silence				
• Using empathy				
• Expressing genuineness				
• Demonstrating unconditional positive regard				
• Problem solving				
• Identifying problems				
• Setting goals				
• Generating alternative approaches				
• Weighing alternative approaches				
• Choosing an approach				
• Developing implementation strategies				
• Implementing				
• Evaluating outcomes				
• Concluding the work				
• Recognizing ethical issues				
Roles and Responsibilities				
• Conducting an initial/intake interview				
• Note taking				
• Performing as a case manager				
• Phases of the helping process				
• Beginning				
• Middle				
• Ending				
• How agency services reflect cultural awareness				

(Continued)

(Continued)

Assessment as a form of dynamic orientation represents both a recognition of the importance of self-awareness and self-reflection; both indicate a commitment to continuing professional development. Even though we describe this process in the first section of the text, at the beginning of the internship, ongoing assessment will help guide your education and professional growth.

We now turn our attention to the direction of your professional growth during the internship experience.

Interns can anticipate that during the first week or two their work will follow a pattern reflecting to their growing knowledge of the site and the responsibilities they have assumed. Box 4.2 describes the increasing responsibility of the internship work.

Box 4.2 Studying the Text: The Increasing Responsibility of the Internship Work

Studying the text: The following outline will help you read and study the text material in this next section.

The increasing responsibility of the internship work

1. Shadowing

2. Human service roles and responsibilities

3. Making models work for you (human service roles and responsibilities)

4. Incremental increase in responsibilities

The Increasing Responsibility of the Internship Work

During your internship, you will note, over time, that your responsibilities at your placement site will steadily increase. As we discussed earlier, when you enter your site you will be forming a relationship with your site supervisor, learning about the site, and developing an initial understanding of professional work. As most internships continue, interns move gradually from orientation to full participation in the agency work. At the beginning of the internship experience, one way interns learn about the agency work is through an activity called **shadowing**.

Shadowing

Shadowing is a way that many site supervisors like to introduce interns to the agency and to the work of the agency. Shadowing may begin with participating in orientation, observing, and performing small tasks during the first few weeks. As interns learn more about the agency and they begin to work with clients under direct supervision, they assume multiple responsibilities which in time includes working with clients without direct supervision.

Observation or shadowing occurs when you follow your site supervisor (and other professionals in the agency) from activity to activity and learn by watching. Observation is a powerful way to begin to understand the human service professional's job and the multiple roles and responsibilities it entails. Your participation at this stage involves your being an active, rather than passive, learner. A good way to begin a day of observation is to have a short meeting with your site supervisor to review the day's schedule. Of course a day in the life of a human service professional rarely goes as planned, so you will have the opportunity to see how your site supervisor prepares for and responds to both scheduled and unscheduled events and requests for help.

Here are some suggestions for making the shadowing experience a productive one. Even though you are shadowing you are rarely just observing your site supervisor in interactions with clients and staff. A conversation with your site supervisor about your role as an observer will help you understand how active you can be. Here are questions you can ask your site supervisor about how to be an effective observer.

- How will we explain my presence to others in the room? (e.g., administrators, peers, clients)
- Can I take notes during our meetings? Can I take notes during our work with clients?
- I plan to record observations, questions, and ideas for my own work. Are there others aspects of what I observe to which I should attend?
- When I have questions, would you prefer I ask them *in the moment* or wait until after the meeting or session?

Human Service Professional Roles and Responsibilities

One way to better understand the work of your site supervisor during these early weeks of internship is to begin to describe your site supervisor's work. We propose you use the description of human service professional roles and responsibilities to help you understand both an overview and the details of the work. Shadowing the site supervisor during the first weeks provides you with an opportunity to view how your site supervisor carries out specific human service professional roles and responsibilities. In this chapter, we introduce **human service roles and responsibilities** to help you categorize your site supervisor's work.

Human Service Roles and Responsibilities

We introduce a set of human service roles and responsibilities described by Woodside and McClam (2015) in their *Introduction to Human Services* text. The authors characterized responsibilities in terms of **providing direct service, performing administrative focus,** or **working with the community,** and then presented roles that reflect each of the three responsibilities. These roles and responsibilities reflect one aspect of professional identity (introduced in Chapter 2) for human service professionals. Performing them illustrates the way that professional identity is acted out or practiced in the human service profession. We assume that earlier in your human service education you studied this way of practice in more depth. For more information see Woodside and McClam's *Introduction to Human Services* text or the National Organization of Human Service website for more information.

We present in Table 4.7 a list of these roles and responsibilities and provide a brief description of the roles that fall into each of the three categories. We then suggest you use Table 4.8 to categorize the roles and responsibilities in which your site supervisor engages.

Table 4.7   Categories of Roles and Responsibilities

Categories of Roles and Responsibilities	Roles and Responsibilities
Providing direct service	Behavior changer—facilitates client change
	Caregiver—provides help such as day-to-day support and 24/7 availability
	Communicator—establishes rapport and trust with the client
	Crisis intervener—provides short-term response for clients who experience sudden and difficult turning points
	Participant empowerer—focuses on the confidence and self-efficacy of the client
	Teacher/educator—guides the client using a variety of approaches
Performing administrative work	Broker—is the connection between client and needed services
	Data manager—makes assessments based upon information collected, numbers, and other descriptive data
	Evaluator—gathering data and making assessments based upon those data
	Facilitator of services—matches clients to services and supports them during the helping process
	Planner—devises a strategy for the near future or longer future for care of the client
	Report (documentation) and grant proposal writer—prepares accounts about client in writing
	Resource allocator—determines how agency resources are spent for client care, staff, operations, and overhead
Working with the community	Advocate—speaks in favor of or for clients in various arenas such as legal, political, and economic
	Community and service networker—links professionals with common interests together to work on behalf of clients in need
	Community planner—works with community services staff so clients receive quality services
	Consultant—provides expert advice and guidance
	Mobilizer/Community organizer—advocates for effective and quality services for those in need
	Outreach worker—provides help *where the need is*, usually outside an office setting

Exercise 4.3 Human Service Roles and Responsibilities

The description of human service roles and responsibilities described provide a structured way you can learn about your site supervisor's job. This also helps you to understand some of the responsibilities you will assume during your internship and think about how you can contribute to agency work.

Step 1

Using Table 4.8, record your observations of your site supervisor's work during the initial shadowing. Categorize your observations according to the roles and responsibilities presented in Table 4.7.

Step 2

As you document what you observe, we encourage you to share this information with your site supervisor and discuss your observations with your faculty supervisor and student peers.

Increasing Responsibilities in Internship

Many times, becoming involved in the work of the agency occurs incrementally. In other words, you will decrease the amount of time you spend observing and increase your responsibilities. In all likelihood, you will move from performing simple tasks to carry out more advanced ones. As you spend more time at your site, your site supervisor may ask you to accept more responsibility. Site supervisors ease their interns into the work in different ways, and you can often influence how quickly you are given more responsibility. In fact, interns may expect to accept responsibility as early as the first day at their internship. In Chapter 2, you met Tomas, an internship student from Brooklyn who was anticipating his internship at a local drug and alcohol rehabilitation center. Tomas has now completed his first two weeks in internship. He shares with us his experience during those first two weeks.

Tomas

I began my internship earlier this month. In fact my first day marked the first day of classes for the spring semester. Heavens, it was a cold day here in Brooklyn. I took the subway and then walked about five blocks all in the snow. The snow

Table 4.8 Shadowing: Observing the Site Supervisor

Observation and date	Roles and responsibilities Providing direct service Performing administrative work Working with the community

helped calm me, and the cold wind helped clear my head. Even though I visited my agency twice in December, once for the initial visit and confirmation of the site and the second for a daylong orientation, I was really nervous. As I write this reflection, I realize I am less nervous today than I was that first day. I did not know what to expect because my supervisor, Ms. Paseattoe, told me I would just follow her around for the first week. I am at my site for 30 hours each week, and she thought I would have a better idea of the job and the responsibilities that I would assume if I watched her work. Boy, she was right about that. Crazy to think you can learn so much by watching. Ms. Paseattoe tries to have a weekly routine, although she explained that rarely does a day go as planned. She does have some meetings and client work that she cannot miss. She laid out the schedule for me the first day, letting me know what the week would look like. This is a copy of what Ms. Paseattoe gave to me that first day.

> *Monday: staffing, reports from weekend staff, individual sessions, paperwork*
>
> *Tuesday: staffing, individual sessions, family meetings, intake sessions, paperwork*
>
> *Wednesday: staffing, individual sessions, family meetings, group sessions*
>
> *Thursday: paperwork, group sessions, intake sessions, group sessions*
>
> *Friday: staffing, client evaluations, individual sessions, group sessions, site supervision (mine)*

During that first week, we followed a schedule, but Ms. Paseattoe sandwiched in phone calls, referrals, suicide risk assessments, and an emergency budget meeting in between her other responsibilities. By Wednesday, she and I had unscheduled supervision time where we talked about what I had learned. She outlined the responsibilities she wanted me to assume on Thursday and Friday. Ms. Paseattoe wanted us to conduct intake sessions together. We made a plan: She would begin the intake session, then I would conduct the middle of the session, and she would close the session. Actually I would have a part in the beginning because we both would provide information from our professional disclosure statements to the client. During our morning staffings on Friday, Ms. Paseattoe asked that I add a few comments about the client sessions I observed. My thought at that point was "Well, here goes." Shadowing felt safe. But, quite frankly I was really nervous.

Now at the end of my second week, I have even more responsibility. And I just finished talking with Ms. Paseattoe in our regularly scheduled site supervision meeting about my client work under supervision. In our time logs we have to list all of our activities and then note whether these activities are direct or indirect hours. Here is what my time log looked like for the first three days. This gives you some ideas about what my experience was like.

In the next section we describe assignments required early in the internship that help you frame your internship.

Table 4.9 First Days of Internship: Tomas's Time Log

Date/Activity	Time Commitment	Summary Reflection
1/12 Attended staffing	120 minutes	Interesting to see people working together. I also got to hear more about clients and the challenges they face. The staff also reviewed reports from weekend staff. Sunday staff members remain on site for this staffing. Ms. Paseattoe is part of this group. She also takes the notes and makes sure documentation is in order.
1/12 Talked with supervisor about preparing for work with clients	30 minutes	This is a time Ms. Paseattoe usually prepares for her individual sessions. Each of the sessions is 30 minutes, and on Monday she sees at least 6 clients. She has her own caseload, and she also sees clients when other staff members are not available. Ms. Paseattoe was scheduled to see a very challenging client passed on to her from another staff member. We reviewed files, and she helped me see how she planned each session. Ms. Paseattoe sees clients back to back so she has to be prepared.
1/13	180 minutes	Observed Ms. Paseattoe work with six clients. What a range of individuals, including teen girls, boys, and adult males! In one session, the client was very aggressive. It scared me because I wouldn't know how to handle that situation. One thing I need to know is how to calm down a client or how to call for help. I noticed that Ms. Paseattoe used different approaches depending upon the client. She was also consistently warm and firm—at the same time.
1/13	70 minutes	Ms. Paseattoe answered phone calls and filled out paperwork for the day. I read through the case files of two of the clients I met today. There was so much information in the file, I only had time for two of them.
1/14	120 minutes	We traveled to juvenile court for a hearing that involved a past client at the agency. The judge called my supervisor and asked that she attend the court hearing. Ms. Paseattoe invited me to come with her.

Box 4.3 Studying the Text: Framing the Internship

Studying the text: The following outline will help you read and study the text material in this next section.
Framing the internship experience

1. Considering student reflections
2. Structuring the internship
   a. Professional disclosure
   b. Internship contract
   c. Confidentiality and permission to tape
   d. Keeping a record of your work: logs, notes, and weekly reflections

Framing the Internship Experience

At the beginning of the internship, there are documents that help structure your internship as each represents an agreement among the multiple participants: the academic program and faculty supervisor, the internship site and site supervisor, and the intern. Usually, it is the intern's responsibility to generate these documents. The faculty and site supervisor will review these documents and suggest revisions. Finally all three participants acknowledge or sign the documents. Then we follow with four additional documents: the intern's professional disclosure, the internship contract, the confidentiality and permission to tape agreement, and the logs, notes and weekly reflections.

Before we talk specifically about structuring the internship documents, internship students share their reflections about beginning the internship and preparing the documents that guide their work.

Box 4.4 Students Reflect on Beginning the Internship

Preparing the Professional Disclosure

Steve: When writing my professional disclosure statement, I consulted the Internship Handbook, resources online, and my site supervisor. I included my educational background, my purpose, my duties, confidentiality, and my site and faculty supervisors' information.

Maria: I was able to update my professional disclosure from the one I created during practicum. I know it is an important document to use in explaining my purpose to other colleagues and clients. I was nervous to show it to my supervisor, but she spent time reading it and helped me with it.

Al: The process of writing my first professional disclosure was pretty simple. I followed a template that made sense to me. There's no sense in trying to reinvent the wheel. I listed my education, my experience working with children or in education, my goals, my hopes for the semester, and my contact information.

Shasha: I made the professional disclosure more of a letter. That felt more comfortable to me. That helped put more of *myself* into the document. I used a picture and also talked about my hobbies. And I talked about how excited I was working in the agency.

What was your experience writing the internship contract?

Steve: Creating the internship contract provided a good opportunity for me to share my goals and learning objectives with my site supervisor. That way we could develop goals that fit both of our needs. We were able to collaborate and come up with a plan for me this semester.

> **Maria:** It would have been helpful to start this discussion the first week and begin creating the contract. I was really nervous and afraid that I could not get it right. It was also beneficial in that it kept me focused and directed towards some specific goals that I thought would benefit me the most. Nothing I ever do goes smoothly.
>
> **Al:** Preparing my internship contract was difficult for me, but only because I really wanted to challenge myself. I also had a tough time coming up with creative ways to measure my progress. It was a positive experience because it led to some great conversations between me, my cohort, my site supervisor, and my program supervisor.
>
> **Shasha:** Creating the contract was a very helpful and meaningful experience. Discussing our goals for internship beforehand was extremely helpful. My site supervisor really helped me when she suggested, "When creating your contract, think of one way or one project that will be your mark or contribution to leave with the school."

Structuring the Internship

As indicated earlier, many of the legal issues related to risk are linked to the professional services you promise. Writing a professional disclosure statement and sharing it with the client is one way to communicate with clients about your knowledge, skills, and experience. It states the services you are able to provide as an intern and as a representative of your internship site. Let's look at the components of a professional disclosure statement and then write one of your own to share with the individuals with whom you work at your internship site.

Professional Disclosure Statement

Now that you will be meeting clients in your internship setting, you will want a formal way that you can introduce yourself to the clients with whom you will work. A **professional disclosure statement** will provide you a consistent way of conveying to both colleagues and clients information about your professional self. A professional disclosure statement meets several goals. First, it is a formal way that you can introduce yourself to the clients with whom you work. Then, it helps them begin to know you and learn what they can expect from you. You convey to them your status as an intern working in the internship site. Second, because a professional disclosure statement is written and includes several sections (e.g., name, education, experience, philosophy, position as intern, supervision), it describes your professional self in an organized way. Third, providing a copy of this document to your clients allows them to take the document with them. They can reread and study it after their first visit. They don't have to remember all the information you provide in your professional introduction. Fourth, the professional disclosure allows clients to know the relevant areas which you are competent to help them. Fifth, the statement affirms that you have professional training and supervision. It specifies that you will act in a professional manner. Finally, such a statement can also detail the limitations of your education and expertise.

In most internship experiences, you will write a professional disclosure statement prior to working with clients. You will want to check your internship handbook for suggested formats for such a document. Once you have written a draft of the professional disclosure statement, share it with your faculty and site supervisors. Then ask for their suggestions.

In the following section we will answer several questions you may have about the professional disclosure statement.

What is included in the professional disclosure statement?

In your professional disclosure statement you will include many or all of the items listed:

- Name
- Contact information (at the site)
- Previous education, current educational experience (e.g., enrolled in human service program), and areas of study
- Status as an intern working at an internship site
- Current supervisors (e.g., faculty and site supervisor)
- Philosophy of helping and services you will provide
- Confidentiality and what are exceptions to confidentiality
- Any professional codes or agency policies you will follow

How personal do I make the professional disclosure statement?

Even though there are standard (and at times mandatory) components of a professional disclosure, you may also want the disclosure to have a welcoming tone. It will also reflect the expectations of your faculty supervisor and your site supervisor. You want a personal and factual statement about your education, experience, abilities, and position as an intern.

Options that make the professional disclosure more personal include using agency letterhead, a photograph, and less professional jargon. It is important to remember that this is an official document, and these guidelines apply:

- Establish yourself as a professional (e.g., I am studying to be . . .).
- Provide information about the conditions of your internship (e.g., serving as an intern, working at the agency for XXX hours a week, available XXX days of the week, from XXX Month, day, year to XXX Month, day, year).
- Provide information about your supervision and include contact information about supervisors.
- Use language that the reader can understand.
- Cover information about confidentiality and exceptions to confidentiality.
- Provide contact information about yourself, if the reader has any questions.

Is there an example or template I can use?

Before you write your own professional disclosure statement, it may be helpful to look at an example. In the professional disclosure statement shown in Box 4.5 Tomas introduces himself to his clients.

Box 4.5 Tomas's Professional Disclosure Statement

Tomas

Brooklyn Drug and Alcohol Rehabilitation Center

Phone: 000-000-0000

Address: Brooklyn, NY

Dear Clients,

My name is Tomas and I am a human service rehabilitation intern from Brooklyn Community College. My anticipated date of graduation is May 20XX. I earned my high school diploma from Brooklyn High School # 4 in 20XX. My previous work experiences include working with children and youth at a local Boys and Girls Club.

I am excited to be working with you during the next 6 months. I immigrated from Puerto Rico when I was 9. I am a U.S. citizen. I speak English and Spanish. I also speak limited Haitian Creole. I am looking forward to working with clients. I believe that everyone has the capacity to change and grow, and I want to work together with clients to find ways to make their lives better.

As part of my human service rehabilitation program internship experience, I am working as an intern. I am required to complete a 600-hour internship in a local agency. I chose the Brooklyn Drug and Alcohol Center for my internship. My site supervisor is Ms. Paseattoe, who is a Team Leader and Case Coordinator (phone: 000-000-0000). My faculty supervisor is Dr. Hank Highland (phone: 000-000-0000). I plan to be at Brooklyn Drug and Alcohol Center from Monday through Friday for the entire spring semester. My last week at the Center will be May 15, XXXX.

During this semester, I will work under supervision. When working with clients, my responsibilities will include gather intake information, write intake reports, work with my supervisor to develop a case management plan, work one-on-one with individual clients, work with groups of clients, and work with my supervisor to prepare a discharge plan.

I will provide individual and group counseling and classroom guidance for students.

As part of my training, I will be audiotaping all individual counseling sessions. The purpose of taping is to allow my faculty supervisor, Mr. Highland, to help me develop my skills. Tapes will be strictly confidential, and client permission will be required before taping occurs. I will erase each taped session 3 weeks after the taping occurs.

I am a member of the Mid-Atlantic Human Service Organization and adhere to the National Organization for Human Services Code of Ethics in my work. The information clients share with me will be held in confidence except for the following reasons: My supervisor needs to be aware of the nature of the issue to provide the best care to the

(Continued)

(Continued)

client; the client requests, in writing, that I share the information with a specified person; the client shares information that implies danger to self or others; the client tells me about a situation where child or elder abuse is occurring or if a court orders the agency to present information about a client.

I look forward to working at the Brooklyn Drug and Alcohol Rehabilitation Center this semester!

Sincerely,

Tomas

E-mail: tomasintern@gmail.com

Phone: 000-000-0000

Exercise 4.4 Your Professional Disclosure Statement: Writing Your Own Story, Entry 12

Step 1

Take a moment and make notes about what you would include in a professional disclosure statement. Save this work to show your faculty and site supervisors. They will have suggestions and feedback.

Step 2

Write a draft of a professional disclosure statement. This statement will change as you gain more experience as an intern.

Internship Contract

One of the most important documents that interns develop with their site supervisors and their faculty is the human services **internship contract**. The purpose of the internship contract is to document an agreement among all three parties related to expectations and responsibilities for the student during the internship experience. The faculty and site supervisors agree to support the student's stated goals. Often the internship contract also provides the frame for midterm and final evaluation of the intern's performance.

Although internship contracts may take many forms, we have listed many common components here:

> **Student information**: This may include student's name, identification, school term, date, name of internship site, name of internship site supervisor, and name of internship faculty supervisor.

> **Specific goals**: The goals reflect the priorities of the program. They may be divided into areas of performance such as professional work-related behaviors, work with clients, and work with staff.

Activities and tasks to meet goals: These may be stated as objectives and be specific to the work of the agency. Examples might include (a) meet with eight clients each week, (b) begin and conduct three adolescent groups, and (c) prepare two newsletters.

Measurement of performance: The intern and the site and faculty supervisors will agree how the student's work will be evaluated. Often students are encouraged to create surveys, interviews, and rating scales to assess their work, especially their work with clients.

Site supervisor comments: At times there is a designated place where site supervisors can explain the nature of the internship work and what contributions they hope the intern can make to the agency and to clients. Also site supervisors may have specific goals and tasks that match the individual student's skills with the needs of the agency.

Student comments: Students are encouraged to provide information about their own experience—that is, what they would like to accomplish. They might want to add tasks and activities that meet their individual goals as well as those set by the agency or the program.

Signatures: Agreement among all three parties is critical. The signatures reflect each party supports the expectation and plans articulated in the document.

Figure 4.2 illustrates one format for the internship contract. The one for your program may differ slightly or considerably.

Figure 4.2 Example of a Template for Internship Contract

Internship Contract

Background information

Student name

Student I.D.

Semester enrolled in internship

Site placement

Site supervisor

Faculty supervisor

The internship student is committed to working toward and accomplishing the goals listed:

1. Promoting client self-sufficiency

Goal 1 _____

Activity or Task _____

2. Communicating orally and in writing

Goal 1 _____

Activity or Task _____

3. Gathering information, planning and delivering services

Goal 1 _____

Activity or Task _____

(Continued)

Figure 4.2 (Continued)

4. Networking and making referrals

Goal 1 _____

Activity or Task _____

5. Evaluating and documenting work

Goal 1 _____

Activity or Task _____

6. Advocating for client

Goal 1 _____

Activity or Task _____

7. Demonstrating multicultural competence

Goal 1 _____

Activity or Task _____

8. Demonstrating ethical decision making and behavior

Goal 1 _____

Activity or Task _____

9. Setting intern specific goals

Goal 1 _____

Activity or task _____

Student signature and date _____

Site supervisor signature and date _____

Faculty supervisor signature and date _____

Negotiating the Internship Contract

During the first two weeks of internship, you will want to review the internship contract form with your site supervisor, noting the date that it is due to your faculty supervisor. Establish a time to talk to your site supervisor about the internship contract. Before the meeting, make notes about goals that you would like to accomplish during the internship. Ask your site supervisor to do the same. You can use the form in Exercise 4.5 to begin to think about the goals you have for internship.

We recommend a meeting that focuses solely on the internship contract. In this meeting, you can learn specific ideas your supervisor has for your internship work and what the agency expects from its interns. You can use the form in Exercise 4.5 to begin to think about the goals you have for internship.

In this conversation, you can move from understanding the site and your place in it, in general terms, to more specific expectations and responsibilities. For each goal that you and your site supervisor record, you want to ask, "How will you (the site supervisor) and I know when I meet this goal?" This question helps you in two ways: First, you can see what tasks and responsibilities you need to accomplish to meet the goal. Second, you can begin to understand how you and your supervisor will evaluate your progress towards these goals. You will probably not receive answers to all of your questions in this first meeting to discuss the internship contract, but hopefully, you will begin to see expectations for your work become clearer.

After this first meeting to discuss the internship contract, it is always a good idea to ask for another meeting to discuss the future work. You and your supervisor will need the time to think whether the goals are realistic, whether they can be measured, and how and whether they can be achieved. Sometimes a first discussion of goals reflects more enthusiasm than a realistic picture of what is possible during the semester. Also, given some time to reflect, you and your site supervisor may think of additional goals you wish to add. And don't forget to review your internship contract with your faculty supervisor. He or she will have some good ideas about how to improve it. Figure 4.3 provides you with an overview of the internship negotiation process.

Exercise 4.5 Negotiating Your Internship Contract

Step 1

1. When you first begin to think about the goals you wish to establish for internship, you can use the internship contract form in Figure 4.2 or adapt one that's according to your program's internship contract.

2. Begin to formulate your goals prior to meeting with your site supervisor. This will help structure your work and provide a concrete way you can introduce some of your ideas.

Figure 4.3   Negotiating the Internship Contract

Source: Created by Gwen Ruttencutter, 2015. Used with permission.

Audio or Video Taping of Your Work With Clients

In Box 4.6 Tomas describes his intentions to record his work once he receives clients' permissions to tape their interactions. Many faculty and site supervisors believe that review of the intern's work on tape provides an opportunity for feedback which can greatly enhance the intern's growth and development. Three positive outcomes can occur from taping one's work and then listening to it and/or watching it with a supervisor. First, from a macro prospective, listening to a tape allows intern and supervisor alike to understand the flow and content of an individual or group session. Early in helping skills classes, students are taught that sessions with clients have a beginning, middle, and end. Reviewing a tape allows interns to identify these three segments of a session. They see the varying skills each requires. Second, from a micro perspective, interns and supervisors can identify key moments or elements in the session. They can share thoughts and reflections about themselves and their clients during these moments. Third, because listening to a tape is a retrospective activity, interns may be less critical of themselves and more objective as they listen to and think about a past activity.

Not all academic programs require internship students to tape their work with clients. But for those who do, interns will use a form for *Permission to Tape*, which is either an essential requirement of agency documentation or suggested by the academic program. The academic program handbook is usually the source for this form. In most cases, internship sites require that interns ask individual clients for permission to tape. In the case of children, interns must gain consent from parents to tape and assent from the children themselves. Interns will discuss the permission to tape during the first meeting with a client or with a group. We suggest a way you can structure this discussion.

- Ask for permission to tape in the first session. Allow clients to talk about their feelings related to taping and hear any concerns or objectives. Taping is their decision.
- Let clients know they can change their decision about taping at any point in the session or in the helping process.
- Clarify to clients there is no taping without permission.
- Describe in detail the purposes for taping (it is used in supervision for professional development). Assure clients that when the intern and the supervisor listen to the tape, the focus is the intern not the client.
- Outline who will hear the tapes. Explain that the site and faculty supervisor will hold the information they hear in confidence.
- Describe how the tapes will be stored and who has access to the tapes.
- Describe how long the intern will keep the tapes and when they will be destroyed.

Taping your work with clients is an especially valued way of learning about how to work with clients. It allows supervisors to provide specific feedback. As important as this practice is, there are serious ethical dimensions of taping that you need to address even before you ask clients for permission to tape. You need to determine if taping is congruent with agency policy. There are some client groups that are regarded as too vulnerable to tape. One such example is a domestic abuse shelter. Many women and children live in protective shelters; knowledge of their whereabouts is secret information. In Box 4.6 we provide an example of a **Permission to Tape Release Form.**

Box 4.6 Permission to Tape Release Form

Release Form/Permission to Tape

(Name of the College or University)
(Name of Academic Program)

Hello. My name is _____ (name of student) and I am a student in the _____ program (name of academic program) at the _____ (name of the college or university). You will be participating in helping interviews with me as I train to be a _____(name of professional at agency) under the direction of the _____ (name of the academic program) faculty at the _____(name of the college or university). These interviews will be audiotaped, and portions of these interviews will be used only for evaluation and/or supervision of the intern. Three weeks after taping, the tapes will be erased.

If you are willing to give permission to assist with this training, please sign below. If you have additional questions, you can contact my site supervisor, _____ (name of site supervisor), at _____ (phone number of site supervisor or e-mail of site supervisor).

_____   _____

Client signature   Date

_____   _____

Student intern signature   Date

_____   _____

Site supervisor   Date

You may need to revise this form if you are working with children and youth. You would include client names and dates and parent or guardian names and dates.

Keeping a Record of Your Work: Logs, Notes, and Weekly Reflections

During your internship you are accountable for maintaining a record of your work. Most faculty members require documentation on a weekly basis, at midterm, and at the conclusion of the term. Each week your faculty supervisor will review your hours spent and activities engaged during internship. In most cases, you will provide this information in the form of a weekly **log**. Table 4.10 provides one example of a log. In this particular example, there is an opportunity for interns to make notes about the activity or task and document the amount of time spent in each. At the conclusion of internship, your faculty supervisor will need this documentation of your daily activities and hours and a summary sheet of your total hours.

In addition, faculty supervisors may also want to read about your personal and professional reflections for the week. Some faculty ask interns to write a **journal** or diary of your thoughts about the internship experience. These reflections can take several forms.

1. Sometimes these reflections are free flowing, and faculty ask interns to respond to a general prompt such as, "When you think about your internship experience this week, what stands out for you?"

2. Other requests for reflections ask for more structured responses. A more structured journal assignment could include, "Describe the most significant learning experience this week. Detail your emotional response. Detail how you linked this learning experience to previous academic work. Describe how you will use what you learned in your future work."

3. Another type of journal reflection might be specific to the time in the semester. Questions may reflect how the faculty understand the developmental process of learning in internship. In other words, each prompt represents what the faculty believe you should be learning at the beginning, in the middle, and at the conclusion of your internship. An early prompt might be, "Describe your first interaction with a client." A later prompt might be, "Discuss the most challenging work you faced this past week."

4. An additional type of journal reflection might invite you to, "write your own story," instructing you to link the text material to your current work in internship. Consider for example, *Exercise 4.1 Your First Two Weeks: Writing Your Own Story: Entry 11* described earlier in this chapter. We asked you to begin your reflection about your first two weeks in internship and the practical ways you managed your experiences.

Two other types of documentation are important to note here, agency reports and case notes. Both of these present additional ways that you record and reflect on your work. We present ideas about how to develop your writing skills related to internship in Chapter 10.

Table 4.10   Sample of an Internship Log

Date	Activity	Notes	Time Spent
Total Number of Hours			

Now that you are more aware of the first week or two of internship and the ways to prepare for it, let's look at ways you can deepen your understanding by hearing from the experiences of others in Box 4.7.

Box 4.7 Deepening Your Understanding

1. Peer-to-peer dialogue
   a. Alicia: The first two weeks
   b. Lucas: The first two weeks
   c. Tamika: The first two weeks
2. Faculty and site supervisors dialogue
   a. Dr. Bianca: Helping students begin
   b. Ms. Bellewa: Being intentional
3. The professional voice and tips for practice: Gwen
4. Terms to remember
5. References

Deepening Your Understanding

Alicia, Lucas, and Tamika share their experience of internship during the first two weeks. Although many of their experiences may differ from yours, we believe that, as you compare their experiences with yours, you will draw new insights about your own internship. Dr. Bianca, Ms. Bellewa, and Gwen provide faculty, site supervisor, and professional perspectives about the beginning of internship.

Peer-to-Peer Dialogue: Alicia, Lucas, and Tamika

We asked Alicia, Lucas, and Tamika to share their experiences. The goal in the summaries is for you to learn about their experiences as interns during the first two weeks of their internship.

Alicia

Hello. I am writing today upon completion of the first two weeks of my internship placement at the Department of Human Services. Preparing for and beginning this new professional journey was exciting, challenging, and inspirational. I am going to share details about preparing for the first week, those I met, what we did, and what I look forward to in the coming weeks.

As I met with Dr. Davis prior to officially starting my 300-hour internship, I gained a basic understanding of my role and responsibilities at the site. I also was paired up with Jarryn, a case manager who has worked with the department for a few years. She reviewed a more detailed job description and told me that I would be working alongside her until I am ready for my own cases. We also reviewed technicalities about the work including documentation, people who are involved with the foster care and adoption process, and legal issues that I need to be aware of. There is a lot to learn and many people to meet. This is exciting, but also intimidating. It's hard for me not to worry about forgetting something or doing something wrong; I'm working with kids and their lives are very much my responsibility. I know with Jarryn's support and with time I'll get comfortable and familiar with all of it.

In our first internship class meeting, Dr. Lynn explained some professional expectations she has for us during internship. We discussed the concept of our professional identity. She provided examples of professional disclosure statements, contracts, and permissions to tape. I remember reading about those documents in the Introduction to Human Services *textbook. We also learned what to include in our portfolios, which we are to submit upon completion of our internship. The portfolio will include a number of professional documents, personal reflections, and some creative component. We are to create our professional documents the first week at our sites and work on the portfolios throughout the semester.*

The first week at my internship site was very exciting. The first day, I met with Dr. Davis upon arrival. We talked about my professional disclosure statement, signed my contract, and verified my permissions to tape. Writing the professional disclosure statement was a bit odd since I had minimal work experience. The contract was relatively straight forward. It detailed my role as an intern and detailed my responsibilities. Dr. Davis, Jarryn, and I discussed my role and responsibilities. To begin, I will need to complete the mandatory trainings that are required for all state employees and interns. This process should take approximately a week. I will continue working alongside Jarryn for at least 1 to 2 weeks following that. I will be learning about the cases, the documentation, all the meetings and people who need to be involved, and the overall process. During this time, I will begin completing some of the documentation for those cases, under Jarryn and Dr. Davis's supervision, of course. After that point, I will carry two to four cases on my own.

After the first two weeks, I was excited to be where I would do more hands on work with the kids and families. I was a little bit overwhelmed by all the administrative trainings involved and all the information I needed to study and learn. I took home a Department of Human Services manual that covered the scope of the work that I would do and the ethical guidelines involved. I am excited and anxious to really start my fieldwork. For the first time in a while, I feel like I am exactly where I need to be.

Written by Allie Rhinehart and Dareen Basma, 2015. Used with permission.

Lucas

Hello! I hope all is well with you. Right now, I am relaxing at home and reminiscing on my first two weeks of internship. All I have to say is, "Where did the time go?" These past 2 weeks my emotions were up and down. In the beginning, I was really excited to begin my internship and now I feel more anxious because I am starting my work with clients next week. What I would like to share with you today is what the past 2 weeks looked like for me. I hope knowing about my experience helps lessens your anxiety.

I still remember the week before internship. I was really nervous at the start because I didn't know what to expect. I consulted with James, my student mentor, on how to prepare for the internship. Given the advice of

James and my adviser, Dr. Franks, this is how I prepared. I first reviewed the notes I took during my initial visit to the site when I met Dr. Kim, my site supervisor. In that meeting Dr. Kim explained to me how to check in each morning. She also described my responsibilities there. Most mornings I am to check in with the security guard, take the elevator to my office, and check in with Dr. Kim. Each morning she will provide me with a list of things to do for the day. On the first day, as an assignment for internship class, I have to give to Dr. Kim a draft of my professional disclosure form and internship contract.

My faculty supervisor told me that my internship couldn't officially begin until I complete the initial drafts of my professional disclosure form and my internship contract. The professional disclosure form is a document to share with my site supervisor and employees at the Tampa Bay Justice Center who are unfamiliar with my background, roles, and responsibilities at the facility. The form included my name, education, my site and faculty supervisor's name, a statement that I am pursuing licensure as a professional counselor in Florida, and a list of my roles and responsibilities at the Tampa Bay Justice Center. In addition, as part of my professional disclosure form, I had to provide a copy of my liability insurance to give to my site supervisor.

For the internship contract, I am to specify my objectives, responsibilities, and the intended outcomes of my human service work. I also included suggestions about how I will be evaluated. For example, one of my objectives for internship was to gain an understanding of victims of abuse and to advance my helping skills to support them. Under responsibilities, I listed (a) conduct individual sessions, (b) participate in treatment team meetings, (c) attend advocacy events sponsored by Tampa Bay Justice Center, and (d) review some of the literature of victims of abuse. I was not sure about the intended outcomes, so I made notes to talk with Dr. Kim about them. Sources of evaluation included tape reviews made at my site, observations by my site and faculty supervisors, a self-evaluation, and evaluation from clients. Once I completed my forms, I started to feel more confident about the internship. I understood better what I wanted to accomplish. I was also more organized.

To be honest, the first day felt like the first day of high school. I was unsure where the client rooms were located, exactly what I needed to do, or who to ask for help. At first I couldn't find Dr. Kim. After the first hour, Juliana, a therapist at Tampa Bay Justice Center, helped me. I spent the day by her side. Juliana is my site mentor, and we met to discuss my caseload and the clients I will be seeing. On day two, Dr. Kim and Juliana described to me the front desk client check in process, gave me background information on my clients, and showed me how to access the database to complete progress notes. I gave them my professional disclosure form and internship contract. Both of them had comments about how to revise these forms. I then revised the forms and they signed both. I was lucky James, my peer mentor, helped me with the forms. He gave me feedback so that my internship contract was realistic.

As the week progressed at internship, my main responsibilities were administrative because the Tampa Bay Justice Center was behind on its paperwork. I gathered the past week's intake and progress notes from all the therapists, made sure they were signed, and then put those documents in each client's folder. This was not how I dreamed of beginning my work, but it helped me understand how the facility tracked its services to clients. At end of the first week, Juliana brought three clients to the Tampa Bay Justice Center to meet me. And I held a short meeting with each of the three, introducing myself. It helped that Dr. Kim and Juilana were present in the meeting. I felt awkward and I was not sure what to say. I was fearful I would be prying into their lives and be perceived as nosey. Instead my clients were extremely nice. They asked me questions about my education and why I wanted to work at the Tampa Bay Justice Center. After I met my clients, I felt more motivated to help them. My anxiety and nervousness turned to excitement and motivation. I am thankful that for the session with my clients, my site supervisor and mentor were there. Their presence and participation broke the ice for conversation and made me feel more comfortable. I think my clients felt more comfortable too.

Well I hope this gives you an understanding of my experiences as the internship began and my first couple of weeks at Tampa Bay Justice Center. Good luck with everything and I look forward to sharing more of my experiences of internship with you. Have a blessed day!

Written by Jorge Roman, 2015. Used with permission.

Tamika

Well, I've been at my internship for about 2 weeks now and the time is just flying by! I'm learning so much during my time at the justice center that sometimes I feel overwhelmed trying to keep up with everything going on. But my supervisor and the other staff members have been really great about showing me the ropes.

On the first day of orientation, I was so nervous! I really didn't know what to expect and I was so worried that I wouldn't know anything. Fortunately, my orientation leader was super. She taught us all about the history of the justice center and about all the different kinds of work that goes on there. There were a couple of new employees and a few interns from different departments in my orientation group, which helped me to feel less alone. Every night after orientation, I spent about an hour reading over the materials we'd been given that day. This really helped me to stay focused and feel prepared each morning. By the end of the orientation week, my nerves had been mostly replaced by excitement. I felt like I really knew my way around the justice center and that I had a great foundation for understanding all of the different things that people do there. I was ready to learn more about my actual duties as an intern.

Once I completed orientation, I worked with my supervisor to develop an internship contract, which I then turned in to my faculty supervisor for review. The basic terms of the contract had been outlined already by my school (number of service hours needed, skills I should practice, etc.) and because my supervisor has worked with our interns before, she knew what to expect. I was pleasantly surprised that she allowed me to collaborate with her on fleshing out the parameters set forth by my school, so that my internship experience would best meet my individual needs, as well as the needs of the justice center. It was neat to explore with my supervisor all the different activities I could be a part of and to be able to tailor some of my duties to my own personal interests. For example, my supervisor let me incorporate a wide variety of activities into my schedule so that I would have the most well-rounded experience possible. I'll be doing some individual work, some group work, and also a little bit of administrative and programmatic work. This will give me great insight into all the facets of the job and will help me to further develop my own professional interests. We made sure to be very clear in the contract about what would be expected of me and how I would accomplish tasks as they were assigned to me. We also contracted to meet regularly for site supervision, which I know will be critical to my development at this stage. I felt great about the final contract, and it was nice to know that my supervisor valued my input.

I also spent some time outside of class and internship working on my first professional disclosure statement. This was a bit more difficult, because I developed it on my own, using only a basic guideline provided by my faculty supervisor. Because I haven't actually worked in the field yet, I didn't have a lot of experience to discuss, but I did write about my passion for serving others and what my current professional interests are. I also made sure to note my status as a student intern, because I think it's really important that colleagues, supervisors, and clients know that I'm still in training. Developing this document really helped me to begin to conceptualize myself as a new professional. I was really proud of the final product. I know that it will continue to develop as I gain more experience but I think I have established a solid foundation from which I can build.

Once orientation and the initial paperwork were out of the way, my supervisor told me that I would spend a few days shadowing her and some of her staff, to get a better idea of exactly what they did and how they went about working with clients. This was going to be my first time interacting with clients in any way, and I was very nervous. I wanted to show my supervisor that I was eager and engaged, but I also wanted to be careful not to overstep any boundaries. During this phase, I really focused on listening and observing. I made sure to take really good notes that I could refer back to, once I was working on my own. I spent a couple of days in court with my supervisor and watched some of the hearings her clients had to attend. I also spent a couple of days with some of the staff therapists and sat in on their individual and group sessions with clients. I didn't really participate in any of these activities during my first week, which gave me a chance to really settle into the environment. I got a better sense of how each different element contributed to the whole of the justice center. At the end of each day, my supervisor spent some time with me reviewing and processing the events of the day, and she gave me plenty of time to ask questions. This was invaluable because I had lots of questions.

Now that I'm moving into my third week at this placement, I can already see a lot of growth within myself. I have a much better idea of how things are run at the justice center and how everyone works together to best serve each client. It's been really helpful to observe each of the areas in which I'll be working and to not have immediate pressure to perform as an intern. My supervisor has been supportive every step of the way, and although I know she won't be available to meet with me every day from here on out, I know she'll always be willing to answer my questions and give me guidance when I need it. I've also developed quick rapport with a couple of the therapists on staff and they'll be great resources as I start working with clients on my own.

The next couple of weeks are going to be really exciting for me, and I'm starting to get a little bit nervous about actually putting my skills to use. My supervisor has arranged for me to begin cofacilitating a group with one of the therapists next week. Eventually, I may even get to run the group on my own. I'm really interested in group dynamics and really like being in a leadership role, so this opportunity is probably what I'm looking forward to the most. I'll also be taking on two clients of my own next week, which makes me feel pretty anxious. Both of my supervisors have reassured me that I'll do just fine, but at this point, I have a lot of questions running through my head. Questions that keep coming like: What if I say the wrong thing? What if I don't know what to do? What if my clients don't want to work with an intern? And this is just the tip of the iceberg. I have learned a lot in my classes and I know that this is supposed to be a learning process . . . but I'm still not as confident at this point as I'd like to be. I just have to remember that it's OK to ask questions. Hopefully with the continued support of my supervisors and by remembering to observe and listen to everything going on around me, I'll soon start to feel like I know what I'm doing. I look forward to sharing the next steps of my journey with you and will report back in a few weeks.

Written by Brittany Pollard, 2015. Used with permission.

Exercise 4.6 Writing Your Own Story, Entry 13

You just read short summaries of the personal development of Alicia, Lucas, and Tamika. Now it is your turn.

- Think about the ways you prepared for your first week at your internship site.
- Describe the ways you demonstrated your professional identity during the first week or two.
- Share what it was like to write your professional disclosure statement and to develop your internship contract.
- Describe your first week or two at the internship (include your reflections on supervision and the trajectory of your work).

Faculty and Site Supervisor Dialogue: Dr. Bianca and Ms. Bellewa

In addition to hearing from Alicia, Lucas, and Tamika, we asked Dr. Bianca, a human service faculty member, and Ms. Bellewa, a human service site supervisor, to talk about their experiences as faculty and site supervisors during the first week or two of the internship experience.

Dr. Claude Bianca

The semester began 2 weeks ago. It is spring term and the time of the academic year when our human service students begin internship. It is exciting for the students and for me to begin this very important part of their education. This semester started well, but not as smoothly as I would like. I had hoped to finalize all of the internship placements by the time the fall semester ended and before students left for the break. But, by the time school closed for the winter break, I was still working on internship placements. Thank goodness school didn't begin until January 21st. I used the first two weeks in January to complete the placement process. I had two students who didn't receive their placements until early January. Once they received information about their placements, they made their initial visits to their agencies right away. By the time we met for our first class of the semester, everyone had a placement.

In our program we have a preinternship seminar for the upcoming internship students. We meet with them three times during the fall semester. Our goals for the seminar include describing the purposes of internship, outlining the process to begin the internship, and discussing professional knowledge and skills we expect from interns. Highlights for the students are the two panel presentations and questions and answers. During one of our meetings before internship begins, students previously engaged in internship talk with our students about their own experiences and answer questions. We also have a panel of site supervisors talk to students about their expectations and tips for success. During the last panel discussion with the site supervisors, two of the supervisors presented very different philosophies of supervision. One proposed a very laissez faire approach and suggested how important it was for the interns to organize their own internship, while another supervisor laid out a 10-week plan he uses for easing an intern into the work of the placement site. The students were wide-eyed during this discussion. Even I hadn't expected the supervisors to present such diverse approaches. In the midst of all this variety of approaches, I remembered the multiple ways we can do human service work.

The beginning of internship is intense for all of us: faculty, students, and site supervisors. For our internship class during the first two weeks, we have a very full agenda. I lay out for students the basic requirements and help them understand their first four assignments: documenting their liability insurance; preparing a professional disclosure statement (they write an initial one in the preinternship class); drafting an internship contract; and beginning to grapple with weekly logs, client notes, and reflections. I assign to students the "write your own story" entries presented in this textbook. (See each chapter in this text book for "Write Your Own Story Exercises.") I also ask interns to share their entries with at least two peers. They share their entries electronically and their peers provide feedback.

I think it is a tender time for interns, and I am very careful to answer any questions they may ask, listen closely, and provide as much support as I can. I try to e-mail each student at least three times a week, especially in the first two weeks, just so they don't feel isolated from support of the faculty. In addition, all of us in internship class share text information with each other. So if there is a need to consult, we can alert one another. My approach to texting has altered over the past 4 years. At first I asked students to e-mail me with concerns. Now we use texting in a professional manner to ask for a phone call check in. I tried this approach last semester, and I think it increased my interns' willingness to talk with me about issues and challenges.

Finally, I wanted you to know that Ms. Bellewa is one of our site supervisors this semester. She agreed late in the fall semester to serve as a supervisor. She will also have an interesting perspective to share with you.

Ms. Zu Bellewa

I had no idea how quickly I would become involved in the human service program as a site supervisor, but I am thrilled that the program needed me as a site supervisor. As you know from my last writing, Dr. Bianca was coming to visit me last semester to begin the process of setting up an internship site placement. By the end of the semester, the site was established. In late December, my assigned intern, Amy, called to introduce herself and to schedule her visit. She came to the office and spent the morning with me. I asked her to bring a description of the human service program and to be prepared to tell me what she knew of the internship. We planned her morning, and it included time with me, time with my associate director, and time with one of our human service professionals who toured the building with her.

At the initial visit Amy also attended a group meeting with some of our clients, recent immigrants to the United States and to Syracuse. Four of our clients are working with a team of community professionals to plan an event to celebrate their coming to this city. We envision an official welcome, somewhat like a party! It will also include tables of community services that we can offer these families that help them with services and help them build skills to better understand the community. A value I brought from Niger is the importance of developing a sense of community. We try not only to function as a family of professionals, but we also try to include clients in the family circle.

In the spring we will have another party. This time the immigrant families will host the event and invite the folks from the community. The purpose of the event is to help the members of the community understand more about culture of origin, traditions, food, customs, and what the life of an immigrant is like. My thought is that Amy will be involved in both of these activities. Finally, I shared with Amy the basics of belonging to the agency. This includes information about clocking in, parking, security badges, and other practical matters.

I spent a great deal of time from December until the second week of January getting ready for Amy. At the conclusion of Amy's second week here as an intern, I believe things are going well. Amy began by working with me throughout the day. But by the second day, there were some tasks that arose for which she volunteered. We needed someone to confirm the log of our clients from the past week matched our client notes. Amy coordinated information from client files with the log. By the end of the first week Amy and I had a draft of her internship contract. I asked her to take the lead since she is my first intern. Dr. Bianca had good suggestions for revisions. Basically, I think that Amy could try to take on too much rather than too little. But, that sure makes my job supervising easier. The one difficulty for me will be to make time for Amy to do supervision. She seems more like a colleague already. We need to have time set aside just for her to talk about her internship work. It is my job to make that happen. All of this to say, we are well into this adventure together!

Written by Dareen Basma, 2015. Used with permission.

The Professional Voice and Tips for Practice: Gwen

One area of communication that is changing very rapidly is social media and social communication. How electronic communication is used in human service agency work continues to develop. Gwen Ruttencutter provides us with tips regarding the place of social media in your internship work.

Gwen

In this chapter, Marianne provides practical tips for surviving and thriving the first few weeks in your new internship site. One of those tips, don't use social media during working hours, addresses electronic devices and social media in the workplace. Given social media's prevalence in all aspects of our lives, and its potential to impact our professional identity, perhaps it's worthy of a bit more discussion. Here are a few more tips about social media, the workplace, and maintaining professional behavior:

- *If you access social media using the equipment of your placement site, you should have no expectation of privacy about what you post to social media. Some companies reserve the right to monitor employees' online activities when employees are using company computers.*
- *A best practice is to not post about your work. If you do, take extreme care not to talk about any of your clients. Even without using a client's name, there could be other identifiers that would jeopardize a client's privacy (and jeopardize your internship!). Similarly, don't complain about your work in an online post. Even if no one from your internship site sees your post, complaining online is unproductive and unprofessional, and is not the image that you want to project of yourself. Plus, you never know when a prospective employer, who is a friend of a friend, might be reading something you posted. Networking online should work to your benefit (showing your best self!), and not work to your detriment.*
- *Assume that anything you post to social media never really goes away, even after you delete the post or photo. Posted photos that seem perfectly appropriate for your college friends may compromise your credibility when viewed by colleagues and clients.*

Written by Gwen Ruttencutter, 2015. Used with permission.

Terms to Remember

Dynamic orientation

Internship contract

Journal

Log

Performing administrative focus

Permission to tape release form

Professional disclosure statement

Providing direct service

Shadowing

Working with the community

References

Bajic, E. (2013). Tips for stress-free first day on the job. *Forbes*. Retrieved from http://www.forbes.com/sites/elenabajic/2013/10/28/tips-for-a-stress-free-first-day-on-the-new-job/

McKay, D. R. (2014). Survive your first day of work: Starting a new job. About Career Planning. Retrieved from http://careerplanning.about.com/cs/firstjob/a/new_job_2.htm

Roos, D. (2014). 10 tips for your first day at work. How Stuff Works. Retrieved from http://money.howstuffworks.com/business/starting-a-job/10-tips-for-your-first-day-of-work.htm

Salpeter, M. (2014). First day on the job: 9 ways to make a great impression. Jobs.AOL. Retrieved from http://jobs.aol.com/articles/2013/06/12/first-day-on-job-make-good-impression/

Woodside, M., & McClam, T. (2015). *Introduction to human services* (8th edition). Pacific Grove, CA: Brooks Cole/Cengage.

PART II

Involving Yourself in Human Service Work

5

Understanding Ethical Perspectives in Internship

Reading this chapter will help you do the following:

- Identify questions to help you determine if a challenge or an issue is a legal one, an ethical one, or both.
- Identify challenges or issues that include a legal dimension.
- Define ethics.
- List the sources of ethical perspectives.
- List and define ethical values and principles that guide ethical practice.
- Understand generally the importance of professional codes of ethics.
- Describe the categories included in the human service professional code of ethics.
- Briefly describe the steps of Kenyon's ethical decision-making model.
- Describe the ways that contextual factors influence the ethical decision-making process.

- Describe the questions you can use to reflect on your own ethical decision-making process.
- Understand professional liability and its importance in internship.

As you remember, Part I, *Introduction to the Internship Experience*, focused on your beginning work as an intern. Now, after completing the first few weeks of internship, you are assuming more responsibility, including more in-depth work with clients and additional work within the agency. As your responsibilities as an intern increase, you will begin to experience the complexities of professional work as reflected in Part II of this text, *Involving Yourself in Human Service Work*. The chapters in Part II focus on various dimensions and complexities of the human service work. These include (a) developing an ethical perspective in internship, (b) developing a multicultural perspective in internship, and (c) engaging in supervision.

This chapter, Chapter 5, focuses on developing an ethical perspective, especially as it relates to internship work. This chapter is divided into three sections. First, we introduce the idea that self-reflection, both personal and professional, provides one way to begin to think about the ethical aspects of professional work. Self-reflection includes considering your motivations to become a human service professional. We show how thinking about who you are as a helper and how your own **use of self** influences the helping process (Heydt & Sherman, 2005). We provide exercises that help you link your use of self to your work as an intern.

Second, after engaging in the self-reflection about personal beliefs, we describe human service professional work from an ethical perspective. To do this, we first describe the ethical values that guide human service delivery, introduce the goals of a professional code of ethics, and then outline the Ethical Standards for Human Services Professionals. We propose an ethical decision-making model that will help you recognize and address ethical challenges and issues. Finally we provide information about competence, professional liability, and the importance of both. We close with terms to remember and references.

Box 5.1 describes the organizational framework of the first section of this chapter, that of personal beliefs.

Box 5.1 Studying the Text: Personal Beliefs and the Use of Self

Studying the text: The following outline will help you read and study the text material in this next section.

Personal beliefs and the use of self

1. Introduction
2. Personal beliefs

Personal Beliefs and the Use of Self

Introduction

As you remember, we introduced the concepts of professional identity in Chapter 2. In this chapter, we focus on one of the seven components or aspects of professional identity: personal beliefs (refer to Figure 2.2). As stated earlier in Chapter 2, personal beliefs become especially relevant to interns during the first week or two of their internships. During this time, interns watch their site supervisors and other professionals who work at the site and then begin to reflect on what they observe. From such reflections, new views of professional identity begin to emerge and develop. Considering personal beliefs from the perspective of professional identity provides a framework for increased reflection and helps interns identify ethical issues and engage in ethical decision making.

Personal Beliefs

Personal beliefs, especially as they are related to helping, are those concepts, ideas, or characteristics that provide the foundation for our professional work in human services. We consider Arthur Combs's list of five personal beliefs. As helpers, we hold these beliefs as they relate to positive work with clients. We ask you to think about these beliefs in relationship to your work as an intern. Human service educators continue to suggest the importance of these beliefs in supporting the work of helping professionals (Neukrug, 2012; Woodside & McClam, 2015).

Arthur Combs's (1999) five beliefs link directly to professional performance. He based his five beliefs on a meta-analysis of research documenting effectiveness of helpers (Combs & Gonzales, 1994). From his analysis, he concluded that effective helpers demonstrate the following five qualities/beliefs/characteristics.

Demonstrates empathy: Human service professionals must be able to understand a client's perspective. Here, the old adage "to walk a mile in their shoes" applies. An effective helper needs to understand the meanings clients attribute to their experiences without having had that experience. In short, the helper demonstrates **empathy.**

Demonstrates positive views of others: For helpers, such a positive attitude translates into hope and optimism that individuals wish to change and can change. Effective helpers view others in a good light and tend to characterize them as honest, trustworthy, virtuous, and responsible.

Demonstrates positive views of self: Effective helpers feel positively about themselves. They trust themselves and have confidence in their own beliefs and abilities. They strongly believe that they can help others.

Maintains people-oriented goals: Helpers learn what is important to the clients. Helpers are able to align their professional goals with client goals.

Uses helping approaches that reflect self: Each helping professional has a special connection to methods of intervention and ways of helping.

An effective helper understands his or her own natural effective approaches and is able to adapt and change these to meet the needs of the clients.

You met Tomas earlier in the text. He is an intern working at the Brooklyn Drug and Alcohol Rehabilitation Center. We asked Tomas if he could comment on his own **use of self** and how he sees his own use of self as he works with his supervisors and his clients. He talks to us primarily about his work with Dr. Highland, his faculty supervisor. They meet once a week to review one of his taped sessions with individual clients.

Tomas

Dr. Highland asks me to prepare for our supervisory session by summarizing the tape I am sharing. The preparation includes noting five aspects of my work. As I listened to my tape for our last supervision meeting, here is what I wrote:
I note the questions in regular text and put my responses in italics.

1. How I demonstrated empathy with the client? What were my feelings? What were my thoughts?

I get confused about empathy and I just think that the client and I merge together. This client is so much like me. I know part of this comes from my own history of addiction. One specific time the client said, "How can I give up my use; it is what holds me together." I thought I would cry on the spot. I didn't expect to have such an emotional response.

2. Describe when I felt positive about the client. Describe when I experienced negative feelings about the client.

I really like this client because of his honesty. But sometimes I think that he uses honesty as an excuse. Listen to what he told me, "Mr. Tomas, I don't really think that it is my fault that I use. I told you all about my family. I have no place to turn."

3. Describe when I felt positive about myself as an intern and a helper. Describe when I experience negative feelings about myself as an intern and helper.

I wanted to tell him, "Look, straighten up and take responsibility. That is your only hope."
Dr. Highland, I resisted telling my client to "straighten up" and I just reflected his feeling. Listen to my response and tell me what you think. What else do you think I could have done?

4. Describe my goals for the client.

I want to meet my client's goals, one of which is not using. He is unsure he can stop using. Agency goals and my goals focus more on addressing his using. We do use motivational interviewing and try to figure out where the client is in the change process. I asked Ms. Paseattoe for help with all of my clients. She seems to be flexible in setting goals for her clients.

5. Identity times with the client when I felt I was myself (authentic).

I tried to find a place in the tape where I felt authentic and I am not sure I can find it.

Tomas provides us a window into how to address the use of self in your work with clients. Read Exercise 5.1 and describe how you think your own personal beliefs play out during your work with clients.

Exercise 5.1 Personal Beliefs: Writing Your Own Story, Entry 14

Exploring your own personal beliefs related to your role as a helping professional expands how you understand yourself in relation to your human service work.

Step 1

For each of the five qualities/beliefs/characteristics suggested by Combs (1999), describe your thoughts, feelings, and behaviors during these early weeks in internship. Remember as you describe your thoughts, feelings, and actions, you are articulating one aspect of your professional identity.

Demonstrates empathy:

_____

_____

_____

Demonstrates positive views of others:

_____

_____

_____

Demonstrates positive views of self:

_____

_____

_____

Maintains people-oriented goals:

_____

_____

_____

Uses helping approaches that reflect self:

_____

_____

_____

Understanding personal beliefs helps you assume responsibility for your own professional development. One important aspect of development focuses on an ethical approach to human service delivery. Although you may have studied ethics earlier in your program, experiencing the ethical dimensions of human service internship will lead to new insights and questions related to understanding yourself, your clients, and your agency.

Box 5.2 describes the organizational framework of the next section of this chapter. The goal is to help you more clearly understand what an ethical perspective in human service delivery means, especially as you experience it in internship.

Box 5.2 Studying the Text: Understanding an Ethical Perspective in Human Services

Studying the text: The following outline will help you read and study the text material in this next section.

Understanding an ethical perspective in human services

1. Developing and ethical perspective
2. Ethical values and principles in human services
3. Codes of ethics in the helping professions
4. Model of ethical decision making
5. Kenyon's ethical decision-making model

Understanding an Ethical Perspective in Human Services

Understanding the ethical dimensions of human service work represents an important aspect of the human service professional identity that we introduced in Chapter 2. You will understand the ethical dimensions of the work by identifying ethical challenges and issues and knowing how to apply professional guidelines to real-world situations. As you assume the roles and responsibilities of a human service professional during your internship, you will have multiple opportunities to act in an ethical manner. In this chapter, for the most part, we discuss primarily ethical, rather than legal, perspectives. We do note challenges and issues that have legal dimensions. We urge you to talk with your faculty and site supervisors about the legal frameworks that relate to your internship work.

As a way of beginning a conversation with your supervisors related to legal issues, the questions listed may help you (and your supervisor) determine whether an issue is a legal issue, an ethical issue, or both a legal and ethical issue. These questions are (Francis, 2014)

- Does the event or situation revolve around a legal course of action?
- Does the event or situation include an attorney or court-appointed individuals?
- Does there appear a possibility someone could bring charges against you?

If you suspect the issue in which you are involved meets any one of these three criteria, or you have questions, you should consult with both your faculty and site supervisors as soon as possible. These supervisors will provide the type of assistance you need to address any possible legal dimensions of your work as an intern.

In addition, some issues might include both ethical and legal dimensions. These issues include suicide risk assessment, duty to warn so to prevent harm to client or others, any written reports that could harm clients or their families, termination of services, and multiple relationships (or sexual relationships) (Francis, 2014).

Developing an Ethical Perspective

To begin to talk about how to develop an ethical perspective in internship work, first, we look at a definition of **ethics** and then talk about what an **ethical perspective** means for human service professionals. The authors of the Community Tool Box (2014), developed by the University of Kansas Work Group for Community Health and Development, provided a definition of ethics, especially as it relates to the human services. They indicated that ethics "is a code of thinking and behavior governed by a combination of personal, moral, legal, and social standards of what is right" (Chapter 19, Section 5). Within the human service profession, we suggest several sources interns can use to gain an understanding of "the code of thinking and behavior" referenced in the Community Tool Box's (2014) definition of ethics. These resources include

- personal beliefs (use of self) introduced earlier in this chapter,
- articulation of values and principles provided by human service scholars,
- helping professions' codes of ethics, and
- model of ethical decision making.

An ethical perspective represents the point of view we take when considering various ethical challenges and issues. Each of the sources of ethics in the previous list represents one such viewpoint. When considering ethical challenges and issues, it is important to be able to recognize that there are multiple sources to guide ethical behavior and to generate viewpoints from each of the sources. The multiple sources, for the most part, provide only guidelines and sometimes are in contradiction with one another. It is helpful to have an ethical decision-making model when considering these contradictions. We will briefly consider each of the ethical sources available to the human service professional. Much of this information you have encountered during your coursework or previous field-based experience. We cannot overstate the importance of understanding the ethical dimensions of human service work.

Ethical Values and Principles in Human Services

Members of the human service profession have long supported six ethical values and principles (Neukrug, 2012; Woodside & McClam, 2015). These values have guided professionals across various human service settings (e.g., education, child and youth services, child and adult corrections, work with the homeless). In this chapter, we will introduce each of the six: autonomy, nonmaleficence, beneficence, justice, fidelity, and veracity. In Chapter 6, we explore the use of these principles as they guide your work as an intern. These principles influence the way you define an ethical issue and how you think it through.

Autonomy reflects the importance of allowing the client to participate fully in the helping process. This means the client can state his or her own challenges and issues, help plan interventions, and then work with the human service professional to determine the outcomes of the helping process.

Nonmaleficence means that the human service professional will do no harm to the client.

Beneficence expands the notion of nonmaleficence and directs the helper to provide services that are in the client's best interest.

Justice as a value reminds human service professionals that clients are entitled to equity of treatment beginning with access to services. It represents a commitment to eliminate oppression and bias—which we will address in Chapter 7 with its focus on multicultural dimensions of human services.

Fidelity guides the human service professional to establish a trusting relationship with the client, a relationship based upon understanding, dependability, and honesty.

Veracity extends fidelity by emphasizing honesty; this means providing information clients need and keeping the helping process open and transparent.

Before we provide specific examples of how these values and principles guide your human service work as an intern, let's look at the professional codes of ethics that guide the helping professions.

Codes of Ethics for Helping Professions

One important aspect of becoming a professional is understanding the **professional code of ethics** that governs it. Each of the many human service professions (e.g., human services, psychology, social work, corrections, and addictions) has a code of ethics that represent and guide professional practice. Reasons for developing these codes are numerous. They include protecting the public; helping members of the professions understand what emotions, thoughts, and actions represent ethical (and unethical) practice and providing a way to assess whether professionals remain accountable to these standards. In addition, ethical standards help professionals better serve clients and the communities in which they practice (Remley & Herlihy, 2015). Finally, codes of ethics help professionals define themselves and differentiate themselves from other professionals. Across the many fields of professional helping, there exist many standards held in common; in addition, there are differences between professions.

Professional organizations continually revise their codes of ethics to respond to changing social contexts in which human service practice always occurs. One area most evident in recent codes of ethics relates to technology. With the increased use of technology in service delivery and its pervasiveness, ethical guidelines must address technology-related challenges and issues such as the role of social media and issues related to confidentiality and challenges related to professional boundaries, to name a few (American Counseling Association, 2014).

The National Organization for Human Services (NOHS) developed Ethical Standards for Human Service Professionals (NOHS, 2015). You can read the code in its entirety on the NOHS website. The major areas of focus include the human service professional's responsibility to the clients, public and society, colleagues, employers, profession, and self. We list the major areas of focus and list the standards addressed in each area in Table 5.1.

Table 5.1 Ethical Standards for Human Service Professionals

Categories of Ethical Standards	Standards for Categories
Responsibility to clients	– Providing strength-based services – Providing informed consent – Observing client's right to confidentiality – Protecting safety of clients – Considering harm of dual or multiple relationships to clients – Not engaging in sexual or romantic relationships with clients – Providing secure storage of client records – Considering multiple ways that use of technology can harm clients
Responsibility to the public and society	– Providing services without discrimination – Respecting client and community culture – Staying current with social issues that influence their clients – Being aware of the sociopolitical issues that influence client's lives and client's issues – Advocating for client's unmet needs – Working to eliminate oppression – Honestly communicating to the public one's own credentials and competencies – Using evidence-based interventions when possible – Representing their abilities accurately to the community
Responsibility to colleagues	– Consulting with other professionals when client is being served by multiple human service professionals – Working directly with a colleague with whom there are issues, consulting and asking for help when appropriate – Addressing a colleague's unprofessional behavior – Maintaining confidentiality of peer consultations
Responsibility to employers	– Understanding the limit and scope of the professional's knowledge and skills – Working with integrity, honesty, and objectivity when performing job-related tasks – Supporting promises made to employers – Helping to provide effective client services and client satisfaction – Advising agency and client when the needs of both are contradictory
Responsibility to the profession	– Seeking ways to provide culturally sensitive services – Understanding the limit and scope of their knowledge and skills – Seeking consultation for ethical or legal issues – Cooperating and collaborating with other disciplines – Advocating for the development of the human service profession – Seeking out ways to develop professionally – Conducting research that abides by standards of care for human subjects – Using social media responsibly
Responsibility to self	– Continuing to development an awareness of the cultural self and how it influences the helping process – Fostering personal and professional self-care – Continuing self-awareness and personal growth throughout the professional career – Committing to lifelong learning related to knowledge and skill development in the helping professions

Exercise 5.2 Understanding the NOHS Professional Code of Ethics

During internship you may be confronted with various ethical challenges and issues. One of the key skills in ethical decision making, which we will talk about in more detail later in this chapter, is being able to identity when an ethical issue or challenge emerges.

As a way of learning to consider your work from an ethical perspective, we want you to develop sensitivity to ethical aspects of practice. One way to do this is to reflect on your current internship experience and note when you have seen or have experienced examples of (a) following the ethical standard, (b) not following the ethical standard, or (c) when two or more standards of the code were in conflict. We provide instructions to help you begin this exercise.

Step 1

Choose one area of the NOHS Ethical Standards for Human Service Professionals guidelines (e.g., responsibility to clients, responsibility to public and society). Reflect on your internship experience and describe a time when you (a) were following the ethical standard, (b) were not following the ethical standard, or (c) had two or more standards of the code in conflict.

Area of the NOHS Ethical Standards for Human Service Professionals

_____

Example of when the ethical standard was followed.

_____

_____

_____

Example of when the ethical standard was not followed.

_____

_____

_____

Example of when two or more standards of the code were in conflict.

_____

_____

_____

Step 2

Choose an additional area of the NOHS Ethical Standards for Human Service Professionals guidelines (e.g., responsibility to clients, responsibility to public and society). Reflect on your internship experience and describe a time when you (a) were following the ethical standard, (b) were not following the ethical standard, or (c) had two or more standards of the code in conflict.

Area of the NOHS Code of Ethics

_____

Example of when the ethical standard was followed.

_____

_____

Example of when the ethical standard was not followed.

_____

_____

_____

Example of when two or more standards of the code were in conflict.

_____

_____

_____

Beginning to think about your work as an intern from an ethical perspective helps sharpen your ability to see the ethical dimensions of your work. For many challenges and issues, you are aware of the ethical guidelines and how to act. Confidentiality serves as a relevant example here. For instance, you may practice many of the following actions to ensure client confidentiality:

- Conducting conversations with clients in a private space
- Keeping client records in a locked file
- Securing electronic files with password protection
- Talking about clients with professional peers in a private space

Unfortunately, not all ethical challenges and issues are easy to understand and many are difficult to apply to professional practice. Even considering confidentiality presents challenges and complications. Human service professionals, at times, face situations where they must consider if breaking confidentiality is warranted. The key to understanding this sentence is the term *consider*—indicating to both interns and professionals that the decision is not always clear. And even if human service professionals make a case for breaking confidentiality, sometimes it is at the expense of the helping relationship and the trust and rapport established between the helper and the client (Woodside & McClam, 2015).

In the next section we introduce a way that interns can engage in the ethical decision-making process.

Model of Ethical Decision Making

Most researchers, scholars, and human service educators recognize that working through ethical challenges and issues and deciding courses of action are difficult for a student engaged in internship. In fact, these very challenges and issues are difficult for the seasoned professional. Hence, using an **ethical decision-making model** supports the process of determining a course of action, especially in challenging situations. There are numerous ethical decision-making models that interns might use when thinking through and acting upon an ethical challenge or issue. Many of these models include similar steps and provide a specific approach that interns can use to look at an ethical challenge or issue in a logical manner. In reality, for human service professionals, deciding how to address an ethical issue evokes both emotional and cognitive responses. Using a rational step-by-step method helps interns and professionals alike to be more objective about the issue(s) they confront.

We present an ethical decision-making model with 10 steps. These steps were presented by Pat Kenyon (1999) in her workbook, *What Would You Do? An Ethical Case Workbook for Human Service Professionals*. Then we ask you to complete an exercise that familiarizes you with the Kenyon model. We present this model for both human service professionals and interns to use as they address ethical challenges and issues (see Figure 5.1).

Kenyon's Ethical Decision-Making Model

Step 1. *Describe the issue*—the first step is about perspective taking. You want to list all of the institutions and individuals involved. Once you have this list, then summary the perspective that each holds on the issue. Finally, summarize your own perspective of the issue.

Step 2. *Consider the ethical guidelines*—In this step you want to review the guidelines of relevant codes of ethics. You will want to write down each of the ethical standards that might apply to this issue. There will be, in many cases, more than one. It is important to look at any laws or rules that may apply. It is also important to record values that various individuals and institutions may have that apply to the issue.

Figure 5.1   Kenyon's Ethical Decision-Making Model

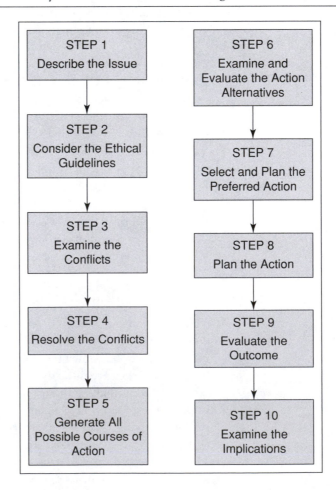

Step 3. *Examine the conflicts*—In this step you will review the information that you generated from Steps 1 and 2. There are some conflicts that are more obvious than others. For example, sometimes it is easy to see how rules conflict. How values conflict may be less obvious. Describe each of the conflicts and see if you can resolve it.

Step 4. *Resolve the conflicts*—When you think about resolving the conflict(s), you may need to decide which will be the most difficult conflict to resolve. Then you want to consider all of the guides available to you such as codes of ethics, laws, state regulations, institutional and policies and decide which of these is most important to you.

Step 5. *Generate all possible courses of action*—This is a time to explore the many ways to address conflicts. List each of the conflicts, and work on each, one-by-one. You want to brainstorm multiple ways that each of the conflicts can be addressed. Be sure to include all of the possible approaches that all parties involved might support. Include what actions might fulfil the intentions of codes of ethics, laws, as well as individuals or institutions involved.

Step 6. *Examine and evaluate the action alternatives*—For each of the alternative actions proposed, look at each and determine if it is doable. You want to provide a short summary of the action required to test if the alternative is realistic and the parties involved will support it and participate in its resolution.

Step 7. *Select and plan the preferred action*—During this step, you are evaluating each course of action that it proposed in Step 6. This means looking at the pros and cons of each. It is important to consider the outcome of each approach. Finally you make the decision about the approach to take for the issue.

Step 8. *Plan the action*—In this step you make an action plan to carry out the chosen approach. Make sure that you monitor the action. You may need to revise it. And you may need to consult during this action phase.

Step 9. *Evaluate the outcome*—evaluation is important at each stage of the implementation of the action plan. There may need to be a revision of the plan depending upon the results of the beginning action. For this reason you evaluate at the beginning of the plan, several times during the action, and when the action concludes.

Step 10. *Examine the implications*—Evaluating the outcome is important for each individual involved in the process. Evaluation also helps you better understand the ethical decision-making process and your place in it.

Exercise 5.3 Using the Ethical Decision-Making Model

Step 1

Return to Exercise 5.2 and choose one of the issues that you identified in that exercise.

Step 2

As a way to practice using the ethical decision-making model, make notes related to your initial thoughts of the issue for each of the 10 steps. Because you may not be involved in working through the issue you chose, use this exercise as a "what if" scenario.

(Continued)

(Continued)

Step 1. Describe the issue.

_____

Step 2. Consider the ethical guidelines.

_____

Step 3. Examine the conflicts.

_____

Step 4. Resolve the conflicts.

_____

Step 5. Generate all possible courses of action.

_____

Step 6. Examine and evaluate the action alternatives.

_____

Step 7. Select and plan the preferred action.

_____

Step 8. Plan the action.

_____

Step 9. Evaluate the outcome.

_____

Step 10. Examine the implications.

_____

═══

Contextual Factors

When interns encounter ethical challenges and issues, we believe there are two special considerations, both related to **contextual factors**. First, we want you to remember that during your internship experience, both your academic program faculty and the staff at your internship site want to support your work. And they are responsible for your professional actions. Because of this commitment, both expect to provide you guidance and support, especially when you are confronting difficult issues. This means that as you learn how to identify challenges and issues that are ethical in nature and negotiate their complexities, we suggest that you work with your faculty and site supervisors to engage in the ethical decision-making process. In Chapter 1, we introduced the two worlds that the intern bridges during internship, that of the academic program and of the internship site. Making ethical decisions requires you to consider, consult, and bridge between both worlds.

Second, in relation to contextual factors, we know that human service work requires a constant juggling of laws, regulations, values, principles, and guidelines, as well as agency mission, goals, and policies. This juggling occurs within the daily realities of the professional work. Adding to this complexity of the factors just listed, there exist other items that influence ethical decision making. These influences could include your own personal beliefs, such as those described in the beginning section of this chapter, and the client's context and worldview, client and community cultural views, and the agency culture.

Although Kenyon's Ethical Decision-Making Model (1999) helps approach issues in a self-reflective and objective manner, contextual factors are significant in determining the outcomes of the decision-making process. As we discuss specific ethical considerations that you may encounter in your internship, we will help you think about the importance and influence of these contextual factors. We include Table 5.2, the contextual factors that influence the ethical decision making that presents a visual of the multiple factors you will consider.

Final Considerations

In Step 10 of Kenyon's (1999) Ethical Decision-Making Model, she recommends taking time to examine the implications of the action you chose and implemented. This step allows you to reflect on the issue and the contexts in which the issue occurred, and determine what you learned from participating in the ethical decision-making process and working through to its resolution. The Department of Counseling and Human Services (n.d.) at the University of Syracuse outlined several questions to guide your self-reflection as shown in Figure 5.2.

Table 5.2 Contextual Factors in Ethical Decision Making

Factors	Agency	Professional	Client and Community
Laws	x		
Regulations	x		
Guidelines	x		
Codes of ethics		x	
Values	x	x	x
Worldview		x	x
Personal beliefs		x	x
Culture	x	x	x

Figure 5.2   Examining Ethical Decisions

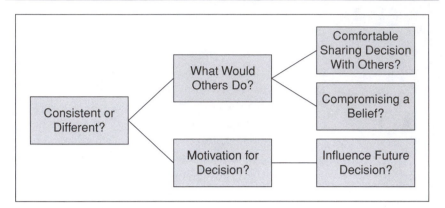

Exercise 5.4 Examining Ethical Decisions

- Did I make consistent decisions when encountering similar situations? If I made different decisions, how do I account for these differences? Are there other options I did not consider?
- If another counselor were facing a similar issue, would I recommend my decision making and resolution?
- Did I make this decision because it was easy, it was politically smart, or was best for me?
- With whom am I comfortable sharing this situation, my thinking about it, and my responses? If am comfortable, why? If not, why not?
- Am I compromising a standard that I believe in? How might this influence a future decision? (adapted from Department of Counseling and Human Services [n.d.], University of Syracuse).

We have considered the ethical values in human services, the helping profession's code of ethics (Human Service Professional Code of Ethics), and Kenyon's model of ethical decision making. In Chapter 6, we will address specific ethical issues you will likely confront during your internship.

We end this chapter with a discussion of professional liability, terms to remember, and references. This box, Box 5.3, outlines an abbreviated Deepening Your Understanding section. Alicia, Lucas, Tamika, Dr. Bianca, Ms. Bellewa, and Gwen return in Chapter 6 to share their perspectives related to ethical decision making and internship.

Box 5.3 Studying the Text: Deepening Your Understanding

Studying the text: The following outline will help you read and study the text material in this next section.

1. Professional liability and professional liability insurance

2. Terms to remember

3. References

Deepening Your Understanding

Professional Liability and Professional Liability Insurance

In assuming any position as a human service professional, the foremost commitment is to help those in need. Competence as a helper is essential as a professional assumes responsibility for delivering services to clients. Unfortunately and unavoidably, there is some legal risk associated when delivering such services. For example, it is possible that clients will perceive the care they receive as flawed in some way. They may believe that they have actually been harmed by their care or that the care provided was less than what they were led to expect.

One common term associated with this possible risk is **malpractice**. Within the realm of civil law, malpractice represents a lawsuit filed by a client against a professional or an agency delivering services and generally represents instances where professionals are thought to have acted in ways that harm a client (Remley & Herlihy, 2015). **Professional competence** relates directly to malpractice. Professional competence refers to an ability to perform responsibilities and tasks according to professionally accepted standards of care established or articulated by academic programs, professional organizations, ethical codes, and/or agency practice. Malpractice reflects instances when professionals fail to meet the accepted standards of care. While professionals may willfully hurt a client, malpractice also includes times when, through ignorance or a lack of knowledge or skills, clients may suffer injury, loss, or damage ("Professional liability", 2015).

Why liability insurance? As stated earlier, when clients claim errors or omissions, these claims may at times result in civil or criminal legal action. If the parties involved (universities or colleges, agencies, professionals, and interns) hold **professional liability insurance**, then the insurer agrees to provide financial coverage for legal advice and defense. We see it as critical for all human service providers, whether as practicing professionals or interns, to obtain professional liability insurance. In fact, procuring such insurance is mandatory for most internship programs.

Where and how to purchase such insurance? In all probability your internship handbook will describe where you may purchase liability insurance. You will want to have the insurance for the entire length of your internship. In addition, once you purchase the insurance, be sure to make and provide copies of the insurance forms to both your faculty and site supervisors to verify your coverage. Also copies should be placed in your permanent academic program file and your internship notebook/portfolio. Keep hard copies and electronic copies for your personal use.

Thinking about professional risk and issues related to risk often evokes stress and anxiety. But this risk is inherent in *all* professions that provide services and offer counsel and advice. A professional response to this stress is to provide human service delivery as conscientiously as you can and to procure professional liability insurance as a protection for you, your academic program, your agency, and the clients you serve.

Terms to Remember

Autonomy

Beneficence

Code of ethics

Contextual factors

Empathy

Ethical decision-making model

Ethical perspective

Ethics

Fidelity

Justice

Malpractice

Nonmaleficence

Personal beliefs

Professional code of ethics

Professional competence

Professional liability insurance

Use of self

Veracity

References

American Counseling Association. (2014). 2014 ACA code of ethics. Retrieved from http://www.counseling.org/docs/ethics/2014-aca-code-of-ethics.pdf?sfvrsn=4

Combs, A. W. (1999). *Being and becoming: A field approach to psychology.* New York, NY: Springer.

Combs, A. W., & Gonzales, D. M. (1994). *What makes a good helper: Concepts for the helping professional* (4th ed.). Boston, MA: Allyn & Bacon.

Community Tool Box. (2014). Section 5: Ethical issues in community interventions. Retrieved from http://ctb.ku.edu/en/table-of-contents/analyze/choose-and-adapt-community-interventions/ethical-issues/main

Department of Counseling and Human Services, Syracuse University. (n.d.). Ethical decision making. Retrieved from http://soe.syr.edu/academic/counseling_and_human_services/modules/Preparing_for_Supervision/ethical_decision_making_model.aspx

Francis, P. (2014, August). *2014 revisions to the ACA code of ethics.* PowerPoint presentation made by Robin Lee and Shawn Spurgeon at Tennessee Licensed Professional Counselors Association, Knoxville, TN.

Heydt, M. J., & Sherman, N. E. (2005). Conscious use of self: Tuning the instrument of social work practice with cultural competence. *Journal of Baccalaureate Social Work, 10*(2), 25–40.

Kenyon, P. (1999). *What would you do? An ethical case workbook for human service professionals.* Pacific Grove, CA: Brooks/Cole.

National Organization of Human Services. (2015). Ethical standards for human service professionals. Retrieved from http://www.nationalhumanservices.org/ethical-standards-for-hs-professionals

Neukrug, E. (2012). *Theory, practice, and trends in human services.* Pacific Grove, CA: Brooks Cole/Cengage.

Professional liability. (2015). In *Free dictionary: Medical dictionary.* Retrieved from http://medical-dictionary.thefreedictionary.com/professional+liability

Remley, T. P., & Herlihy, H. P. (2015). *Ethical, legal, and professional issues in counseling* (4th ed.). Boston, MA: Pearson.

Woodside, M., & McClam, T. (2015). *Introduction to human services* (8th ed.). Pacific Grove, CA: Brooks/Cole, Cengage Learning.

6 Addressing Ethical Issues in Internship

Reading this chapter will help you do the following:

- Understand these ethical issues in human services: informed consent, confidentiality, competence, suicide risk assessment, dual/multiple relationships, boundaries and limit setting, and certain uses of technology.
- Describe a self-test to evaluate your ethical decision-making process and resolution.
- Become acquainted with some of the ethical issues that Alicia, Lucas, and Tamika experience in internship.
- Learn about the faculty and site supervisors' perspectives related to ethical decision making.
- Describe the tips that Gwen provides for the use of reflection during the ethical decision-making process.

Part II of this text focuses on the nature and characteristics of the work of helping during your internship. In Chapter 5, you read about the values that guide human service practice. These values are described in the Ethical Standards for Human Service Professionals developed by the National Organization for Human Service (NOHS, 2015). We presented Kenyon's (1999) ethical decision-making model to use as you consider the ethical issues and challenges you may encounter as an intern.

In this chapter, Chapter 6, we identify various ethical challenges and issues that are especially related to the interns experience and suggest ways interns can address these. Issues presented include informed consent, confidentiality, competence, suicide risk assessment, the nature of helping relationships (dual and multiple relationships, including boundaries and limit setting), and issues related to technology.

In addition, we suggest ways interns can recognize concrete ethical issues when they are confronted with them. We then provide an opportunity to use an ethical decision-making model to address at least one issue. We also present a self-test that helps interns and professionals carefully think about the decisions they make and the actions they take in response to ethical problems. In the final section of this chapter, we provide peer-to-peer dialogues, students, faculty, site supervisor, and human service professional dialogues. Alicia, Lucas, Tamika, Dr. Bianca, Ms. Bellewa, and Gwen share their own experiences of the ethical challenges they faced during their internship work.

Actually, we consider ethical issues throughout this text. For example, in Chapter 3, we suggested the specific ways that students can fill out their internship applications in a forthright and honest manner. In Chapter 4, we described ways to structure an internship that addresses the ethical dimensions of competence related to client consent and assent. In addition, we discuss the ethical dimensions of multicultural helping in Chapter 7. Finally, in Chapter 8, we present the ethical aspects of supervision.

Box 6.1 lists ethical issues such as confidentiality, boundaries, and suicide risk assessment, to name a few. We include in the section examples and exercises that help you use Kenyon's (1999) Ethical Decision-Making Model for issues you are currently confronting in internship.

Box 6.1 Studying the Text: Identifying Important Ethical Considerations in Internship

Studying the text: The following outline will help you read and study the text material in this next section.

Identifying important ethical considerations in internship:

1. Informed consent
2. Confidentiality
3. Competence
4. Suicide risk assessment
5. Relationships
    a. Dual and multiple relationships
    b. Boundaries and limit setting

6. Ethical and legal issues related to technology

7. Making models work for you

Identifying Important Ethical Considerations in Internship

A constant challenge for human service professionals is how to integrate the ethical values, principles, and codes of ethics into human service practice. One of the first steps is to recognize when an ethical challenge or issue exists. A second step is to think it through, determine an appropriate ethical approach, and then act accordingly. We present five issues that you are likely to confront during your internship experience. We also caution that you may encounter others. Before we talk about these issues, let's read about how other human service interns describe their experiences with ethical dimensions of human service practice.

Box 6.2 Students Reflect on Ethical Experiences During Internship

Steve: We read the code of ethics in our introduction to human service class. One thing that I liked about the topic was the case studies that we worked on in class. I am going to talk with my site supervisor about the ethical dilemmas that she faces in her work. Maybe she can give me some insights.

Maria: I think I already have an ethical dilemma at my site. My uncle used to be the director of my agency and I already knew many of the staff. People keep coming by to talk with me about my uncle. They also treat me like a friend and sometimes not like a professional. I am not sure how to handle this.

Al: I feel that my site is so different from the other sites where my peers are placed. I am not sure how much I can tell them about the site and my clients so that they understand what my experiences are. Most of my ethical issues are related to my supervisor.

Shasha: This might sound weird but I keep the code of ethics with me all of the time. Sometimes I can find the answers to my questions by reading through the code. Other times, especially when I am dealing with confidentiality, it is difficult. We have a break room at my agency. The talk that goes on in the break room, I think, violates lots of the standards in the codes.

Informed Consent

One critical aspect of a helping relationship is gaining **informed consent** from the clients with whom you work. In fact, informed consent is fundamental to the helping process and important to developing rapport and trust. The NOHS Ethical Standards for Human Service Professionals, in the section on *Responsibility to Clients*, state the importance of informed consent (NOHS, 2015). Informed consent is both a process and a product representing a communication that occurs between the helper and the client. It includes a discussion of the nature of, and details of, the services the client will receive. Communication during the informed consent process is two-way: Both the helper and client identify the client's values, goals, and needs; discuss service options including benefits and risks; and establish an understanding of the client's role in decision making. There is ample opportunity for dialogue and questions. The outcome of informed consent is a signed document in which the client indicates an understanding of the terms of the helping process and agrees to them. To gain a client's informed consent, the helper provides the following information:

- Options of services
- Risks and benefits of services
- Manner in which the services are provided (e.g., length of time and helper availability)
- Type of services (e.g., play therapy, group therapy, case management; concrete services such as food, clothing, housing)
- Options for refusing services (and a discussion of what happens if the client does not want services)
- Provisions for and circumstances of confidentiality related to
  o intern work with the client,
  o client records,
  o site and faculty supervision of intern (taping or on-site observation, note taking), and
  o limitations of confidentiality
- Training and competence of the intern (i.e., the client's understanding that the intern is in training and under supervision)

We recommend that interns work with their site supervisors to develop a plan to obtain informed consent from the clients with whom they work. The process of gaining informed consent will include both the university and the agency's requirements. For example, as described in Chapter 4, interns will review with clients their professional disclosure statements (sample shown in Box 4.5) and their permission to tape work with clients (as seen in Box 4.6). These two documents indicate training and competence of the intern, position of the intern in the agency, confidentiality related to supervision, and limits of confidentiality related to harm to self and others.

In addition, each agency will also have its own documents that address informed consent. Agency informed consent requirements may include record keeping and policies related to confidentiality of records. Agencies may also have established standards for informed consent, such as

- taking time for the client to understand the information presented,
- providing the client all of the information needed to make an informed decision,
- helping the client to understand the value of the informed consent process and his or her place in the process (client participates in the decision making),
- communicating in a language the client can understand,

- communicating in a way that respects the client's culture, and
- taking time to determine if the client understands the information communicated about the agency and service provision

---

Exercise 6.1 Processing and Obtaining Informed Consent

It is now your turn to describe your own process of obtaining informed consent in your agency setting.

Step 1

Describe in detail how you combine the professional disclosure statements and permission-to-tape forms you prepared in Chapter 4 and the informed consent process with forms your agency uses for explaining and obtaining informed consent.

_____

_____

_____

Step 2

Share these processes with your peers in internship class. Identify similarities and differences in the processes and the forms you see among your peers' experiences. Discuss the strengths and weaknesses you see related to your own and others informed consent processes and outcomes.

_____

_____

_____

Confidentiality

Confidentiality is a fundamental component of the helping process. The helper and the client generally agree that "information the client divulges will remain between the two of them" (Woodside & McClam, 2015, p. 280). But there are limits to confidentiality. We introduced the exceptions to that confidentiality in Chapter 4. These limits include (a) when the client indicates harm to self or others, (b) there are indications of abuse or neglect, (c) the client charges the helper with negligence, or (d) the helper receives a court-ordered subpoena for information. The NOHS Ethical Standards for Human Service Professionals identify guidelines regarding confidentiality under the category of Responsibility to Clients (NOHS, 2015). Nevertheless, in spite of what appear to be clear guidelines, human service work presents professionals with situations in which confidentiality represents an issue or challenge. Because of the many complexities related to client information and confidentiality, it is not surprising that interns often encounter dilemmas related to confidentiality. In fact, interns often wonder how they obtain a client's permission to share information with supervisors, other agency personnel, faculty supervisors, and members of client's families (See Figure 6.1). We present questions that interns ask, and then we suggest possible approaches.

Figure 6.1   Confidentiality: How Much Do I Share?

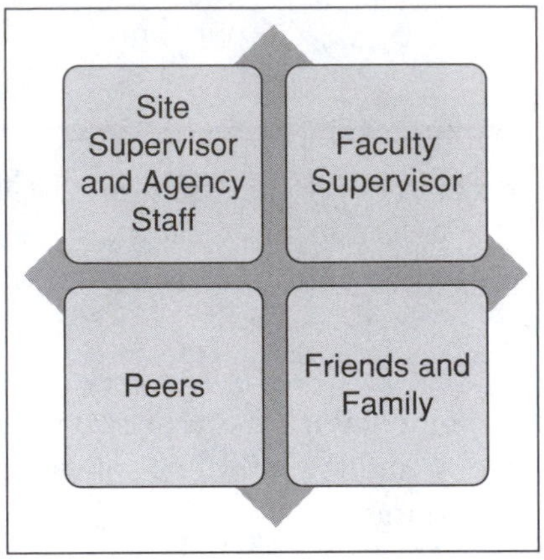

*What information about my clients can I share with
my site supervisor or other colleagues at my site?*

Assuming the role of an intern in an agency or organizational setting places you in a special position and role. Though you are not an employee of the agency, nevertheless, as an intern, the agency accepts responsibility for your supervision and your professional behavior. One key aspect of the internship experience includes being under supervision. Thus, your supervisor assumes responsibility for your professional work. You will want to create a time to talk with your supervisor about your work with your clients. Chapter 8 provides additional information about supervision.

Interns speak of difficulties when a client says to them, "I want to talk with you about X, but I don't want you to tell anyone else." Your response, as an intern, is to describe your role as an intern and explain that in this role you have a responsibility to your supervisor to disclose information about your work with clients. Specifically, you might respond by saying, "I am glad that you trust me with important information about yourself and I want you to talk with me openly. But you do need to understand that any information you share with me, I may share with my supervisor."

You might feel that the client's desire to share information with you demonstrates the rapport and trust you have built; you also might fear that the rapport will be diminished if you violate client trust. These feelings are important to note. But in spite of your desire to kept client confidences, you must share client information with your site supervisor. You might say to the client, "I am learning how to be a helping professional. My supervisors can only assist me to learn more about how I can help you if they know what we are talking about. My supervisors need to know what I am hearing and thinking so they can make suggestions about my work."

What information can I share with my faculty supervisor?

It is impractical for your faculty supervisor to know all of the details about your work with clients, but your faculty supervisor is also responsible for your work with clients. And you do indicate to your clients in your permission-to-tape form and professional disclosure statement that you expect to discuss your work with both your site supervisor and your faculty supervisor.

Because both supervisors are valuable resources and may have varying perspectives, you want to develop the habit of asking both about issues for which you have questions or difficulties.

There exists one instance, we believe, where it is critical to talk with both your site supervisor and your faculty supervisor—that is when a client talks about doing harm to self or others, or describes behavior that suggests possible abuse or neglect. In many programs, it is policy that students must inform their faculty supervisor if either of these issues arises. For that reason, you will want to have your faculty supervisor's contact information readily available. And you want to know how to contact your site supervisor if he or she is away from the work site for an extended period of time.

What can I share with my peers during internship class?

We believe that this is a complicated and difficult question to consider. Rather than provide an easy answer, let's consider the purpose of internship class and guidelines you might follow when discussing your work in class. First, let's look at the goals and outcomes for internship class in terms of what you learn from your peers and what you provide to them.

During internship class you can expect to gain information about issues and challenges that other peers face, learn about a variety of human service settings and supervision, and explore distinctive aspects of providing services to different client groups. Being able to bring issues to an internship class allows you to learn to articulate issues related to work setting, relationships at your agency, and work with clients. You are also noting your strengths and limitations publically, asking for help, and receiving feedback. Playing tapes and role-playing in class support the learning process.

But when talking with peers during internship class, you will need to be thoughtful and careful about how you describe both the clients with whom you work and the context in which you work. As you consider how best to talk about a situation or an encounter so others may understand, there is a range of how much information you might share about the setting, your supervisor, and the clients. We recommend, when speaking about your clients, you use pseudonyms rather than their actual names. Helping maintain the confidentiality of your clients reinforces the promise of confidentiality already discussed earlier. If you are discussing your clients, you will want to provide enough information so you can seek supervision, but limit the information to what peers need to know to understand the situation.

Regardless of your experience at your site, you will want to speak respectfully about the individuals you encounter and the experiences you have. What does "speaking respectfully" mean? The following two guidelines will help you talk to your peers about your internship experiences (Fredman, Anderson, & Stott, 2010).

Guideline 1: Offer a gracious invitation to your peers to talk about a situation you have encountered and are now asking for help. Language that offers an invitation might begin with "I am having difficulty with . . ." rather than "My coworkers are . . ." Words that indicate graciousness might include "When we have time, I would like to talk about . . ." or "I need your help with . . ." Note that this approach demonstrates respect of your peers and also suggests that you are having difficulty, rather than beginning with how difficult others are. Two examples follow:

Gracious example

Open with this "I am frustrated with the supervision I am receiving . . ."

Rather than this "My supervisor is driving me crazy . . ."

Gracious example

Open with this "I have an issue that I would like to bring to the group . . ."

Rather than this "I must have time today to talk about an issue with a client . . ."

Guideline 2 Using respectful language when describing others will help peers respond to both your emotional reaction to the situation and the context and content of the situation. You want to present workplace issues or client challenges in a way that clearly articulates the issues without indicating causation, labeling, blaming, or negative descriptions. For example, you might demonstrate respect for the client and for your work with the client by stating, "I am unsure how to work with one of my clients . . . let me talk you through my case notes about our last session." A less respectful statement might be, "The teen I am seeing is a problem client and refuses to follow treatment plans . . ." uses labels and blame to convey your message. Two examples follow:

Respectful example

Describe this way "I felt embarrassed yesterday while I was working with my client. I didn't know that I needed to fill out specific paperwork to prepare my client for his visit home. I wish my supervisor had told me about this procedure."

Rather than this "My supervisor never tells me what I need to know about agency procedure and practice. He caused me to look bad and incompetent in front of my client yesterday."

Respectful example

Describe this way "Yesterday, at the beginning of our session, my client told me that his mother was living with her boyfriend. Then, at the end of our session, he told me that his mother was living with her sister. I was unsure how to ask him to clarify."

Rather than this "My client is totally untrustworthy . . . he told me a lie in yesterday's session . . ."

Can I talk with my trusted family members about my internship? Can I talk with my spouse or significant other? Can I talk with my best friend?

We believe that this question represents a struggle that interns, as well as most human service professionals, experience when sharing both emotions and content-related experiences about their professional work. For some, it is common practice to talk about work with friends and family.

This sharing helps individuals share important aspects of their lives and seek assistance for professional issues and challenges. However, there exist clear boundaries about what human service professionals (including interns) can share with others. A guideline we suggest is to separate talking about the personal dimensions of work related to self and the professional dimensions of work related to clients. You also saw this guideline in operation when we discussed graciousness and respect. We provide a few examples related to several aspects of work individuals are likely to share:

Nature of work

<u>Describe this way</u> "My day goes really fast. There are 10 clients waiting outside the door of our building when I arrive for work. They are waiting to enter the building and sign up to see a case manager. It seems like the day of work begins even before I arrive. The pressure is constant all day."

<u>Rather than this</u> "Yesterday when I arrived at work, three of my clients, Shakisha, Crystal, and Sam were there waiting for me. I knew things would start fast because Crystal needed me to go to court with her. She is asking DHS for times she can visit her daughter, Trixie, who is in foster care. And I knew I would immediately be behind in my work."

Volume of work

<u>Describe this way</u> "I don't know what to do. I am working all day and still I am behind on my paperwork. I try to complete it on Sundays. But then I can't spend time with my family."

<u>Rather than this</u> "I need to fill out the paperwork for all of my clients. Seven of my clients need special paperwork from the VA. Both George and Tom require so much more time. They live down the street from us and I hate to let them down. Whether they get services or not depends upon me."

Skills related to work

<u>Describe this way</u> "I am not sure that I have the skills to work with one of my clients. She comes from another culture and it is one I know nothing about."

<u>Rather than this</u> "Just last week a client from the Ukraine walked in the door. Tasha and her son just arrived last month. They live in the East Rutledge neighborhood and attend the Evangelical church in that neighborhood Ms. Travis from the church brought them to our agency. I don't know much about the culture or the country they came from."

In each of these examples, you begin to see a pattern of appropriate ways that you can talk with your family and trusted friends about your work. The first guideline is to talk about your work in terms of yourself, rather than in terms of your clients. The second guideline is to provide very few details about the clients you serve or the supervisor with whom you work. Following these two guidelines may help you share information about your work while respecting the confidentiality you promised to maintain related to your clients.

Exercise 6.2 Maintaining Confidentiality During Internship: Writing Your Own Story, Entry 15

We identified the various situations where maintaining confidentiality may be tested.

Step 1

To complete this exercise, write about your experiences of talking about your internship experience with your site supervisor, faculty supervisor, peers, and family and friends. Describe times when you believe you followed appropriate guidelines for maintaining confidentiality. Note times when you are unsure about the information you disclosed or how you shared it.

Competence

Competence for the human service professional means having the knowledge, skills, and values necessary to perform the assigned roles and tasks effectively, especially those related to human service delivery. The NOHS Ethical Standards for Human Service Professionals presents standards related to Responsibility to Clients, Public and Society, Colleagues, Employers, Profession, and Self (NOHS, 2015). Although competence remains a challenge for all human service professionals, there exists a unique tension related to it during internship. Specifically, during internship, as interns assume a learning and training role, there are special considerations. First, remember that you, as an intern, do enter the internship experience with recent academic training, previous service learning, and volunteer experiences. This preparation provides a foundation for your work in internship. Second, you are in a learning role and you are developing as a professional. You can periodically monitor your development of knowledge, skills, and values and note your strengths and limitation. We recommend three ways you can address the issue of professional competence: assessment, supervision, and professional disclosure as shown in Figure 6.2.

Assessment

In most internships, the faculty describe in the course syllabus the midterm and the final evaluations the knowledge, skills, and values they expect you to learn. In fact, you and your internship faculty and site supervisors alike assume that you will grow professionally during your internship experience. To monitor your own competency, we suggest that you conduct a preassessment of your knowledge, skills, and values prior to the midterm evaluation.

Figure 6.2   Ways to Address Ethical Issues of Competence as an Intern

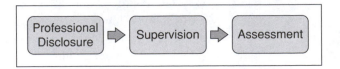

You can either refer to the assessments you completed in Chapter 4, Exercise 4.2, or you can use the evaluation forms suggested by your academic program and described in your internship syllabus. Once you have completed one or more of these assessments, then you can review each with your site supervisor. This early assessment activity helps your site supervisor understand how much support or supervision you will need. You can also use this information to add goals and strategies to the internship contract introduced in Chapter 4 and shown in Figure 4.2.

Supervision

A second approach to addressing competence involves seeking supervision and focuses on your work with your site supervisor. As we noted in Chapter 4, our hope is that you receive orientation to your agency during your initial visit and that you have subsequent opportunities to continue to learn about your agency and the clients it serves. In addition, during our discussion of orientation, we suggested that you engage in the process of dynamic orientation or continual professional development. We encourage you to see dynamic orientation as a lifelong effort to increase your knowledge, skills, and values related to human service work.

Since, during your internship, you will assume an increasing responsibility for clients and agency work, your expectations for and levels of competence will change. Exercise 4.2 and Tables 4.4, 4.5, and 4.6 can guide your work with your site supervisor to continually assess the knowledge, skills, and values you need as an intern.

Professional Disclosure

The professional disclosure statement you share with your clients represents a third approach to addressing issues of competence. In Chapter 4, we presented in-depth information about the professional disclosure statement. It is in the professional disclosure statement that you clarify to your clients and your colleagues your previous experience and training, your position as an intern, the nature of the supervision you will receive, and the roles and responsibilities you will assume.

At times interns are reluctant to disclose the fact they are interns and that they are working under supervision. One aspect of this reluctance is the fear that clients will think less of them as professionals and will be unwilling to trust their lives and care to them. While sometimes clients do not want to work with interns who are learning and training, oftentimes clients are reassured when they understand that interns receive faculty and site supervision. And clients often indicate that they see interns as approachable and less intimidating to work with.

The quality of supervision matters to both the intern and to the client. We discuss supervision, the nature of quality supervision, and provide practical suggestions about how interns may seek and encourage good supervision in Chapter 8. In relationship to competence, quality supervision means regularly scheduled time with your site supervisor to talk about clients and focus on how to meet client needs. Supervisors need also to be available to consult in crises. In fact, the more the supervisor knows about your work with the clients, the more the supervisor can help you.

Since competence is at the heart of the education and training experience for the intern, we suggest the following exercise. We based this exercise on the initial work interns begin in the first few weeks of their internship.

Exercise 6.3 Developing Competence as a Human Service Professional

Step 1

As we suggested earlier in this section, working with your site supervisor, review the midterm evaluation and your internship contract to assess the knowledge, skills, and values on which you wish to continue to work during the academic term.

_____

_____

_____

Step 2

Disclosing to client your role as an intern can increase anxiety during the beginning stages of the helping process. Talk with your supervisor about what this experience is like for you. In addition, regularly discuss with your supervisor your behaviors, thoughts, and emotions related to your feelings of competency as a human service professional.

_____

_____

_____

Suicide Risk Assessment

We believe that the **suicide risk assessment** is a fundamental responsibility of all human service professionals. The NOHS Ethics Standards for Human Service Professionals (2015) suggests its importance in guidelines related to Responsibility to Clients. Suicide represents the 10th leading cause of death for Americans. Many human service professionals work with populations vulnerable to risk of suicide, including senior adults, men, Caucasians, Native Americans, and those living in specific Western states (American Foundation for Suicide Prevention, 2012). But in fact the risk increases when clients have vulnerabilities beyond their current or immediate reasons for seeking services. For instance, a client may face losing her children to state custody. Although the loss of her children represents a devastating occurrence, this loss is heightened by previous vulnerabilities linked to her own childhood neglect and spousal abuse.

One way to begin to assess your competence with handling this area of focus is to talk with your site supervisor about his or her experiences, the agency's policy, and any suggested ways you might learn more about suicide risk assessment. Ask your site supervisor for his or her reactions to the following goals you might establish for yourself related to suicide risk assessment.

Talking about these goals will, perhaps, open the discussion to an acknowledgement between the two of you of the importance of ongoing dialogue about this topic.

- What do I do in my position as an intern when I think a client is at risk for suicide?
- How can I gain competence in assessment of clients who may be at risk for suicide?
- What is the difference between an informal suicide risk assessment and a formal suicide risk assessment?
- How do I tell a client that I am concerned about him or her and will conduct a suicide risk assessment?
- How do I conduct an assessment? What skills do I need?
- How do I document the suicide risk assessment?
- Once I have conducted the suicide risk assessment and documented the assessment, what do I do next?
- How do I help develop a client safety plan?
- Throughout an informal or formal assessment, how do I weigh the commitment to confidentiality that promotes trust with my responsibility to protect the client from self-harm?
- What is my legal responsibility to report? Is there mandated reporting?

It is also important to talk about suicide risk assessment with your faculty supervisor.

Many times an internship syllabus and subsequent conversation with the faculty supervisor confirm that your faculty supervisor wants to know if you suspect it is necessary to conduct a suicide risk assessment or if you or your site supervisor conducts such an assessment. Providing information and gaining consultation with your faculty supervisor may provide an additional perspective on this important work.

Tomas shares with us a discussion he had with his site supervisor about suicide risk assessment and his struggles with the concept as it related to himself and his clients.

Tomas

Suicide risk assessment is difficult for me. I shared my fears with my supervisor. She told me that she sees a possible suicide risk in every client. For some reason, I don't want to see this in any of my clients. I know how important it is for me to perform either an informal or formal suicide risk assessment with each client I see. Ms. Paseattoe and I decided together that for me this is an ethical challenge and issue. She and I decided that we would focus on this challenge and issue in every meeting we had. One of the first exercises we did was trying to define suicide risk assessment. Ms. Paseattoe views suicide risk assessment as a complex issue. She categorizes the issue as ethical, legal, or moral. She thought if I understood more about the concept, I might be more comfortable talking about it. Here is a summary of the discussions we had about suicide and suicide risk assessment.

Tomas and Ms. Paseattoe's Words

We began the discussion of suicide risk assessment and decided it was easier to use a real life example rather than talk about this assessment in the abstract. I (Tomas) showed Ms. Paseattoe the Kenyon model of decision making and asked for her help in thinking through what suicide risk assessment means for one of my clients. We tried to decide if suicide risk assessment appeared to be ethical, value driven, or legal. For suicide risk assessment, here is what we decided to use as a guideline for our thinking:

<u>Ethical</u>—We also found that there is a standard in the NOHS Ethics Standards for Human Service Professionals that addresses suicide risk assessment. In the section that addresses confidentiality as a fundamental promise a helper makes to the client, one exception to maintaining confidentiality is an assessment that the client intends to harm self or others. Because of the responsibility of the helper to protect the client from harm, sometimes the helper breaks confidentiality.

Ms. Paseattoe talked to me about how truly difficult the decision to break confidentiality can be. She explained that suicide risk assessment is an imperfect assessment. Sometimes she has to weigh the harm *the client might do to self against the harm of the* consequences of *declaring a client at risk and the potential difficulties it causes in the client and perhaps family's life. Hence, at times, the least invasive intervention may be considered.*

<u>Value driven</u>—One of the basic values in human services is nonmaleficence. Even though this essentially means do no harm, we found that several helping professionals suggest that this also means keeping clients from harm (Gladding, 2004).

<u>Legal</u>—There is also a legal dimension to the suicide risk assessment. The law in our state and, I think but am not sure, in most states, is that helping professionals have a responsibility to protect clients from harming themselves and others. If the professional fails to keep the client from harm, then the helper may be seen as negligent. This means that the helper did not perform according to professional standards and the result was harm to the client (Remley & Herlihy, 2015).

<u>Consultation</u>—Finally Ms. Paseattoe and I agreed that consultation with others in the agency or with Ms. Paseattoe throughout a suicide risk assessment is critical. She told me that she continues to consult with her colleagues when confronted with a client she believes is at risk for suicide. Consultation with peers during suicide risk assessment is recommended in most professional codes of ethics.

Wellness and Self-Care

There is a self-care dimension to working with clients with suicidal ideation. In other words, research in helping tells us that clients are not the only ones at risk. Helpers are vulnerable too (Woodside & McClam, 2015), and helpers may experience personal and professional stress. In fact, the stress may negatively influence a helper's ability to work with clients, as well as negatively impact a helper's personal mental and physical health (Knox, Burkard, Bentzler, Schaack, & Hess, 2006). Trainees or interns in the helping professions are especially at risk to experience strong or vivid emotional reactions to working with suicidal clients. In fact, interns experience these strong reactions including fear of failure and thoughts of guilt and anger influencing their personal lives (Kleepsies, Penk, & Forsyth, 1993; Knox et al., 2006; McAdams & Foster, 2000). This makes self-care all the more important.

Exercise 6.4 Thinking About Conducting a Suicide Risk Assessment, Entry 16

As we indicated earlier, working with clients who may be suicidal is a very difficult aspect of the helping process. It is also a critical piece of caring for clients and ensuring their safety.

Step 1

Assess your behaviors, thoughts, and feelings about conducting a suicide risk assessment. This can include your personal and professional history and experience with the risk of suicide, personal fears you have about working with suicidal clients, and any personal beliefs or dispositions that you believe will help or hinder your work.

Step 2

Second, share the written statement in Step 1 with your site supervisor. Include in this conversation the questions listed earlier that will help you explore with your site supervisor the topic of suicide risk assessment. Make a plan to address questions or challenges that arise from this conversation.

Exercise 6.5 Conducting a Suicide Risk Assessment

Step 1

To help you prepare to conduct a suicide risk assessment, make notes about the information you need from your client. Ask your site supervisor or faculty supervisor to role-play with you a suicide risk assessment.

Step 2

After the role play, discuss the suicide risk assessment from the client perspective and from your perspective as the helper.

Relationships: Multiple Roles/Multiple Relationships, Boundaries and Limit Setting

Early in your human services program you learned about the unique nature of the helping relationship. Characteristics of this relationship include (a) begins with an agreed upon, common purpose, (b) is focused on a goal, (c) occurs within a specified period of time, (d) ends when the agreed upon goals are reached, (e) includes a helper with professional or specialized knowledge, skills, and values and a client who has self-knowledge, and (f) exists to help and support the client's growth, development, and problem solving (Woodside & McClam, 2015). Not only is it important to understand what constitutes a helping relationship, it is equally important to understand its limits. The NOHS Ethical Standards for Human Service Professionals suggests guidelines related to relationships in Responsibility to Clients (NOHS, 2015).

Professional ethical codes clarify the terms of the helping relationship, as they provide standards related to **dual and multiple relationships**, **boundaries and limit setting**, and shifting roles (See Figure 6.3). The purpose of these standards is to protect clients, recognize the unequal power dimension of the helping relationship, and minimize the risk of harming the client. Harm can come to the client for many reasons and in many ways. We consider several types of relationships and provide guidelines from various ethical codes of different helping professions. Ultimately, the purpose of the guidelines is to protect clients.

The ethical codes of various helping professions, such as the NOHS, the American Counseling Association (ACA), and the National Association of Social Workers (NASW) address directly concerns related to professional conduct as it relates to sexual and romantic relationships. There are several types of sexual and romantic relationships to consider. We examine three codes of ethics in an effort to describe the various perspectives that relate to each type of relationship (ACA, 2014; NOHS, 2015; NASW, 2008).

Sexual and/or romantic relationships with clients—NOHS, ACA, and NASW Codes of Ethics each prohibit helping professionals from engaging in sexual or romantic relationships with clients.

Previous sexual and/or romantic relationships—ACA and NASW Codes of Ethics prohibit helping professionals from engaging in helping relationships with individuals with whom they have had previous sexual and/or romantic relationships. The NOHS Ethical Standards for Human Service Professionals, Standard 5, addresses this relationship while recognizing the reality that dual or multiple relationships will occur in daily personal and professional life (NOHS, 2015).

Sexual and/or romantic relationships with former clients or members of their families—ACA ethical code prohibits these relationships for a period of 5 years from the last helping interaction. NASW prohibits these relationships, noting that if exceptions occur, responsibility and consideration of client safety rests with the professional. We caution interns to avoid these types of relationships. The NOHS Ethical Standards for Human Service Professionals, Standard 6, addresses this relationship and prohibits sexual or romantic relationships with clients with whom human service professionals are working. This standard further limits these relationships with previous clients and family members. The caveat is harm to the client or family members involved (NOHS, 2015).

Family members and friends—ACA does not prohibit establishing a helping relationship with family or friends; rather, they prohibit the engagement if the professional is unable to be objective. NASW prohibits the professional from engaging in a helping relationship if there may be harm to the client or if the power differential leads to exploitation of the client. The NOHS Ethical Standards for Human Service Professionals, Standard 5, described earlier addresses this relationship (NOHS, 2015).

Figure 6.3   Aspects of Ethical Standards Related to Relationships

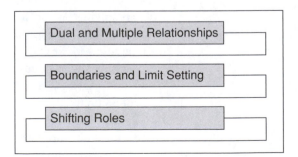

Members of the community or past or distant relationships—ACA's Code of Ethics addresses these relationships in several standards. One especially relevant standard suggests any helping relationship of this type be undertaken only after serious consideration of potential harm to or advantage for the client. According to the NASW code, helpers must consider and inform clients when a conflict of interest exists or arises and protect client interests. The NOHS Ethical Standards for Human Service Professionals, Standard 5, addresses this relationship (NOHS, 2015).

Extending boundaries—Extending boundaries, related to professional relationships, refers to ways that helpers can engage or support clients beyond the helping relationship. Examples of extending boundaries may include, but are not limited to, attending important events related to the client or the client's family, giving of or receiving gifts, or assuming the role of a power of attorney. ACA's Code of Ethics addresses extending boundaries explicitly by indicating the counselor would approach such actions with caution (e.g., informed consent and consultation) to ensure that helper judgment is not damaged and no harm comes to the client. NASW standards for social workers reiterate consideration of dual or multiple relationships that may cause harm to the client. Under the concern for conflicts of interest, the code warns that care should be taken to protect the client and establish clear boundaries. The NOHS Ethical Standards for Human Service Professionals, Standard 6, specifically addresses the circumstances when dual or multiple relationships may exist and, like the ACA and NASW codes, suggests caution be taken to protect client welfare (NOHS, 2015).

Shifting Roles

As we discussed earlier in other relationship ethical issues, the ultimate goal for the human service professional is the protection and safety of the client. One ethical aspect of relationships occurs when professionals change or expand their roles and responsibilities as they work with a client. We believe that, as interns, shifting roles while working with a client is likely to occur, especially as the intern becomes increasingly familiar with the agency, the clients, and the work of the agency. We talked about the increasing responsibility of the work during internship in Chapter 4. In fact, interns, as well as faculty and site supervisors, anticipate that interns will increase their responsibilities throughout the internship. We see this expansion or shift in responsibilities as a part of informed consent, related to what the client can expect from treatment, and the competencies of the helping professional to provide said treatment.

The ACA Code of Ethics directly addresses shifting roles and responsibilities as role changes (ACA, 2014, p. 5). In the ACA code, when counselors shift from the initial role to an additional one, informed consent is considered. Helpers must explicitly clarify the role change and its consequences, and then the client must agree to the change. The NASW and human service professional codes do not address change of roles directly, but we believe the guidelines related to informed consent apply to the role shift.

In this section, we present various ways that ethical challenges and issues may arise related to multiple boundaries and multiple relationships. Interns and human service professionals negotiate these every day in the encounters they have with clients. We think that faculty and site supervision provide opportunities for exploring this area of professional practice. In fact, supervision provides an important place to protect the client from harm, to support the helper/client relationships as a positive place for human service delivery, and to consider the influences of power and privilege. See Chapter 7 for a more detailed discussion of power and privilege.

Exercise 6.6 Considering Issues Arising From Multiple Boundaries/Multiple Relationships

Professional development is a key aspect of addressing issues related to multiple boundaries and multiple relationships. We suggest reading, personal reflection, consultation, supervision, and documentation as ways to extend your personal development. This exercise will help you learn how to negotiate these ethical issues and challenges.

Step 1

First, for each of the issues we described previously, describe a hypothetical or current circumstance where you can see a dilemma that may possibly harm a client.

Sexual and/or romantic relationships with clients

_____

_____

Previous sexual and/or romantic relationships

_____

_____

Sexual and/or romantic relationships with former clients or members of their families

_____

_____

Family members and friends

_____

_____

Members of the community or past or distant relationships

_____

_____

Extending boundaries

_____

_____

Shifting roles

_____

_____

Exercise 6.7 Considering Issues Arising From Multiple Boundaries/Multiple Relationships: Writing Your Own Story, Entry 17

Step 1

Begin to document your confrontations with the challenges and issues related to multiple relationships and multiple boundaries. What were the specific issues? The measures you took to consult? The actions you took to address the issue and challenge?

Ethical and Legal Issues Related to Technology

The influence and use of technology in the helping professions continues to increase, and with the increase comes a need to consider both ethical and legal ramifications of its use. Within the history of helping, the use of technology is still relatively new. As such, we highlight ethical and legal issues related to technology in a separate section, even though many of these issues fall within dimensions of ethics such as competency, **informed consent**, confidentiality, and relationships. Specific to the three codes we used for illustrative purposes earlier in our discussion, ACA provides a specific section focusing on "distance counselling, technology, and social media." The NASW offers guidelines we consider relevant to the use of technology in helping, but are not specifically related to distance helping or social media. The NOHS Ethical Standards for Human Service Professionals presents Standard 9 that addresses technology directly (NOHS, 2015). Standard 9 suggests caution when considering confidentiality with client service delivery and client records. The focus broadens to include how technology might harm the client or the helping relationship.

Because the ACA focus on technology related helping is presented in such detail, we present the guidelines from this code of ethics. Please also refer to the NOHS Ethical Standards for Human Service Professionals, Standard 9, for guidelines related to technology and ethical standards (NOHS, 2015).

Competence—The ACA Code of Ethics states that helpers need to develop special knowledge and skills if they deliver services using technology. In addition, the ACA code cautions professionals to understand and inform clients about legal restrictions that relate to providing services electronically, especially as they relate to working across state or international boundaries. The NOHS Ethical Standards for Human Service Professionals, Standard 5, addresses this issue (NOHS, 2015).

Informed consent—The ACA Code of Ethics suggests that professionals provide clients the choice whether to receive services face-to-face or within an electronic framework.

Confidentiality—The ACA Code of Ethics outlines the terms of a secure communication with clients. In a section entitled "Informed Consent and Security," the guidelines include the terms of informed consent described above. In addition, the guidelines suggest sharing with clients the parameters of confidentiality of records (e.g., supervisor or staff access), possible limits of security of information, use of security systems to protect client information (e.g., encryption), and verification of client identity during the helping process. The NOHS Ethical Standards for Human Service Professionals, Standard 5, addresses this issue (NOHS, 2015).

Relationships—The ACA Code of Ethics describes six guidelines for what they term "distance counseling relationships" (ACA, 2014, Section H.4a–f). These include outlining benefits and limitations of distance counseling, professional boundaries, capability of clients to use the technology required for services, effectiveness of services, access to technology, and differences between face-to-face and technology-provided services. A discussion of each of these benefits and limitations helps the professional helper and the client determine if technology-delivered services will address client needs. The NOHS Ethical Standards for Human Service Professionals, Standard 5, addresses this issue (NOHS, 2015).

Records and Web Maintenance—The ACA Code of Ethics provides four guidelines that recognize the increasing use of the World Wide Web (WWW) in professional work (ACA, 2014, Section H.5 a–d) and suggests ways that the web can be used in an ethical manner. In this standard, the ACA Code of Ethics suggests the following actions: providing informed consent about security of records, sharing with clients a web-based professional disclosure (e.g., education and training, certificates and licensure, expertise), maintaining an updated and working web presence, and addressing multicultural needs such as translations of web-based material. The NOHS Ethical Standards for Human Service Professionals, Standard 5, also addresses this issue (NOHS, 2015).

Exercise 6.8 Technology, Internship, and You

Step 1

In this exercise, we ask you to think through how technology influences your work as an intern. Consider the following questions or prompts, develop your response, and share and discuss your responses with your supervisor.

What is your personal social media presence today? What is your agency's social media presence today? How do you address the personal and the professional presence?

_____

_____

_____

What will you do if your clients find your Facebook or other social media presence and refer to it? What if your clients ask you to engage with them on social media?

_____

_____

_____

Should you look for your clients on the web? What will you do if you find your clients on the web?

_____

_____

_____

Your internship site supervisor asks you to create a more creative agency presence on the web.

_____

_____

_____

Your clients want to text you and communicate in other technology-related ways.

_____

_____

_____

Add other issues related to technology that you encounter.

_____

_____

_____

Making Models Work for You

In many of the chapters in this text, we ask you to use a model to help you focus in more depth on a specific topic. This chapter is no exception, and as suggested in Chapter 5, we recommend Kenyon's (1999) Ethical Decision-Making Model.

Exercise 6.9 Using Kenyon's Ethical Decision-Making Model

Step 1

We would like for you to use the model to work through a current ethical challenge or issue that you or your supervisor is confronting, or anticipating confronting, at the internship site. Since the model encompasses multiple steps, choose a challenge or issue that is important to you, your work, and your professional growth.

Step 2

Once you create a rough draft of your decision making related to the issue, share your thinking process with your faculty and site supervisors. If you do have a challenge or issue that warrants use of the model, return to this assignment at the appropriate time.

1. *Describe the issue.* _____

   _____

2. *Consider the ethical guidelines.* _____

   _____

3. *Examine the conflicts.* _____

   _____

4. *Resolve the conflicts.* _____

   _____

5. *Generate all possible courses of action.* _____

_____

6. *Examine and evaluate the action alternatives.* _____

_____

7. *Select and evaluate the preferred action.* _____

_____

8. *Plan the action.* _____

_____

9. *Evaluate the outcome.* _____

_____

10. *Examine the implications.* _____

_____

Step 3

Consider the context factors that influence ethical decision making. We introduced the importance of contextual factors in Chapter 5, Table 5.2.

What is the perspective of the university and human service program? The agency?

_____

_____

What are the contextual factors present in this issue? How did you consider these in your decision making?

_____

_____

Step 4

In Chapter 5, we presented final consideration when evaluating your ethical decision making. This self-test is a way you can further evaluate what you learned during the process. To complete this assessment, answer the following questions from the Department of Counseling and Human Services (n.d.) at the University of Syracuse:

- *Did I made consistent decisions when encountering similar situations? If I made different decisions, how to I account for these differences? Are there other options I did not consider?*

_____

_____

- *If another counselor were facing a similar issue, would I recommend my decision making and resolution?*

_____

_____

- *Did I make this decision because it was easy, it was politically smart, or was best for me?*

_____

_____

- *With whom am I comfortable sharing this situation, my thinking about it, and my responses? If am comfortable, why? If not, why?*

_____

_____

- *Am I compromising a standard that I believe in? How might this influence a future decision?*

_____

_____

We now look at more personal aspects of ethical decision making in internship. Box 6.3 describes the ways that you will deepen your understanding of ethics and internship.

Box 6.3 Deepening Your Understanding

Deepening Your Understanding

1. Peer-to-peer dialogue
   a. Alicia: Ethical challenges
   b. Lucas: Ethical challenges
   c. Tamika: Ethical challenges
2. Faculty and site supervisor dialogue
   a. Dr. Bianca: Awareness of ethical issues
   b. Ms. Bellewa: Ethics and culture
3. The professional voice and tips for practice: Gwen: Ethical issues and self-reflection
4. Terms to remember
5. References

Deepening Your Understanding

Alicia, Lucas, and Tamika share their experiences of internship as it relates to identifying and addressing ethical challenges and issues they are encountering during their internships. Although many of their experiences may differ from yours, we believe that, as you compare their insights with yours, you will draw new insights about your own internship. Dr. Bianca,

Ms. Bellewa, and Gwen provide faculty, site supervisor, and professional perspectives about ethical issues and how to address them.

Peer-to-Peer Dialogue: Alicia, Lucas, and Tamika

We asked Alicia, Lucas, and Tamika to talk about ethical perspectives related to their own internships.

Alicia

Hello all—I hope your experience in Human Services is going well. I am happy to tell you about my experience preparing for and working with individuals from an ethical perspective. Probably the most important issue that I encounter every day is confidentiality. My clients are so vulnerable, both the children and the parents. At the same time, I am so emotionally challenged by the work, I feel like I need to talk with others about the difficulty of the work. Let me give you an example. Last week, my job was to help my site supervisor move three children from their mother's care to a foster family. The mother was devastated and the children cried and cried when they have to leave their home. I came home and I could still hear the cries of all involved. It took all that I could do not to break down in front of them. I talked with Jarryn, my site supervisor. She listened to me talk about my own feelings and also about how conflicted I was about taking children from their mother. She also suggested that I talk with my faculty supervisor, Dr. Lynn. I was afraid to call Dr. Lynn. I thought I might not be able to even discuss what had happened and my strong reactions to it without crying. So I called my mother first. I didn't use the names of my clients to describe what had happened that day, but I did tell her what happened when the children left their home. She listened to me tell the story. Just having her listen helped me immensely. She also suggested that I called Dr. Lynn. I still wasn't sure if I wanted to do that.

I went home directly after the end of my day in internship. Picking up Thomas and attending to his needs helped me refocus my emotions. After my day, Thomas seemed more precious than ever to me. Once I fed him, we played, and I settled him down for the night, I call Dr. Lynn. She wanted to hear about my day and what was troubling me as a way to begin our conversation. When I reflect on our conversation, I felt better about my internship work and about my reactions to today's interactions with clients. Dr. Lynn didn't minimize my difficulties; rather, she shared how glad she was that I called her. I worried about bothering her with my tender feelings. She encouraged me to explore those feelings and indicated that my response was typical of many interns. And indeed, she acknowledged what a difficult issue child custody is, especially when parents lose the rights for a time to see their children. We scheduled a time for me to see her in her office later that week to talk again. She asked me if I would write a brief reflection about why this issue was so difficult for me. I am to consider (a) personal factors that might evoke such strong emotions, (b) ethical issues that arise for this situation, and (c) the relationship between laws regarding child custody and agency policy. This reflection will help prepare for our meeting at the end of the week.

One other issue that I am struggling with right now relates to paperwork and documentation of my work in the agency. I am concerned about signing any agency documents regarding evaluation of parent-child relationships and evaluation of foster care settings. I think documenting my interactions and having my supervisor review the written files is quite appropriate. But I don't think that I have enough knowledge or experience to conduct evaluation interviews and visits. My supervisor assures me that this is common practice with interns. But I don't feel confident. After reading about the issue of competence, I feel more strongly than ever. In our next supervisory meeting, I am going to talk to both to Jarryn, Dr. Davis, and Dr. Lynn.

Written by Allie Rhinehart and Dareen Basma, 2015. Used with permission.

Lucas

Hello, this is Lucas again! I hope you are having a great day! Today, I would like to talk to you about my experiences focusing on ethical situations during internship. Ethics, to me, as I am continuously learning to be a helping professional, is an ongoing learning process. I still remember the ethics course I took a year ago, and it was overwhelming for me. There were so many ethical codes and information to be an ethical counselor. Therefore, if you are feeling overwhelmed, I can relate to your feelings. My most important skill, especially at internship, is to seek supervision when I need assistance. For instance, to see if I am helping or hindering client progress, if I am doing notes correctly, or if I start to have reactions or feelings during sessions when client's talk about their experiences. I was taught, during training, that when in doubt, seek supervision.

When I think about ethics, one thing my supervisor and I talk about during supervision are the values pertaining to nonmaleficence, beneficence, justice, autonomy, and veracity. These are just the common values, among others; we mainly discuss to make sure I am providing effective services to my clients. The easy part is having an understanding of these ethical values, but the difficult part is making sure I am applying these values during sessions. For example, I was working with a client who wanted me to dictate the helping process. My client wanted me to have full control of the therapeutic process and help her, ultimately, get better. After a couple of sessions, I started to realize I was taking control of sessions by planning interventions and therapeutic goals without allowing my client to be a part of the process. I noticed my client shutting down during sessions, and upon supervision I realized I was not promoting autonomy to my client. I knew what the ethical value of autonomy states, but applying it, especially when a client is in need, was very difficult for me. However, if I did not seek supervision, I could have caused harm to my client and possibly reinforced similar behaviors of power and control. After reflecting on my behaviors during supervision, I promoted autonomy during sessions; now my client feels empowered in the therapeutic process, and she is applying the same principles in her own life.

Not only did autonomy play a role during sessions, I realized I was potentially imposing my own values to my client. Growing up, my mother taught me to help others when they are in need. In my family, helping involves doing things for other people, so they do not feel the harm. It is similar to removing the stimulus that is causing harm. During supervision, I realized I was trying to rescue my client by imposing my familial values on my client, by controlling sessions, in hope of removing the pain she was suffering. Consequently, I was not promoting autonomy during sessions. I was in shock about how my own personal and familial values influenced sessions. I remember in my ethics course, my professor would teach us self-awareness exercises to avoid imposing your own biases, values, and/or assumptions during sessions. However, removing your own experiences and values in sessions was very difficult for me, and still is. I consider this an ongoing learning process and development as a helper.

Another ethical issue I experienced, and you may experience this too, is the use of technology to provide services. Recently, a client of mine who was traveling, e-mailed me to provide services via e-mail, due to a minor discomfort reported by my client. I did not recognize his e-mail address, but I recognized his name. I was confused because I was not sure if this was my client, and secondly, this was my first experience of a client requesting services via e-mail. I was nervous and confused on how to respond, and ultimately, I did not know if I was on the border of an ethical dilemma. On supervision, my supervisor advised me to verify if it was my client by calling my client and asking identifying information, and then to discuss issues about maintaining confidentiality via the Internet. When I called my client for identifying information and to talk him about issues of confidentiality, my client decided he did not want to participate in online counseling because of the lack of security on the internet that could not preserve confidentiality. My client stated he felt the Internet was not a safe means to talk about private information, so he refused online services.

These are just a couple of examples, among others I experienced, that challenged my skills as a helper, especially when I was on the border of an ethical dilemma. I hope my experiences will alleviate your anxieties during internship, as it pertains to ethical issues. One thing I am learning is that I do not have all the answers, and you may not either; so I would recommend seeking supervision as much as possible. This will help you grow, and, at the same time, avoid situations that can cause harm to clients. I hope this information helps you and good luck with internship!

Written by Jorge Roman, 2015. Used with permission.

Tamika

Ethics is a topic within my field that I have simultaneously felt both nervous about and grateful for. Having been at my internship for a while now, I see ethical issues on a daily basis, and while I am still a bit anxious about learning all that there is to learn about ethical considerations within human services, I am grateful to recognize how my own personal beliefs align with the ethical values I am learning about. I am also grateful that my professors and supervisors have taken the time to so strongly emphasize ethics during class and supervision time to help me figure out how to be the most ethical helping professional I can be.

Thinking about my own personal beliefs as a future human services worker really helps me to frame the ethical decisions I sometimes have to make at my internship. The five beliefs outlined earlier in this chapter describe many of my own values in working with clients, particularly in the correctional setting. I find that many of the clients with whom I work encounter empathy and positive support very infrequently, so it is important to me to convey to them that I have respect for their perspectives and for who they are as individuals. Focusing on their experiences, including their wants and needs for the future, really helps me to develop goals with them in a collaborative, supportive way. I think my clients really appreciate my willingness to use an ethics-based approach that helps them to explore their own best interests and figure out ways to reach the goals they set for themselves.

As an intern, one of the beliefs I struggle with is feeling consistently confident in myself and in my ability to help clients. Although I generally hold a positive view of myself as an individual, I am still working on developing a strong identity as a helping professional. I know that this will come with time, but ethical decisions can be particularly hard to make as an intern because I have not yet fully developed confidence in my competence and ability to always make the most ethically sound decision. Fortunately, I have the support of my supervisors to help me work through the process of making these decisions at internship and I am grateful to be able to use this time to learn and grow as a helping professional.

At the justice center where I'm currently working, I encountered my first ethical situation while co-facilitating a group session with my supervisor. During break, one of the clients approached me and asked me to pass a private letter to his girlfriend who was incarcerated in another part of the jail. He told me it was really important and that he would be grateful if I could just help him out this one time. He also said that other counselors did this kind of stuff all the time and it wouldn't be a big deal. I really wasn't sure how to handle the situation, so I took the note and thought about it for the rest of that day's group session. On the one hand, I felt really uncomfortable and my gut instinct told me that something didn't seem right about the situation. On the other hand, however, I really wanted my new clients to trust me and like me, and my personal belief in giving people the benefit of the doubt put me in a position of wanting to believe this client had good intentions.

Fortunately, I remembered my faculty supervisor talking about the importance of using consultation and supervision, especially when faced with ethical dilemmas. As such, I took the note and talked to my internship supervisor immediately after the group session ended. We talked through what had happened and she introduced me to an ethical decision-making model that she's used in the past when faced with tough decisions. It was really helpful to me to have a guide for thinking ethically through each step of the decision I had to make, until ultimately I was able to identify and defend what choice would be in the best interest of my client—which was not to pass his letter on to his girlfriend. My supervisor processed with me how it felt to work through the steps of the model and my feelings about the conclusion I reached. She sat with me the following day when I met with the client individually and together we talked to him about the boundaries of my work. I think even though he didn't get what he wanted, my client developed respect that day for my ethical approach to my work. In this way, I ended up building trust and rapport with him, after all.

With regard to technology, I've only encountered one major ethical issue so far at the justice center. A coworker asked me to share my computer password with her so that if she needed to, she could access my private notes and compare them with her own when we shared clients. Again, I felt immediately uncomfortable and after the client incident that had taken place, I was quick to trust my gut. I consulted with my supervisor about my coworker's request and we talked about the ways in which sharing my password could cause major breaches of confidentiality for all of my clients. My clients' rights to confidentiality and privacy are of the utmost importance to me, so I ended up telling my coworker that I would be happy to compare notes with her as appropriate for individual clients but that I was ethically uncomfortable sharing my private password with her. She hadn't even thought of the problems that sharing passwords could cause and we were able to have a great discussion about ethics and keeping one another in check. I know that future ethical dilemmas may be a bit stickier than what I've encountered so far at the justice center, but I'm confident that sticking to my personal beliefs will help me to make thoughtful, ethical decisions as issues come up.

Written by Brittany Pollard, 2015. Used with permission.

Exercise 6.10 Confronting Ethical Issues: Writing Your Own Story, Entry 18

You just read about how Alicia, Lucas, and Tamika address ethical issues they encounter during their internship experience. Now it is your turn!

- Think about the ways you identify ethical challenges and issues. Describe your thoughts, emotions, and actions that alert you to the presence of them.
- In what ways are your personal beliefs integrated with how you identify ethical challenges and issues.
- Share what it was like to confront an ethical challenge or issue (be specific).
- Review Kenyon's Ethical Decision-Making Model. Discuss which aspect of the decision-making process best supports your decision-making process. Which aspect is least helpful or most difficult?

Faculty and Site Supervisor Dialogue: Dr. Bianca and Ms. Bellewa

In addition to hearing from Alicia, Lucas, and Tamika, we asked Dr. Bianca, a human service faculty member, and Ms. Bellewa, a human service site supervisor, to talk about their experiences and perspectives of identifying and participating in the ethical decision-making process, especially during internship.

Dr. Claude Bianca

It is hard for me to think about ethics and ethical practice without thinking of several roles that include helping professional and faculty member. Ethics also includes my role as a faculty supervisor. One of the most important things that I worry about for my interns is the ability to actually see that an ethical situation exists. If they cannot identity a situation as ethical, then they cannot use values, codes of ethics, and an ethical decision-making model to work through the issue. Suicide risk assessment is one issue that comes to mind. When we all come together in class to discuss what is happening with our work with clients, one of the first things that interns do is describe the client they are working with. I always ask the intern, "When you performed an information suicide risk assessment, what were your thoughts?" No matter how many times I ask, many of them indicate that the possibility of suicide risk never occurred to them. Most interns fear the thoughts about suicide, their proximity to the possibility, and their responsibility to this type of assessment.

Another issue many of my students have is seeing what they think of as unethical behavior with their supervisors. It comes as a surprise to them when they see confidentiality broken or supervisors working outside their area of competence. This presents quite a dilemma for them. They want their supervisors to be the "perfect" role models and students express disappointment when they see flaws too. I see my role as helping them process the supervisor's behavior, their own reactions to that behavior, and ideas about how to think through the issues presented. Sometimes reality in the human service professional work is different from what is presented in the textbooks they studied.

Finally, although we teach our students Kenyon's Ethical Decision-Making Model, I encourage my students to develop their own model. By the end of our internship class, they each present a variation of that model as one that they use most often. Allowing the flexibility of ethical decision making helps the interns create an intentional way of addressing ethical issues that works for them.

Ms. Zu Bellewa

Working at a site that encounters a wide array of cultural diversity is not only rewarding, but also requiring of numerous ethical measures to be in place. The interns at this site face unique struggles when working with some of our immigrant and refugee clients. At the core of the struggles are major cultural differences that at times overlap with ethical concerns in the United States.

One of the biggest struggles that I have seen come up frequently is a clash in worldviews between the agency's services and requirements and the client's. We have worked with many clients who have been exposed to war-related trauma and have resided in areas of conflict for years. While we as an agency recognize the mental health implications that this could mean for our clients, which can include depression, posttraumatic stress disorder, and anxiety, our clients may not want to address that or feel the need to focus on it. This could partly be because of the role mental health plays in their country of origin, which, many times, is muted and not as encouraged as it is here. The ethical dilemma that many of us face is this: Should we continue pursuing mental health needs and services if the client does not feel the need for it or value it? If their culture views mental health services as taboo and shameful, should we avoid discussing mental health needs at all? This clash in cultural values occurs on many different levels and is something that requires constant self-awareness and cultural awareness. My agency recognizes its ethical duty to not impose the Western norms and expectations on individuals who are not from here.

When discussing this with my interns, my role as a site supervisor is to encourage them to take the time and do the research on the cultural background of the individual they are working with. The reason for this encouragement is because it is crucial to understand the foundations and components of who the clients are. Many of the immigrants and refugees whom we work with come from a very collectivistic culture, one that is made of a social fabric that can be easily differentiated from a Western form of culture. I firmly believe that it is the ethical duty of every one of my interns to be proactive in gaining an awareness of that background during their work with their clients. There have been times where I recognized that an intern did not do the necessary research and it hindered her work because she struggled with understanding her client's worldview. Not only is it crucial that they gain awareness of their clients' cultural background, but it is also highly important that they gain awareness of their own cultural backgrounds as it may impact the work that they do.

I acknowledge the relationship that culture and ethics have and I'm very mindful of incorporating it into my supervisor relationship. While it is a difficult conversation to have, I try to ensure that my interns and I talk about possible ethical and cultural dilemmas at every supervision meeting. I feel like the more I encourage my interns to talk about it, the more comfortable they become in sharing their experiences and overcoming many of those ethical dilemmas.

Written by Dareen Basma, 2015. Used with permission.

The Professional Voice and Tips for Practice: Gwen

Gwen Ruttencutter provides us with ideas about ethical decision making and self-reflection.

Gwen

In this chapter, we have learned about ethical decision making and have gained a deeper understanding of its importance and its process, such as Kenyon's (1999) model. Ethical quandaries can arise regularly in life and can arise particularly frequently when we are working within a dynamic environment like the helping professions. As we read about and practiced with in Exercise 6.9 in Kenyon's model, evaluating our decisions after the fact is an essential step in the decision-making process. This type of reflection-on-action (Schön, 1983) helps practitioners develop deeper insights into and connections among motivations, actions, and outcomes.

In addition to using an ethical decision-making model for the quandaries that arise, daily reflection-on-action is another strategy practitioners employ. Practitioners who reflect regularly are constantly seeking to learn from their actions and to use what they have learned to inform their work going forward.

In an effort to foster regular reflection on ethical decision making, Thomas Shanks (n.d.) of the Markkula Center for Applied Ethics at Santa Clara University offers five daily reflective questions, How did I live today?

- *Did I practice any virtues (e.g., integrity, honesty, compassion)?*
- *Did I do more good than harm?*

o *Did I treat others with dignity and respect?*

o *Was I fair and just?*

o *Was my community better because I was in it? Was I better because I was in my community?*

As you continue on your internship, consider using these five daily reflective questions not only to foster your own reflection, but also to keep the ethical stance of your practice at the forefront of all you do.

Written by Gwen Ruttencutter, 2015. Used with permission.

Terms to Remember

Boundaries and limit setting

Competence

Confidentiality

Dual and multiple relationships

Informed consent

Suicide risk assessment

References

American Counseling Association. (2014). 2014 ACA code of ethics. Retrieved from http://www.counseling.org/docs/ethics/2014-aca-code-of-ethics.pdf?sfvrsn=4

American Foundation for Suicide Prevention. (2012). Facts and figures. Retrieved from https://www.afsp.org/understanding-suicide/facts-and-figures

Department of Counseling and Human Services, Syracuse University. (n.d.). Ethical decision making. Retrieved from http://soe.syr.edu/academic/counseling_and_human_services/modules/Preparing_for_Supervision/ethical_decision_making_model.aspx

Fredman, G., Anderson, E., & Stott, J. (2010). *Being with older people: A systemic approach.* London, UK: Karnac Books.

Gladding, S. T. (2004). *Counseling theories: Essential concepts and applications.* Boston, MA: Pearson.

Kenyon, P. (1999). *What would you do? An ethical case workbook for human service professionals.* Pacific Grove, CA: Brooks/Cole.

Kleepsies, P. M., Penk, W. E., & Forsyth, J. P. (1993). The stress of patient suicidal behavior during clinical training: Incidence, impact, and recovery. *Professional Psychology: Research and Practice, 24,* 293–303.

Knox, S., Burkard, A. W., Bentzler, J., Schaack, A., & Hess, S. A. (2006). Therapists-in-training who experience a client suicide: Implications for supervision. *Professional Psychology: Research and Practice, 37,* 547–557.

McAdams, C. R., & Foster, V. A. (2000). Client suicide: Its frequency and impact on counselors. *Journal of Mental Health Counseling, 22,* 107–121.

National Association of Social Workers. (2008). Code of ethics of National Association of Social Workers. Retrieved from https://www.socialworkers.org/pubs/code/code.asp

National Organization for Human Services. (2015). *Ethical standards for human service professionals.* Retrieved from http://www.nationalhumanservices.org/ethical-standards-for-hs-professionals

Remley, T. P., & Herlihy, H. P. (2015). *Ethical, legal, and professional issues in counseling* (4th ed.). Boston, MA: Pearson.

Shanks, T. (n.d.). Everyday ethics. Retrieve from: http://www.scu.edu/ethics/publications/iie/v8n1/everydayethics.html

Schön, D. A. (1983). *The reflective practitioner: How professionals think in action.* New York, NY: Basic Books.

Woodside, M., & McClam, T. (2015). *Introduction to human services* (8th ed.). Pacific Grove, CA: Brooks/Cole, Cengage Learning.

7

Developing a Multicultural Perspective in Internship

Reading this chapter will help you do the following:

- Define the concepts of multiculturalism, culture, cross-cultural experience, and culture-centered helping.
- Understand a multicultural perspective of helping.
- Describe the importance of assuming a multicultural perspective of helping.
- Articulate the ways that the National Organization for Human Services (NOHS) Ethical Standards for Human Service Professionals (2015) supports a multicultural perspective.
- Describe how power and oppression influence the helping process.
- Define culture from a focused and a more broad perspective.

- List several dimensions of your cultural identity.
- Represent your own personal view of one aspect of your culture.
- Investigate the types of clients your agency serves.
- Learn about several aspects of your client's environment using an ecological model.
- Become acquainted with some of the experiences of multicultural helping that Alicia, Lucas, and Tamika experience in internship.
- Learn about the faculty and site supervisors' perspectives related to multicultural helping.
- Describe the tips that Gwen provides that guide working with different cultures.

Chapter 7 is the third chapter in Part II, *Involving Yourself in Human Service Work*. We began our discussion of working in the human service system in Chapters 5 and 6 by focusing on the ethical aspects of human services and the ethical issues and challenges that are particularly relevant to the internship experience. This chapter, Chapter 7, focuses on developing a multicultural perspective that will guide your own work with clients. First, we review the concepts of multiculturalism, culture, **cross-cultural experience**, and culture-centered helping and describe a multicultural perspective of helping. We include a rationale for the importance of maintaining a cultural viewpoint and present the aspects of the NOHS Ethical Standards for Human Service Professionals (2015) that guide a human service professional's work. Second, we look at culture from a narrow and a more broad perspective and then examine the roots of power and oppression that influence the helping process.

Third, we suggest two **multicultural competencies** that are essential to effective work with clients: understanding your cultural self and learning about other cultures. We provide exercises that help you develop these competencies, especially as they relate to your internship placement and the clients your serve. Finally in this chapter's peer-to-peer, faculty, site supervisor, and human service professional dialogues, Alicia, Lucas, Tamika, Dr. Bianca, Ms. Bellewa, and Gwen share their own experiences related to developing their own multicultural perspectives of helping.

Box 7.1 describes the organizational framework of the next section of this chapter that introduces a multicultural approach to human service delivery.

Box 7.1 Studying the Text: An Introduction to a Multicultural Perspective

Studying the text: The following outline will help you read and study the text material in this next section.

An Introduction to a multicultural perspective

1. Definitions

2. Defining a multicultural perspective

a. History and rationale

b. Considering the whole person

c. Ethical dimensions of multicultural helping

d. The influence of power

An Introduction to a Multicultural Perspective

Two foundational tasks of helping clients are first, to understand them and second, to deliver services to them. Understanding clients and then providing services to them represents a significant challenge because of the inherent complexities of the task. Many of these complexities involve culture and its multiple dimensions. Using a cultural viewpoint or lens requires continual efforts by human service professionals to learn more about the cultural aspects of their own lives and the lives of their clients. In addition, specific components of the helping process, such as knowing the client, defining the client's challenges and problems, exploring possible interventions, choosing and implementing interventions, and evaluating outcomes of these various interventions are also influenced by culture. Hopefully, agency policies and procedures also reflect cultural perspectives of those providing the services and attend to aspects of the client's culture.

We assume that in past courses you have learned about the multicultural dimensions of helping. Therefore, we begin the discussion of the multicultural focus with a summary of the knowledge that guides this work. To do so, we provide information that will help you integrate multicultural considerations into your internship. After considering the definitions related to multicultural helping, we define the multicultural perspective, present information about its history, and provide a rationale for importance. We demonstrate how a multicultural approach to helping is linked to other key concepts in human services such as serving the whole person, the ethical approaches of helping and the influence of power and prejudice.

Definitions

Culture, multiculturalism, cross-cultural experience, and **culture-centered helping** are four terms that are essential to understanding the multicultural perspective. In this section and others that follow, we define and describe this concept in more detail so that you will comprehend how each relates to your work as an intern, and later, as a human service professional.

Culture

"The beliefs, customs, arts, etc., of a particular society, group, place, or time" is the definition of culture ("Culture," 2015). Helping always occurs within a context, and culture suggests specific aspects of that context. Interns who understand their own culture and the culture of their clients are more likely to develop empathy for and establish rapport with them.

Multicultural

Multicultural is defined as, "Of, relating to, reflecting, or adapting to many different cultures" ("Multicultural", 2015). During internship we believe that it is important to consider helping within the framework of culture. We add the term "multi" to the term "culture" because of the multidimensional influences that culture has on our lives and the lives of our clients.

Cross-Cultural

"Related to or involving two or more different cultures or countries" defines cross-cultural ("Cross-cultural," 2015). The basis for helping is interacting with clients and establishing meaningful relationships. Since each individual represents a unique set of cultural influences, a helper's communication and interaction with a client represents an exchange across at least two cultures.

Culture-Centered

Participating in an activity that uses the uniqueness of an individual's culture and diversity of experiences as a foundation for that activity defines culture-centered (Pacific Oaks College, 2014). The act of helping is grounded in an appreciation of who the client is as a member of a culture and a collaboration with the client that reflects the cultural aspects of his or her strengths and needs. Considering the client's culture at each stage in the helping process demonstrates respect for individual uniqueness. *Culture-centered* was a term coined by Dutta (2007) who, as an expert in communication practices in health care organizations, posits that minority or disenfranchised populations often cannot access the health care system on their own cultural terms. We discuss culture-centered helping in depth in Chapter 9.

Exercise 7.1 Multicultural Terms and Your Internship

Step 1

As you begin to think about your internship in terms of multicultural helping, we think it is important to record some of your first thoughts and considerations. For each of the terms listed, briefly write about how you believe each relates to your internship experience.

Culture

_____

_____

_____

Multiculturalism

_____

_____

_____

Cross-cultural experience

_____

_____

_____

Culture-centered helping

_____

_____

_____

Defining a Multicultural Perspective

A multicultural perspective in human services represents a particular way in which helpers view themselves and their clients. Our focus on developing a multicultural perspective is rooted in two beliefs: one, that every helping event is multicultural and two, that helpers should deliver culture-sensitive services to their clients. The multicultural perspective emphasizes the importance of culture, a diversity of cultures, and a respect for that diversity. Many organizations and scholars provide a range of insights about multiculturalism. For example, the American Psychological Association (2002b) says, "Multiculturalism, in an absolute sense, recognizes the broad scope of dimensions of race, ethnicity, language, sexual orientation, gender, age, disability, class status, education, religious/spiritual orientation, and other cultural dimensions. All of these are critical aspects of an individual's ethnic/racial and personal identity." Wong (2013) described multicultural perspectives as a political force and as essential in achieving a greater understanding of those we intend to help. Embedded in a multicultural perspective is a recognition of the rights of minority cultures which may involve basic challenges to majority cultures.

We believe that assuming a multicultural perspective is essential to the delivery of human services. However, viewing helping as a cross-cultural experience is a relatively new idea in the helping professions.

Background and Rationale

In the early 1990s, Paul Pederson described multicultural helping as a fourth force of understanding and helping others. He believed that culture was a common and important dimension of human behavior, whether one defined that behavior in terms of any of the other three forces—the psychodynamic, humanistic, or behavioral perspectives (Pederson, 1998). In fact, he claimed that any work that occurs during the helping process, including relationship building, assessment, planning, intervention, and evaluation, reflects and interacts within a cultural context.

This focus on the cultural dimensions of helping is relevant for and related to the increasing diversity in the U.S. population today. The U.S. Census

Bureau (2011) speculates by 2043 no **majority population** will exist in the United States. In fact, the U.S. Census Bureau also projects that by 2019, there will be no majority population of children under 18. Another area of increasing diversity relates to the growth of the aging population, which will also continue to increase; the U.S. Census Bureau projects 20% of the population will be 65 or older by 2050. In addition, **foreign-born** populations (including illegal immigrants) in the United States, coming predominantly from Mexico, represent another aspect of increasing diversity within the United States. Larger numbers of foreign-born persons also come from China, India, the Philippines, Vietnam, and El Salvador (Associated Press, 2013; Center for American Progress, 2014).

An additional aspect of the growing diversity is reflected in an increase in the number of multiracial individuals living in the United States (Stone, 2012; Wang, 2012). Specifically, according to the U.S. 2010 census reports, individuals who identified themselves as two or more races increased by 32% (U.S. Census Bureau, 2012). In the United States there is also an increase in the ability to speak more than one language with the highest percentage of multilingual individuals speaking Spanish and English. There are more than 350 languages and dialects spoken in the United States (McGabe et al., 2013; Stewart, 2014).

Finally, the provision of services through technology will continue to increase the ability to serve diverse populations, erasing local and global boundaries. Specifically, technology provides us knowledge of and, at times, the ability to provide help to individuals in need who either have limited access to transportation to a local site or live a considerable distance from the sources of various services. For example, at a local level, in New York City, human service professionals developed an online system to help women experiencing domestic violence to file an order of protection (NPower, n. d.). In this instance, technology promoted advocacy to help women, across diverse populations, by supporting their use of the judicial system.

Considering the Whole Person

Ideally, human service professionals assume a viewpoint that acknowledges and respects the commonalities and uniqueness of ethnicities and cultures. This perspective reinforces the idea of knowing clients holistically and recognizes the multidimensionality of individuals. Early scholars in human services provided an initial definition of the whole person which included the social, psychological, medical, financial, educational, vocational, and spiritual aspects of individuals. The intention was to develop an expanded view of clients (Eriksen, 1981; Neukrug, 2012; Woodside & McClam, 2015). Today in the human service profession, this initial definition of the whole person has been extended to include the cultural dimensions of the client's identity and environment.

The importance of multicultural helping is also one aspect of the NOHS Ethical Standards for Human Service Professionals (2015). Standards address the following: (a) understanding values and biases and their influences upon clients; (b) providing services to all populations in need; (c) gaining knowledge of cultures of clients and respecting these cultures; (d) understanding how social issues influence clients from various cultures; (e) recognizing the influence of oppression and advocating for social justice; (f) developing multicultural competencies regarding work with clients and communities; (g) using research approaches that recognize and eliminate cultural bias, when possible; and (h) seeking awareness of the influence of one's own cultural background on human service delivery.

The Influence of Power

As indicated in the NOHS Ethical Standards for Human Service Professionals (2015), one motivation for the human service profession's recognition of the importance of multicultural sensitivity reflects the consequences of power expressed by those in the dominant culture who, wittingly or unwittingly, denigrate and even oppress individuals of the less dominant culture, sometimes with devastating effects. Many scholars believe that **oppression** comes from a basic human tendency to form in-group and out-group associations. Individuals self-identifying as *in*, tend to see others as *out* or less worthy (Brammer, 2011). Moreover, the *in* dominant groups or associations assume power and privilege for themselves and discriminate against *out* nondominant groups. **Discrimination** means controlling nondominant groups' access to or participation in economic, educational, or cultural opportunities (Ancis & Chang, 2008). Not only are members of the nondominant group viewed as less worthy and less able, but as a result of this judgment by others, they see themselves as having less value (Hayes, Montes, & Schroeder, 2013).

Internalizing the viewpoint of others is called the **self-fulfilling prophecy** (Jones, Dovidio, & Vietze, 2014). When individuals in a minority culture accept the stereotypes of the majority group about their culture or race, **internalized oppression** results. One example is an individual who changed their physical characteristics (characterized by their race or ethnicity) because they believe they are ugly. For example, on the campus of a Predominantly White Institution (PWI), African American women talked about one of the keys to success is "acting like those perky white girls" (Hannon, Woodside, Pollard, & Roman, in press).

Forming prejudicial notions that result in stereotypes arises from the human need to process information efficiently (Jones et al., 2014). The results can be devastating for some groups. **Prejudice** is understood as a "preconceived opinion not based upon reason or actual experience . . . against a race, sex, or other class of people" ("Prejudice," 2014). Individuals form **stereotype**s of groups by race, ethnicity, gender, age, and other characteristics. We then judge individuals by our stereotypical assumptions. Members of the dominant culture use **macroagressions** and **microaggressions** to express their power by means of prejudicial attitudes and treatment of individuals in nondominant cultures (Sue et al., 2007).

Macroaggressions are so named *macro* because they represent the discriminatory actions or attitudes when they occur on a large scale. This means aggressions that, either visible or invisible, reflect discrimination toward minority populations. Assumptions of criminal intent of young African American men and subsequent reactions by Whites (e.g., fear, aggressive response) provide just one example. A second example occurs within the business sector, where there is an unwillingness to hire immigrants (Sue et al., 2007).

Microaggressions are distinguished from macroaggressions because they occur at the individual level. According to Sue et al. (2007), instances of microaggression manifest themselves in "brief and commonplace daily verbal, behavioral, or environmental indignities, whether intentional or unintentional, that communicate hostile, derogatory, or negative racial slights and insults toward people of color" (p. 271). Many of these occurrences happen because White individuals do not understand how deeply ingrained their biases and prejudices toward People of Color are. Sue et al. (2007) described "microaggressions in everyday life" (p. 271) as a way to heighten our awareness of the ubiquitous nature of these behaviors. Microagressions can be expressed in a variety of ways. For example individuals may use verbal or behavioral action to assault an individual by referring to an individual of another race or culture using derogatory language or ignoring the other's physical presence. Individuals of the majority race or culture also may invalidate another by discounting bias. For example, a White male may exclaim to a Black female, "I don't see you as either Black or female. I just see you as another person I work with." White individuals often tell individuals of another race or culture, "I am an X [mother, father, teacher, student] too. I know exactly how you feel."

An awareness of how power and oppression influences the helping process is important to consider. Approaching the helping process from a multicultural perspective will help you increase this awareness. Using this approach, you as a human service intern will better recognize and respect each individual client's worth and dignity. Furthermore, assuming a multicultural approach assists each of us to uncover, confront, and hopefully, counter the prejudices and stereotypes that may undermine the help we are trying to provide.

In the next section, we introduce two multicultural competencies that will support your personal and professional growth and development while in internship as shown in Box 7.2.

Box 7.2 Studying the Text: Developing Multicultural Competence

Studying the text: The following outline will help you read and study the text material in this next section.

Developing multicultural competence

1. Multicultural competency: Understanding your cultural self

2. Multicultural competency: Exploring new cultures

Developing Multicultural Competence

If you as a human service intern would like to provide help that is sensitive to multicultural considerations, there are several **multicultural competencies** you may want to develop and practice. These competencies focus on (a) increasing your awareness of your own cultural self, (b) learning about new cultures, and (c) using culture-centered interventions when you work with clients. In this section, we help you develop the first two competencies. First, we summarize the concept of culture and suggest ways that you might explore your own culture. Internship provides you an opportunity to view your own culture vis-à-vis the cultures of your faculty and site supervisors, your coworkers, and your clients. Second, we suggest guidelines you can use to explore cultures that are new to you. These include learning about history, cultural identity, differences among the group members, the nature of families, socioeconomic characteristics, educational trends, worldview, spirituality and religious perspectives, health (physical and mental), and the need for advocacy. Third, in Chapter 9, we introduce ways to help in a culture-centered way during the helping process. This includes ways you provide culture-centered helping to the individual client throughout the helping process. It also includes ways you can assess the culture-centered features of your agency and learn aspects of service delivery that help organizations respond to clients and client groups in a culture-centered way.

Before we introduce the first two multicultural competencies, here in Box 7.3 are student comments about their multicultural experiences in their internship.

Box 7.3 Students Reflect Multicultural Experiences During Internship

Steve: I try to monitor my first impressions. Like yesterday, I was at the Department of Human Services and a mother with her 11-year-old son walked in. I was taking families without appointments. The mother was upset; the boy was sullen. It was hard to get past the first read of the family. I thought *poor* and *uneducated* and *Black*.

Maria: I am White and from a rural area. Yet here I am working in an urban area. I feel that I don't belong. I want to say to my clients, "I know how you feel about being a minority, I feel that way right now." I also know that I don't know how they feel at all. I try to remember when I am so nervous and shy, that I come from privilege.

Al: I work with immigrants. I try not to make too many assumptions and just listen to them talk about their lives—where they came from and what life is like for them now. They are not all the same. I do have trouble understanding some of them. I have not yet used an interpreter. Maybe I should.

Shasha: We have children from 20 different countries in my child-centered day care. Sometimes the language barriers get in the way of communication. We also have a difficult time feeding everyone. Like no one eats the same breakfast in their country of origin. What we feed them just doesn't look like a morning meal.

Multicultural Competency: Understanding Your Cultural Self

To understand multicultural dimensions of helping, first, it is important for you to understand your own cultural self. We will not explore this issue in detail, but present a focused definition of culture and an exercise that helps you explore your own culture.

A Focused Definition of Culture

A focused definition of culture includes considerations of "race, ethnicity, and/or nationality" (Mio, Barker-Hackett, & Turnambing, 2011). But even these cultural considerations are in flux. Today race and ethnicity are no longer clear categories. Rather, both race and ethnicity are now considered to be multifaceted. Scholars suggest the use of the term *race* is no longer sufficient to capture the multifaceted racial and ethnic backgrounds in our society (Brammer, 2011; Patten, 2015). Historically, race was used to describe physical characteristics of individuals (Lott, 2010). But today the term race is used as a political term and represents an indicator of the inferior status of a minority group. Although race does not capture today's cultural reality, racism as a bias against a particular group of individuals continues to exist (Lott, 2010).

As an example of the complexities of dealing with the concept of race, you can explore how your own campus identifies and provides services to biracial and multiracial students (Literte, 2010). Campus responses include special services for biracial students and care with which students are labeled. In fact, as individuals in the United States and globally are revising their racial and ethnic identities, it is important to avoid labeling. Rather, a new way of talking about race and ethnicity is through self-identification.

In an attempt to capture a view of race and ethnicity and its realities of individuals living in the United States, in 1997 the White House Office of Management and Budget (OMB) developed a new method of **designating race/ethnicity status** (U.S. Census Bureau, 2011). The goal of the OMB was to provide flexibility in the way in which individuals could describe the racial and ethnic groups to which they claimed membership. The categorization reflects a two-step process. First, individuals indicate their ethnicity as Hispanic or Latino *or* non-Hispanic or non-Latino. By definition, Hispanic or Latino may refer to the "heritage, nationality group, lineage, or country of birth of the person or the person's parents, or ancestors before their arrival in the United States" (U.S. Census Bureau, 2011). Those identifying themselves as such may be any race.

Second, individuals could identify their race by marking multiple categories, thus recognizing the complexities of racial identity. The racial categories included American Indian or Alaskan Native, Asian, Black or African American, Native Hawaiian or Other Pacific Islander, White, or Some Other Race. In addition, there is a broader view of culture that includes more than race, ethnicity, or nationality. For instance, culture broadly conceived, may include linguistic expressions, history, beliefs, race, religion, families, and even hobbies. Aspects of culture may also include arts, music, dance, food, clothing, and other expressions or traditions (Mio et al., 2011 Barker-Hackett & Turnambing, 2009).

The **place of the family** within the culture helps illustrate the unique expressions of this specific human universal. In fact, what family includes varies within populations living in the United States. In Table 7.1, we look at the notion of family for Arab American, Latina/o, European American, and European American Appalachian cultures.

Table 7.1   The Place of Family

Arab American Culture	Latina/o	European American	European American Appalachian
Arab American culture, defined as those individuals who describe their heritage from the Arab Middle East (Lee, 2013), reflects a patriarchal society and views the family as central to its culture. Within this population, family is more important than other relationships such as friends or peer groups. The importance of family reflects a sense of belonging and living together in homes or neighborhoods. Within both Arab American and Latina/o cultures, there exists an expectation that group values and traditions are important; hence individuals should follow them.	The place of family within the Latina/o culture reflects both similarities and differences from the Arab American culture. Within a Latina/o culture the family is also central and includes nuclear and extended family (Hipolito-Delgado & Diaz, 2013). Different from the Arab American culture, the Latina/o culture includes a concept of fictive kin. The term reflects an expanded view of family to include godparents and especially valued friends of the family. Within both Arab American and Latina/o cultures, there exists an expectation that group values and traditions are important; hence individuals should follow them.	The European American notion of family differs from the Arab American and Latina/o cultures, in part, because of the influence of or importance of the individual. For this group, the family provides the basic needs and care for young children and adolescents; the goal is to raise independent and self-sufficient young adults (Lee, 2013). Early in the preteen and teen years, peers and close friends become paramount in their influence. And often, non-familial mentors, such as spiritual leaders, teachers, and coaches become important influences (Arnett, 2013). But even within the European American notion of the place of family, cultures differ. At times these are regional differences (e.g., the urban northeast, the rural Midwest, the Appalachian mountains, the west, and the northwest).	Within the Appalachian culture, "cultural area along the Appalachian Mountains in the eastern United States," (Russ, 2010, p. 1), the importance of family reflects less influence on the individual. Values center on the family and the community. As a result, individuals are less likely to strive for independence, seek awards and marks of achievement, and compete with others. Rather individuals focus on how they can contribute to the good of the community and the good of their family (Wagner, 2005).

You and Your Culture: Describing Your Multiple Cultural Identities

We stress throughout this text self-awareness as a critical part of becoming a professional helper. Engaging in the process of understanding your own culture represents one aspect of this self-awareness. We prefer to think of gaining self-awareness as an ongoing, lifelong, developmental process instead of a task. Rather than a one- or two-step exercise that you can complete in an afternoon, a week, or a semester, professional helpers continually examine, throughout their lives, thoughts and beliefs about their own culture and how it influences their work with clients. An illustration of the multiple aspects of you related to your culture is represented in Figure 7.1. Note that "who you are" is at the center of this representation. You can add as many circles as you would like to describe aspects that help define you and your culture.

Figure 7.1 Who Am I? Multiple Cultural Identities

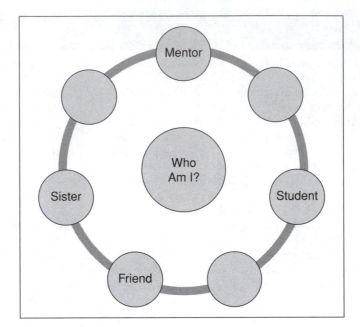

With this long-term process in mind, we suggest two interesting and different ways to approach the process of thinking about one's own culture and **multiple cultural identities**. The first is an exploratory naming of your culture and describing its many aspects. This is an exercise you may have completed in an earlier class. We include Exercise 7.2 because it allows you to think about the many aspects of culture that reflect who you are at the present time.

Exercise 7.2 Describing Your Multiple Cultural Identity: Writing Your Own Story, Entry 19

One way to begin to think about how culture shapes who you are is to think about the many dimensions of your identity as reflected by the groups or associations to which you belong. These dimensions may include those related to groups or associations such as race, ethnicity, and gender that we introduced earlier. You may want to expand into areas such as spiritual orientation, sexual orientation, or a person with a disability. The areas may also include other groups or associations that reflect socioeconomic status, educational background, country of origin, region of the country, urban or rural background, or others. Identities may also encompass the roles you assume (past or present) such as mother, father, child, sibling, place in family (e.g., birth order), student, employee, professional or others.

Step 1

a. Write about all of the groups, associations, or roles that you think are important in describing you or that others might think are important in describing you.

b. Choose five of these groups, associations, or roles from the list you generated. Describe some of the customs, beliefs, language, dress, habits, behavior, rituals, beliefs, and social rules that exist for each of these five groups, associations, or roles.

    c. Highlight three that you consider most influential or important in your work as an intern. Provide at least one example of the way in which each of the three expresses its influence or importance.

Step 2

You can return to this exercise as often as you wish. There will be times when you revise the list of groups, associations, and roles that describe you. As we stated earlier, self-reflection as it relates to culture is a lifelong process. A deeper understanding of self is a first step in understanding helping from a multicultural perspective.

Step 3

Sue, the intern working in the homeless shelter in Oklahoma, wrote about her family and then about its possible influence on her as an intern. Sue's description provides you with one example of how to explore your own culture and its relationship to internship work.

My Family

My family is a close knit one. There is my big sister, my little brother, and my mom and dad. Well, my mom is not really my mom. My real mom left us when my sister was seven, I was three, and my brother was one. My dad got remarried the same year my mom left. What I remember is when my dad remarried, we began to do everything together as a family. Other families I knew didn't do that. We had dinner every night at 6 pm and had breakfast together before we went to school. We all went to the same school and we walked to school. My new mom walked us to school, and then she walked my brother to day care, and then she walked to work. She walked home and picked up my brother, and then she walked home with my sister and me. On Sundays, we went to the temple together. We were the envy of many of our friends because everyone saw our family as perfect. They forgot that my mom actually left our family. Today, my sister and my mom are also two of my closest friends. And we all take care of my brother, even though now he is big enough to take care of himself.

My Family's Influence on Internship Work

I thought about my meeting with my three clients last week. None of these clients had any family support or not much support. I felt so sorry for them. I was depressed over the weekend because I realized what they are missing. I also don't know how I just lucked into a terrific family. I want all of my clients to be in a great family where everyone does things together. And this morning I met with a client who has family support. His mom supports him but she does not like him and she does not want him to live with her. How can a mother be like that!

    Now that you have considered your own culture and its influence on your internship work, let's turn to how you learn about the culture of your clients.

Multicultural Competency: Learning About Other Cultures

The second approach to increasing your multicultural competence is to begin to learn about other cultures, and in doing so, develop ways to understand the distinctive ways cultures influence clients. We suggest two ways you can prepare for learning about other cultures. One approach focuses on understanding the cultures of the clients your agency serves. The second is to learn about specific aspects of a particular client's culture which will help you understand the client and the groups or associations she or he belongs to. Both approaches provide a foundation for developing an understanding of culture-centered helping.

The Clients Your Agency Serves

It is difficult to prepare for all of the cultural groups and associations you will encounter during your internship and later employment. That said, a good place to begin is to learn about the specific client groups with whom you will be working. We recommend three ways to approach this information gathering: Talk with your site supervisor, review agency reports, and learn about the environment in which the clients live.

Talk With Your Site Supervisor

Site supervisors can provide a wealth of information about the nature of clients served by the agency. Indicate to your supervisor your interest in learning about the cultural aspects of the clients with whom you will be working. Questions or prompts for your supervisor might be

- Describe a profile of a client the agency typically serves.
- Describe three or four occasions when you were surprised by clients and/or their unique needs.
- Tell me about clients who were unlike any others you have encountered.

Each of these questions will help you understand the range of clients with which your site supervisor works and which your agency serves.

Reviewing Agency Reports

A second way to learn about the demographics of the populations your agency serves is to review current reports and documents that describe the agency's work. Many of these reports will include details about the clients served and provide an account of characteristics such as ethnicity, race, gender, age, veteran status, disabilities, and more. Other information might include socioeconomic status, educational level, and family status. Exercise 7.3 helps you organize the information you learn from the written reports about the clients. This knowledge will help you better understand the client population. You may have already reviewed some of the reports on the agency web site to prepare for your initial interview or during your agency orientation. This second review is more focused on identifying the culture or groups and associations of the client population.

Exercise 7.3 Clients Your Agency Serves

Step 1

In this exercise you will identify knowledgeable individuals (such as site supervisor, the agency director, and other coworkers) and ask them the following questions about the agency's clients.

Describe a profile of a client the agency typically serves.

_____

_____

_____

Describe three or four occasions when you were surprised by clients and/or their unique needs.

_____

_____

_____

Tell me about clients who were unlike any others you have encountered.

_____

_____

_____

Step 2

Locate one or two agency reports written in the last year that include demographics about the clients served by the agency. This information provides you a more detailed picture of agency work. Make notes on the client data available. In this exercise, we leave room for additional information you may discover in the document(s) you reviewed.

General description of the client population

_____

_____

_____

Specific characteristics (note numbers and percentages)

Ethnicity_____

Race_____

Gender_____

Age_____

Disabilities_____

Veteran status_____

Education_____

Socioeconomic status_____

Family status_____

Other_____

Other_____

Other_____

Understanding Your Client's Environment

Another way to expand your knowledge about the culture of your clients is to begin to learn about and understand the environment in which they live (Berg, 2009). Although this is not an easy task, this type of knowledge provides you with insights about clients, their daily lives, the strengths, and the barriers that exist for them in their environment. You will also begin to understand how that environment helps define, reinforce, and sometimes challenge your clients' cultural identities.

Making Models Work for You: Understanding Your Client's Environment

We use an **ecological perspective** that helps us clarify the type of information we need to better understand the world and culture in which our clients live. This perspective will help us integrate the salient aspects of several ecological models to describe the environmental features that influence clients' lives in Figure 7.2 (Brofenbrenner, 1979; Hays, cited in Shallcross, 2013; McAuliffe & Eriksen, 1999; Woodside & McClam, 2015).

In the model presented in Figure 7.2, generally speaking, the closer the aspects of the client's environment are to the inside of the circle, the more powerful the influence on the individual. For instance, most of the time an individual's most powerful influence is the family. Yet in other instances, neighborhood and friends might also have a major influence in the life of a youth whose membership begins in a gang. For some children and youth, especially in Native American cultures, grandparents may extend their role outside the traditional family role and assume the role of cultural conservator (Weibel-Orlando, 2009). Grandparents assuming this role become the primary teachers of culture, traditions, and beliefs of their ethnic group. This role as cultural mentor can involve family, neighborhood and friends, social institutions, the arts, and the wider community.

Figure 7.2   Aspects of the Client's Cultural Environment

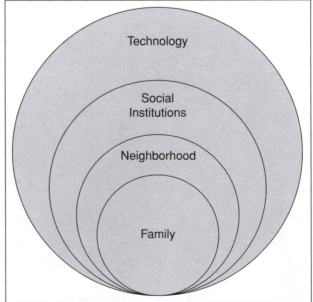

Source: Created by Gwen Ruttencutter, 2015. Used with permission.

We suggest there are at least eight important aspects of influences: (a) family, (b) neighborhood and friends, (c) social institutions (e.g., schools, religious institutions, social organizations, and sports), (d) technology and the arts (e.g., music, art, and social media), (e) the local community, (f) the regional community, (g) the national community, and (h) the global community. Although we present these aspects within concentric circles, we acknowledge the power of each influence varies according to the individual and the setting. We describe each of these salient aspects of influence briefly.

Family influences—At the heart of the individual's early living conditions is the family. These are the influences that children experience on a day-to-day basis. The family takes many forms and can include two parents, a single parent, grandparents, blended families, and families that include extended members (aunts, uncles, and cousins), fictive kin (friends with family influence), and others. But families are not always stable and are never simple.

Neighborhood and friends—The neighborhood represents an influence beyond the family: It often establishes behavioral role models and positive and negative support. Positive support includes stability and support within a safe environment. A strong sense of the *neighborhood as family* and public gathering places illustrates such a positive environment. Neighborhood adults also help transmit traditions and values including the importance of education, the meaning of work, and opportunities for leisure and recreation. The values and activities of child and youth peer groups are also important. A more negative environment provides less sense of the neighborhood cohesion, less support for education or for work, and in some instance, less safety.

Social institutions (e.g., schools, religious institutions, social organizations, and sports)—These are institutions that serve clients, and they may or may not be neighborhood based. If clients served by your agency are located in the same neighborhood or segment of the city or town, it will be easier for you to learn about the social institutions important to them. But if your agency services clients from a wide geographic area, in-depth knowledge of these institutions may be difficult.

Technology and the arts (e.g., music, art, and social media)—The influence of technology and the arts is a unique feature of this ecological model. We believe that technology and art are present throughout today's culture. For example, the use of technology continues to increase and is continually changing. Art, a human universal introduced earlier in this chapter, transmits culture and values, fosters self-awareness and creativity, develops positive self-identity, encourages wellness, and reduction of stress.

Geographical communities—Each of the communities listed below represents a spatial community that begins within a smaller geographic area and extends globally. Common to each and all are (a) location, (b) common experiences, (c) use of common resources, (d) social interactions, and (e) dependence and interdependence. For each of these communities, we suggest ways they might influence the client.

The local community is distinguished from a neighborhood in spatial terms, such as size and proximity. A local community is closely related to a town, small city, or designated area within a larger city or county. This is the area in which the client lives, uses its resources, and participates in its social institutions.

The regional community is more inclusive than a local community but is still smaller than a country. While countries may have their traditions and laws, there also exist regional differences within them. Regional differences develop from a variety of factors: different histories, traditions and values, economic practices, geographical features, and educational institutions (Hays, cited in Shallcross, 2013). Many times rivalries and/or bias develop within regions. Examples include designations such as urban or rural, north or south, and rich or poor.

The national community represents a country with traditions, rules, and laws that governs its citizens and those living in its geographical area. Countries influence an individual's worldview. Customs of a country represent specific traditions, written or unwritten, that influence how individuals think and behave (Hays, cited in Shallcross, 2013). For example, the U.S. Bill of Rights guides the country's laws and many of our traditions. In contrast, the Basic Law of Governance in Saudi Arabia reflects written tradition, rules, and laws of that country.

The global community and its influences continue to increase as the world becomes more interconnected. We are becoming more economically dependent and interdependent. Also occurring is the increase in diversity in many countries and the spreading of Western culture across the globe. In addition, with worldwide immigration, there exists a reciprocity of cultural exchange between native citizens and the foreign-born immigrants.

You can use Exercise 7.4 to help you use this ecological model presented in Figure 7.2 to learn more about the culture(s) of your client(s). For each client, you will discover one or more aspects of the culture that appear to exert a major influence.

Exercise 7.4 Making Models Work for You: Learning About Aspects of Your Client's Environment

This exercise will help you better understand the clients that you serve using the ecological model described above.

Step 1

Choose one of the following: (a) a client with whom you work currently, (b) a client population that lives in a specific area of your city, or (c) a client you hope to work with before you complete your internship.

Step 2

Describe the eight aspects of influence for the client or client population you choose. In this initial data gathering, you may not be able to describe each of the aspects. For example, if you choose a population rather than a specific client, you will not be able to provide information about the family. But you may be able to identify information about the neighborhood, though less about specific friends.

Family

_____

_____

Neighborhood and friends

_____

_____

Social institutions (e.g., schools, religious institutions, social organizations, and sports)

_____

_____

Technology and the arts (e.g., music, art, and social media)

_____

_____

Local community

_____

_____

Regional community

_____

_____

National community

_____

_____

Global community

_____

_____

Step 3

Review the information you gathered with your site supervisor. Talking with your supervisor may provide you with additional insights about clients. And don't be surprised if your supervisor informs you that she or he learned some things from you too!

In this final section of Chapter 7, peers, supervisors, and a human service professional share their experiences of internship and their work with clients from a multicultural perspective as presented in Box 7.4.

Box 7.4 Deepening Your Understanding

1. Peer-to-peer dialogue

    a. Alicia: Assuming a multicultural perspective

    b. Lucas: Assuming a multicultural perspective

    c. Tamika: Assuming a multicultural perspective

2. Faculty and site supervisor dialogue

    a. Dr. Bianca: Helping students with assuming a multicultural perspective

    b. Ms. Bellewa: Our work is multicultural

3. The professional voice and tips for practice: Gwen: How to expand your multicultural awareness

4. Terms to remember

5. References

Deepening Your Understanding

Alicia, Lucas, and Tamika share their experience of internship and are assuming a multicultural perspective is influencing their work. You can use their own experiences to help you better understand your own. Dr. Bianca, Ms. Bellewa, and Gwen provide faculty, site supervisor, and professional perspectives about the importance of understanding your culture and your clients' cultures.

Peer-to-Peer Dialogue: Alicia, Lucas, and Tamika

We asked Alicia, Lucas, and Tamika to share their multicultural experience in their internship programs.

Alicia

Hello all. I hope your experience in Human Services is going well. I am happy to tell you about my experience preparing for and working with individuals from diverse backgrounds. In my academic training in Human Services, I learned the definition and meaning of the word culture. In my mind, culture is automatically the obvious differences, like nationality, ethnicity, and race. I never considered that culture would mean much more than just that. In my mind, race was very clear and easy to process. This was, primarily, due to my experience growing up in a region that lacked cultural diversity.

In my training, I observed a variety of cultures present in one location. I also began seeing aspects of my own culture that I had previously accepted as normal. This awareness was heightened at my internship site and in the discussions I had in my Human Services courses. As we read the chapter about multicultural counseling, I recognized that not only did different cultures exist, but also that every individual stepped into a room with their own personal culture. One of the hardest things I had to come to terms with was related to power and privilege. What I mean by this, is regardless of my personal hardships and the struggle of my journey, I still maintained a position of power and privilege just by being Caucasian. I have to admit—that was a hard pill to swallow. I denied it at first, telling myself that just because I was White didn't mean that I had it easy. I was a teenage single mother— there's nothing easy about that! The more I learned, the more focused my observations were and the more I felt myself become aware of the reality of what it means to be White. It means being a part of the dominant culture.

When I started my internship at the Department of Human Services, I immediately noticed that the population we served generally came from lower socioeconomic backgrounds. That's where the cultural similarities ended. We served clients from a wide array of racial and ethnic backgrounds, differing religions as well as family traditions and values. Working with DHS was at times a struggle because I sensed that many of the counselors and case managers had a hard time working with our clients. This struggle manifested itself in their cynical attitude towards clients. And I thought sometimes my peers were culturally insensitive. For example, many times, I heard comments like "those people will never get their kids back" when referring to some African American families, who had kids in foster care and struggled to maintain DHS requirements to get them back. Other times I would hear comments like "they just don't understand how America works" when Latino families were struggling to adjusting to this country. I didn't know how to process those comments at first and chalked it up to burnout. I thought to myself, "These professionals have been working in the field for years, and we all know this is not an easy field to be in." In our classes we were warned that the work can be emotionally draining.

It wasn't until I mentioned these signs of burnout in my multicultural counseling course that I was able to recognize what their comments meant—at least from a multicultural perspective. On one end, it was a form of prejudice and microaggression. On the other end, it was a manifestation of burnout. The combination of the two resulted in the lack of insight and awareness about culture. The statements were insensitive. Hearing professionals make those types of comments scares me. I worry that I too will one day reach a state of burnout that would make me so insensitive. When discussing my fears with my supervisor, she gave me some ideas about how to try to avoid this type of insensitivity. She suggested that I first needed to recognize I have biases and prejudices. And she asked me to be continually aware of these. My supervisor told me that I needed to be aware of who/ what I can and cannot work with. Taking the required classes for my major has really helped me understand and process many of the issues that I've never quite considered before. I know now that there is a lifetime worth of work to do in order to become a culturally competent individual and that cultural awareness does not happen overnight.

Written by Allie Rhinehart and Dareen Basma, 2015. Used with permission.

Lucas

Hello this is Lucas again, and I hope you are having a great day! I am really excited to share some of my current experiences related to multiculturalism in my work at internship. To be honest, before I started internship, I did not focus on race/culture in the helping process. To me, my main concerns were working with clients to identify current problems, making sure I am applying counseling skills, and ultimately, help my clients live better lives. However, what I did not realize is how different I am, from a race/culture perspective, from my clients. For example, right now I am currently interning at the Tampa Bay Justice Center working with victims of domestic violence. With my work at internship, the majority of my clients are minority women that live in a low SES environment. I have an understanding of my clients and their cultural background; however, I remember one day at internship I realized I neglected knowing about a specific cultural group.

I am going to use a pseudonym to preserve confidentiality for my client. Last month in internship, my supervisor wanted me to work with a client named Adrienne. My supervisor provided me with current issues and symptoms of Adrienne before I met her. With the information, I had a perception of Adrienne because of my previous clients. My perception of Adrienne was a heterosexual female who lives in a low SES environment. Nevertheless, when I entered the office, I was shocked when I saw Adrienne. All I can say is that my perception was completely wrong. Adrienne was not a female, but a male, who lives in an upper class rural environment, and self-identifies as gay. My whole perception of Adrienne changed after the intake, and my anxiety levels were extremely high. The reason why I started to feel anxious was the lack of knowledge I knew about the LGBT community, males who are victims of domestic violence, and working with upper class individuals. From this experience, it was the first time I ever considered multiculturalism in counseling.

After my session with Adrienne, I met with my supervisor to talk about the session. At the Tampa Bay Justice Center, I am very blessed to work at an agency that is nonjudgmental and appreciates you as an individual. With the comfort and safety to be genuine, my supervisor makes it easy for me to express myself and share my concerns. During supervision, I told my supervisor what I observed during the session, and explained to her how uncomfortable I am working with Adrienne, due to my lack of knowledge regarding members of the LGBT community and upper class. I was afraid what my supervisor would say, but she was supportive, and encouraged me to become culture-centered. In our session, she had me first reflect on my race and culture, and how my cultural factors influence the counseling relationship. My supervisor helped me identify my prejudices, biases, and assumptions of people who self-identify as gay and upper class individuals. I felt awkward saying my prejudices of Adrienne, but my supervisor said that by addressing these issues during supervision, this would help me avoid these issues during sessions. Afterwards, she recommended to me to join an LGBT community group to learn more about this community, due to my lack of knowledge and information. By applying these methods to help Adrienne, I realized I am more empathetic of his situation and have a better understanding of his experiences. More important, with the methods I learned, I am currently applying these techniques to all races and groups I am unfamiliar with, in order to become culture-centered.

The last aspect I want to share with you is how I see power, prejudice, macroaggressions, and microaggressions at the Tampa Bay Justice Center. At the Tampa Bay Justice Center, we are taught to see power as control of another person, which is usually the abuser. When I work with clients at internship, and since I am a male working with predominantly female clients, my goal is to empower my clients. Therefore, I view my client and myself as having equal power when we work together and while I try to empower them to direct treatment. When it comes to prejudices in my internship site, I do not see this having a big impact as I work with my clients or colleagues. The reason why is the training from my supervisor. We are consistently doing self-reflective practices to address personal prejudice or acting on preconceived opinions regarding race and other cultural factors.

When it comes to macroaggressions and microaggressions this is a different story at my internship site. I remember one day when an African American male was pacing outside of the Tampa Bay Justice Center. The cops felt threatened by the male, and due to abuse rates with minority males, the cops discriminated against the male, and ended up questioning him. This was weird because the following week, I saw a White male doing the same thing, and no one approached him. Therefore, macroaggressions are prevalent at my internship site. I think this is due to the nature of our work at the center. Everyone assumes that violence is connected to race and gender.

From a microaggressions perspective, I sometimes hear derogatory comments from people in my community. They talk about the high rates of women of Color and their experiences of domestic violence. I even heard one professional at the Tampa Bay Justice Center say the same thing. When I heard this, I confronted the person and educated him, as my supervisor taught me, on his behaviors and biases. Overall, when it comes to these concepts, I am taught by my supervisor to consistently reflect on my views of power, prejudices, macroaggressions, and microaggressions. She says that this continual self-assessment will help me build positive relationships with clients and avoid causing harm to them.

Well I hope you enjoyed hearing about my experiences at the Tampa Bay Justice Center. One thing I would recommend is to continue the journey to become culture-centered by doing self-reflective practices. It has been important for me to seek supervision. I always learned more about why I am thinking or acting in a certain way when I share my work with my site supervisor. She challenges my thoughts and beliefs about race and culture. If you continue the path of self-understanding, it will definitely help you be the best human service professional you can be, and ultimately, give your client the best chance to improve their lives. Have a great day!

Written by Jorge Roman, 2015. Used with permission.

Tamika

One of the most interesting things about my time so far as an intern has been my work with people from so many cultures that are different than my own. My colleagues, my supervisors, and my clients have taught me so far that everyone comes from his/her own unique cultural background. It has been really fascinating to see some of the issues we talked about in my multicultural class play out in real life. While recognizing and addressing cultural issues can sometimes make me feel uncomfortable, it has been a critical part of the learning process for me. I am starting to feel much more culturally competent as a member of the human services profession.

I was a little bit nervous before this internship thinking about how my own culture would impact my experience and how my clients might view me. I know that African Americans are incarcerated at disproportionate rates in our justice system. Therefore, I was somewhat anxious that my African American clients would view me as entitled or different. I thought this difference make it difficult for them to relate to me. I know this comes partially from feeling marginalized in most settings—sometimes it feels like I'm working constantly to prove myself as an African American female student, worker, and member of society in general. I wondered if I would have to prove myself to my clients on a cultural level. I tried to prepare myself for the possibility that, at times, I may feel that way. Talking to my faculty supervisor and my multicultural course instructor helped me to explore this anxiety before I began internship. They really worked with me to identify what exactly I was nervous about and how I could manage my concerns while working at the justice center.

Another one of the biggest anxieties I was able to uncover during my conversations with faculty members was worrying about how I would connect with clients from cultural backgrounds with which I was completely unfamiliar. I discussed with my supervisor the importance of building solid rapport with all clients and of addressing culture openly, including both similarities and differences. My supervisor reassured me that asking cultural questions is generally preferable to pretending that I fully understand where a client is coming from. This made me feel a lot better, because I was somewhat shy about asking questions about race and culture that would help me better understand my clients. After role-playing cultural scenarios with my supervisor however, I became much more comfortable thinking about how to ask appropriate questions of clients in order to grasp their experiences as fully as possible.

In actually working with my clients and colleagues, I've found it really important to keep culture in mind and to remember that everyone's culture is at least a little bit different. It's been helpful to remind myself that culture includes so much more than race and ethnicity—and it's present every single time I'm talking with somebody! Gender, religion, sexual orientation, education level—all of these things, along with other cultural factors, impact people's thoughts, behaviors, and experiences. I realize that it is imperative that I consider these dynamics when I work with clients.

My peers and supervisors at the justice center have been really supportive as I explore culture in my internship work and have talked openly with me about how their cultural experiences influence their own work. I've become especially close with a colleague who comes from a cultural background similar to mine, and it's been really valuable to hear about her experiences as an African American female professional.

One way I've really seen elements of power and prejudice play out at the justice center is during interactions between front line workers and clients. Many of the guards and correctional officers are verbally disrespectful toward inmates and that has been a difficult adjustment for me. At times, I've felt ill equipped as an intern to stand up for what I think is right and it's difficult for me to know how to balance the culture of the justice center itself with my own personal ethics and values. I've heard some of the correctional workers use racial, ethnic, and sexual slurs when addressing inmates, and it feels really inappropriate and unprofessional to me at times. It's easy to see how these workers use power to control clients and remind them who's in charge. This use of power has been an important focus during my supervisory sessions. I find it really important to process what's going on around me with someone I feel safe being open with, and my clinical supervisor has really become that person for me. While I also witness prejudice amongst inmates themselves, it seems to bother me less because of my preconceived notion that they would discriminate against one another. My supervisor has helped me to process this perspective as well. I'm learning a lot about how culture, power, and discrimination intersect on multiple levels in this type of setting. I'm also recognizing more and more the importance of supervision and consultation in doing this type of work, particularly when it comes to issues of culture.

Written by Brittany Pollard, 2015. Used with permission.

Exercise 7.5 Considering Culture-Centered Helping: Writing Your Own Story, Entry 20

You just read short summaries of the personal development of Alicia, Lucas, and Tamika related to their consideration of delivering human services in a multicultural environment. Now it is your turn to share your own experiences working as a human service intern in a multicultural environment.

- Think about the ways you prepared for working with different races and cultures. Describe these ways.
- Provide examples of how you considered race/culture during the helping process.
- Share what it was like to work in your agency and how you gain assistance in working with peers and clients of different races and cultures.
- Share the way you see power, prejudice, macroaggressions, and microaggressions play out in your setting.

Faculty and Site Supervisor Dialogue: Dr. Bianca and Ms. Bellewa

In addition to hearing from Alicia, Lucas, and Tamika, we asked Dr. Bianca, a human service faculty member, and Ms. Bellewa, a human service site supervisor, to talk about their experiences as faculty and site supervisors and how the concept of culture influences their work as supervisors.

Dr. Claude Bianca

My own development as a human service educator continues in relationship to my own self-identity development. Honestly, when I think about my own development, my mind and heart flood with images of how I used to think about race, mine and others. I never think about how far I have come; rather, with each interaction, I realize how dynamic my own development continues to be. Let me provide an example. I am working with an intern right now. Su Chin is Asian and a minority in our human service program, in her internship, and in her community. Just last week, she appeared to be very anxious about working at her internship site. She was not sure how her site supervisor accepted her. She never mentioned her race. She is a terrific student, has wonderful skills, and relates well with her clients. One of her classmates asked if she thought that her feelings/reactions to site staff reflected her race/culture. In that moment I recognized I was guilty of not recognizing her culture; I made it invisible. Because I thought so much of Su Chin's skills and ability to establish rapport with clients, I failed to consider the race/cultural perspective. I shared this oversight with my students.

As you can tell with this example, as a faculty supervisor, I keep race/culture as a consideration in all of our classes. Students now ask each other about multicultural issues and how they can provide helping that works for their clients. Some of my students are still very uncomfortable with this type of discussion. I encourage them to express their discomfort. In my mind being able to share anxiety, fear, prejudice, and a lack of understanding of their own identity development—all of this is far better than saying the right things during our time together.

During class we also return time and again to the information in this chapter and we balance the focus between our own cultural awareness and racial identity development and the race/culture of the client. We also try to balance talking about how we feel as we deal with race/culture and concrete ways we see macroagressions and microagressions. And when we talk about the helping process, we always focus on race/culture implications of the work of helping. At the end of each session we remind ourselves that we are all learning and we try to remain open to our personal and professional growth. Some days for this work are better than others.

Ms. Zu Bellewa

When interns look at me they immediately think "stranger." I don't look like I am from the U.S., and I am not. My skin color is black, and I wear the Niger female dress. I am also a very large woman, very tall and broad. All of this can be intimidating for interns on their first internship site assignment. In the long run, I think working with me helps them break down their fear of talking about cultural issues. My cultural experiences are so numerous, and my parents always talked about race and culture. It was a part of our own family culture. My dad was from Niger and my mother was from Angola, so I have a biracial and bicultural identity. I speak French, Portuguese, and English, and I am fluent in each language. In my home we spoke and studied in French and Portuguese. I attended British boarding schools. With this type of background, race and culture is part of every conversation. This is the reason I think that Dr. Bianca was willing to trust me to supervise his students. Although we have different cultural backgrounds, we resonated with each other when we talked about the importance of establishing a comfortable culture for staff and clients. Of course this includes interns.

One of the best things about working with interns is they have the cutting edge knowledge about helping. And that includes courses in multicultural helping. It also includes self-awareness and the importance of handling complex issues. Dealing with culture requires all of these things.

Right now, our agency is working with immigrants. The term immigrant encompasses an incredibly wide array of populations. I always tell interns that when working with immigrants, it is important to consider three questions. First, what was the reason for their immigration? Working with a client who immigrated to the U.S. voluntarily for reasons such as education or financial prosperity can look very different than when working with a client who immigrated for involuntary reasons. Involuntary immigration, or forced migration, can include displaced individuals who had to leave their home for extraneous variables and refugees who had to flee their countries due to war and political turmoil. This leads us to the second question to consider. Has their immigration impacted their daily life? If so, how? Immigration can increase stressors that an individual faces due to culture shock, loss of support systems, changing roles, and possible discrimination. As stressors increase, coping becomes difficult and the individual's mental health begins to suffer. Those stressors are exacerbated for involuntary immigrants, who many times, have faced trauma related incidents that can include kidnapping, torture, and violence. Not only would they have to cope with the trauma they faced, but they also have to do it in a new and very different environment, while also coping with the regular stressors of immigration. The third question to consider addresses varying acculturation levels. Understanding their level of acculturation is vital when working with this group. How much does your client want to assimilate into their new host culture? While some may want to fully embrace the new culture that they are a part of, others remain disconnected and resistant, choosing to hold onto their culture of origin. Others try to find a balance between their culture of origin and their new host culture. It is crucial to acknowledge that not all immigrants look the same. Not only do they come from varying cultural backgrounds, but they immigrate for different reasons and hold different expectations of their new host culture. I tell my interns that recognizing those components of their client's immigration provides a rich and layered painting of the journey their client is on.

Written by Dareen Basma, 2015. Used with permission.

The Professional Voice and Tips for Practice: Gwen

Gwen, a human service professional, provides us with advice about how to maintain a culturally sensitive perspective when working with clients.

Gwen

In this chapter, Marianne introduced us to multicultural awareness and competency and the essential roles these play in the helping professions. Throughout the chapter, Marianne encouraged us to consider our own cultures and then, in Exercise 7.3, she provided an activity that you can do to learn about the culture of the clients your agency serves. Now that you have begun to develop your own awareness of self and others' cultures, let's look at ways that you can employ that awareness and competency in your internship.

The American Psychological Association (2002a) offers the following "tips for culturally informed communications:"

- *Learn by asking: Generally, people respond positively when we authentically want to know more about them and their culture. So when you don't understand aspects of your clients' cultures, it's okay to ask, just make sure you're respectful. And if clients aren't comfortable sharing about their cultures, then be sure to respect their privacy.*
- *Avoid insensitive comments: As a helper, you already understand the foremost importance of protecting and respecting your clients. But we sometimes forget that what is acceptable in our own cultures may not be acceptable someone else's culture. For that reason, take particular care to choose your words wisely, particularly when referencing clients' cultures. And if you do err, be quick to apologize and ask your client what is culturally appropriate to him or her.*
- *Tune in to nonverbal behaviors: Different cultures have different behavioral expectations. In some cultures, such as the American business culture, direct eye contact is a sign of paying attention and being respectful. In other cultures, direct eye contact can appear confrontational and disrespectful. Be mindful of your clients' nonverbal cues and consider their cultural contexts. Likewise, keep in mind that your nonverbal cues may be culturally confusing to your clients.*

Written by Gwen Ruttencutter, 2015. Used with permission.

Terms to Remember

Cross-cultural experience

Culture

Culture-centered helping

Designating race/ethnicity status

Discrimination

Ecological perspective

Foreign-born

Internalized oppression

Macroaggressions

Majority population

Microaggressions

Multicultural competencies

Multiculturalism

Multiple cultural identities

Oppression

Place of family

Prejudice

Stereotypes

Self-fulfilling prophecy

References

American Psychological Association. (2002a). *Guide to cultural awareness for public education campaign and disaster response network members.* Retrieved from http://www.apapracticecentral.org/update/2008/12-17/cultural-awareness.pdf

American Psychological Association. (2002b). *Guidelines on multicultural education, training, research, practice, and organizational change for psychologists.* Retrieved from http://www.apa.org/pi/oema/resources/policy/multicultural-guidelines.aspx

Ancis, J. R., & Chang, C. Y. (2008). Oppression. In F. T. Leong (Ed.), *Encyclopedia of counselling.* Thousand Oaks, CA: Sage. doi: 10.4135/9781412963978

Arnett, J. (2013). *Adolescence and emerging adulthood* (5th ed.). Boston, MA: Pearson.

Associated Press. (2013, September 23). U.S. illegal immigration may be increasing, study shows. *The Guardian.* Retrieved from http://www.theguardian.com/world/2013/sep/23/us-illegal-immigration-rising

Berg, C. J. (2009). A comprehensive framework for conducting client assessments: Highlighting strengths, environmental factors, and hope. *Journal of Practical Consulting, 3*(2), 9–3. Retrieved from http://www.regent.edu/acad/global/publications/jpc/vol3iss2/JPC_V3Is2_Berg.pdf

Brammer, R. (2011). *Diversity in counseling.* Pacific Grove, CA: Brooks/Cole, Cengage Learning.

Brofenbrenner, U. (1979). *The ecology of human development.* Cambridge, MA: Harvard.

Center for American Progress. (2014). The facts on immigration today. Retrieved from http://www.americanprogress.org/issues/immigration/report/2013/04/03/59040/the-facts-on-immigration-today-3/

Cross-cultural. (2015). In *Merriam-Webster dictionary* (11th ed.). Retrieved from http://www.merriamwebster.com/dictionary/cross%20cultural

Culture. (2015). In *Merriam-Webster dictionary* (11th ed.). Retrieved from http://www.merriamwebster.com/dictionary/culture

Dutta, M. (2007). *Communicating health: A culture-centered approach*. Boston, MA: Wiley.

Eriksen, K. (1981). *Human services today*. Reston, VA: Reston.

Hannon, C., Woodside, M., Pollard, B., & Roman, J. (in press). The meaning of African American college women's experiences attending a predominantly white institution. *Journal of College Student Development*. Manuscript submitted for publication.

Hays, D. (2013). Why is becoming multicultural competent as a counselor so important? As cited in L. Shallcross (2013, September 1). Multicultural competence: A continual pursuit. Counseling Today. Retrieved from http://ct.counseling.org/2013/09/multicultural-competence-a-continual-pursuit/

Hayes, C., Montes, A., & Schroeder, L. (2013). Self-fulfilling prophecy not: Using cultural assets to beat the odds. *Gender and Education, 25* (7), 923–937.

Hipolito-Delgado, C. P., & Diaz, J. M. (2013). A conceptual approach to counselling with Latina/o culture in mind. In C. Lee (Ed.), *Multicultural issues in counseling* (4th ed., pp. 67–86). Alexandria, VA: American Counseling Association.

Jones, J. M., Dovidio, J. F., & Vietze, D. L. (2014). *The psychology of diversity: Beyond prejudice and racism*. Boston, MA: Wiley.

Lee, C. C. (Ed.). (2013). *Multicultural issues in counseling* (4th ed.). Alexandria, VA: American Counseling Association.

Literte, P. (2010). Revising race: How biracial students are changing and challenging student services. *Journal of College Student Development, 51*(2), 115–134.

Lott, B. (2010). *Multiculturism and diversity: A social psychological perspective*. Chichester, West Sussex, UK: John Wiley.

McAuliffe, G. J., & Eriksen, K. P. (1999). Toward a constructivist and developmental identity for the counseling profession: The context-phase-stage-style model. *Journal of Counseling & Development, 77*, 267–280.

McGabe, A., Tamis-LeMonda, C. S., Bornstein, M. H., Brockmeyer Cates, C., Golinkoff, R., Wishard Guerra, A., . . . & Song, L. (2013). Multilingual children: Beyond myths and towards best practices. *Social Policy Report, 27*(4). Retrieved from http://fcd-us.org/sites/default/files/Multilingual%20Children%20Beyond%20Myths%20and%20Towards%20Best%20Practices.pdf

Mio, J., Barker-Hackett, L., & Turnambing, J. (2011). *Multicultural psychology: Understanding our diverse communities* (3rd ed.). Boston, MA: McGraw-Hill.

Multicultural. (2015). In *Merriam-Webster dictionary* (11th ed.). Retrieved from http://www.merriam webster.com/dictionary/multicultural

National Organization of Human Services. (2015). Ethical standards for human service professionals. Retrieved from https://nohs.memberclicks.net/ethical-standards-for-hs-professionals

Neukrug, E. (2012). *Theory, practice, and trends in human services*. Belmont, CA: Brooks Cole/Cengage Learning.

Npower. (n. d.). *Technology guide for non-profit leaders: Health and human services*. Retrieved from https://www.att.com/Common/files/pdf/npower_health_and_human_services.pdf

Pacific Oaks College. (2014). Culture-centered education. Retrieved from http://www.pacificoaks.edu/Why_Pacific_Oaks/Culture-Centered_Education

Patten, E. (2015). *Who is multiracial? Depends on how you ask*. Retrieved from the Pew Research Center: http://www.pewsocialtrends.org/2015/11/06/who-is-multiracial-depends-on-how-you-ask/

Pederson, P. (Ed.). (1998). *Multiculturalism as a fourth force*. Philadelphia, PA: Taylor & Francis.

Prejudice. (2014). In *Oxford English dictionary*. Retrieved from http://www.oed.com/view/Entry/150162?rskey=R1KknT&result=1#eid

Russ, K. A. (2010). *Working with clients of Appalachian culture*. Retrieved from http://www.counseling.org/resources/library/vistas/2010-v-online/Article_69.pdf

Stewart, M. A. (2014, February 12). Speak American: Be multilingual. *San Diego Union-Times*. Retrieved from http://www.utsandiego.com/news/2014/feb/12/speak-american-be-multilingual/

Stone, A. (2012, September 27). Multiracial American population grew faster than single-race segment in 2010 census. *Huffington Post Online*. Retrieved from http://www.huffingtonpost.com/2012/09/27/multiracial-americans-2010-census_n_1919070.html

Sue, D. W., Capodilupo, C. M., Torino, G. C., Bucceri, J. M., Holder, A. M. B., Nadal, K. L., & Esquilin, M. (2007). Racial microaggressions in everyday life: Implications for clinical practice. *American Psychologist, 62*(4), 271–286. doi:10.1037/0003-066X.62.4.271

U.S. Census Bureau. (2011). *Overview of race and Hispanic origin: 2010* (2010 Census Briefs). Retrieved from http://www.census.gov/prod/cen2010/briefs/c2010br-02.pdf

U.S. Census Bureau. (2012). *The two or more races populations* (2010 Census Briefs). Retrieved from http://www.census.gov/prod/cen2010/briefs/c2010br-13.pdf

Wagner, M. B. (2005). Connecting what we know to what we do. In S. Keefe (Ed.), *Appalachia: Social context past and present* (4th ed., pp. 55–73). Dubuque, IA: Kendall/Hunt.

Wang, W. (2012). *The rise of intermarriage: Rates, characteristics vary by race and gender* (Executive Summary). Retrieved from Pew Research Center website: http://www.pewsocialtrends.org/2012/02/16/the-rise-of-intermarriage/

Weibel-Orlando, J. (2009). Grandparenting styles: The contemporary American experience. In J. Sokolovsky (Ed.), *The cultural context of aging: Worldwide perspectives* (3rd ed.). Westport, CT: Praeger. Retrieved from http://faculty.usfsp.edu/jsokolov/webbook/weibel.pdf

Wong, Y. (2013). Returning to silence, connecting to wholeness: Contemplative pedagogy for critical social work education. *Journal of Religion & Spirituality in Social Work, 32*(3), 269–285. doi:10.1080/154264322013.801748

Woodside, M., & McClam, T. (2015). *Introduction to human services* (8th ed.). Pacific Grove, CA: Brooks Cole/Cengage.

8 Participating in Supervision

Reading this chapter will help you do the following:

- Describe the goals of supervision in internship.
- Understand the terms related to supervision in internship.
- Describe the roles and responsibilities of the faculty supervisor, site supervisor, and intern.
- Learn about the Supervisee [Intern] Bill of Rights.
- Understand the triad and the quartet model of supervision as it relates to internship.
- Learn how to be a good supervisee.
- Learn how to ask for good supervision.
- Learn how to ask for critical evaluations and appropriate feedback.
- Identify poor and harmful supervision.
- Become acquainted with some of the experiences of supervision that Alicia, Lucas, and Tamika experience in internship.

- Learn about the faculty and site supervisors' perspectives on their own supervision and how it supports the internship experience.
- Describe the tips that Gwen provides that guide participating in supervision.

In this chapter, Chapter 8, we focus on interns and the supervisory process. Supervision is an important aspect of the human service internship; for interns this means both being supervised and engaging in supervision. Helping interns learn about the topic of supervision is the fourth chapter in Part I, "Engaging in Internship During the First Week or Two."

In the first section, we focus on the topic of supervision by defining supervision, presenting the goals of supervision, and introducing terms that relate directly to supervision in the internship. Then, in the second section, we introduce the Triad/Quartet Model of Supervision that defines the primary individuals or participants involved in supervision (Bernard & Goodyear, 2014).

In the third section of this chapter, we discuss the evaluation process in internship from the perspectives of the site and faculty supervisors and the intern. We introduce the responsibility of gatekeeping as a critical aspect of the supervisory process.

In the fourth section, we consider the type and quality of supervision that you as an intern are receiving. We introduce the Intern Bill of Rights. We look at what you can expect from good supervision and introduce the responsibilities you have as an intern. Then, we move to a discussion and assessment of poor supervision and harmful supervision. We then help interns conduct an assessment of the supervision they are receiving at their internship sites and ask them to share this assessment with their faculty supervisor.

In the fifth and final section of this chapter, we provide insights from students, faculty, site supervisor, and human service professional dialogues about supervision. Specifically, Alicia, Lucas, Tamika, Dr. Bianca, Ms. Bellewa, and Gwen share their own experiences with supervision, especially as it relates to the internship experience.

In Box 8.1, we describe the organizational framework of the first section of this chapter, that of defining supervision.

Box 8.1 Studying the Text: Defining Supervision

Studying the text: The following outline will help you read and study the text material in this next section.

Defining supervision

1. Definition and goals of supervision

2. Terms that relate to the supervisory process

3. What students say

Defining Supervision

We believe that supervision provides a unique contribution to professional development in human services, and those professionals who provide supervision for human service interns are particularly important. Understanding what supervision is and what makes it work will help you as you participate in the supervisory process.

Definition and Goals of Supervision

In your role as a human service intern, you work with at least two individuals who perform a **supervisory** role: the faculty supervisor and the site supervisor. Let's look at a simple and direct answer to "what is supervision?" Supervision is a role and responsibility assumed, most of the time, by a more senior member of the profession in order to support the professional development of a less experienced member of the profession. More specifically, the Oxford English Dictionary states that supervision is, "The action or function of overseeing, directing, or taking charge of a person, organization, activity, etc" ("Supervision," 2012). As indicated by the definition, supervision is a critical aspect of your professional growth and development and is an integral component of your academic program.

Terms That Relate to the Supervisory Process

Before we talk more about supervision and the supervisory process, we want to introduce terms that are basic to understanding supervision, especially as we approach it in this chapter. You will learn more about each of these terms as you study supervision in more depth.

Supervision—Providing oversight of another individual's work as he or she assumes the role of a helping professional and perform assigned responsibilities. Primary goals include supporting growth and development of helping professionals and promoting client welfare and safety.

Supervisory process—A course or series of actions occurring, when in a professional capacity, a senior individual provides oversight for the professional work and development of a professional with less experience or expertise. A continuous series of interactions between the supervisor and the intern that focuses on the intern's professional growth and development. Usually supervision occurs over time.

Supervisor—The individual charged with the responsibility to oversee a supervisee or intern's professional development and professional work.

Supervisee or intern—The recipient of a supervisor's teaching, consulting, and counseling related to professional development and work. The supervisee will henceforth be referred to as the *human service intern* or the *intern*.

Supervision triad—The most significant participants in the supervisory process include the supervisor, the intern, and the client.

Supervision quartet—An expanded version of the triad includes the faculty supervisor, the site supervisor, the intern, and the client.

Intern Bill of Rights—Guidelines written by educators that describe expectations that an intern may have for supervisor that reflects good supervision. The Bill of Rights also includes a set of intern responsibilities related to the supervisory process.

Within the field of human services, supervision is both a responsibility and a task or activity essential to the training of the human service student engaged in a field-based experience. Professional organizations, such as the National Organization of Human Services in their Ethical Standards for Human Service Professionals, describe the importance of experiencing supervision, especially as it relates to cultural diversity and ethical decision making (NOHS, 2015). In addition, the Council for Standards in Human Services Education reinforces this importance in its national standards, especially standards related to the field experience (CSHSE, 2013).

Four goals of supervision directly relate to the intern's work within an agency setting. First, supervision supports the professional development of the intern. Interns at the beginning of their field experience may need supervision that differs from the more advanced intern. A second goal of supervision is to protect the welfare of clients (Bernard & Goodyear, 2014). With specific reference to client welfare, the CSHSE recommends that supervision move from observation, to direct supervision, and then to indirect supervision and represents a standard of best practice (CSHSE, 2013). These phases refer to the increasing responsibility of work that is assumed by the intern throughout the internship (see Chapter 4). This progression of responsibility allows the intern to build knowledge, skills, and values needed to deliver quality services to clients.

Gatekeeping is a third goal of supervision and represents the obligation of the supervisor to (a) evaluate an intern's fitness for internship work, (b) identify strengths and limitations, and (c) provide feedback and suggestions and support for growth. If in the role as gatekeeper, site supervisors conclude specific interns are not capable of or willing to fulfill their internship responsibilities, they will work with faculty supervisors to constructively address issues. Finally, the fourth goal of supervision is to help interns learn to self-supervise. Supervisors can teach interns how to support and reflect about their own work in the hope that learning to self-supervise extends through postgraduation employment as a human service professional (Corey, Haynes, Moulton, & Muratori, 2010).

Before we begin to explore the nature of supervision and your experiences in internship, let's look at the experiences of other human service students. These students provide us some insights into how they view supervision.

Box 8.2 Student Experiences of Supervision During Internship

Steve: I am in my field internship. My supervisor this semester is really different from my first supervisor. He is more open and doesn't expect me to be perfect. And he lets me work more independently. I like that.

Maria: My supervisor and I get along splendidly. She and I bonded on the first visit to the internship site. She doesn't give me as much feedback as I would wish, but she is kind and warm.

> **Al:**   I have already talked with my faculty supervisor about my questions concerning my current supervisor. She doesn't have time for me and won't give me anything to do. I try to ask for more responsibility but she acts as if I am not here at the internship site.
>
> **Shasha:** My supervisor is so talented and I am learning so much just watching her work with clients. I hope we can begin to work together with clients next week. I am not sure when she will trust me with my own clients.

Box 8.3 describes the organizational framework of the second section of this chapter, that of describing the supervisory relationship.

Box 8.3 Studying the Text: Describing the Supervisory Relationship

Studying the text: The following outline will help you read and study the text material in this next section.

Describing the supervisory relationship

1. The supervision triad

2. The supervision quartet

The focus of this section is to describe the **supervisory relationship**. The supervisory relationship represents the bond or relationship between the supervisor and the intern (Bordin, as cited in Horvath & Greenberg, 1994). Each supervisory relationship varies and is dependent upon multiple factors, such as the individual characteristics of the supervisor and the intern, how the supervisor views the supervisory role, and the match between supervisor skills and intern needs. To help you understand the supervisory relationship, we present the model of the Supervision Triad/Quartet that describes the participants involved in the supervisory process.

The Supervision Triad

Experts often refer to the supervisory experience in terms of the supervision triad (Bernard & Goodyear, 2014). This triad is so named since the supervisory process reflects work among three primary individuals, (a) the supervisor, (b) the intern, and (c) the client. For each individual in the triad, there are specific roles, responsibilities, and relationships. Figure 8.1 presents a visual aid that helps us to describe the supervision process between the intern, the site supervisor, and the client. Internships in human services include two supervisors, the faculty supervisor and the site supervisor. Each plays different roles and assumes different responsibilities. Because of the important contributions each supervisor makes to your internship experience, we expand the notion of the

Figure 8.1   The Supervision Triad

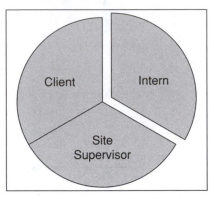

Source: Created by Gwen Ruttencutter, 2015. Used with permission.

Figure 8.2   The Supervision Quartet

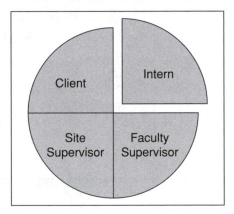

Source: Created by Gwen Ruttencutter, 2015. Used with permission.

supervisory process from the supervision triad to the supervision quartet. And we expand the visual in Figure 8.2 to include the four individual participants.

After studying Figures 8.1 and 8.2, you can see the different participants in the supervisory process. In fact, you, as the intern, are an important part of this group. And note that the client is also a critical participant. We use Table 8.1 to help you distinguish among all four participants and help you better understand the roles, responsibilities, and relationships of all four members. Many of these roles, responsibilities, and relationships relate to the three worlds that intersect during internship, that of the academic program, the agency site, and the intern. We introduced these worlds in Chapter 3 (see Figure 3.1). In Table 8.1 we list each member of the quartet, and then we describe the role, responsibility, and the primary relationships in which each engages.

As an example of an intern's experience of supervision, we look at the experiences of Tomas, a human service intern working at the Brooklyn Drug and Alcohol Rehabilitation Center. In earlier chapters, he shared with us some of his internship experiences. In this chapter, he reflects on the supervisory quartet and how the model helps him understand his own experiences of supervision.

Table 8.1 The Supervision Quartet Roles, Responsibilities, and Relationships

Member of the Quartet	Role	Responsibility	Relationship
Intern	Learning to be a human service professional	Following academic and agency commitments Assuming responsibility for quality client care	Engaging in relationships Primary with client, site supervisor, and faculty supervisor
Client	Receiving therapeutic help and concrete services	Working with the intern Following agency guidelines	Engaging in relationships Primary with intern Secondary with the site supervisor
Site supervisor	Supporting the intern's work and professional development and monitoring client welfare	Teaching intern professional knowledge, skills, and values Ensuring client welfare	Engaging in relationships Primary with the intern Secondary with the client Tertiary with the faculty supervisor
Faculty supervisor	Supporting the intern's work and communicating with and supporting the site supervisor	Providing academic structure for the intern experience Monitor intern work. Serving as a liaison with site supervisor Gatekeeping	Engaging in relationships Primary with the intern Secondary with the site supervisor Tertiary with the client

Tomas

I am just now learning about the triad, and I can see how complicated it can be to describe the roles and responsibilities of all the people involved in the supervisory process. I think that I am closest to Ms. Paseattoe just because I spend so much time with her. I think that Dr. Highland, my faculty supervisor, sets the standards and the assignments for my academic work, but it is difficult for me to remember that I am still a student. If I had to choose my identity, I would think of myself as a human service professional working at the Brooklyn Drug and Alcohol Rehabilitation Center. I am at school only a couple of times a week. Even though I talk with Dr. Highland about my work and review tapes from time to time, most of the week I am working with clients and doing staff work with Ms. Paseattoe. Also Dr. Highland is always ready to help me, but the person that I turn to is almost always Ms. Paseattoe. I described my dilemma with suicide risk assessment earlier. It was Ms. Paseattoe who helped me figure out my issues related to making that assessment. Also she was the one who helped me tie my academic knowledge to the more practical knowledge that I could use with clients. And although we role-played suicide risk assessment in class, I watched Ms. Paseattoe conduct suicide risk assessments with three of her clients. And I observed two other case managers determine if they needed to do a formal assessment. It's happening for me here at the center. When I think about the supervision, the most important supervision is the triad. That is because my site supervisor really knows the clients I am working with. Dr. Highland can help me with my clients, but Ms. Paseattoe has more detailed knowledge of the agency and the client's situation.

Before moving to the next section of this chapter that focuses on the supervisory relationship, we ask you to write about your current experience of supervision. Exercise 8.1 provides you the opportunity to describe the supervision you are receiving.

Exercise 8.1 Describing Your Experience of Supervision: Writing Your Own Story, Entry 21

Step 1

Take a few minutes to think about your internship experience, make some notes, and then write the story of your experience of supervision thus far at your internship site. Don't worry about creating paragraphs or constructing a paper that is technically correct. Just write down your thoughts as they come. Provide as many examples as you wish that describe you, your supervisor, and your interactions and experiences. This writing exercise is for you. You will not need to share this writing with anyone.

The supervisory relationship or the bond between the intern and the supervisor is an important component of supervision (Bordin, as cited in Horvath & Greenberg, 1994). There are several important parts of the bond that can make it strong (Gallon, Hausotter, & Bryan, 2005). In the following list, we propose several specific characteristics of supervisors that foster strong supervisory relationships. For this list, we adapted elements of supervision proposed by Gallon, Hausotter, and Bryan (2005) and added many of our own. We categorize these important supervisor characteristics into four areas: caring, commitment, intern focused, and style.

Caring

- Providing Rogers's (1980) core conditions (that comprise a positive helping relationship) in supervision: empathy, genuineness, and unconditional positive regard
- Establishing and maintaining mutual respect and trust between the supervisor and the intern

Commitment

- Making time for supervision
- Providing relevant and focused supervision

Intern-focused supervision

- Paying attention to the intern's developmental needs (e.g., beginning intern needs; more advanced intern needs)
- Helping the intern move from dependency to autonomy
- Giving well-defined and clear feedback
- Defining and sharing intern's limits and mistakes
- Allowing the intern to participate in giving and receiving feedback

Style

- Conveying enthusiasm for supervision
- Appreciating what is funny, whimsical, or humorous
- Disclosing one's own mistakes and learning opportunities
- Asking for feedback on supervision and the supervisory process

It may be helpful at this point for you to take a moment and make some more notes about your own experience with the supervisory process during internship. Use the next exercise, Exercise 8.2, to build upon the description of supervision that you began in Exercise 8.1.

Exercise 8.2 The Supervision Quartet and the Bond: Writing Your Own Story, Entry 22

Step 1

With this exercise you will continue your reflections on the supervision you are receiving. In this exercise, we expect you will increase your understanding of supervision and the supervisory relationship. For this exercise answer each of the following questions.

The Quartet

Within the Quartet Model of supervision, my site supervisor performs in the following ways:

_____

_____

_____

Within the Quartet Model of supervision, my faculty supervisor performs in the following ways:

_____

_____

_____

Within the Quartet Model of supervision, as an intern, I perform in the following ways:

_____

_____

_____

Within the Quartet Model of supervision, my clients perform in the following ways:

_____

_____

_____

Goals

This is my perception of how my faculty supervisor and I agree or disagree on the goals of internship:

_____

_____

_____

This is my perception of how my site supervisor and I agree or disagree on the tasks of internship:

_____

_____

_____

Now that you understand the participants in the supervisory quartet, it is important to learn more about evaluation and gatekeeping. In Box 8.4 we outline the focus of the next section of this chapter.

Box 8.4 Studying the Text: Evaluation and Gatekeeping

Studying the text: The following outline will help you read and study the text material in this next section.

1.   Evaluation and gatekeeping

Evaluation and Gatekeeping

In this section, we describe evaluation and gatekeeping and its purposes, the ways in which it occurs, and how you can prepare for it.

Internship and the Evaluation Process

The definition of **evaluation** is, "to judge the value or condition of (someone or something) in a careful or thoughtful way" ("Evaluation," 2015). This reflects two important components of evaluation as it occurs during supervision of an intern. It includes an action, that of gathering data and forming an opinion, and a description of how that action occurs in a careful and deliberate way. During the supervision of a human service intern, the supervisor has a professional obligation to include evaluation as part of the supervisory process. In fact, assessing intern performance and providing feedback are essential for the four goals of supervision we introduced at the beginning of the chapter. First, positive and critical feedback encourages and facilitates the professional growth and development of the intern. Most human service program handbooks or the internship handbooks describe this as an expectation of a site supervisor, and most list evaluation and assessment as a primary role of the supervisor (see Chapter 1). Second, a supervisor also has an ethical commitment to monitor the welfare of the clients the intern serves. During the supervisory process, regular assessment of an intern's work with clients helps the supervisor fulfill this obligation to the clients.

Third, the supervisor serves as a gatekeeper for the human service profession. As such, he or she assumes responsibility for maintaining standards of the human services profession. These include standards dictated by the profession (such as the NOHS, the academic program, licensure or certifying boards such as Human Services-Board Certified Practitioner) and the internship site placement. Ethical considerations also guide evaluation. Because the site supervisor can observe firsthand his or her intern at work, the site supervisor plays a major role in assessing abilities and skills, as well as promise or fit, of an intern for the profession. The site supervisor functions as a gatekeeper in that he or she will evaluate the intern's performance and provide the faculty supervisor with information that influences final assessments and perhaps graduation. Although unusual, at some internship sites, the site supervisor assigns the final grade for the internship.

Evaluation also supports the fourth goal of supervision, teaching interns the importance of self-supervision and describing ways they can promote their own professional growth and development. During the evaluation process, interns gain much more than the feedback about their professional performance. Interns learn the types of professional behaviors, values, helping skills, and helping processes they need to demonstrate and continue to assess when they enter the world of human service professional work. Participating in an evaluation process with a supervisor also teaches the interns the value of seeking feedback from others and demonstrates to them how to ask and accept feedback.

Evaluation and Power

Even in the most collaborative of supervisory relationships, during evaluation, supervisors make judgments about the interns they are supervising. Because of the power differential between supervisor and intern, there exists for the supervisor an ethical obligation to protect the intern from any abuses of this power. Two ways the supervisors can meet this obligation is to conduct evaluations in a respectful way and follow due process. Both respect and due process help balance the power differences between the supervisor as the evaluator and the intern as the individual being evaluated. And respect and due process help maintain the collaborative relationship we introduced in Chapter 1.

Conducting Evaluation in a Respectful Way

Evaluation conducted in a respectful way encourages open and honest communication between the supervisor and the intern. Both supervisor and intern play a part in a successful and respectful evaluation experience. Understanding what to expect from your supervisor will help you respond in a positive way when receiving feedback and being evaluated.

The Supervisor Perspective

We suggest several ways that supervisors can establish a positive environment in which evaluation can occur. These include considering individual factors, establishing a positive environment, facilitating clear communication, and attending to intern development. We think it is important for you to understand the ways a supervisor can lessen the power differential during the evaluation process.

Considering Individual Factors

- Consider the unique position of the intern as a novice.
- Consider the cultural dimensions of the interaction (e.g., nationality, ethnicity, religious affiliation, gender, age, abilities, social class, economic status, language, sexual orientation, physical characteristics, and organizational affiliations).

Establishing a Positive Environment

- Set aside time for evaluation.
- Conduct the evaluation in a private space.
- Make the evaluation a collaborative process.
- Seek information from the intern.
- Include positive and critical feedback.
- Include opportunities for supervisor and intern to agree and to disagree.

Facilitating Clear Communication

- Provide clear, specific feedback and concrete examples.
- Be clear about who has access to the written evaluations.
- Connect evaluation to agreed-upon goals and tasks.
- Use oral and written feedback.
- Consider the possibilities for misinterpretation.

Attending to Intern Development

- Discuss performance at the beginning of internship.
- Establish future goals.

The Intern Perspective

Even though the supervisor has the primary responsibility for providing feedback, we believe you too can support the evaluation process and contribute to its success. We use the same categories related to supervisor behaviors to help you foster a positive evaluation process.

Considering Individual Factors

- Talk to your supervisor about what it is like to be a novice or intern.
- Talk to the supervisor about the impact that your own culture and the culture of your supervisor has on your experience of supervision.

Establishing a Positive Environment

- Ask for a meeting time to discuss the formal evaluation. Suggest a time when both of you are least likely to be interrupted.
- Ask for a private space where you and your supervisor can talk freely.
- Ask your supervisor to collaborate with you on filling out the evaluation form.
- Seek information from the supervisor by asking questions or making prompts such as "How have you viewed my work in [specific area]?" "When you think about my work doing [specific work] what stands out to you?"
- Ask your supervisor for positive and critical feedback.
- When appropriate, say to your supervisor, "Here are some times that I did [specific behavior, work, feelings] that may differ from your observations."

Facilitating Clear Communication

- When preparing your evaluation of your work, provide concrete examples as evidence of when your work is going well, as well as areas where you need help.
- Communicate to your site supervisor how the academic program will use the evaluations.
- Bring your contract to the evaluation meeting. Connect the evaluation to components of the contract.
- Bring written notes to the evaluation meeting of thoughts you wish to share.
- If your supervisor says something that you don't understand, ask for clarification or specific examples.

Attending to Intern Development

- Discuss how you view your performance at the beginning of the internship.
- Talk about your current knowledge, skill, and professional development level; indicate how your work has changed since the beginning of the internship.
- Discuss future goals.

Evaluation With Due Process in Mind

Due process is a legal term reflecting a set of procedures that protect the rights of an individual. Due process, as it relates to evaluation during internship, reflects what we consider best practices in evaluation. In their handbooks and syllabi, most human service programs include written policies that address due process for students in their internships, especially related to evaluation. These include

1. Students help establish the goals and tasks included in their internship contract. The academic program (faculty), agency site, and students agree on the internship contract. The internship contract is a written document.

2. Internship goals relate to specific tasks to meet those goals.

3. The academic program (faculty) describes in writing the process by which the intern is evaluated. The site supervisor and the student both have a written copy of the formal evaluation process and forms to be used prior to the beginning of the semester.

4. The intern receives regular feedback prior to the midterm and final evaluations. This feedback includes positive and critical information about intern performance. This means during the formal evaluation, there are few surprises.

5. Both supervisor and intern discuss each evaluation standard and provide examples. Even though the evaluation reflects the supervisor's assessment, both participants have input into the evaluation process.

6. If the intern disagrees with the evaluation received, there exists a formal process to appeal the evaluation.

7. The intern appeals any disagreements according to the academic program and academic institution processes. This usually means a route of appeal through the faculty member, department head, dean, and chief academic officer.

8. Whether the evaluation is positive or negative, supervisor and intern agree upon next steps based upon the assessment. These reflect a revision of the internship contract or a letter of remediation possibly signed by the intern, site supervisor, or faculty supervisor.

We discuss two types of evaluations that may occur during the internship experience, formative and summative. Both are important during the internship experience.

Types of Evaluation

Formative Evaluation

Formative evaluation occurs between the supervisor and the intern on a regular, and often, daily basis. It represents the give and take between supervisor and intern as they discuss the intern's work with clients, other peers, and members of the outside community. Interactions viewed as formative evaluation might include the following:

- Can you tell me the reasons you chose that intervention with the client?
- In your case notes, let's look at words that describe and words that label or blame.
- Tell me what just happened when you worked with the group. What went well? What might you change next time you see the group?
- How did your interaction with staff go? Were you able to speak up as you wished? Here are some ways you could try participating.
- I like the way you are thinking about this client. Look at this list of aspects of thinking about clients. Which ones might you include in your next write-up?

Many times formative evaluation does not look like an assessment. Some interns consider the discussion as a part of good supervision. These interns respond in a positive way because their supervisors took the time to pay attention to their work and talk with them about it. On many occasions, formative evaluation focuses on the process and in-the-moment feedback rather than outcomes. Often, this type of evaluation causes less distress than a more formal outcomes-based evaluation.

Even though much of the formative evaluation occurs in an informal way, most internships also have a formal midterm evaluation. Sometimes the midterm evaluations resemble semistructured interviews, while others use formal assessment protocols. Regardless of the approach, most midterm evaluations are less outcome-based and focus more on process. We present an example of a less formal midterm evaluation in Figure 8.3.

Figure 8.3   Semistructured Midterm Evaluation of Human Service
Internship

Midterm Evaluation of Human Service Internship

Student _____

Site supervisor _____

Placement site _____

Semester _____

Please fill out the following questions about the intern's performance of roles and
responsibilities in the internship. Review this form with the intern. Sign and date the
form and deliver to the faculty supervisor by this date.

Briefly describe the intern's roles and responsibilities at the internship site.

Next, summarize the strengths of the intern in the following areas:

1. Work-related qualities such as dependability, work with others, quality
   of work, quantity of work, organization, initiative, analytic abilities, and
   ethical behavior.

2. Personal dispositions such as commitment, openness, respect, integrity,
   and self-awareness.

3. Work-specific skills, such as developing rapport with clients, setting
   client goals and linking with services or interventions, evaluating client
   progress, using community resources, advocating for clients, responding to cultural needs, developing professional relationships, engaging
   in professional development, and networking.

4. Supervision-specific skills such as following instructions, working as a
   team, consulting, taking on new tasks, asking for feedback, and responding
   to critical feedback.

Outline the roles and responsibilities for the last half of the internship. List the
knowledge and skills upon which the intern should focus.

_____Site supervisor signature and date

_____Intern signature and date

_____Faculty signature and date

Tomas shares his thoughts on his experiences with the midterm evaluation. His supervisor used a copy of the final evaluation as a way to prepare
Tomas for the expectations of that assessment. His assessment resembled
the final evaluation as presented in Figure 8.4.

Tomas

*Well I am a little bit up and a little bit down from my evaluation. Maybe
we can talk about our goals for internship. For agreement on goals we*

agreed that my work with clients and the quality of work with clients was a primary goal. Our specifics about that goal were a little different. I listed being able to conduct an intake interview, being able to help clients set goals and develop plans, and being able to help the clients implement the plans. So Ms. Paseattoe agreed with me about work with clients as a primary goal. But she was much more specific about my interaction with clients, like learning to help the client participate in the process, being silent and giving the client a chance to speak, learning to paraphrase, and reflect client emotion not just content. She sounded more like Dr. Highland than I expected. She also expanded her list of goals to include several of mine. By the time we finished our conversation about goals, we both agreed that we learned a lot about each other. And we agreed that we had a strong relationship.

Then came the evaluation. There were times I felt really good and other times I felt like I was a child. I was so surprised by what she said and by my reaction. I am still going over what happened. I read about what I could do to prepare for the midterm evaluation. I rated myself and tried to be realistic. I wrote down the things that I thought I needed help with and provided examples of what I thought I did really well. It was not like we disagreed. But I received some lower scores than I expected. The ratings are Exceptional, Average, Needs Improvement.

I'll admit that I gave myself a few Average scores, but, in my mind, I thought Ms. Passeattoe would say, "Oh I don't think you are "Average," I rated you as "Exceptional." Instead, she gave me "Average" on several items. Ms. Passeattoe could see my disappointment with my evaluation. We ended with a discussion of what the next few weeks would look like and how she wanted to help me improve my skills and also my organizational ability. And my case notes. I know I will be better about this tomorrow, but right now I am sad, disappointed in myself, and I am afraid that Ms. Passeattoe doesn't think that I will be a good human service professional.

Exercise 8.3 Your Thoughts About the Midterm Evaluation: Writing Your Own Story, Entry 23

Step 1

In this exercise, record your thoughts about how you prepared for the midterm evaluation.

Step 2

Then describe your experiences of the midterm evaluation.

Step 3

Finally detail how the midterm evaluation refocused your internship work.

Summative Evaluation

The **summative evaluation** differs from the midterm evaluation in several ways. It focuses on outcomes of work or experience. The summative evaluation of the internship occurs at the conclusion of the internship. This evaluation represents a formal way that the supervisor, in conversation with the intern, documents the progress the intern has made during the academic term. Most academic programs use a standard final evaluation form to guide the assessment of intern performance and professional development. This final evaluation is similar to the final or comprehensive examination required in most academic courses. This final evaluation often uses objective measures and more subjective methods for assessment. The evaluation lists specific standards, behaviors, or competencies and the site supervisor assesses the degree to which the intern's work reflects these competencies. We note that no matter how site supervisors strive for objectivity, there will always be a subjective judgment. By using examples of the intern's work, the site supervisor supplies evidence. However, how the supervisor or the intern interprets this evidence may differ.

There may be an opportunity during the summative evaluation for the supervisor to provide examples of the intern's work. By the conclusion of the summative evaluation, the site supervisor and the intern should be able to discuss the change the intern experienced during the internship experience. Interactions in a summative evaluation may include the following supervisor feedback and remarks:

- I enjoyed working with you during your internship this semester. The purpose of the final evaluation is for us to discuss your current knowledge and skills as a human service intern.
- On Standard 2 of the final evaluation, I marked your performance as a 4 on a scale of 1 to 5. Let me give you my reasons for this assessment.
- How would you rate yourself on Standard 2? I would like to hear from you some examples of where you met this standard and how you struggled to meet this standard.
- For Standard 3, where do you think you started at the beginning of the internship? Where do you think you are now?
- Standard 4, I see it relates directly to a goal in our contract and two of the specific tasks we listed. I am not sure you had ample opportunity to develop this skill. We kept trying to give you this experience, but other experiences seemed to take precedent.
- For Standard 5, I realize that I didn't have opportunity to observe. What are your thoughts on this standard and your experience?
- Here are the areas where I think you exceed expectations. Here are the areas where I think you need continued professional development.
- Overall, I think . . . What do you think?
- What strengths do you think you will bring to your first job as a human service professional? Where do you think you need to continue to grow?

It is important to note the formality of the final evaluation. Even if the site supervisor establishes a comfortable atmosphere for assessment, the final evaluation represents a report on the quality of your work and your development as a human service intern. And a positive evaluation retains a critical element that records your current knowledge and skills and provides suggestions for future growth and development.

Gatekeeping

The final evaluation also marks a time the supervisor's evaluation becomes an integral part of **gatekeeping**. For example, a positive evaluation from the site supervisor reinforces the message to the faculty supervisor and the intern that "This intern [You] is ready to join the ranks of other human service professionals." A less positive evaluation may communicate to the faculty supervisor and to the intern that "This intern [You] will need more work before you are ready to join the ranks of other human service professionals."

When the site supervisor indicates a less than satisfactory performance, the two supervisors and the intern work together to plan the next steps. The goal of this meeting is to devise a plan to help the intern gain the necessary knowledge and skills to become a successful human service professional. That work, appropriately matched to the areas where intern needs work (e.g., personal beliefs and values, professional behavior, work with clients, ethical practice), should help the intern move toward a more positive set of outcomes and evaluation. Interns might also receive less than satisfactory final evaluations for personal circumstances, such as illness, difficult family situations, or other personal situations beyond the intern's control. Again, faculty, site supervisor, and intern may work together to plan how the intern will successfully complete internship work and hours.

A final or summative evaluation in Figure 8.4 illustrates how assessment can combine the evaluation of specific standards and skills with more subjective descriptions and concrete examples.

Figure 8.4   Final Evaluation of Intern

Final Evaluation of Human Service Internship

Student _____

Site supervisor _____

Placement site _____

Semester _____

Supervisor: Take time to match the intern's work with the following competencies and criteria. Your evaluation is information that influences the intern's academic evaluation this term and provides information for referrals. Also, as you evaluate the intern, think about the developmental level of the individual (e.g., beginning internship experience, final internship experience.)

Rate each on a scale of 1 to 5

1. Poor

2. Below average

3. Average

4. Good

5. Exceptional

Work-related qualities

Demonstrating initiative and motivation 1 2 3 4 5

Being punctual and maintaining regular attendance 1 2 3 4 5

Getting along with others 1 2 3 4 5

Submitting work that is complete and accurate 1 2 3 4 5

Working efficiently 1 2 3 4 5

Anticipating problems 1 2 3 4 5

Following rules and procedures 1 2 3 4 5

Demonstrating good judgment 1 2 3 4 5

Demonstrating organizational skills 1 2 3 4 5

Submitting well written reports 1 2 3 4 5

Specific examples of work-related skills:

Personal beliefs and values

Demonstrating commitment 1 2 3 4 5

Demonstrating openness 1 2 3 4 5

Demonstrating respect 1 2 3 4 5

Demonstrating integrity 1 2 3 4 5

Demonstrating self-awareness 1 2 3 4 5

Specific examples related to personal beliefs and values:

Work-specific skills

Developing rapport with clients 1 2 3 4 5

Setting client goals 1 2 3 4 5

Linking clients with services or interventions 1 2 3 4 5

Evaluating client progress 1 2 3 4 5

(Continued)

Figure 8.4 (continued)

Using community resources 1 2 3 4 5

Advocating for clients 1 2 3 4 5

Responding to cultural needs 1 2 3 4 5

Developing professional relationships 1 2 3 4 5

Engaging in professional development 1 2 3 4 5

Networking 1 2 3 4 5

Specific examples related to work-specific skills:

Supervision-specific skills

Using supervision appropriately 1 2 3 4 5

Demonstrating ability to follow instructions 1 2 3 4 5

Working as a team 1 2 3 4 5

Engaging in consultation 1 2 3 4 5

Taking on new tasks 1 2 3 4 5

Asking for feedback 1 2 3 4 5

Responding to critical feedback 1 2 3 4 5

Specific examples related to supervision-specific skills:

Additional comments

_____Site supervisor signature and date

_____Intern signature and date

_____Faculty signature and date

Exercise 8.4 Your Thoughts About the Final Evaluation: Writing Your Own Story, Entry 24

Step 1

In this exercise, record your thoughts and feelings about the final evaluation of your internship.

Step 2

Talk about how you will prepare for the final evaluation. How does completing this exercise reframe your remaining weeks in internship?

Your Thoughts and Feelings About the Final Evaluation

_____

_____

_____

Preparing for the Final Evaluation

_____

_____

_____

Reframing Your Remaining Weeks in Internship

_____

_____

_____

We indicated in this section that the supervisor's evaluation of the intern is an important aspect of the internship experience. It is also important that you as the intern have the opportunity to provide feedback to your site supervisor and faculty supervisor about your view of the supervision you received. To do so in an informed and fair way, we provide ways you can consider the quality of your supervisory experience in the next section.

Box 8.5 Studying the Text: Considering the Quality of Supervision

Studying the text: The following outline will help you read and study the text material in this next section.
Considering the quality of supervision

1. Intern Bill of Rights

2. Rights of intern

3. Responsibilities of intern

4. Poor supervision

To help you begin to reflect on the supervision you are receiving, we want to introduce you to the concept of the **Intern Bill of Rights**. This Bill of Rights will help you be clearer about the expectations you may have for supervision.

The Intern Bill of Rights

By its very nature, the act of being supervised places an intern in a vulnerable position. For example, site supervisors assume the responsibility to support the professional development of the intern by structuring the

Figure 8.5 Intern Bill of Rights: Supervisor Responsibilities

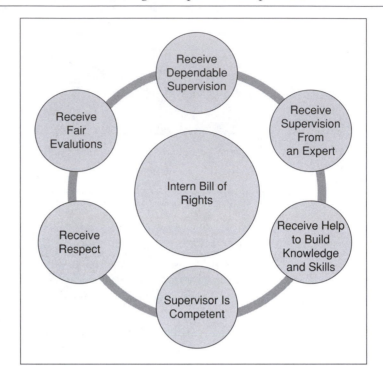

internship. And as we discussed in the earlier section, they also evaluate the intern's performance. Faculty members view site supervisors as more senior and as experts. In fact, at the outset, faculty see site supervisors as trustworthy. Because of the importance of supervision, and in relation to the inherent vulnerability of the intern within the supervisory process, we introduce the Intern Bill of Rights. Knowledge of the Intern Bill of Rights will help clarify the rights and responsibilities you have as an intern.

Munson (2002) introduced the concept of a Supervisee Bill of Rights as a way to describe the legitimate expectations you, as an intern, have as you look forward to or participate in supervision. We adapted Munson's (2002) expectations to describe what you can expect of supervision. We call these **supervisor responsibilities.** Note these expectations are written from the intern's perspective and shown in Figure 8.5.

You should expect to

- receive dependable supervision at regularly scheduled times;
- receive supervision that helps you develop knowledge, skills, and values;
- receive supervision that demonstrates respect;
- receive an evaluation based upon clear expectations, standards, and observable data;
- receive supervision from a supervisor who has expertise in helping and demonstrates effective helping skills; and
- receive supervision from a supervisor with training in supervision.

In a sense, this list of expectations represents what good supervision looks like. In addition, alongside the rights you have relating to supervision, there exist concurrent responsibilities you assume as a participant in the supervisory process. These are the duties or obligations that help you become a reliable participant and support your own professional growth and development and, ultimately, prepare you for professional human service work. We call these **intern responsibilities**.

What do intern expectations and responsibilities to the supervisory process actually look like during internship? We address this question in Table 8.2, where in the first column, we present each of the expectations listed. Then, in Column 2 we describe possible ways supervisors might meet each expectation. Column 2 allows you to reflect more clearly on the supervision you are currently receiving in light of your expectations. Finally, in Column 3 we add the intern's responsibilities related to each expectation. Again, we use specific behaviors to define the intern responsibilities.

Table 8.2   Intern Bill of Rights

Intern Rights	Desirable Supervisor Behaviors	Intern Responsibilities
Receives dependable supervision at regularly scheduled times	– Schedules regular supervision times – Is available for questions and consultations – Is available for crisis intervention – Makes plans for alternative site supervision when unavailable for assistance or consultation – Is clear about how intern prepares for and delivers services – Provides appropriate developmental supervision (observation, direct supervision, indirect supervision) – Provides opportunities to practice interventions	– Attends supervisory sessions. – Arrives on time to supervisory sessions – Asks supervisor for instructions prior to providing services or assuming agency tasks or projects – Asks supervisor for feedback after client work – Reviews case notes and other assignments with supervisor and asks for feedback – Attends relevant professional development meetings to learn about innovative interventions
Receives supervision that helps develop knowledge, skills, and values	– Develops a supervision plan reflecting what the intern should learn and what the intern should do – Plans supervision sessions based upon intern development and overall plan – Merges supervision plan with intern's expressed goals	– Asks questions that facilitate learning – Probes for clarity related to supervisor instructions or suggestions – Make notes about work and follows up with questions
Receives supervision that demonstrates respect for intern	– Listens to intern's description of experiences – Seeks intern's opinions and thoughts – Respects confidential information shared by intern – Discusses difficulties and challenges related to supervisory relationship promptly – Encourages intern to try new skills	– Shares internship-related experiences with supervisor – Remains open about strengths and limitations – Shares thoughts and opinions about internship work – Uses personal disclosure as a way to gain insight about professional growth and skill development – Discusses challenges with the supervisory relationship

(Continued)

Table 8.2 (Continued)

Receives evaluation based upon clear expectations, standards, and based upon data	– Matches internship goals with evaluation measures – Reviews goals and evaluations – Conducts informal evaluations regularly – Provides clear, positive, and constructive feedback – Conducts evaluations in a timely manner – Reviews formal evaluations with intern – Seeks intern's input into evaluations – Creates a plan for growth based upon evaluation	– Shares professional and personal goals for internship – Seeks experiences that meet goals – Prepares questions for supervisor and asks for specific feedback – Provides examples of ways intern believes he or she is meeting supervisor goals – Keeps a list of goals to add or subtract from your internship contract – Reviews the academic program evaluation forms prior to formal evaluation – Identifies any areas of work for which student believes he or she needs additional work
Receives supervision from supervisor who has expertise in helping and demonstrates effective helping skills	Related to clients – Demonstrates good attending skills – Establishes rapport with clients – Uses a variety of assessment techniques – Formulates clear client conceptualizations – Understands theories and approaches to helping – Formulates treatment goals and plans – Uses a variety of interventions effectively – Assesses client cognitive and affective communication – Responds with respect and equity to client's individual differences – Behaves in a professional and ethical manner	Related to supervision – Learns intervention skills – Practices good assessment skills – Understands how to use client conceptualizations – Recognizes clients' individual needs and differences – Evaluates different treatment goals and plans – Makes ethical decisions on issues
Receives supervision from individual who is a trained supervisor	– Understands the roles and responsibilities of supervision – Assesses what type of supervision the intern needs – Attends training related to supervision – Asks for feedback from intern on performance as a supervisor	– Asks for help that facilitates professional growth and development – Uses academic program's list of responsibilities to assess supervisor performance – Provides faculty supervisor information related to supervisor performance and supervisory process – Seeks supervision from others, when supervisor cannot provide support needed – Consults faculty, supervisor, and peers

During the time you are in internship, the intern rights and responsibilities establish the standards for quality supervision. But, the realities of internship, at times, make these behaviors difficult to demonstrate consistently. Some days you may feel you are receiving quality supervision and believe you are performing responsibly. At other times, you may be less sure of your supervisor's commitment or uncertain about the value of your own work. For example, your supervisor may convey respect for your work with clients by allowing you to work with clients independently and support your work within the agency by assigning you responsibility for projects and programs. Yet, in a crisis situation or during a threat assessment, you may play a limited role in the agency's response. And your supervisor may not have time to talk with you about what it happening or to answer questions you have about agency responses.

You can expect this unevenness of the experience of supervision because of the dynamic nature of human service work. Yet, in spite of some inconsistency in supervision you receive, you still may be able to offer a positive assessment of your supervisory experience. You should also expect your supervisor to be generally positive about your performance as an intern, even though, from time to time, you make mistakes or fail to understand the nuances of the professional work.

After studying Table 8.2, you begin to understand what expectations you can have for the supervisory experience, as well as learn about ways you can participate in the supervisory experience in a positive way. Interns often ask the following questions as they begin to think about and assess the quality of their supervisory experience.

- "How do I judge the quality of experience I am receiving?"
- "Am I fulfilling my responsibilities in the supervisory process?"
- "How do I ask for good supervision?"

These questions begin with an assessment of the nature of the supervisory experience, extend to advocacy for good supervision, and, at times, confront difficult supervisory situations. Exercise 8.5 helps you address these questions. With this exercise we intend for you to explore the strengths and limitations of your supervisory relationship and the supervision you are receiving. We repeat the idea that both quality work as a supervisor and work as an intern may take many forms, yet we assume that no supervisor's or intern's performance is flawless. There exist many ways to provide good supervision, just as there are many ways interns may perform their responsibilities.

Exercise 8.5 Supervisor Desirable Behaviors/Intern Rights and Responsibilities

In this exercise, we would like for you to assess the supervision you are receiving. You will use Table 8.2 to guide your assessment.

Step 1

Before you begin this exercise, read through your responses to Exercises 8.1 and 8.2 where you described your current supervision.

Step 2

Read through Table 8.2 again. Review each of the supervisor desirable behaviors and list those your supervisor practices and those your supervisor does not practice.

Answer the following questions or prompts:

> What are the behaviors your supervisor demonstrates that you value most?
>
> What behaviors do you wish your supervisor demonstrated?
>
> In your estimation, what does you supervisor think you need?
>
> How does your supervisor meet those supervisor-driven needs?
>
> What do you need from your supervisor?
>
> How does your supervisor meet your needs?
>
> Which of your needs go unmet?

Step 3

Review the intern responsibilities and list those you practice and those you do not practice.

Answer the following questions or prompts:

> Within the context of supervision, what responsibilities do I assume?
>
> In my opinion, which of my behaviors best support the supervisory process?
>
> In my estimation, what are the limitations of my participation in supervision?
>
> In my estimation, how do these limitations influence the supervisory process?

Step 4

Talk with you faculty supervisor about how you can ask your supervisor for what you need, based upon the list of desirable supervisor behaviors. Talk with your faculty supervisor about your list of intern responsibilities you believe you are not assuming. Ask your faculty supervisor for help related to how you might assume your intern responsibilities more effectively.

Addressing Poor and Harmful Supervision

We talked earlier about expectations for supervision and the intern's responsibilities related to supervision, indicating that most supervision is dynamic and, at times, imperfect. Helpful supervisors recognize the challenges in supervision, their own limitations, and the constraints of the internship site. These supervisors talk openly about the realities of professional work and, relevant to the internship, indicate their ongoing assessments of their supervision, the supervisory process, and intern performance.

Because supervisors make major contributions to the interns' professional growth and development, **poor supervision** or **harmful supervision** negatively impacts this potential for growth (Ellis, 2001; Ellis et al., 2014). Whether faculty or the student establishes an internship site, they both hope for a good supervision experience. In spite of the care taken, supervision does not always meet the academic program or faculty expectations. Interns may express uncertainty about the quality of the supervision they are receiving when they ask these questions:

- "When do I share with my faculty supervisor my doubts about supervision?"
- "When is the supervision so poor that I need to request another placement?"

We help interns answer these two questions as we describe poor supervision and harmful supervision, although it is difficult, at times, to distinguish between the two.

The Question of Poor Supervision

As stated earlier, a description of intern rights and responsibilities helps us understand what good supervision looks like in practice. On the other hand, the lack of these behaviors indicates poor supervision. Ellis (2001) describes "bad" supervision as that carried out by a supervisor who "is unable or unwilling" (p. 402) to help the intern grow and develop. To better understand what some of the behaviors are that reflect poor supervision, we use the intern rights from Table 8.2 (Munson, 2002) and provide a list of a few behaviors that illustrate poor supervision.

- Receive dependable supervision at regularly scheduled times. *Poor supervision means supervisors*
  - maintain an irregular supervision schedule,
  - consistently arrive late to supervision meeting,
  - consistently come to supervision ill prepared, and
  - communicate using an aggressive tone.
- Receive supervision that helps develop knowledge, skills, and values. *Poor supervision means supervisors*
  - assign most tasks and activities on an ad hoc basis,
  - relate all assignments to supervisor needs rather than internship contract and goals,
  - disregard intern's interests, and
  - refuse to share ethical decision-making process.
- Receive supervision that demonstrates respect for intern. *Poor supervision means supervisors:*
  - maintain communication at a surface and business level,
  - criticize intern in front of others,
  - demand intern's work mirrors supervisor behaviors,
  - disregard intern's concerns about discrimination and oppression related to client work, and
  - ignore any ruptures in the supervisory relationship.
- Receive evaluation based upon clear expectations and standards and based upon data. *Poor supervision means supervisors*
  - evaluate intern without observation,
  - evaluate intern without reference to established goals,
  - evaluate intern without reviewing criteria for evaluation,
  - discuss only intern's limitations, and
  - surprise the intern with strong criticism at the final evaluation.
- Receive supervision from supervisor who has expertise in helping and demonstrates effective helping skills. *Poor supervision means supervisors*
  - see only their strengths and do not see their limitations,
  - discuss only their own strengths with intern,
  - practice outside their areas of competence, and
  - rarely ask other colleagues to work with intern.

- Receive supervision from an individual who has training in the practice of supervision. *Poor supervision means supervisors*
  - do not talk with intern about how to improve supervision,
  - do not seek training in supervision, and
  - do not consult with faculty supervisor about how to match intern experience with academic program goals.

Sometimes interns have supervisors who, whether intentionally or not, do harm during the supervisory process. Sometimes telling the difference between poor and harmful supervision is not easy. While poor supervision reflects an ineffective way of working with an intern, we suggest that harmful supervision exists when the intern is hurt or traumatized in some way by the supervision received. In other words, we can, in part, determine harmful supervision by the way it affects the intern (Ellis, 2001; Ellis et al., 2014). This includes "psychological, emotion, and/or physical harm or trauma" (Ellis et al., 2014, p. 435). According to Ellis (2001), these types of harm may be related to making sexual approaches, demonstrating sexual harassment behaviors, acting in a discriminatory way (e.g., microaggressions—see Chapter 7), crossing intern professional or relationship boundaries, and acting in an abusive way. In many ways harmful supervision may represent violations of professional and ethical standards of supervision practice (Dye & Borders, 1990).

Ellis (2001) proposed four ways that interns might be harmed by supervision:

- Psychological harm resulting in intern feelings of guilt, shame, fear, and mistrust
- Impairment in professional or personal life resulting in the intern's inability to maintain relationships, organize daily tasks, or follow a schedule
- Emotional harm to the intern related to the development of an aggravation of expressions of anxiety, depression, or posttraumatic stress syndrome
- Physical debilitation in the intern resulting in issues such as chronic illness, sleep disorders, or increased use of alcohol or substance abuse

As a way to concretize harmful supervision, we believe that harmful supervision can occur either when the supervisor is negligent or behaves with malicious intent, or acts unethically (e.g., sexual harassment or intimacy). As you think about the supervision you receive, it is important that you identify aspects of supervision that are either poor or harmful and share these with your faculty supervisor. We ask you to look at Exercise 8.6 as a way to identify aspects of poor or harmful supervision related to the supervision you are receiving.

Exercise 8.6 Identifying Poor or Harmful Supervision

Step 1

For each of the characteristics listed below, describe your supervisory experiences:

- Receive dependable supervision at regularly scheduled times
- Receive supervision that helps develop knowledge, skills, and values

- Receive supervision that demonstrates respect for intern
- Receive evaluation based upon clear expectations and standards and based upon data
- Receive supervision from supervisor who has expertise in helping and demonstrates effective helping skills
- Receive supervision from individual with training in supervision.

Step 2

Review the characteristics of harm that you may have experienced due to supervision. Indicate if you are experiencing any of these. Explain.

- Psychological harm resulting in intern feelings of guilt, shame, fear, and mistrust
- Functional impairment in professional or personal life resulting in the intern's inability to maintain relationships, organize daily tasks, or follow a schedule
- Emotional harm to the intern related to the development of an aggravation of expressions of anxiety, depression, or posttraumatic stress syndrome
- Physical debilitation in the intern resulting in issues such as chronic illness, sleep disorders, or increased use of alcohol or substance abuse

Step 3

Review the supervisor behaviors that may have occurred during your time at your agency. Indicate if you have experienced any of these. Explain. Supervisor

- Engages in sexual intimacies
- Demonstrates sexual harassment
- Acts in a discriminatory manner
- Crosses professional boundaries between supervisor and intern (e.g., friendship or social relationship)
- Acts in an aggressive way (or refuses to help the intern)

Step 4

Discuss the results of this exercise with your faculty supervisor. Plan next steps.

Now that you have learned about your rights and responsibilities as an intern and reviewed the quality of the supervisory you are receiving, it is time to hear from your student peers, supervisors, and a human service professional. You can review Box 8.6 for the familiar close of this chapter.

Box 8.6 Deepening Your Understanding

1. Peer-to-peer dialogue

   a. Alicia: Experience of supervision

   b. Lucas: Experience of supervision

   c. Tamika: Experience of supervision

2. Faculty and site supervisor dialogue

   a. Dr. Bianca: The roles of faculty supervision

   b. Ms. Bellewa: My experience as a supervisor

3. The professional voice and tips for practice: Meet Gwen: Sexual harassment

4. Terms to remember

5. References

Deepening Your Understanding

Alicia, Lucas, and Tamika share their experience of internship as it relates to asking for and receiving supervision. Although many of their experiences may differ from yours, we believe, as you compare their insights with yours, you will draw new insights about your own internship. Dr. Bianca, Ms. Bellewa, and Gwen provide faculty, site supervisor, and professional perspectives about the supervisory process, its goals, and their experiences.

Peer-to-Peer Dialogue: Alicia, Lucas, and Tamika

We asked Alicia, Lucas, and Tamika to talk about their experiences in supervision. They share information about the supervisory relationship, their own understanding of the supervisory process, how supervision meets their expectations, and what they wish for that they are not receiving. They present supervision in a realistic way.

Alicia

Hello, again! I am excited to tell you about my experience in supervision. I see it as one of the most rewarding aspects of human services training. I am currently supervised by my faculty supervisor, Dr. Lynn, and site supervisor at Cal State's career center, Dr. Davis. Group supervision with Dr. Lynn occurs during our internship class meeting. I enjoy this process, as I am able to reflect upon my experience, receive feedback from Dr. Lynn and my fellow students, while learning from their experiences. I feel like this setup is particularly advantageous, as we learn about various populations and, even, differing supervisory approaches. Furthermore, Dr. Lynn does a great job of providing each of us individual attention with equal opportunities to speak, while maintaining group cohesion and overall lessons in human services. Individual supervision with Dr. Davis is very helpful, as we discuss my growth, goals, and strategies for conquering developmental challenges. I also feel an overall sense of collaboration between Dr. Lynn, Dr. Davis, and myself, as we openly discuss my evaluations. Each supervisor understands my apprehension regarding evaluation, and we work together to focus on learning opportunities and strengths.

Written by Allie Rhinehart and Dareen Basma, 2015. Used with permission.

Lucas

Hello, I hope you are having a great day! Today, I am going to share with you my experiences of supervision from the Tampa Bay Justice Center. One thing I want to say is, "I LOVE SUPERVISION!" The reason why I say this is the knowledge I get from Dr. Kim, my site supervisor, and Dr. Franks, my faculty supervisor. This is my first placement, and before I started, I had a lot of anxiety and self-doubt about my skills to help people. However, supervision alleviates my anxieties, and my supervisors give me the confidence to help my clients. More importantly, the supervision I am receiving is helping me develop my skills as a therapist, helps me understand myself and how I am influencing my clients, and I can consult with my supervisors when I need help.

In my opinion, what is making supervision work is the relationship I have with my supervisors. For instance, at every session when I am having difficulties helping my clients, my supervisors do not judge me, they listen to me, and they are honest with their feedback. Our relationship works because I believe we are a good match because of our growth mind-set, personality characteristics, and we have clear expectations of the supervisory process. For example, for every supervision session, I bring in a tape. We review the tape, and my supervisors help me process my work with clients. They provide me feedback. At the end of each session, they allow me to express my feelings and thoughts of the session, give me opportunities to ask questions. They ask me what I learned about my clients and myself. Additionally, throughout the supervisory process, we evaluate each session, not only to evaluate my performance, but also to evaluate my supervisors.

One thing I am disappointed about in supervision is the lack of counseling I am receiving. For example, there was a session where I started to get emotional when a client was telling me her story because it reminded me of an experience I had. I did not show any emotions during the session, but during supervision, I told my supervisors how I felt. They normalized my feelings of the situation, but they did not delve deeper to my issues as it related to my client's experiences. I felt I needed support, and help understanding my feelings. I asked for assistance, and they told me I needed to see a therapist to delve deeper into my feelings and experiences. I was disappointed when they told me this because I feel comfortable around them, and they do have the skills to help me but did not want to. At least that is how I felt. I did ask them both, after I evaluated our supervision session, and they said they do not believe supervision involves counseling. They said some supervisors support counseling as part of the supervisory role or expectation; however, they said they do not want to cross that boundary with me. I was disappointed, but I respect their supervision philosophies.

Overall, I truly enjoy supervision at the Tampa Bay Justice Center, and with my faculty supervisor. It is a safe place for me to express how I feel, what concerns I have, and ask for help, without being judged. I hope my experience gives you insight to supervision and what it looks like. I have a good experience of supervision, and I hope you do too!

Written by Jorge Roman, 2015. Used with permission.

Tamika

Before beginning my internship, I was really worried about the supervision aspect of the process. I had lots of questions running through my mind—what if my supervisors didn't like me or think I wasn't doing a good job? What if I didn't feel comfortable asking them for help or accepting their feedback? Fortunately, my faculty and site supervisors have both been great and my fears were quickly relieved. At this point, supervision is actually a topic I feel totally comfortable talking about because during this internship, I have gotten lots of it!

As a student intern, I'm required to go to group supervision class once a week, meet alternately every other week with my faculty supervisor for individual supervision, and my faculty supervisor and a peer for triadic supervision, and meet with my site supervisor once a week. That is a lot of supervision. At first, it seemed like kind of a hassle to work all these extra meetings into my schedule and I wondered why I couldn't just be assigned one supervisor and stick with him or her. I quickly learned, however, the value of meeting with multiple people to discuss my work. Not only does doing so expand my support network, but it also gives me multiple clinical perspectives to consider when I think about how to better help my clients.

My faculty supervisor talked in class about the Supervisory Working Alliance and its three main elements (Bordin, as cited in Horvath & Greenberg, 1994). Boy, did I luck out. Both of my supervisors have been extremely supportive in helping me to navigate goals and tasks that will help me to develop as a human service professional. They both contributed to my internship contract and have worked hard to help me stay organized and make sure that most of the work I do at my site is significant to my overall professional development. I have also formed a solid bond with both of my supervisors. While we don't always immediately agree on everything, I really trust them to help me figure out clinical solutions that work for my clients, as well as for me. I feel especially close to my site supervisor, who has helped me work through some tough dilemmas and has encouraged me to ask questions as they arise. I know that my supervisors check in with each other from time to time regarding my work, and I look forward to hearing their collaborative feedback because I know that our working alliance is strong.

Although I feel positive about the supervisory process these days, I can't lie. My first formal evaluation made me pretty anxious. My program requires that my site supervisor complete a written evaluation for me at midsemester and again at the end of the internship. I loved how my site supervisor structured the experience for my midterm evaluation. She asked me to take the form provided by my school and complete a self-evaluation while she completed one on me at the same time. During one of our weekly supervision meetings, we shared our evaluations with one another, and it was such a neat experience. It really gave us the opportunity to discuss similarities and differences in how we each viewed my work, and it made me a lot more comfortable to explore openly with her my strengths as an intern and the areas in which I can improve. In the end, it wasn't scary at all and I found it to be a really valuable experience.

The consequences of my first evaluation were mostly positive, but it also presented a few challenges. The advantages were that it allowed me to reflect on my own performance as an intern, invest more in the evaluation process than I might have otherwise, and discuss openly with my supervisor how to put her constructive feedback and suggestions into action. One disadvantage was that I think her evaluative method spoiled me a bit. I need to remember that it's possible not all supervisors will take the same collaborative approach.

Overall, I have really enjoyed the role of intern and the responsibilities that I have assumed. I recognize now the value of supervision and truly appreciate the time and effort my supervisors have dedicated to fostering my professional development. Who knows? Maybe one day I'll even want to be a supervisor. But I suppose I better finish my internship first!

Written by Brittany Pollard, 2015. Used with permission.

Exercise 8.7 Your Thoughts About the Supervisory Experiences: Writing Your Own Story, Entry 25

You just read about Alicia, Lucas, and Tamika and their experiences of supervision. Now it is your turn to write about your own supervisory experiences! This exercise will help you integrate the material you learned in this chapter.

- Review the Triad/Quartet Model and the Intern Bill of Rights. Discuss how you will use the two together to make sense of the supervision you are receiving or you wish you were receiving.
- What are your highs and lows of supervision? Describe these. Review the personal beliefs discussed in Chapter 5 and relate these to the highs and lows you describe.
- A primary purpose of supervision is to promote client welfare. How is supervision helping you to better serve the clients with whom you work?

Faculty and Site Supervisor Dialogue: Dr. Bianca and Ms. Bellewa

In addition to hearing from Alicia, Lucas, and Tamika, we asked Dr. Bianca, a human service faculty member, and Ms. Bellewa, a human service site supervisor, to talk about their experiences with supervision, especially with an intern.

Dr. Claude Bianca

I know that I talked earlier about the quality of supervision that I try to provide for my internship students, both in our group supervision class and at their site. I have certain standards for my own supervision, but I fully understand that I am not going to be a great supervisor for everyone. First, I feel that I am really limited about the skills I know my students are gaining in their internship site. Sometimes they can tape at their site and sometimes not. Some semesters, students bring me multiple tapes and I am able to listen to them on a regular basis, sometimes I just don't have time to listen to as many tapes as I would like. Sometimes my internship class has 15 students in it. At our group meetings, I don't get to hear from every student, and that means that, on a week-to-week basis, I don't know what is going on with their work at the site or their work in agencies. Where I am especially strong, I think, is helping students dealing with crisis in their placements to crisis in the supervision they are receiving.

The fact that I can rarely count on quality supervision is one of my struggles with the site supervisor/intern match and the supervisory process. First, I have some site supervisors that are really good supervisors. This means that they understand the role, they relate well to interns, they provide excellent feedback, and they help students move from novices to accepting their place in the profession. In spite of all of these assurances, there are still times when a placement does not work. Sometimes, there is just not a match between the supervisor and the intern. For example, the intern might remain resistant to serving the population or never feel competent to assume a professional role. At other times, this same quality supervisor might, for any number of reasons, not have time for good supervision.

Other times, there might be a personality clash between the supervisor and the intern—oh they can make the supervision work—but neither supervisor nor intern feels the comfort level necessary for critical feedback and positive growth. But in my experience, most of the time, the quality supervision our site supervisors provide our students is better than adequate and, at times, there exists a magical quality in the bond between site supervisor and intern that occurs in internship and extends beyond it.

Ms. Zu Bellewa

Providing supervision to my interns is one of the most enjoyable parts of my work as a site supervisor. During my work with this agency and its interns, I noticed that the students generally start supervision with a sense of confusion about what its purpose is. As a result, I started utilizing my first and second meeting with them to outline expectations for supervision and negotiate a contract. I use the word negotiate because it truly is indicative of what I feel supervision needs to look like: a discussion of what my expectations are, what my intern's expectations are, what goals we both have for our time together, and how we can develop items we both agree on. I will outline those two meetings because I believe it lays out a solid foundation for my relationship with the interns.

The first meeting can be uncomfortable for my interns. I focus this meeting on three specific things. First, we review what they perceive my role and purpose in supervision is; we then discuss what my role and purpose in supervision really looks like. I've noticed that interns begin their work at the agency with the preconceived notion that I am their manager, so to speak. In their minds, I am the one they get in trouble with if they do anything wrong. While their work with clients must be reported to me and I have to hold them accountable for the work they do, I try to immediately dispel the idea that I am in a managerial role. I explain to the interns that the supervision meeting is a time for us to develop our relationship in order to best meet the needs of the clients. As such, my role as a supervisor is not to tell them what to do, when to do it, or how to do it; instead it is to guide them through their journey in the human services internship in order for them to gain enough confidence to make those decisions themselves.

After I explain to them the purpose of supervision, I ask them to consider two different things for our following meeting. First, I ask them to think about a list of three of their strengths and three areas they would like to develop throughout the course of their internship. I often ask them to think about what specific things they think they will need from me. I recognize that every intern has different needs and different ways of meeting those needs. Some interns prefer a larger amount of support than others; some require more emotional support, while others require direct and concrete feedback.

We review those two items during our next supervision meeting and really delve into the supervision contract. I recognize that interns' needs, strengths, and areas for growth shift and change as they undergo their process of development and let them know that this conversation is one that occurs several times throughout their work with the agency. Overall, supervision for me is a working relationship that is constantly changing and requiring adaptation from both my interns and myself. Ultimately, my role is to help interns' meet their needs in order for them to best meet their client's needs.

Written by Dareen Basma, 2015. Used with permission.

The Professional Voice and Tips for Success: Gwen

Gwen

In this chapter, Marianne wrote about harmful supervision. In that discussion, she referenced sexual harassment and the deleterious effects of being harassed, including experiencing feelings of shame, guilt, fear, and mistrust, as well as experiencing anxiety and an inability or difficulty in organizing your daily life. In this tips for success, we're going to examine what is sexual harassment, what are some of the behaviors commonly associated with it, and, lastly, we'll consider the next steps of responding and reporting sexual harassment.

According to the U.S. Equal Employment Opportunity Commission (EEOC, n.d.), "It is unlawful to harass a person because of that person's sex. Harassment can include 'sexual harassment' or unwelcome sexual advances, requests for sexual favors, and other verbal or physical harassment of a sexual nature." An important note here is that harassment doesn't have to be of a sexual nature, necessarily; harassment can include offensive remarks about someone's sex (EEOC, n.d.). For example, saying that men can't be good mental health counselors because they are not in touch with their emotions is an example of sexual harassment. It's also important to note that sexual harassment can happen to anyone, regardless of gender; however, women are far more likely to be victims of sexual harassment (National Women's Law Center, 2000). Additionally, sexual harassment perpetrators are not limited to people in supervisory positions. Anyone who perpetrates these behaviors—supervisors, student peers, agency staff, or clients—is committing sexual harassment and is breaking the law. As such, you have a right to legal protections and redress.

Sexual harassment can take many behaviors and can range widely—such as, but not limited to, the following:

- *Discussing sexual activities*
- *Telling off-color jokes*
- *Unnecessary touching*
- *Commenting on physical attributes*
- *Displaying sexually suggestive pictures*
- *Using crude language or demeaning or inappropriate terms*
- *Using indecent gestures*
- *Engaging in hostile physical conduct (Westminster College, n.d.)*

If you, or another intern you know, experience any form of harassment, first, know that it is not your fault. No one asks for or deserves to be harassed. And no one should have to tolerate those behaviors, particularly in the workplace. Here are some guidelines for your next steps if you are being harassed:

- *In the moment of being harassed, name the behavior and tell the perpetrator, "No! Do not do [name behavior] again. I feel very uncomfortable with [name behavior]."*
- *Record the incident in writing, being specific with who did what to whom. Write down date, time, and location of incident.*
- *Immediately report the incident to your site and faculty supervisors, assuming neither is the perpetrator.*
- *If the behavior is not addressed, contact the human resources department of your site (if such exists) and contact the office of social equity and diversity at your university.*

*Please note, the above are responses for harassment behaviors; if you are being sexually assaulted and in eminent physical danger, protect yourself and report the incident to police immediately. And, of course, you should always contact your faculty supervisor.

Written by Gwen Ruttencutter, 2015. Used with permission.

Terms to Remember

Due process

Evaluation

Formative evaluation

Gatekeeping

Harmful supervision

Intern Bill of Rights

Intern responsibilities

Poor supervision

Summative evaluation

Supervisee (intern)

Supervision

Supervision quartet

Supervision triad

Supervisor

Supervisor responsibilities

Supervisory

Supervisory process

Supervisory relationship

References

Bernard, J. M., & Goodyear, R. K. (2014). *Fundamentals of clinical supervision* (5th ed.). Boston, MA: Pearson.

Corey, G., Haynes, R. H., Moulton, P., & Muratori, M. (2010). *Clinical supervision in the helping professions: A practical guide* (2nd ed.). Alexandria, VA: American Counseling Association.

Council for Standards in Human Services Education. (2013). National standards: Associate degree in human services. Retrieved from http://www.cshse.org/pdfs/Standards-Associate.pdf

Dye, H. A., & Borders, L. D. (1990). Counseling supervisors: Standards for preparation and practice. *Journal of Counseling & Development, 69,* 27–32. doi:10.1002/j.1556-6676.1990.tb01449.x

Ellis, M. V. (2001). Harmful supervision, a cause for alarm: Comment on Gray et al. (2001) and Nelson and Friedlander (2001). *Journal of Counseling Psychology, 48*(4), 401–406.

Ellis, M. V., Berger, L., Hanus, A. E., Ayala, E. E., Swords, B. A., & Siembor, M. (2014). Inadequate and harmful supervision: Testing a revised framework and assessing occurrence. *The Counseling Psychologist, 42*(4), 434–472. doi: 10.1177/0011000013508656

Evaluate. (2015). In *Merriam-Webster dictionary* (11th ed.). Retrieved from http://www.merriamwebster.com/dictionary/evaluate

Gallon, S., Hausotter, W., & Bryan, M. A. (2005). What happens in good supervision? *Addiction Messenger, 8*(9), 1–5. Retrieved from http://www.unodc.org/ddt-training/treatment/VOLUME%20D/Topic%202/4.2-What_happens_in_good_supervision.pdf

Horvath, A., & Greenberg, L. (Eds.). (1994). *The working alliance: Theory, research and practice.* New York, NY: Wiley.

Munson, C. E. (2002). *Clinical social work supervision* (3rd ed.). New York, NY: Hayworth Press.

National Organization of Human Services. (2015). Ethical standards for human service professionals. Retrieved from https://nohs.memberclicks.net/ethical-standards-for-hs-professionals

National Women's Law Center. (2000). Fact sheet: Sexual harassment in the workplace. Retrieved from http://www.nwlc.org/resource/frequently-asked-questions-about-sexual-harassment-workplace

Rogers, C. (1980). *A way of being.* Boston, MA: Houghton Mifflin.

Supervision. (2012). In *Oxford English dictionary.* Retrieved from http://www.oed.com/view/Entry/194558?redirectedFrom=supervision#eid

U.S. Equal Employment Opportunity Commission. (n.d.). Sexual harassment. Retrieved from http://www.eeoc.gov/laws/types/sexual_harassment.cfm

Westminster College. (n.d.). *Harassment policies and procedures.* Retrieved from https://www.westminstercollege.edu/pdf/career_center/Harrassment%20Policies.pdf

PART III

Expanding Your Skills

Working With Clients

Reading this chapter will help you do the following:

- Outline the guidelines for working with clients using a culture-centered approach.
- Provide an example of how to implement each of the guidelines.
- Describe several aspects of agency practice that facilitate an environment of culture-centered helping.
- Define strengths-based helping.
- Describe how to implement strengths-based helping in the helping process.
- Learn about how peers, a faculty supervisor, a site supervisor, and a human service professional work with clients.

This chapter, Chapter 9, is the first chapter in Part III, Expanding Your Skills. The purpose of the chapter is to help you integrate a culture-centered approach with the helping process. We also suggest ways that you can extend your work with the helping process by focusing on culture-centered approaches to helping. We also help you think about how agencies review, and then respond to, their clients' cultural needs. We provide guidelines for integrating a strengths-based approach during the helping process. In the final section, we return to Alicia, Lucas, and Tamika to hear about how they implement culture-centered helping and a strengths-based approach in working with clients. Dr. Bianca and Ms. Bellewa share their experiences of interns expanding their skills while working with clients. Finally, Gwen provides her perspectives on facilitating change in an internship site.

Box 9.1 describes the organizational framework of the first section of this chapter, that of delivering to clients culture-centered helping.

Box 9.1 Studying the Text: Delivering Culture-Centered Helping

Studying the text: The following outline will help you read and study the text material in this next section.

Delivering culture-centered helping

1. The helping process

2. Guidelines for the helper

3. Guidelines for the organization or agency

Delivering Culture-Centered Helping

We discussed in Chapter 7 two multicultural competencies important to providing services to clients, those of understanding your cultural self and learning about other cultures. An additional multicultural competency, presented in this chapter, relates to your work in internship. This competency reflects your ability to use a culture-centered approach in the helping process. We base this approach on the idea that the helping process is embedded in an ecological and cultural context (see Figure 7.1). To describe the **culture-centered approach** to helping, first, we present a brief review of the helping process (Woodside & McClam, 2015), and then we describe ways you can integrate each stage of the helping process with its cultural context. Second, we present ways that organizations and agencies can provide culture-centered helping to their clients.

The Helping Process

You have studied the **helping process** as one way to prepare for your internship experience. In Figure 9.1 you can view the main features of the helping process. First, the helping process begins when the client enters the human service delivery system. The first helper/client encounter is often an initial or intake interview. Second, the helping process continues as the helping professional gathers additional information from the client and others in order to identify client issues and challenges. Third, once much of the information is gathered, the helper and the client together set goals and priorities, and then generate possible actions or **interventions** that address them. Fourth, helpers and clients then select the intervention(s) of choice and plan the steps or phases of the intervention. Fifth, the helpers and the clients begin the intervention, making adjustments based upon the changing client needs and outcomes. Sixth, ideally helpers and clients together determine when termination occurs. Often termination ends, when the agency fulfills its responsibilities, reaches its limits of service provision, or when the client no longer participates in the helping process. Regardless of how the termination occurs, hopefully both the helping professional and the client assess the outcomes. Of course the helping process is not as linear or as simple as this description suggests. But it does include these six stages, and each stage relates to the work that occurred in the previous one.

What makes Figure 9.1 unique is that we ground the entire helping process within the framework of culture-centered helping. In other words, every aspect of the helping process takes place within multiple cultures. For simplicity's sake, we focus on only three of those cultures here: the culture of the client, the culture of the helper (intern), and the culture of the agency.

To help you develop ways to provide culture-centered help to your clients, we suggest three approaches to consider: working within your own culture, working within the client culture, and working within the agency culture. In Chapter 7, we described the lifelong process of understanding your own culture and how it influences the helping process. Here we

Figure 9.1 The Helping Process Within the Cultural Context

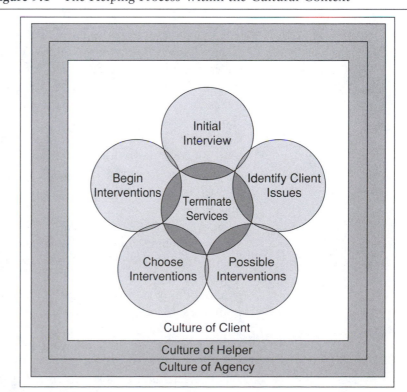

Source: Created by Gwen Ruttencutter, 2015. Used with permission.

address working within the client culture and working within the agency culture in this section.

At the heart of providing culture-centered helping is the helper's knowledge of and familiarity with specific cultures. These cultures include, but are not limited to, American Indians, people of the African Diaspora, individuals from Asia and Pacific Islands, individuals identifying as Latina/o, Arab Americans, and those who self-identify as biracial. In addition, there are important cultural considerations related to gender, age, sexual minorities, those with disabilities, and those with veteran experiences, as well as others. As we discussed in Chapter 7, it would be difficult for you as an intern (or as a human service professional, for that matter) to have an in-depth understanding of the cultures of all the clients you may encounter. We recommend several textbooks, such as Sue and Sue's (2012) *Counseling the Culturally Diverse* and Lee's *Multicultural Issues in Counseling* (2013), that provide detailed information about cultures and how culture influences the helping process.

As an alternative way of helping you, as an intern, think about engaging in culture-centered helping, we present guidelines for integrating the client's culture into the helping process. Then we illustrate ways you can use these guidelines as you plan your work with clients. The guidelines and process we suggest can help you begin to understand how to demonstrate cultural awareness and respect for your clients. Furthermore, as you base your work within the client's cultural framework, you will likely increase empathy, trust, and positive outcomes (Lee, 2013).

Guidelines for the Intern: Delivering Culture-Centered Helping

The guidelines we present in this section will help you in your work with clients. Each will help you engage in a cross-culture encounter. These principles provide a sound approach, regardless of the client you encounter. As we stated earlier, the guidelines do not describe for you the exact interactions you should have with clients or the specific interventions you should choose. Rather, the guidelines help you think about your professional work as you plan for, engage with, and later reflect on your work with clients. The following guidelines represent knowledge and advice about culture-centered counseling from various experts in the field of multicultural counseling (Atkinson, 2003; Brammer, 2012; Lee, 2013; Sue & Sue, 2013).

Continue to learn more about your cultural self. Earlier, in Chapter 7, we talked about culture and its influences, especially as it relates to your own culture. Understanding your own culture represents the first multicultural competency. This self-awareness helps you identify many basic assumptions you carry and helps you seek to uncover your biases and prejudices. In Exercises 7.2 through 7.5 you explored your cultural self and its influences on internship. In preparation for any cross-cultural encounter, you can ask yourself the following questions:

- What cultures does this client represent?
- What are my preconceived understandings of this culture?
- How does my culture and my experience influence these understandings?

Questions such as these allow us, as professionals, to assume some responsibility for considering the cultures of our clients.

Be curious about other cultures. In Chapter 7, we discussed both an academic and a personal approach to learning about other cultures. Commit to making each day one in which you learn more about others and their cultures. This curiosity includes better understanding the cultures of the clients with whom you work, traveling that allows you to learn more about other cultures, reading professional literature about different cultural environments, and reading nonfiction and fiction that helps you experience vicariously the cultures and cultural influences individuals experience. This curiosity can extend to the type of work represented in Exercises 7.2 through 7.5. These exercises help you focus on the cultures of the clients you are serving in internship.

Be aware of the power dimensions between you and the client. We believe that each helping event reflects **power**, including past, present, and future. Notions of power are complicated. For instance, for the client, you may introduce yourself as an intern, yet you come to the helping event as a representative of an educational institution and the authority of the agency. You may feel less power, since, in your position of the agency, you are an intern rather than full-time staff. Your status as an intern is only one aspect of power. Your race, gender, age, experience, and other groups, associations, or roles may place you in a more dominant or less dominant group. Also, don't forget the clients' views of you in relation to their own groups, associations, or roles. Keep concepts such as power, oppression, bias, prejudice, stereotypes, self-fulfilling prophecy, and internalized oppression in the forefront of your mind. Examine your feelings, thoughts, and actions, as well as those of the clients, and reflect on how these influence the helping process.

As an intern, here are some specific ways that you can consider dimensions of power and its aspects in work with clients.

- Let your client know of your intern status and what being an intern means. Explain that you are a student and that you are working with your faculty supervisor and site supervisor to become a helping professional.
- Early in the relationship talk to your client about the control he or she can have in the helping process. This can include statements such as, "We need to complete an intake session together. The purpose of this session is for me to know you better. You are the expert here." In addition, asking clients to work together with you to establish goals helps give power to the client. You might begin a discussion about goals by saying, "I want us to work together to decide what type of help you need."
- During goal setting, you can ask your client about his or her experience of his or her environment, either feeling in control of it or feeling powerless. Consider including statements such as, "This sounds like a good goal you are suggesting. Are there people or places you can go for support?" or "Do you think being 'race or ethnicity' or being 'gender' will make this process easier or more difficult? What is that difficulty like for you?"

Acknowledge your interest in the client's culture and note cultural differences early in the helping process. At times the cultural differences will be obvious to you and to the client. And many times, during the initial or intake interview, clients will disclose information that clarifies at least some of their cultural perspectives.

- To introduce the notion of culture, you might state, "I want us to work together and form a good helping relationship. For this to happen, I need to understand the world from your perspective. I will provide you with lots of opportunities to share who you are and the culture you live in."
- To begin to explore the similarities and differences in culture, you might ask clients to join you in constructing a list of the ways you are similar and the ways you are different. Refining and referring to that list from time to time allows helpers to keep a focus on culture.

With care, place the client in the position of the expert. Many helpers involve their clients in the helping process.

- To do so they state to the client, "You know yourself and your situation better than anyone else. I am going to rely on you to help us determine what you need and how we can provide you the help you need."
- Many clients do suggest to us they don't want to be seen as speaking for their race or their gender, so avoid questions such as, "What would be the Black perspective on this issue?" or "How do you think women would respond to this intervention?"

Think carefully about defining the issues and challenges. We know that issues and challenges are, in part, defined within a cultural context. For example, the definitions of dysfunction or impairments are, many times, culturally dependent. For example, within the Native American culture, dimensions of spirituality include visions and cultural metaphors (e.g., nurturing from the healing forest) (Coyhis & Simonelli, 2008). At times, the Eurocentric approach to helping considers visions an indication of illness rather than spirituality. Similarly, integrating the use of metaphors into the helping process does not fit with many more behavioral or scripted interventions.

Think carefully about planning the intervention. Just as defining the issues and challenges clients face has a cultural aspect(s), interventions also reflect a more standard Eurocentric approach. As we introduced the background of multicultural helping, we mentioned earlier of traditional models of helping such as psychodynamic, humanistic, or behavioral perspectives. Today, scholars, researchers, and practitioners are introducing models of helping that are more sensitive to working with specific cultures or to adapting current interventions to match the unique needs of the clients and the clients' environments. These include strengths-based helping (Berg, 2009), narrative therapy (White, 2005), feminist therapy (Brown, 2008), positive psychology (Seligman & Csikszentmihalyi, 2000), and integrated therapies (Prochaska & Norcross, 2010), to name a few.

Exercise 9.1 helps you think about ways you might vary how you use the helping process. This exercise walks you through the entire process and then helps you think about how to vary it depending upon the client and the client's culture.

Exercise 9.1 The Helping Process and Culture-Centered Helping: Writing Your Own Story, Entry 26

In this exercise, we want you to identify your own approaches to the helping process and then modify those approaches depending upon the culture of a client with whom you are working. The steps listed below help you work through this process.

Step 1

Using Table 9.1, in Column 2 describe how you would approach each of the stages of helping.

Step 2

Describe a client with whom you are working. Be as specific about that client's culture as you can be.

Step 3

Review your description of each stage of helping. In Column 3, adapt your approach for each stage of helping to better reach your client, based upon what you know about the client.

Step 4

In Column 4, note how power, oppression, internalized oppression, and biases influence the helping process.

Step 5

Spend time reading about the client's culture, the culture-centered approach, and spend time consulting with your faculty and site supervisors about how to approach this client in a cultural-centered way. Record these insights in Column 5.

Table 9.1   Clients and Culture-Centered Helping Process

Stages of the Helping Process	Your Approach	Your Approach With Your Client	Considerations of Oppression	Consultation
Initial interview				
Information gathering				
Setting priorities and goals				
Generating choices				
Intervention				
Termination				

Just as it is important to consider how you can provide culture-centered helping to your clients, it is also important to understand the way an organization or agency can maintain this culture-centered focus for its clients.

Guidelines for the Organization or Agency: Delivering Culture-Centered Helping

As we indicated in Figure 9.1, human service delivery usually occurs within an **organizational or agency context**, such as your internship site. Just as you, as an intern or other human service professional, can develop multi-cultural competence, there is also a way an agency or organization can be a welcoming, sensitive, and culture-centered environment. Different organizations and agencies promote the development of culture-centered helping in various ways. Each agency will demonstrate strengths as they deliver culture-centered helping. And there will be ways these same agencies can improve their abilities to serve various client groups.

There are several ways that agencies can develop cultural sensitivity (see Figure 9.2). These can occur at various levels of agency functioning, such as, developing mission and policy, hiring and training diverse staff, delivering methods of culture-centered helping, providing a welcoming physical environment, attending to language, promoting **outreach**, and developing continual assessment of **client satisfaction** and attention to cultural aspects of service delivery. To help you understand the ways agencies may better serve various client cultures, we summarize the seven levels of agency functioning. We illustrate each with specific examples of how a culturally sensitive agency might, or might not, function, by returning to Sue and her internship experience at the Oklahoma Homeless Shelter. You previously read about Sue and her internship experiences in Chapters 1 and 7.

Figure 9.2   Culture-Centered Agency Considerations

Mission and Policy

If cultural sensitivity is incorporated into a **mission statement** and various agency policies, one might see language in agency publications or on their website that articulates commitment to "providing services to culturally diverse populations" or "helping clients in a culturally respectful way." Culture-centered mission statements might also promise to deliver services that "value the beliefs, traditions, of individual and family practices" of the clients. In addition, an agency's mission and policies might commit to advocate for needs of the communities in which it serves. **Agency policies** might reflect input from a broad representation of the clients served and include client representation on a board of directors, as well as yearly focus groups, whose purpose is to gather information from clients served. Read the homeless shelter's mission statement and governance policy statement and decide, if either or both are culture-centered.

The homeless shelter's mission statement reads as follows: To help those without housing find a home.

The homeless shelter's governance policy states this: The Board of Directors, who are committed to represent diverse perspectives of community leaders, neighborhood representatives, staff, and clients, will consider policies and issues related to each of the aforementioned individuals involved.

Staffing and Training

One aspect of providing culture-centered helping is hiring staff that represents the culture of the clients the agency serves. In addition, including cultural competence in a job description is one way to emphasize how strongly the agency values delivering culture-centered helping.

Having a **culturally diverse staff** supports the commitment to providing culture-centered helping in two ways. First, a culturally diverse staff helps an agency meet the needs of the clients served. These staff may be able to more quickly establish rapport with clients, interpret agency policy in a cultural context and language that clients understand, adapt interventions to fit the clients' culture and belief system, and more effectively help clients identify barriers they encounter during the helping process and within their environment. Second, a culturally diverse staff may provide valuable knowledge and insights to professional peers about understanding client cultures, assessing the cultural sensitivity of agency practice, developing systematic outreach, and assessing and confronting power and bias of an agency's work.

A second aspect of developing an agency approach to culture-centered helping is **staff training. Cultural sensitivity** is a continuous process requiring ongoing discussions and training that are focused on individual racial/cultural identity development and agency awareness of client perceptions of agency practice. We present information about the cultural diversity of the staff at the Oklahoma Homeless Shelter. What are your assessments of their success in hiring and training diverse staff?

At the Oklahoma Homeless Shelter, a majority of staff are White females. Many of these professionals are entry-level professionals from the ages of 23 to 45. The clients served are African American, Native Americans, and White males, ages 40 to 60. There are an increasing number of veterans, women, and children who use the services. Currently there is little attention given to culture-centered helping at the agency level, although several case managers attend workshops about serving minority clients.

Methods of Service Delivery

To deliver culture-centered helping, the methods of service delivery must reflect client values, beliefs, and cultural practice. They also must take into consideration individual racial/cultural identity, especially as it relates to power and internalized oppression. To deliver culture-centered helping, an agency must continually assess its methods of service vis-à-vis the culture of the clients it serves. The complexities of this process require ongoing attention and flexibility of service delivery. We suggest a very concrete approach to an assessment of agency methods of intervention in relation to the culture of its clients.

> Step 1—Agency professionals develop a chart or model of the client experience of the agency, from first contact through termination.
>
> Step 2—Agency professionals ask several clients to describe their experiences of the agency services.
>
> Step 3—Using both sets of perceptions, agency professionals construct a revised model of service delivery.
>
> Step 4—Agency professionals review each aspect of the revised model, according to their client's cultural perspectives related to the following aspects of culture-centered helping shown in Table 9.2.

Sue asked her two site supervisors, Carmello Jones and Maria Rodriguez, about the ways the agency thinks about delivering services to the different racial and cultural groups they serve. Carmello talked about never knowing what cultures they would be serving. He indicated that the types of clients keep changing, so it is difficult to make any changes. He did talk about trying to find interpreters when clients did not speak English. He kept a list of those interpreters in his office. Also case managers had the same list. He encouraged case managers to determine if interpreters were needed prior to their initial appointment.

Maria provided a different answer to Sue's question. She stated, "Although I don't know much about the Native American culture, our state is emphasizing the contributions this culture made to our heritage. So I try to be respectful when I am working with Native American clients. I am working with this one man whose mother lived on the reservation about 50 miles from here. He doesn't want to live there and he doesn't have any support to live here in town. I see he doesn't feel he has support in either place. I need some education about how to help my Native American clients."

From the information that Sue gained from her two supervisors, it appears that the homeless shelter provides little focus on adapting services to provide culture-centered helping. Scholars have suggested that because interns are learning about current practices in the helping professions, it may be the case that they know more about the multicultural dimensions of helping than their supervisors (Bernard & Goodyear, 2014). Here

Table 9.2 Agency Considerations of Culture-Centered Helping

Aspects of helping	*Agency responses*
Racial/cultural identity • Racial or cultural self-identification • Experience of culture as support • Experience of culture as stressor • Level of acculturation	
Beliefs and values • Meaning of time • Meaning of religion and spirituality • Cultural specific healing practices • Locus of control (internal and/or external)	
Aspects of social life • Meaning of family and family roles • Meaning of gender roles • What are social rituals (e.g., introductions, greetings, farewells)	
Helping-related beliefs • Meaning of having a problem • Meaning of help • Meaning of asking for help • What effective help looks like	
Intervention or service-based beliefs • Meaning of praise • Meaning of challenge and confrontation • Meaning of self-disclosure • Meaning of silence • Meaning of verbal communication	
Communication • Communication style • Meaning of physical space • Ways respect is conferred • Appropriate behavior between strangers • Appropriate behavior with professionals	

are some additional perspectives about the delivery of culture-centered helping and then Sue's assessment of the culture-centered helping at the homeless shelter.

Language

Many times different racial/cultural groups speak different dialects or languages other than English. In fact, language proficiency varies from client to client. For example, the Interagency Language Roundtable (ILR, 2014) uses a 5-point scale to measure levels of language proficiency: no proficiency in the language, elementary proficiency, limited working proficiency, professional working proficiency, full professional proficiency, and finally, native or bilingual proficiency. For example, an individual with no proficiency has a small vocabulary to communicate basic needs, while an individual with full professional proficiency would be able to respond to familiar and unfamiliar situations but would not speak as a native. Since a primary foundation of helping is communication, it is difficult to ask clients who do not speak English, or do not speak it well, to talk about their experiences and identity issues and to brainstorm possible solutions. Having staff that have a sufficient proficiency in the client's native language or using bilingual translators are essential for effective client interface.

Written documents represent another way that human service professionals communicate with clients. If possible, translating agency forms and announcements into multiple languages helps clients better understand the terms of the services, and it allows them to take full advantage of what the agency offers. These **translated documents** also help the process of gathering information and making assessments. Using written documents that the client understands places the emphasis on the helping, rather than on the translation process.

Sue noted that, even though the staff at the homeless shelter was not attuned to racial and cultural aspects of their clients' lives, on the sign outside the agency, the name of the agency was written in English, Spanish, and Choctaw. These names were also on a sign over the front door of the agency. The agency also had a sign in the main hallway where clients enter the agency that described the agency's mission and goals in these three languages. As indicated earlier, in the community in which the homeless shelter was located, there was a strong pool of interpreters from which to draw. The intake interview forms were written in six different languages. And currently members of the local community were helping translate assessments into these six different languages.

As Sue indicated, the homeless shelter is able to use community resources to provide interpreters and translators. Having these resources helped the director and the case managers communicate more freely with clients and deliver services. This effective communication reduced the stress for both professionals and clients.

Physical Environment

Constructing an environment that is welcoming to a diverse array of clients is important. As a helping professional, you want your agency to be accessible and respectful; you want clients to feel they are valued from the moment they walk into the agency. For some clients, coming to the agency represents entering unfamiliar, if not, foreign territory. Creating a **welcoming environment** represents a nonverbal way to say to clients, "We are glad that you are here." Specific ways to do this are to display positive images of members of client groups, provide printed and visual material in various languages representing client groups, incorporate refreshments that reflect various cultures, and provide representative toys and books for children of various cultures. In addition, having meeting rooms that facilitate conversation, provide enough room and seating for a client and his or her family members, and provide opportunities for clients to talk in private all convey respect for client needs.

At the homeless shelter, clients can enter through the front door or through the back door. Intake rooms are private spaces and can accommodate at least five individuals. Once clients have a case manager, they have an assigned room in which to talk with their case manager. This provides them both privacy and consistency of space. The day and evening programs are both individual and group based.

Sue noticed that the physical environment of the homeless shelter is continually changing to meet client needs. For example, one Hispanic male, Jorge, was homeless and unemployed for about 2 months. During that time five individuals from his family in Mexico joined him. It seemed like he had a new member of his family every week. A flexible agency policy that examines client needs on a weekly basis allowed the agency to expand his living quarters from a single bunk in the group room to a living suite for families by the end of his stay. Individuals who receive services enter into a reciprocity agreement with the agency where they give back to the agency in small ways. As Jorge's family increased, many of them joined the kitchen crew to feed lunch to clients receiving food services.

When Sue asked Carmello Jones and Maria Rodriguez about their agency's attention to culture-centered helping, they only described small ways the agency demonstrated attention to a client's race and culture. But, as we can see in this example, in responding to client needs, they show respect for the family values of this Hispanic client.

Focus on Outreach

A critical aspect of service delivery that demonstrates respect for clients and their cultures is **outreach**. This means seeking clients in their community and neighborhood settings. Agency leaders and helping professionals that build a strong network of neighborhood leaders, business owners, families, and individuals allows an agency to better understand the culture and the needs of clients. This networking can occur when agency staff attend community meetings, support local businesses, and participate in community recreational activities.

The nature of the work of the homeless shelter requires that agency staff be involved in outreach activities. In fact, the work of the homeless shelter began as outreach work. Ten years ago, two individuals, who had recently graduated from a social work and a human service program, wrote a small grant funded by the city to canvas four neighborhoods in the town center and identify homeless adults who needed help. The two graduates partnered with assisted living facilities, the office on aging, the criminal court, legal aid, and a local coffee shop to provide needed services. After 18 months, the grantees provided data to the mayor and his staff about the homeless population and its needs. The need for the homeless shelter was established.

Outreach becomes a critical element of providing culture-sensitive services. It moves the focus of services from agency driven to client driven. We believe that the potential of outreach activity is limitless and, at times, unpredictable. The history of the homeless shelter nicely illustrates this point. In addition, finding time to spend in the community helps agency staff to learn more about cultural dimensions of their clients and helps the staff better understand their strengths and challenges.

Assessment

As agency and staff integrate culture-centered helping into agency practice, it is important to assess both the **client satisfaction** and the outcomes of these efforts. Considering culture is important; understanding how that consideration is received and its effectiveness is as essential.

The homeless shelter gathers information about client satisfaction in two ways. Every time individuals walk through the door of the shelter, they pick up a quick paper survey asking them for feedback in three areas: if they found the shelter welcoming, if their needs were met, and if they would return or recommend the shelter. The surveys are available in four languages. Also exit interviews are possible for clients who cannot read. For individuals receiving case management services, they fill out surveys at the end of their first, third, and sixth month of receiving services. They also receive surveys 6 months after they transition from case management care. Surveys are about quality of care received (e.g., promptness, empathy, privacy, competence), nature of contacts (e.g., walk-in, appointments, community meetings), services that made a difference, services that made little difference, and recommendations for improvement of services. The homeless shelter also tracks housing and employment for its clients who are receiving case management. These are the primary outcomes that reach the long-term goals of the shelter.

The homeless shelter uses fairly standard ways to assess client satisfaction and track client outcomes. In their assessments, they do not ask clients directly about culture-centered helping. There are ways to seek information from clients about the cultural sensitivity of an agency (e.g., surveys that ask about staff sensitivity to racial or ethnic background, effective communication, treated with respect and acceptance of cultural differences). It is more difficult to link outcomes to culture-centered helping.

As we discussed earlier, internship provides an excellent opportunity for you to learn how agencies develop and implement culture-centered helping approaches. As you can probably guess, in some agencies, attention to cultural issues is of primary concern and talk about cultural sensitivity is routine. In other environments, attention to culture is of less importance. One way to approach a discussion of the agency's culture-centered helping is to schedule a formal or informal interview with your site supervisor. You can use the following interview described in Exercise 9.2 to begin to understand the way your internship site focuses on serving its diverse client populations.

Exercise 9.2 Understanding Your Internship Site's Cultural Sensitivity

In this exercise, you begin to learn about your internship site's cultural sensitivity. To complete this exercise, set up a time with your site supervisor to talk about how your internship site incorporates a multicultural perspective with regard to culture-centered helping.

Mission and policy

_____

_____

_____

Staffing and training

_____

_____

_____

Methods of service delivery

_____

_____

_____

Language

_____

_____

_____

Physical environment

_____

_____

_____

Focus on outreach

_____

_____

_____

Assessment

_____

_____

_____

Next, Box 9.2 describes the organizational framework of the next section of this chapter, that of providing strengths-based helping.

Box 9.2. Studying the Text: Providing Strengths-Based Helping

Studying the text: The following outline will help you read and study the text material in this next section.

Providing strengths-based helping

1. Defining strengths-based helping
2. What students say
3. Implementing strengths-based helping

Providing Strengths-Based Helping

Strengths-based helping represents a relatively new approach to service delivery. An example of its wide use would be providing help to a client experiencing mental illness, substance abuse and addiction issues, and chronic physical illnesses. In addition, human service professions engage families and children using strengths-based strategies and intervention (Abdullah, 2014; Rangan & Sekar, 2006). Serving clients with multiple needs that require case management work often employs a strengths-based approach. In this section, we define strengths-based helping and we provide concrete ways to represent the approach in the helping process. We introduce an exercise that helps you explore how to use a strengths-based approach.

Box 9.3 What Students Say: Students Use a Strengths-Based Approach

When did you first learn about a strengths-based approach?

Steve: We read a little about asking about client strengths when we were in our first Introduction to Human Service class. I remember wondering why we were talking about this. It seemed like a natural thing to do to me.

Maria: When I was in my first internship, I worked in juvenile probation. Each of our clients had a case manager. When the case manager first worked with a youth, she conducted an intake interview. There was one question on the intake form that asked youths to talk about their strengths.

Al: I really didn't know anything about a strengths-based approach. My agency does not use that approach. Once

I learn something about the approach I am going to talk with my site supervisor about it and how we might incorporate it with our work with clients.

Shasha: My site supervisor believes in the strength-based approach. She uses a brief intervention with the adults she sees in the shelter. The brief intervention she uses, helps clients identity their strengths and build on these strengths.

What are the positive benefits of using a strengths-based approach with clients?

Steve: I am not sure, but I think it might help the clients think I am really interested in them and see them in a positive light.

Maria: I am used to helping young boys think about their strengths, the things that they do well. Usually they first cannot identify any strengths. Once they start—and sometimes I need to help them—I think we have begun to build more trust.

Al: Well it seems like a good way to begin a helping relationship. I think that I need to experience the strengths-based approach myself, maybe have one of my friends conduct an interview with me, just so I can see what it is like.

Shasha: One of my concerns is how the strengths-based helping fits with trying to work within the context of the client. My clients have such difficult home lives and not a bit of support. So I am not sure it is completely realistic.

Now that we have read about human service students and their experiences and hopes for using strengths-based helping during their internship, let's describe this perspective and outline its goals.

Defining Strengths-Based Helping

Strengths-based helping represents a specific perspective that the helper assumes when delivering services. In part, this approach guides the helping process. Foundations of this perspective are fourfold: (a) a focus on client growth, (b) a collaboration between the helper and the client, (c) a commitment to client-determined and client-driven change, and (d) a commitment to advocacy to promote positive change in the client's environment (Saleeby, 2012). What you see in the four foundations represents a positive view of individuals who are resilient and able to help themselves within an environment that also has strengths and supports (Abdullah, 2014). For many this means that the individual is able to face difficulties, handle stress, overcome difficulties, and find others to help when difficulties occur (McQuaide & Ehrenreich, 1997). However, what is viewed as a strength in one circumstance may be less of a strength in another circumstance. Therefore, how a human service professional uses the strengths-based approach may differ from one situation to another. Also, the approach may vary from one client to another.

Implementing Strengths-Based Helping

At each stage of the helping process, the strengths-based approach consistently reinforces the four foundations described above. In doing so, human service professionals promoting the strengths-based approach hope to enhance the helping process in the ways we describe below. In addition, Sue provides us with an example of her use of the strengths perspective with one of her clients at the homeless shelter.

Initial Interview

During the **initial interview** the helper inquires about the strengths of the client and the strengths of the family and the environment. Questions, such as, "How have you managed to survive (or thrive) thus far, given all the challenges you have had to contend with?" and "What people have given you special understanding, support, and guidance?" (Saleeby, 2012), reinforce an emphasis on the positive aspects of the client's accomplishments and environment assisting the helping professional build rapport with the client. The information gained provides a basis for later stages of the helping process.

I had studied about the strengths perspective in my skills class and in my theories class before I started my internship. The perspective is not one that my peers used at the homeless shelter, but I talked with my supervisor, Maria. She helped me think about how I could use the approach with one of my clients just to see how it would work in practice. I told her that I would use Saleeby's (2012) five categories of strengths-based questions that we learned in class to structure my work with a client. For our clients, we have a process laid out; really, it is a five-step process that we follow for each of our clients. So I looked at the process and tried to integrate the strengths perspective into the shelter's process. The first of the processes at the shelter is the intake interview. We have a standard intake form that we need to fill out. Although it is on the computer, I usually have my client sit with me and we fill out the form together. I added several questions to the intake form that helped my client and I get to thinking about his strengths. Four weeks ago today, I met George for the first time. I spent about an hour with him and we filled out the form together. One of my primary responsibilities is to discover his type of homelessness—trying to distinguish between sleeping on the streets, moving from place to place, or living in short-term temporary housing. The survival question, "How have you managed to survive (or thrive) thus far, given all the challenges you have had to contend with?" seemed to change the conversation we were having (Saleeby, 2012). George looked me in the eye for the first time as if no one had ever acknowledged that his survival was a good thing.

From that question we returned to a discussion of the intervention that the agency uses to address the challenges of homelessness. I outlined a 4-week plan, if he decided to accept our services. We have three options that clients can choose. Regardless of options, there is quite a bit of information gathering that occurs for each of our clients. Under the housing-first option, we encourage our clients to stay with us so we can ensure they have a safe and secure place to live.

Information Gathering

As the helper continues **information gathering**, information emerges about positives for the client, and at times, his or her family and/or his or her environment. The helper can ask more in-depth questions that focus on the client's perspective, including times and opportunities when things were going well for the client. Questions or prompts that highlight exceptional times for the client are appropriate. The efforts attempt to pull out strengths that have been forgotten or overlooked. Examples of these questions include, "When things were going well in life, what was different?" or "In the past, when you felt that your life was better, more interesting, or more stable, what about your world, your relationships, your thinking was special or different?" One result intended is to provide encouragement to the client to participate fully in the helping process.

During the process of additional information gathering, we try to assess the client from various perspectives that include both strengths of clients and the limitations. We try to pinpoint some of the individual factors that might lead to homelessness. We use a model that looks at structural reasons for homelessness, such as unemployment, inadequate employment, and short- or long-term poverty. In addition, we try to determine about family and social networks, their strengths, and where they might break down. We also consider two other factors that may influence the homelessness of our client. These include any personal factors, such as mental health issues, health issues, substance issues, or intellectual disability issues. It also means assessing any culturally linked factors, such as discrimination, lack of cultural support, and any cultural barriers.

Support questions, such as "What people have given you special understanding, support, and guidance?" and "Who are the special people on whom you can depend?", appear to work during this time in the helping process" (Saleeby, 2012). It is also a time that I pay particular attention to their culture and ask questions about cultural supports. I learned that George's grandparents live on the reservation. But his mother and father, now divorced, live in a small town close to but not on the reservation.

Setting Priorities and Goals and Generating Choices

From the strengths-based perspective, the collaborative effort between the helper and the client enables them to **set priorities and goals** that are **client centered**. The helper encourages the client to use strengths as building blocks for establishing goals and outlining choices about how to achieve those goals. The identified strengths become incentive in this stage of the helping process. In other words, clients view past successes and use them as a beginning point for achieving other goals. Questions or prompts, such as, "What now do you want out of life?" and "How can I help you achieve your goals or recover those special abilities and times that you have had in the past?" encourage the client to reach beyond the present moment and to think of change and growth as possible. These questions also indicate to the client that the process represents work between the client and the helper.

The third stage of the helping process at the homeless shelter is helping clients determine their own goals. However, the shelter is clear about its own priorities. A match between client and shelter priorities helps clients determine which of the service packages they want. All of the services offered are very concrete, tangible. The first type of support is crisis support, the second is early support (for individuals with temporary housing), the third is ongoing support, and the fourth is nonintrusive "standing-by" support. Housing for clients is important in all of these areas. Since George had housing, although it was temporary, he was not in crisis. But he wanted more services than just housing, and he wanted more stable housing. Along with the more stable housing we offered, George described the life he wanted and the services he needed. Exploring with George possibility questions such as "What now do you want out of life?" and "How far along are you toward achieving these?" (Saleeby, 2012) helped George say what he wished for. The question "What people or personal qualities are helping you move in these directions?" helped us see how much he was willing to commit to interventions (Saleeby, 2012). I also reinforced my role as a partner in the delivery of services.

Intervention

As we described earlier, the **interventions** and services can be delivered with client strengths in mind. Within the context of identified client strengths, it is more likely that clients will see the interventions as meeting their own goals, such as (a) addressing issues and challenges and (b) developing new skills and talents. Since the intervention is created with a specific client in mind, no two client interventions will look the same. This requires flexibility on the part of the helper, as well as patience, as the client begins to see possibilities of change and positive outcomes. This requires interventions that build upon the client's previous successes (Madsen & Gillespie, 2014). And within the collaboration with the helping professionals, clients are inclined to accept some responsibility for the intervention, to work alongside the helpers involved, and to engage in doing many things for themselves, rather than asking others to accept this responsibility.

I am just beginning our plan with George and I am excited about it. Together, we determined that he needs health services and educational services. He also wants to study and learn skills that will help him get and hold on to a steady job. He will have a case manager and I will stay on his team. I hope to continue to provide the strengths-based perspective for his care and for his team. Maria encouraged me to share information about this perspective with the team so they would understand my use of the strengths approach as well as my beliefs in George's abilities and strengths.

Termination and Evaluation

Ultimately, within the strengths perspective, clients end their work with a human service professional. **Termination** occurs for many reasons such as client circumstances, agency eligibility or limitations of service, or success in meeting the client's goals. Helping professionals who use the strengths-based approach believe that working from strengths may facilitate positive outcomes, regardless of the reasons for termination.

Although not all client interventions have positive outcomes, there are several goals that might be met by identifying and building on client strengths during the helping process. Possible outcomes from this process might be (a) a client's increased sense of an ability to change, (b) a client's expanded knowledge of himself or herself and circumstances, (c) a client's belief in his or her ability to overcome hardships, (d) a client's ability to discover groups to which he or she belongs, (e) a client's ability to identify and accept his or her strengths, and finally, (f) a client's capacity to experience positive interventions that lead to change. When engaging in an **evaluation** of the outcomes of the helping process, questions or prompts such as, "When was it that you began to believe that you might achieve some of the things you wanted in life?" or "What people, events, and ideas were involved in your sense of success?" may help the client continue to articulate strengths (Saleeby, 2012).

Of course I hope that we are not even near the end of our work with George. But our 4-week plan to begin to involve him in a plan of services is on track. I do have permission to go with his case manager to her meeting with George every week. I told her it was not too early to ask questions about outcomes and George's assessment of his progress—what he thinks about how he is meeting his goals. And as he discovers new strengths in himself and in his environment, it is important for all of us to notice them.

Five Areas of Strengths-Based Questions

Saleeby (2012) suggests questions in five areas that help both helper and client assess strengths: survival, support, exception, possibility, and esteem. Answers to these questions will provide you with ideas about how to structure an initial interview, additional information gathering, setting priorities and goals, generating choices, intervention, and termination—all steps in the helping process. Earlier we illustrated how many of these questions could be used by professionals engage in the helping process. Here are a few questions that illustrate each of Saleeby's (2012) categories: survival, support, exception, possibility, and esteem.

Survival Questions

- Clearly you have survived the difficulties you have encountered. Why do you think you have survived?
- Think about the challenges you have faced. What have you learned from these? What have you learned and what skills have you acquired because of these challenges?

Support Questions

- Think about the people you have encountered in your life. Which ones have been special? Which ones have provided you with help and assistance?
- Which individuals can you count on when you need help?

Exception Questions

- Can you talk to me about the times in your life when things were good for you? What was that like? How does that time differ from the present? When things were going well in life, what was different?
- When you think about the past, can you talk about things you would like to recover?

Possibility Questions

- When you think about the present, what would you like your life to look like?
- When you envision a positive future, what does that future look like?

Esteem Questions

- Think about the people you know. What are the positive ways those people would describe you?
- If today was the perfect day for you, what would it be like?

Exercise 9.3 The Helping Process and the Strengths-Based Perspective: Writing Your Own Story, Entry 27

By now you are working with various clients at your internship site. A strengths-based perspective may be one approach with which you are familiar and even one you are currently using, or it may be, for you, a new approach to helping. In this exercise you will describe how you are integrating a strengths-based perspective into your internship work or describe how you might plan to do so.

Step 1

Choose one client and write a description, similar to Sue's, of how you integrated or might integrate a strengths-based perspective into the helping process.

Initial Interview

Information Gathering

Setting Priorities and Goals and Generating Choices

Intervention

Termination and Evaluation

Step 2

You can evaluate the ways in which your work with a client is strengths based. We use several guidelines for strengths-based client assessment proposed by Cowger (1994) to help you assess your use of this perspective. Identify a client with whom you are working and ask yourself the following questions:

- Did I pay attention to how the client understands the situation?
- Did I believe what the client tells me?
- Did I learn what the client's goals are?
- Did I help the client look at both client strengths and context strengths (rather than just issues and challenges)?
- Was I able to identify strengths from a variety of sources, including the client's relationship skills, values, motivations, as well as from the client's context, including the family, friends, and social institutions.
- Did I look at the client's culture and determine the role of power and oppression in the client's life?
- Did I communicate using words and phrases that the client could easily understand?
- Did both the client and I work through the helping process (assessing the goals, possible approaches, intervention, and assessment of outcomes) together?
- Did the client and I avoid blaming, and rather, assuming the client could make changes and facilitate change?

Step 3

Another way to know if you are using a strengths-based lens is to ask for feedback from your site supervisor, your coworkers at the internship site, or your clients. You might formally or informally ask for feedback in the following areas:

- Was I helpful?
- Was I fair?
- Was I sensitive to your culture and family background?
- Did I ask about strengths?
- Did I suggest positives?
- Did we together use strengths in our planning?
- Did we together use strengths in our intervention and service delivery?
- Did we together involve members of your family for support?
- Did we together involve the community for support?
- Was our plan positive?
- Did we together focus on good changes for the future?
- Did we together focus on a positive sense of self for the client?

We conclude our discussion of strengths-based helping and how you might use this perspective in internship in the final section of this chapter by allowing you to read accounts of how Alicia, Lucas, and Tamika worked with their clients. You also learn from Dr. Bianca, Ms. Bellewa, and Gwen about cultured-centered helping within their human service contexts. You can review Box 9.4 for an outline of the closing section of this chapter.

Box 9.4 Deepening Your Understanding

1. Peer-to-peer dialogue

    a. Alicia: Using culture-centered approaches

    b. Lucas: Using culture-centered approaches

    c. Tamika: Using culture-centered approaches

2. Faculty and site supervisor dialogue

    a. Dr. Bianca: Challenges I face with clients and culture

    b. Ms. Bellewa: My interaction with clients

3. The professional voice and tips for practice: Gwen

4. Terms to remember

5. References

Deepening Your Understanding

We now turn to our peer-to-peer dialogues and see how Alicia, Lucas, and Tamika are using their skills in their work with clients. Also, Dr. Bianca, Ms. Bellewa, and Gwen share their perspectives about culture-centered helping and how it can be integrated with using a strengths-based perspective.

Peer-to-Peer Dialogue: Alicia, Lucas, and Tamika

We asked Alicia, Lucas, and Tamika to talk about their experiences working with clients. They share with you information about the ways they tried to deliver culture-centered helping to their clients. They also describe if, and how, they used the strengths approach to helping. They present their experiences with clients in a realistic way.

Alicia

When I started seeing clients, I worried about my ability to say or do the right thing. Added to that pressure, most of my clients are older than I am and have lived through a wealth of experiences that varied tremendously from mine. Working with my supervisors, I learned to conquer my feelings of inadequacy while providing services to the children and parents I worked with. Often times, we tend to focus on what we do wrong, instead of focusing on what we do right. Focusing on my strengths helps me be more aware of my clients' strengths. In this way, I am able to turn something I considered negative into a positive tool for my clients. Beyond this, I started noticing that working with a multiculturally diverse population no longer intimidated me. This was partially due to my recognition that despite some of the glaring and noticeable differences between the clients I saw and myself, such as race, ethnicity, and religion, there were also many similarities. Similar to some of my clients, I have had feelings of distress, sadness, anger, and frustration. I have felt out of control, vulnerable, and overwhelmed with everything around me. While I may have not experienced the exact same circumstance as my clients, our emotions may have mirrored each other, despite all of our differences. Being able to recognize that and use that in sessions helped communicate my empathy and understanding, further strengthening our relationship.

Written by Allie Rhinehart and Dareen Basma, 2015. Used with permission.

Lucas

Hello, I hope all is well with you! Today I want to briefly talk to you about how I use a cultured-centered approach at the Tampa Bay Justice Center. I am still learning how to become culturally-centered, and that is why the internship is so important for me to develop cultural competence, and to understand my cultural self. Right now, since I am in the beginning stages of my counselor development, one thing I am working on is understanding my cultural self, and expanding my knowledge of diverse cultural groups. To do this, I rely on supervision to help me understand my cultural self. My site supervisor has been instrumental on approaching topics about gender, race, ethnicity, sexual orientation, and vulnerable populations. My supervisor approaches these topics by having activities that make me identify the cultural groups I belong to, and then having me discuss how my cultural groups I self-identify with may influence the helping process with clients. Therefore, my site supervisor and the Tampa Bay Justice Center make an emphasis to promote a cultural-centered environment, due to the diverse clients we work with.

Another aspect to promote a culture-centered approach I apply is empowering my clients to be the expert of themselves, and having them educate me on the cultural groups they self-identify with. To me, this the most effective method I apply while working with clients. Just by asking my clients to talk about their familial culture and the cultural groups they self-identify with has helped me avoid imposing my biases and assumptions, because my clients are teaching me who they are and their cultural groups. By empowering my clients, they feel more comfortable, and I even had one client thank me for wanting to know how she sees the world, which was rewarding.

Well I hope this information helps you, and gives you an understanding of how I am currently using a cultured-centered approach with my clients at the Tampa Bay Justice Center. Remember, cultural competence is an ongoing process, and the more you work with clients, the more culturally component you will become. This is what I am learning. Have a great day!!

Written by Jorge Roman, 2015. Used with permission.

Tamika

Culture is one of my favorite reflection topics, because I think it is SO important in working with clients! At my internship, culture is something we discuss a lot in supervision and during treatment team meetings. Two of the greatest lessons I've learned during my internship are that culture is always in the room and that no two individuals share the exact same personal background. I think that's really important to keep in mind as a human service professional, and I find it really helpful to bring culture up during the first or second session with each of my new clients. Lots of times, to help both the client and myself feel more comfortable thinking about and addressing such a sensitive topic, I'll initiate a discussion about the ways in which we might be similar and the ways in which we might differ culturally. This usually provides a great starting point for learning their story, and it often helps me to build solid rapport with clients almost immediately. Showing interest in and respect for clients' varying cultural backgrounds also enhances my strengths-based approach to working with them; it demonstrates that I value their heritage and the abilities, supports, and resources that naturally exist within their cultural framework.

Something I struggle with, related to culture, is feeling like I could never know enough. As I mentioned, everyone has unique pieces to their cultural background and I sometimes feel intimidated when I am assigned to work with a client, whose culture I perceive to be drastically different, in some way, from my own. One way I try to manage this culture-based anxiety is by taking advantage of every opportunity possible to learn more about different cultures and how I might work best with them in a therapeutic sense. My internship site supervisor knows that I find culture fascinating and that I want to be as competent as I can be. She has given me several articles and a couple of books to read and offered to discuss the topic with me whenever I have questions or concerns. During our supervision time, she always makes sure to check in with me about the cultural aspects of my work with clients, which I really appreciate. My school frequently offers guest lectures, many of which focus on or at least address the cultural elements of working in a helping profession. This is an area in which I'd love to see my internship site improve. Although we receive many staff training opportunities, the seminars mostly focus on evidence-based interventions or other more concrete topics. I would love more opportunities to learn about how culture is present and best addressed in the judicial system, where I think it's an especially important consideration. This is a suggestion I felt comfortable bringing up to my site supervisor the last time we met and she seemed really receptive to the idea. Hopefully we will see more culture-centered training opportunities in the future!

Written by Brittany Pollard, 2015. Used with permission.

Exercise 9.4 Writing About Your Work With Clients: Writing Your Own Story, Entry 28

You just read about Alicia, Lucas, and Tamika and their experiences of working with clients. Now it is your turn to write about your own work with clients! This exercise will help you integrate the material you learned in this chapter.

Step 1

Choose at least one client and list five characteristics of this work. List characteristics that seem most important to you and your professional growth.

Step 2

For each characteristic of the work, describe why it is important to you. Was the characteristic important to the client? Why?

Step 3

Relate what you described in Step 2 to culture-centered helping, the strengths-based approach, and the agency culture.

Faculty and Site Supervisor Dialogue: Dr. Bianca and Ms. Bellewa

In addition to hearing from Alicia, Lucas, and Tamika, we asked Dr. Bianca, a human service faculty member, and Ms. Bellewa, a human service site supervisor, to talk about their experiences of working with clients and supervising students who work with clients from culture-centered and strengths-based perspectives.

Dr. Claude Bianca

When I was educated as a human service professional, I was taught to pay attention to the needs of the individual client. Embedded in this concern for the individual was the concept of culture. But I didn't learn about the importance of looking at client culture until much later in my professional development. For me, culture became an important focal point when I worked with clients who were much different from me. Female clients always received my attention because I wanted to be sensitive to the female perspective. I didn't want to ignore the women. During the early days, my clients taught me quite a bit.

One approach that really helped me was to see clients as my teachers. And now I ask my students each week, "What did your clients teach you?" We focus on culture and also on strengths. We also focus on the client's environment. When each of the students talks about the client-as-teacher, there is a powerful message about the client's role in the helping process. Often, during our class meetings, the work with one client has the power to impact the entire group of interns. For example, during the first week of this term, a student told a story of pacing a conversation she had with a client. The client told the student, "Can you work with me? When you speak, I take in your words in English, then I translate into my language, then I think of a response in my language, then I translate my response to English, and then I speak. I just can't go very fast."

Another assignment that builds on the client-as-teacher is the thank you note. *Every other week I ask interns to write a short thank you note to their clients. Although this is an assignment that they share with their peers, some of them share this note with their clients. Others convey the thanks verbally. Both of these activities seem to strengthen the helping process and build a stronger bond between intern and client. It also sets a positive and respectful tone during our class meetings.*

Ms. Zu Bellewa

Often times, students struggle with fully understanding how to take on a culture-centered approach when they've been trained to focus so much on the individual and his or her needs. What I try to communicate to them is that culture, both theirs and their clients, is inevitably in the room; choosing to recognize it allows for the development of a culture-centered relationship. Not only are interns expected to recognize their client's culture, but they are also expected to recognize their own as it interacts with their client's. When interns first start at our site, I find it necessary to have a conversation on cultural differences and similarities, values, and beliefs. In doing so, they become comfortable with recognizing culture as it impacts the work that we do and are open to having those conversations with their peers, supervisors, and clients.

Culture is infused into everything that we do. At times, it is easier for students to recognize differences in culture when they are loud and visible, like the color of one's skin, the traditional clothes they choose to wear, or the language they choose to speak. My role as a site supervisor is to make sure that all my interns understand that culture and cultural differences go beyond what is visible, and extend to our core values and beliefs. My role is to also encourage them to recognize the cultural components that they bring into the working relationship they have with their clients. Ultimately, interns begin to recognize that while cultural differences may appear to be vast, at the core of many of the issues are undeniably similar needs and emotions. I try to emphasize to my interns that culture is different for each of us. Many times I begin with talking with them about my own culture and then explore how my culture is different from theirs. And if I am able to talk about culture in a comfortable way with them, it models for them how they can do this with their clients.

Written by Dareen Basma, 2015. Used with permission.

The Professional Voice and Tips for Practice: Gwen

As we consider culture-centered helping and using a strengths-based approach, we ultimately want to help our clients facilitate change in their lives. Often one way an agency measures change is to consider client satisfaction. The question that arises is how does a human service organization or agency measure client satisfaction. I think that can be done at various points in the helping process. In our agency, we believe the more feedback clients provide the better. We also think that we need to provide easy ways for clients to tell us how we are serving them.

Gwen

I am going to provide several different ways that we ask for client feedback. I hope that these suggestions provide you with some ideas about how you can collect feedback from clients about your work with them.

Feedback Opportunity 1

We ask for client feedback at the end of the initial interview. We ask clients to fill out a five-question survey. We use simple language and have the survey constructed in over 20 languages. Here is the feedback we ask for.

- *Satisfaction of overall services*
- *Satisfaction about the wait time for services*
- *Satisfaction to immediate needs*
- *Satisfaction for referral*
- *Satisfaction for plans for follow-up*

Feedback Opportunity 2

After each individual visit with a client, we ask clients to answer a six-question survey before they leave the office. The survey addresses physical environment, relationships, and quality of service.

- *Timeliness of service*
- *Helpfulness of staff*
- *Attention to your cultural needs*
- *Attention to your immediate needs*
- *Willingness to return*
- *Willingness to refer our services to others*

Feedback Opportunity 3

When clients leave the agency, we like to have an individual interview with them to ask more in-depth questions about the services they received. This information is anonymous. The exit interview usually takes about 15 minutes. The questions focus on the following topics.

- *Reason for seeking services*
- *Helpfulness in establishing goals*
- *Receipt of services needed*
- *Helpfulness of staff*
- *Availability of staff*

- *Attention to culture*
- *Existence of a follow-up plan*

You might want to talk with your faculty and site supervisor about how you can gain feedback from your clients. There are numerous ways that you can gather these data, depending upon the services provided and the types of clients served. I hope that you will incorporate gathering data about client satisfaction as a part of your human service delivery.

Written by Gwen Ruttencutter, 2015. Used with permission.

Terms to Remember

Agency policies

Client centered

Client satisfaction

Cultural sensitivity

Culturally diverse staff

Culture-centered approach

Helping process

Information gathering

Initial interview

Interventions

Mission statement

Organizational or agency context

Outreach

Power

Staff training

Set priorities and goals

Strengths-based helping

Termination

Translated documents

Welcoming environment

References

Abdullah, S. (2014). An Islamic perspective for strengths-based social work with Muslim clients. *Journal of Social Work Practice: Psychotherapeutic Approaches in Health, Welfare and the Community, 29*(2), 163–172. doi: 10.1080/02650533.2014.956304

Atkinson, D. R. (Ed.). (2003). *Counseling American minorities: A cross cultural perspective* (6th ed.). Boston, MA: McGraw-Hill.

Berg, C. (2009). A comprehensive framework for conducting client assessments: Highlighting strengths, environmental factors, and hope. *Journal of Practical Consulting, 3*(2), 9–13.

Bernard, J. M., & Goodyear, R. K. (2014). *Fundamentals of clinical supervision* (5th ed.). Boston, MA: Pearson.

Brammer, R. (2012). *Diversity in counseling* (2nd ed.). Pacific Grove, CA: Brooks Cole/Cengage.

Brown, L. (2008). *Cultural competence in trauma therapy: Beyond the flashback* [Kindle Edition]. Retrieved from http://www.amazon.com/Cultural-Competence-Trauma-Therapy-Flashback/dp/1433803372

Cowger, C. D. (1994). Assessing client strengths: Clinical assessment for client empowerment. *Social Work, 39*(3), 262–268. Retrieved from https://www.preventchildabusenj.org/documents/fop_admin/9407122511.pdf

Coyhis, D., & Simonelli, R. (2008). The Native American healing experience. *Substance Use & Misuse, 43*(12–13), 1927–1949. doi: 10.1080/10826080802292584

Interagency Language Roundtable. (2014). Language Skill Level Descriptions—Speaking. Retrieved from http://www.govtilr.org/Skills/ILRscale2.htm

Lee, C. C. (Ed.). (2013). *Multicultural issues in counseling* (4th ed.). Alexandria, VA: American Counseling Association.

Madsen, W. C., & Gillespie, K. (2014). *Collaborative helping: A strengths framework for home-based services*. Hoboken, NJ: Wiley.

McQuaide, S., & Ehrenreich, J. H. (1997). Assessing client strengths. Families in Society. *Journal of Contemporary Human Services, 78*(2), 210–212.

Prochaska, J. O., & Norcross, J. C. (2010). *Systems of psychotherapy: A transtheoretical approach*. Pacific Grove, CA: Brooks Cole/Cengage.

Rangan A., & Sekar, K. (2006). Strengths perspective in mental health (Evidence-based case study). In V. Pulla & C. Montgomery (Eds.), *Brisbane Institute of strengths based practice papers*. Retrieved from http://www.strengthbasedstrategies.com/PAPERS/16RanganFormatted.pdf

Saleeby, D. (2012). *The strengths perspective in social work practice* (6th ed.). New York, NY: Pearson/Allyn & Bacon.

Seligman, M. E. P., & Csikszentmihalyi, M. (2000). Positive psychology: An introduction. *American Psychologist, 55*(1), 5–14.

Sue, D. W., & Sue, D. (2012). *Counseling the culturally diverse: Theory and practice*. Hoboken, NJ: Wiley.

White, M. (2005). *Narrative practice and exotic lives: Resurrecting diversity in everyday life*. Adelaide, AUS: Dulwich Centre.

Woodside, M., & McClam, T. (2015). *Introduction to human services* (8th ed.). Pacific Grove, CA: Brooks Cole/Cengage.

10 Expanding Your Skills

Reading this chapter will help you do the following:

- Understand what is involved in *case conceptualization*.
- Learn how to view your work with clients in more complex ways.
- Prepare a case study of a client.
- Learn about how to document your work and write reports about it.
- Follow a problem-based learning approach to learn more about client populations and issues clients encounter.
- Learn about how other peers, a faculty supervisor, a site supervisor, and a human service professional respond to the complexities of their professional work.

Part III of this text, focused on Expanding Your Skills, began in Chapter 9 by introducing ideas about how you and your agency's staff can think about and deliver culture-centered services to clients. In Chapter 9, we also suggested how you might, if appropriate, integrate a strengths approach into service delivery.

In this chapter, which is the second chapter in Part III, we focus on helping you work with clients by thinking about them in more **complex ways**. First, we introduce the concept of case conceptualization as a way to consider the complexities of issues and challenges, as well as possible interventions. Second, we describe what a client **case study** involves and suggest ways one can be constructed. Third, we present suggestions about how to thoroughly document your work and write reports about it. Fourth, we introduce a model of learning called the problem-based learning approach. This model will help you explore client populations and client issues and challenges in more depth. In the fifth and last section, we return to Alicia, Lucas, and Tamika to hear about how they view the complexities of their work with clients. Dr. Bianca and Ms. Bellewa also will share their supervision experiences their interns assume more challenging work. Finally, Gwen describes how you can use Bloom's taxonomy of the cognitive domain to advance your thinking about your professional work (Huitt, 2011).

Box 10.1 describes the organizational framework of the first section of this chapter that addresses the complexities inherent in helping clients. To reach this goal, we introduce the concept of case conceptualization and present a way you can perform the three tasks that constitute it.

Box 10.1 Studying the Text: Developing a Case Conceptualization of the Client

Studying the text: The following outline will help you read and study the text material in this next section.

Developing a case conceptualization of the client

1. Case conceptualization and the helping process

2. Engaging in the three tasks of case conceptualization

3. Sue engages in an instance of case conceptualization

Developing a Case Conceptualization of the Client

Defining Case Conceptualization

The purpose of our work with clients is to facilitate change and to help them create a sense of self-efficacy and empowerment for that change. At this stage in your internship, some of your work with clients may be more predictable and less anxiety producing. At the same time, you will also be more likely to see more complexity within your clients and their environments. Such complexities may be more easily perceived in your encounters with multiproblem clients, who face multiple issues and challenges. Work with clients will also become more complex as you increase your own skills as a helper. You may be able to generate multiple ways of representing, and then addressing, client issues and challenges.

Your ability to see clients in more complex ways and to consider interventions that respond to this complexity, in some ways, mirrors your own development as an intern. This development is described in the Integrated Developmental Model (IDM) (Stoltenberg & McNeill, 2011) that we introduced in Chapter 2. According to the IDM, increased experiences in working with clients will lead you to become less focused on yourself as you become more focused on clients, all while the experiences improve your basic helping skills. Your ability to think about clients in more complex ways becomes greater. One outcome of this professional growth is learning how to develop a client **case conceptualization** (Tate & Amatea, 2010).

Simply stated, client case conceptualization centers on determining client needs and considering possible interventions. One of the first steps in adding complexity to understanding and working with clients is to develop the ability to perform Seligman's (2004) three tasks of case conceptualization: (a) representing client needs, (b) making sense of client needs, and (c) determining interventions. We suggest that one aspect of each of these tasks is generating multiple perspectives. The development of multiple perspectives allows you to see your clients beyond stereotypes and categories and to view each of your clients in unique ways. We will teach you to perform these three tasks by describing each task and showing how the tasks fits within the helping process and by illustrating how Sue works with her client, George, to perform the three tasks of case conceptualization.

Case Conceptualization and the Helping Process

For the purpose of your work in internship, we suggest thinking about case conceptualization as it occurs throughout the six-stage helping process. In Chapter 9, we identified the six stages of the helping process: initial interview, information gathering, setting priorities and goals, generating choices, intervention, termination, and evaluating outcomes. Related to case conceptualization, Seligman (2004) suggests that the helping professional engages in three tasks during case conceptualization: representing client needs, making sense of client needs, and determining interventions. We provide Table 10.1 to illustrate how you can integrate the six-stage helping process with Seligman's (2004) model of case conceptualization.

Table 10.1   Working With Clients: Case Conceptualization and the Helping Process

Tasks of Case Conceptualization	The Six-Stage Helping Process	All Individuals Involved
	Initial interview information gathering	Helper, client, others
Representing client needs		Helper and client
Making sense of client needs		Helper and client
	Setting priorities and goals Generating choices	Helper, client, others
Determining the intervention		Helper and client
	Intervention Termination and evaluation of outcomes	Helper and client

These three tasks are adapted from Seligman (2004).

Representing Client Needs

As indicated in Table 10.1, the process of **representing client needs** is a direct result of an initial interview and the information gathering stages of helping. After engaging in these two stages, a helper together with the client combine the information gained to represent the client's needs. The intake interview may include a social history, family history, educational history, medical history, mental health history, and financial history, as well as other pertinent areas. The client provides some of this information. Other sources of information may include family and friends, other community agency records (with client's permission), testing, outreach visits, and other professional reports. The key to defining the client needs is to generate as much pertinent information as possible and to identify multiple needs.

Making Sense of Client Needs

After completing the task of representing client needs, helpers consider critically the information gained and use their professional understanding and experience as a basis of describing and **making sense of client needs.** This includes looking at very specific client needs, as well as developing a more holistic picture of the client. Some helpers refer to developing this holistic picture as putting together pieces of a puzzle (Woodside & McClam, 2013). Often helpers ask clients to help refine the holistic view.

The task of making sense of client needs involves both analyzing data and then generating a creative interpretation of those data that presents the client as a unique individual within a special set of circumstances. In analyzing the data, the helper will generate as many categories of data as are relevant and develop a detailed description that avoids a stereotypical view of the client.

Determining Interventions

The third task of case conceptualization, that of **determining interventions,** is based upon the outcomes of the first four stages of the helping process (initial interview, information gathering, setting goals and priorities, and generating choices) and upon the first two tasks of case conceptualization (defining client needs and making sense of client need) already completed as shown in Table 10.1. The helper and the client want to develop a plan that matches client needs with agency services.

Now that you have an introductory understanding of the tasks of case conceptualization, we provide a step-by-step description about how to perform them and illustrate them in Figure 10.1. We then look at how Sue uses the tasks of case conceptualization as she works with her client, George. Then we provide you with an opportunity to develop a case conceptualization for one of your clients.

Engaging in the Tasks of Case Conceptualization

Representing Client Needs

Representing client needs culminates the process of intake interviewing and additional information gathering. In this first task of case conceptualization, you and your client are simply describing client needs.

Step 1 Complete the intake interview

Step 2 Gather additional information

This information can come from a variety of sources such as the client, family, friends, additional agency sources, outreach visits, tests, and other appropriate sources.

Step 3 Develop a comprehensive list of client needs

Making Sense of Client Needs

Step 1 Analyzing the Data

In this step, you will develop categories or themes of needs. These categories might include personal factors, family and significant others, and/or environmental factors. The agency's mission or the population served or the issues addressed may help you define the categories. Categories might also include culture and strengths.

Step 2 Creative Understanding

During this step, you perform a variety of tasks that allow you to understand the client in new ways.

1. Review the information and identify client characteristics that represent the norm for the population.

2. Identify what characteristics are unique to this client.

3. Identify characteristics that appear to be strongly linked to the client's needs.

4. Identify characteristics that appear to be linked to meeting the client's needs.

5. Write a summary about the client based upon responses to statements 1 to 4.

Step 3

1. Work with the client to answer the same questions you answered in Step 2.

2. Then help the client write a summary of his or her responses in Step 3.

3. Work with the client to identify what seemed important to meeting his or her needs.

Step 4

In this step, you and the client work together to develop a collaborative understanding of client needs.

1. With the client, review your responses and his or her responses.

2. Create one summary about the client and his or her needs.

3. Agree that this will be the basis of setting priorities and goals, as well as for determining interventions.

4. Agree that this summary could be revised.

Determining Interventions

During this task, you and the client generate multiple interventions to meet established priorities and goals.

1. List priorities and goals.

2. For each priority and goal, list as many interventions as possible.

3. Choose interventions.

4. Develop and implementation plan, including a timeline and which individual will be responsible.

Before you develop a case conceptualization of one of your clients, review Sue's description of how she performed the tasks of case conceptualization with her client, George.

Sue Engages in the Three Tasks of Case Conceptualization

Sue describes how she develops a view of the complexities of who George is and the context in which he lives. She uses the three tasks of case conceptualization outlined by Seligman (2004) to illustrate how she creates a more complex understanding of George and his situation.

Sue's Introduction

I wanted to share with you the way that I see my work with George fitting into the three tasks of case conceptualization. Here is a description of how

Figure 10.1   Representing Client Needs

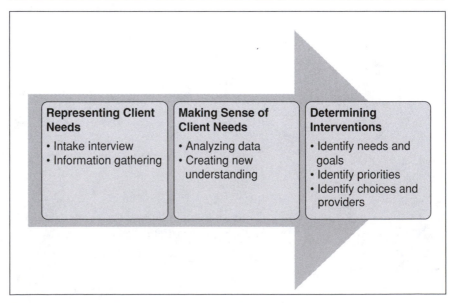

Source: Created by Gwen Ruttencutter, 2015. Used with permission.

I applied the tasks to my work with George. I don't provide you with all of the details of my work. But I include enough information for you to see how each of the three tasks—representing client needs, making sense of client needs, and determining the intervention—guided my work.

Representing Client Needs

George and I started identifying his needs when I met with him the first time. Since our agency's mission is to address and alleviate homelessness in our community, that agency mission was the primary focus of our work. But the agency assumes a more general view of homelessness, and its ultimate goal is to provide the client with multiple services, ultimately permanently ending the client's homelessness.

First, George and I filled out an agency intake form together. We identified his type or category of homelessness (this is the issue that brings him to the shelter)—he is now living in short-term temporary housing, but the search for housing is a long-term issue for him. We talked about various aspects of his life and his situation. During the intake, we discussed his family, educational history, income history, medical history, alcohol/ drug abuse history, mental health history, and legal history. In addition, George helped me record and understand his history of homelessness and the types of services he has received in the past. This included things that had helped him previously and things that didn't. George and I brainstormed about other information we needed before we could set priorities and goals and generate possible interventions. Even though George was clear about his desire for long-term housing, he was less clear about other needs.

During our second meeting, George and I reviewed the intake information and I shared with him the follow-up information I attained, with his permission, from the local hospital, a cousin who lives in the area, his grandparents, and the Bureau of Indian Affairs (BIA) Division of Human Services. I also contacted several of his past employers and two of his past landlords. At one time, George had a case manager who helped him secure temporary housing. Also, he had lived for a short while in two shelters in the county. I located the records of those services.

Making Sense of Client Needs

Once I gathered the information about George, it was time for me to begin to make sense of his needs. I had three reasons that I wanted to understand George in more depth. First, I wanted to be able to link what we know about homelessness to helping George. Second, I wanted to understand George without stereotyping him as either a homeless individual, a male, or a Native American. Third, I wanted to view George as an individual with a unique set of needs. In other words, I wanted my knowledge and experience working with homelessness to inform my work with him. Yet, I didn't want my prior experience to limit my ability to develop new insights about George or what he needed.

To meet these goals, I engaged in two types of thinking: analysis and creativity. Therefore, I analyzed the data I had about George and then developed a description of the data that conveyed my understanding of George and his needs. I knew that making sense of George's needs influences the setting of goals and priorities, generating choices for interventions, and determining interventions.

Step 1

To help me understand George and his situation, first I analyzed the data that George and I gathered by categorizing the information. I also made notes about further information I needed. Here are some of the categories I used.

Individual reasons for George's homelessness—I considered the personal factors, such as mental health issues, health issues, substance issues, or intellectual disability issues that might relate to George's current situation. George had experienced depression in his early teens but indicated that was not an issue for him now. His health issues were few; he had been to the emergency room at least once a year for untreated wounds or pneumonia. George smoked cigarettes and used marijuana occasionally. He indicated he rarely had resources to buy marijuana. George continues to smoke cigarettes.

Structural reasons for George's homelessness—These are factors that our agency considers for each client. It is part of our assessment model. The reason we look at these factors represents our belief that several aspects of the broader society, especially related to poverty and wealth, contribute to the issue of homelessness. These factors include looking at the experience of short-term and long-term poverty, unemployment or inadequate employment, availability of housing, cost of housing, and discrimination. We try to understand and address structural issues in our treatment and advocacy for a client. With George, as we reviewed his employment history, it became clear that, when he was able to find work, he had low-paying employment and few benefits. The employment he did have had no training or promise of advancement; rather, many jobs were part-time and/or temporary. Because of the irregular nature of his employment, he could not secure permanent housing.

Strengths Perspective

As I indicated in Chapter 9, when I talked about my work with George, the homeless shelter allowed me to integrate a strengths perspective into my work with clients. During my work with George, I used several questions from a larger set of questions developed by Saleebey (2002). The categories of questions included survival, support, exception, possibility, and esteem. The specific questions I used with George I have listed here:

- *"When things were going well in life, what was different?" Or "In the past, when you felt that your life was better, more interesting, or more stable, what about your world, your relationships, your thinking was special or different?" (Saleebey, 2002).*
- *Sue Reports George's Response—George was able to share a few times when he felt things went well for him. He talked about two times when he was employed at a local machine shop. The owner was willing to train him and let him live in a small room just outside the shop. He didn't have to worry about housing or transportation. He could concentrate on his job. Unfortunately his two stints at this machine shop were limited because of the owner's difficulty maintaining a steady flow of orders. During the last*

economic downturn, the shop closed. George indicated that both times of employment at the machine shop were good periods in his life.

- *"What people have given you special understanding, support, and guidance?" and "Who are the special people on whom you can depend?" (Saleebey, 2002).*

- *Sue Reports George's Response—I talked about my employer. He trusted me and supported me. He gave me a place to live. I was under his roof. And I didn't worry about each day and how I would take care of myself. It was so great to know where I would be sleeping at night. I also know that I can depend upon my grandparents. I don't see them very often, but earlier in my life I could go to their home. I knew they loved me and they could keep me safe.*

- *"What now do you want out of life?" and "How far along are you toward achieving these?" "What people or personal qualities are helping you move in these directions?" helped us see how much he was willing to commit to interventions (Saleebey, 2002).*

- *Sue Reports George's Response—I want to have a job and have a home. I am tired of worrying about each day. Right now I could go back to the reservation but I don't want to do that. I want to make it in this world.*

Environmental Strengths

In addition, in the agency staff's work with clients, we work with the client to gather information about family and social networks. We want to understand their strength, and also anticipate where they might break down.

I know that George had a good employer at one time. But that employment placement is not a possibility. Some of George's family is not very supportive but his grandparents still would like to help him. George has a limited social network. And some of the limitations exist because he does not want help from the BIA's Division of Human Services.

Culture

The final category we worked to describe was client culture. It also means assessing any culturally linked factors, such as discrimination, lack of cultural support, and any cultural barriers. George is keenly aware of his status as a Native American. When I learned about the importance of George's grandparents in his life, I knew that they were a key to his link with his sense of culture. I also learned how separated he had been from his culture and his family since he left the reservation years ago. In fact, George expressed sadness that he didn't feel he belonged anywhere. He didn't belong outside the reservation. And he didn't want to live on the reservation.

From time to time in his life, he could identify a few friends he spent time with. Those individuals were usually connected with work. But his work experience was so episodic there was little way to continue those relationships. George did value family and friends and talked about the importance of his family when he was a child. But he had been disconnected with his Native American culture since he left home. But he recognizes that outside the reservation, he is considered a Native American. And because of his culture, those outside the reservation treat him as less than an equal.

Step 2

The second aspect of making sense of client needs required me to sort through what I had learned about George and distinguish what is unique about him. I followed a five-step process:

1. *I looked through all of the information that I had gathered about George. I made notes about what characteristics made George similar to what we would consider the norm for the homeless population.*

2. *I made notes about what characteristics or factors that stand out to me and make George unique.*

3. *I made notes about what factors I thought were key to determining George's needs.*

4. *I made notes about what factors were key to meeting George's needs.*

5. *I created a written summary of my findings from Items 1 to 4.*

Step 3

1. *I worked with George to complete the Steps 1 to 4. Together we created a written record of his responses.*

2. *Then I asked him to note what factors were key to meeting his needs. And then I asked him to talk about what was most important to him.*

Step 4

1. *Together we reviewed my responses and his. We created a summary of our discussion that represented how we made sense of his needs.*

2. *We agreed to use this as a basis for setting priorities and goals and determining interventions.*

Determining Interventions

George and I worked together to determine interventions that might help him reach his goals. We used a chart to generate multiple options. Our goal here was to provide as broad a set of choices as possible and then match agency services to George's needs and goals. The chart we used helped us gain a larger picture of what was possible. We had available a list of the services my agency provides and an additional document that details other community services. We worked through the table from columns left to right. For example, we would list a need, determine the goals related to that need, rank the need as a high, middle, or low priority. Then we would describe the services we might use to meet the need and list who would be the service provider. I filled out one line for you to view the results of our work. Once we completed this table, we used it as a way to develop a plan for intervention.

I have used this table to work with six of my clients. The degree of detail depends upon the client needs and the complexity of the issues the client faces. Filling out the table together seems to confirm the helping process as a collaborative effort.

Now that you see how Sue is involved in the three activities of case conceptualization, let's look at one of your own clients and see how you are representing that client's needs and making sense of these needs. In addition, look at ways that you are determining interventions for this client.

Table 10.2 Determining Interventions

Needs	Goal	Priority	Services	Providers
Housing	Maintain current housing	1	Financial support	Homeless shelter
	Achieve permanent housing			Community housing development

Exercise 10.1 Using the Three Activities of Case Conceptualization

Step 1

Identify one client with whom you have worked or are working. Summarize your thinking about how the three activities of case conceptualization—representing client needs, making sense of client needs, and determining interventions—represents your work with this client. You can use Sue's description of her work with George to help structure you own work. Adapt the process to fit your agency's mission, your client, and his or her needs and your knowledge, skills, and experience.

My Client

Representing client needs

_____

_____

_____

Making sense of client needs

_____

_____

_____

Determining interventions

_____

_____

_____

In the following section, we introduce another way to construct a case conceptualization of a client by developing a case study. Box 10.2 introduces this section.

Box 10.2 Studying the Text: Developing a Case Study

Studying the text: The following outline will help you read and study the text material in this next section.

Developing a case study

1. Possible uses of the case study

2. The case study format (See Exercise 10.2)

Developing a Case Study

Case conceptualization assists helping professionals better understand, and communicate to others, their own thoughts about their work with clients. One way to record a case conceptualization is to develop or write a **case study** of a client. Writing a case study allows you to think more formally about what you know about the client, what your experience with the client has been like, and what help you need to support your work with the client.

Possible Formats of the Case Study

During the internship class, sometimes faculty ask their interns to write a case study of a client and submit it, in writing, for review. As an alternative, or in addition, interns may prepare an oral case study and present it to their peers in internship class. This provides interns with opportunities for peer feedback and support. A third way a case study may support the internship experience relates to agency work. Many agencies hold client staffings. In these staffings, one or more staff members may present information about their clients, discuss their cases with other agency staff, and receive feedback about their work with specific clients. Using a case study format is one way interns can prepare for such an agency client staffing.

We introduce a case study format in Exercise 10.2 and ask that you prepare a case study for one of your clients. You may substitute this assignment for a format that your faculty supervisor suggests, if you so choose.

Exercise 10.2 Writing a Case Study, Writing Your Own Story, Entry 29

Step 1

Use the following format to prepare a written case study about a client of your choice. Include the following information in this exercise:

Description of client (this is a brief summary of your impressions)

Statement of the issues (combines both representing client needs and making sense of them)

Client Information

> Family and home background
>
> Ethnic background and identity

Racial background and identity

Cultural background and identity

Exceptionalities

Physical health history

Educational history

Social interaction

Testing and assessment

Occupational history

Hobbies and recreational activities

Sexual adjustment

Client Strengths Assessment and Limitations

Client strengths to face difficulties

Client strengths to handle stress

Client strengths to overcome difficulties

Client strengths to find others to help

Client belief in self

Client belief in change

Client ability to collaborate with helper

Client knowledge, skills, and values

Support from client's environment

Client limitations

Environmental limitations

Client Experience With Human Service System

Summary of client's experience with human service agencies (this is a brief summary you prepare)

History of services

What lead the client to seek help at this time?

Number of times you have seen client

Brief case conceptualization (includes representing client needs, making sense of client needs, and determining interventions)

Intervention and Treatment

What does your work with this client entail?

What are the past interventions and outcomes?

What are the planned interventions and anticipated outcomes?

What are complicating factors?

(Continued)

(Continued)

Consultation

What are the difficulties you are having?

What type of help or feedback would you like or need?

What are your thoughts about future work with client?

Step 2

Prepare a 10-minute presentation to share with your internship class or agency staffing based upon your written case study. Develop a short one-page summary of the in-depth study you prepared in Step 1 to distribute to members of the class. This task provides you with an opportunity to share your work with the client, practice your ability to present salient facts and understandings about the client, and develop your willingness to consult with peers about your internship work.

The case study that you prepared in Exercise 10.2 is one of the many reports, cases, and case note entries that you will write during your internship. The ability to document your work and prepare reports is essential to successful internship work. In the following section, we include some tips that you can use to guide your writing. Box 10.3 describes the organizational framework of the following section that is focused on developing documentation and report-writing skills.

Box 10.3 Studying the Text: Developing Documentation and Report-Writing Skills

Studying the text: The following outline will help you read and study the text material in this next section.

Reviewing documentation and report-writing skills

1. The importance of documentation

2. Guidelines for report-writing

Reviewing Documentation and Report-Writing Skills

Documentation, as it relates to human service work, provides the details of service delivery provided by human service professionals, including interns. In many cases, it also describes the quality of the work. During your internship, you will most likely be asked to write several reports and, in addition, document your work with clients. The reasons for documentation in human service work are numerous. They include describing interactions with clients and describing the services they receive. It is also a written record of how staff follow the policies and procedures the agency has in place. In addition, it helps agency staff account for their time and resources expended to benefit the client and the community. Finally, it helps an agency demonstrate in concrete terms their adherence to ethical and legal guidelines they follow. Let's look at the purposes of documentation and report writing in more details.

First, documentation supports the helping process and the delivery of services. An important component of helping is planning. Clear written records about past work with a client and recommendations about future work help professionals remember and review those past actions and make future plans. This written record is especially important since professionals and interns may be working with a large number of clients. In addition, as you write, you will be thinking about and reconsidering your work. During this activity, you may gain insights about client progress and your own professional work.

Second, good documentation helps support **continuity of care** for the client. As an intern, there are boundaries related to your work with clients, especially in terms of your availability. You enter the internship with a commitment of working at the agency for a limited time that is dictated by your academic program. This means you will not always work with clients through the entire helping process. Many clients may enter the agency and maintain their involvement with the agency long after you complete your internship. Good documentation of your work with clients will help other professionals continue your work after you leave the agency (see Chapter 11 for guidelines for concluding your work with clients).

Third, since good supervision is critical to your own professional growth, a written record of your work with clients helps your site supervisor review your work and provides a basis for supervision. The details of your work may help your supervisor provide the critical feedback you need for your own professional growth and development. In most instances, your supervisor is also responsible for your internship work, especially your work with clients. Therefore it is important that your supervisor is continually aware of this work and can account for your interactions with clients. Finally, good recordkeeping is necessary for **professional accountability** for clients, for the agency, and for you. For instance, clients may have questions about the services they received or about the direction of their treatment. It is well within their rights to review agency records about their involvement with the agency. In terms of accountability, good records will help both interns and professionals articulate to others if legal or ethical questions arise about work with clients. Finally, the agency needs accurate documentation for self-directed data gathering and evaluation, accountability to funding sources, and records requested by state agencies or the courts.

Although we assume that you have received information about how to document client work and write reports during your coursework and from your agency, we provide some tips that may be useful to you as you complete your documentation and report writing. We also encourage you to talk with your site supervisor about the agency guidelines and expectations related to record keeping, especially for documenting work with clients. This may include documentation of information gathering, priority setting, planning and implementation of services, and the time and effort you spent with each client.

We suggest ideas about how to record your work using a client contact report so that your site supervisor and faculty supervisor can review your work with clients. Then we provide ideas about how to write a summary of a client interaction that may help you write a case study report. Finally we suggest guidelines for writing goals and objectives and recommendations.

Client Contact Report

From our experience with human service agency work, a common expectation for human service staff is to record, in writing, each client contact. We follow with the items that might be included in a **client contact report** and a tip on writing each item.

Client information—This information may include the name of the intern or professional staff, date, name of the client, and the purpose of the interaction.

Tip: This information is factual and must be accurate.

Intern or professional staff observations—With the intern or professional **staff observations,** you are summarizing the interaction between and/or observation of the client. This may include the physical location, as well as the mood or feeling of the interaction. You will also include a description of what happened during that time, the client's verbal and nonverbal activity or behavior, as well as your own.

Tip: These observations are your own descriptions of your experiences and observations. You will be both conveying what happened during the time with the client and interpreting your experience.

For example, for a description of how the client entered the room, you might write, "She knocked twice, opened the door, and sat in a chair quickly, keeping her eyes on the floor" (conveying what happened).

"When she looked up she had tears running down her cheeks. I thought she seemed distressed" (interpreting the experience).

You should not try to share any strong feelings you have about the client.

Topics and content—This is a summary of the substance of what occurred during the meeting.

Tip: It helps when conveying content to be as accurate as possible. You want to report the occurrences in chronological order. Quotes add to the account. Here you present the facts.

Perceptions—This is a time when you share your impressions of the interaction.

Tip: You express these as your own thoughts, rather than facts.

For instance, you may say, "He appeared to be . . ." or "She may have felt . . . when we talked about . . ." or "He seemed to believe . . ."

In your writing, you remain clear when you are interpreting client behavior, rather than reporting client behavior.

Summary of Client Interactions

Many agencies maintain files of each client they serve. These represent a **summary of client interactions**. Some of the content of the summary of client interaction is different from the client contact report. These files contain applications for services, information from an initial interview, and case notes from each interaction with the client. If you are working with individual clients and leading client groups, you will be writing summaries of these interactions with clients. The summary is a brief record of what occurred during the interaction. In other words, you provide the facts related to the interaction. The report focuses on the client, is a brief account, is organized by topic, and often includes a summary of your analysis of the session. This summary of client interactions is helpful to your supervisor, to interdisciplinary team members who also work with your client, and to your faculty supervisor who reviews your internship work. A typical summary of client interactions might include the following items: problems and issues addressed, session goals, summary of session, planned actions, and recommendations. Often the agency stores this information in an electronic database. As we discussed earlier, your work will need to conform to agency standards.

In order to help you write a summary of client interactions, we provide guidelines for writing two components of the summary: session goals and recommendations.

Writing Session Goals

Writing **session goals** requires you to review the initial goals established for the client during an earlier step in the helping process. What happens during your work with your clients is directly linked to the priorities and goals previously established and the interventions chosen by the helper and the client. Whether you were involved in the earlier stages of the helping process or are beginning your work with the client during the intervention stage, your work is closely tied to the earlier stages of the helping process. Below, Sue contrasts her work with George with her work with LaTisha and her two daughters, both clients being served by the homeless shelter.

My work with George is going well. I am happy that I was able to begin my work with George when he first came to the agency. I have a sense of continuity with him. Each time I meet with him, he and I plan the session together. We begin with our initial goals and objectives and the priorities that we set together. Each time, I try to plan a session that meets his needs.

I am also excited about my work with LaTisha and her two small daughters, Gracie and Dominica. Gracie is 7 and Dominica is 11. Both attend a local elementary school. This family came to the homeless shelter 3 months before I began my work as an intern. Now, I belong to the team that is helping them. My job is to meet with the girls individually at the school once a week and form a helping relationship with them. I also talk with the school counselor every other week to hear more about how the girls are doing at school. In addition, I meet with LaTisha and the girls once a week at the agency. One of the priorities that LaTisha and her case manager set was to improve relationships among the three of them. For each of our weekly sessions, we work on communication skills and other social skills, such as helping and developing relationships.

As you can see with Sue's goal setting for her sessions, she is very intentional in planning each session. For each session, Sue makes a brief statement of her goal, states her plan, summarizes her plan, reports the outcome, and then makes recommendations for the next session. Here are some ideas about how to establish and document the session goals. All of the information that Sue records is kept on the agency's server. The agency uses a case management database to format the data.

Use a brief statement—The goal should be stated briefly and is a statement of what the helper and the client intend for a session.

Tip: Begin with a verb and include a rationale or outcome for the action.

For example, Sue's goal statement for one of her sessions with LaTisha and her daughters was, "Learn how to ask questions and to help the family talk positively about Gracie and Dominica's school experience." Or "Learn about what characteristics make a good friend, to help gain friendships at school."

Establish reasonable goals—To establish reasonable goals, the helper and the client must understand the goals, the purposes of the goals, and they must believe the goals can be accomplished. The goals must account for both the abilities and the resources of the helper and the client, the time allotted to achieve the goals, and the previous progress made on them. It must also be possible to link goals to action or intervention that will occur in the session.

Tip: Goals should be stated in simple terms that both helper and client can understand. As indicated earlier in Sue's example, use language that the client can understand. In addition, the client needs to be able to see the link between the goals and what occurs during the intervention.

Standards for writing goals—We present a way that you can check the quality of the goals that you establish and then record (Woodside & McClam, 2013).

Tip: Write goals that are easy to understand.

This means using language that the client understands. You should consider the client's language, culture, gender, age, and other aspects of the client's experience. Sometimes you might ask the client to help you write the goals for the session.

Tip: Write goals that easy to interpret. Avoid goals that could have more than one meaning.

At times this is a difficult standard to achieve. We often make statements and assume that if we know what a statement means, then it should be clear to everyone involved. You are much more likely to meet the goals and void confusion if you strive to keep the goals simple, share the goal with clients, and, finally, ask if the clients understand what the goals mean to them.

Tip: Make sure that both helper and client believe that the goal can be reached.

You want the client to read or hear about the goal and believe that obtaining the goal is possible. We suggest that you ask yourself prior to the work with clients if you believe that a goal is realistic. Sometimes larger goals require small steps, and you will need to break your initial goal into smaller ones.

Sue shares her experience working with Gracie and Dominica about developing friendships as a goal they set together. Sue illustrates how she uses these writing tips in her work with Gracie and Dominica.

One of my responsibilities was to help Gracie and Dominica to develop friendships at school. They had moved from school to school depending upon where LaTisha could find temporary housing. Now they were in a stable school setting. I had several challenges with this task. Since Gracie was 7 and Dominica was 11, it was difficult to meet with the two of them and plan a session that would meet both their needs. So I asked my site supervisor if I could meet with each separately. That way I could establish goals that were more suited to each. I was then able to develop smaller goals related to friendship that reflected each of their individual needs. For example, for Gracie I started with three sessions about describing "What is a friend?" I broke this down into describing one friend (drawing and telling a story), describing feelings around friendships (pictures of friends and linking to feelings), and identifying friends at school (using a friendship circle handout). I am not sure what future sessions will look like, because the goals and sessions will depend upon what happens in these three sessions.

Now that you understand more clearly about setting goals for your work with clients, we will present guidelines about another component of the summary of client interactions, that of writing recommendations at the end of the session.

Writing Recommendations

Often at the end of a report of a session, the final section includes **recommendations** of what is to come next. Usually in this section, you provide recommendations for the next steps in the helping process.

Target recommendations—In the recommendations section, you will provide suggestions for the session to come. It is in this section that you want to ensure continuity from one session to the other.

Tip: We suggest that you write these recommendations with the recipient of the report in mind. Individuals receiving the recommendations might include your supervisor, other staff, a referral source, your client, the client's family, or perhaps you are writing the recommendations for yourself, so you will remember how to continue your work with the client.

Suggest action—Because you are advising activity and tasks for the future, focus on action rather than interpretations or summaries. Make your recommendation focused and clear.

Tip: Write recommendations in clear language, use action words, and include the reason for and/or the outcomes of each. Examples of recommendations can include, "Schedule an appointment for Joe with a physician to receive a general medical exam required by this school" (staff). "Meet jointly with mother and father to discuss their career ideas" (client). "Call the college to determine the date Joe's application to college is due" (intern).

Link to client needs—As always, client interactions are planned with goals in mind. Therefore, the recommendations should be connected to the client goals. The connection should be obvious to the reader. If you believe that there should be a change in goals or if the work in the session was less than positive, then in the recommendations be clear about your consideration of this information.

Tip: Recommendations need to emerge from the helping process and case conceptualization we discussed earlier. There should be a clear link between each recommendation, making sense of client needs and implementation of the intervention or service delivery.

Exercise 10.3 will help you review the documentation and report writing guidelines presented in this section.

Exercise 10.3 Documentation and Report Writing

By this time in your internship, you have written various reports and case notes related to your work with clients for agency records and for class assignments. At this point in the term, it is a good time to review your skills and assess how to improve your documentation and report writing.

Step 1

Find a recent report that you wrote about one of your clients. Assess your written work using the following criteria. The format suggests that you record your initial writing and based upon the guidelines and the tips provided, rewrite your work. Use the aspects of the client contact report or the summary of client interaction or a combination of both. How you structure your work for this exercise depends upon the format for documentation of work with clients you use either in your agency or in your internship class.

Client contact report (lengthy summary)

- Client information
- Intern or professional staff observations
- Topics and content
- Perceptions

Summary of client interaction (brief report including problems and issues addressed, session goals, summary of session, and planned actions and recommendations)

- Session goals
  - Use a brief statement
  - Establish reasonable goals
  - Standards for writing goals
    - Write goals that are easy to understand
    - Write goals that easy to interpret
    - Make sure that both helper and client believe that the goal can be reached
  - Writing recommendations
    - Target recommendations
    - Suggest action
    - Link to client needs

Box 10.4 describes the organizational framework of the next section of this chapter, that of using a problem-based learning approach to learn more about client populations and the unique needs of clients.

Box 10.4 Studying the Text: Using a Problem-Based Learning Approach

Studying the text: The following outline will help you read and study the text material in this next section.

Using an problem-based learning approach

1. What students say

2. The problem-based learning approach

Problem-Based Learning Approach

Many fields of study, such as medicine (physicians and nurses), business, and engineering, have used a problem-based learning model as one aspect of professional education and training (Gallow, 2001). We adapt this problem-based learning model used by other professions and suggest a way that interns might use it to expand their knowledge of client populations and to develop new skills to work with those populations. Before we describe this **problem-based learning approach** and illustrate its use, we present several characteristics of this learning approach (Gallow, 2001; Savery, 2006).

The learning model is intern centered. This means that both interns and supervisors have the responsibility for determining the content. Specific to human service internship, interns, after consulting with site and faculty supervisors, determine the area of study.

The learning is context focused. Learning using a problem-based learning approach relates directly to what interns need to know for their specific internship work.

The learning is problem based and begins with a question. Using a problem-based approach means that interns describe a problem or issue encountered in the internship and state that problem in terms of a question. The question then focuses the information gathering and problem solving. Many of the questions are directly related to work with clients.

The outcome is creative. Using this learning approach, interns describe what they know, investigate more in-depth about the question they posed, and create ways they can combine what they know with their new learning to support their work in internship.

The goal is to develop as a human service professional. Ultimately, an important outcome of using the problem-based learning approach is to teach interns how to improve their understanding of and work with clients. This effort advances their abilities as human service professionals. Based upon the ethical standards of competence and a commitment to professional development, interns need to recognize when they need additional information and skills to work with a specific client or client group, continue to develop skills and abilities, and consult with supervisors and others as they encounter new challenges.

One of the most common issues that you face in your work as an intern is working with clients whose experiences and issues are beyond your knowledge and expertise. We suggest that a problem-based learning approach provides one way you can address your need for knowledge

---

Box 10.5 What Students Say: Using the Problem-Based Learning Approach

Can you describe a time when you used a problem-based learning approach?

Steve: Oh my. I was working with children. I had not worked with young children before and one of my clients told me

(Continued)

(Continued)

that his mother was dying. I didn't know how to respond. I just sat there and looked at this small boy. I told him that I was glad that he told me about this. I asked him if he wanted to talk about his mother. That day after I completed my work with him, I went straight to my site supervisor. I was really shaken.

Maria: Working in juvenile probation, many of my clients previously lived with a grandparent. I didn't understand what it was like to be living with someone other than a parent. And I didn't understand the legal aspects of guardianship.

Al: All of my clients are immigrants. They have been in the United States for 6 months or less. They don't speak English very well. I know that I need to understand about the immigrant experience and about these specific immigrants. I don't know if they are political refugees, and I am not sure about the terms of their entry into this country. I don't know anything about their cultures either.

Shasha: I am working in a shelter. I have always had a place to live and very strong family ties. The concept of homelessness is very new to me. I used to be scared of the people on the street. Also many of the men and some of the women are veterans. No one in my family served in the military. This is another area I don't know very well.

How will you used problem-based learning to support your work with the clients you mentioned earlier?

Steve: I defined the focus of my learning as grief and loss, both as experienced by children. I looked up all three topics and I learned quite a bit about the developmental levels of children and how children process grief, especially the death of a parent. I also found some material that I could use with the young boy I was working with. I also realized that this was going to be difficult for me, and I talked at length about it with my site supervisor.

Maria: I didn't even know where to begin, so I talked with my faculty supervisor first about my confusion. I think that my feelings got in the way of my understanding. I just kept thinking about how abandoned I would feel. I read about grandparents raising grandchildren and that gave me new insights into how important living with a family member might be. I also read some information about the experience from the grandparent point of view. And there is not just one point of view. I have a meeting with my site supervisor next week just to focus on guardianship and what that means.

Al: I have been struggling all semester in my work with immigrants. I think that most staff in my agency really work hard. Every day, we serve more and more immigrants. And beginning this new year, we counted clients from more than 22 countries. I realize that I am not going to know a lot about each of the 22 countries. But I have developed a way to look up information and also I changed how I work with the immigrants and I encourage them to tell me more about themselves.

Shasha: There is a lot of information available about homelessness. I am reading the literature that is available in our agency library. I am also reading a first-person account of the experience. One of our staff used to be homeless. I have learned to seek information from him too.

about and skills to work with these clients. In Box 10.5, other interns share with us situations that they encountered during their internship when working with clients for whom they had too little experience or knowledge.

Each of these students described situations that they encountered during internship. They engaged in the problem-based learning approach to support their work with clients. When confronted with a lack of knowledge or skill, we suggest you can use a problem-based learning approach to help you begin to better understand the clients that you serve as shown in Figure 10.2.

Figure 10.2   Problem-Based Learning Approach: Enhancing Understanding of Client

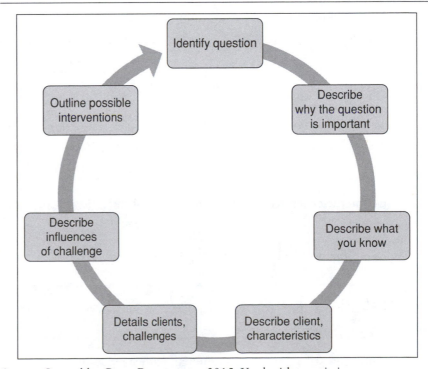

Source: Created by Gwen Ruttencutter, 2015. Used with permission.

Populations and Client Issues

1. Identify the question you have about the client population and/or client issue.

2. Outline why answering the question is important for your work.

3. Describe what you know about this population and/or issue.

4. Define the characteristics or complexities of the topic (client population or client experience).

5. Detail the problems or challenges the client population might experience.

6. Describe how the problem or challenge influences the client's experiences of daily living.

7. Outline possible interventions human service professionals might use with this client population or these client issues.

In the following exercise, Exercise 10.4, you have the opportunity to use the problem-based learning approach to gain more in-depth information about a client population or an issue a client faces.

Exercise 10.4 Using the Problem-Based Learning Approach, Writing Your Own Story, Entry 30

Step 1

Choose a population or a challenge or issue that you believe would further your work with one of your clients. Use the problem-based learning approach (1 to 7) to structure your learning.

1. Identify the question you have about the client population and/or client issue.

   _____

2. Outline why answering the question is important for your work.

   _____

3. Describe what you know about this population and/or issue.

   _____

4. Define the characteristics or complexities of the topic (client population or client experience).

   _____

5. Detail the problems or challenges the client population might experience.

   _____

6. Describe how the problem or challenge influences the client's experiences of daily living.

   _____

7. Outline possible interventions human service professionals might use with this client population or these client issues.

   _____

As we conclude this chapter, we hear from Alicia, Lucas, and Tamika as they describe their work with clients during the latter part of their internship experiences. Dr. Bianca, Ms. Bellewa, and Gwen all discuss how they help students think in more complex ways about their clients.

Box 10.6 Deepening Your Understanding

1. Peer-to-peer dialogue

   a. Alicia: Thinking in complex ways

   b. Lucas: Thinking in complex ways

   c. Tamika: Thinking in complex ways

2. Faculty and site supervisors dialogue

   a. Dr. Bianca: Helping students think in complex ways

   b. Ms. Bellewa: The complexities of the work

3. The professional voice and tips for practice: Gwen: Bloom's taxonomy

4. Terms to remember

5. References

Deepening Your Understanding

We now turn to our peer-to-peer dialogues and see how Alicia, Lucas, Tamika, Dr. Bianca, Ms. Bellewa, and Gwen share their perspectives from their special roles and responsibilities as they work with clients.

Peer-to-Peer Dialogue: Alicia, Lucas, and Tamika

We asked Alicia, Lucas, and Tamika to talk about their work with their clients. They talk about their earlier approaches and how their work with clients changed as they gained more experience.

Alicia

Hi! I hope you are enjoying your training process thus far! When I reflect upon my development of helping skills, I think of the lens through which I view my clients. At the start of this learning process, I found myself comfortable with choosing a primary theme or characteristic for each client. For example, I unintentionally grouped children and families in certain categories. For example, if a child was removed from the home due to any form of abuse, I immediately assumed that that child would want to focus on talking and processing that abuse. I realized quickly that that was not the case and was able to recognize that my assumptions can do more harm than good. A black and white conceptualization was of no benefit to my clients or my own developmental growth process as a helping professional. Regardless of their similarities, each client was very different, with different needs, wants, and stressors. By encouraging the client to choose what he or she wanted to process during our time together, I was empowering them to own the change they make in their life. For internship class, we each prepared a case study. Highlighting the individual characteristics, goals, and progress of one of my clients helped me identify and process my limited conceptualization. Learning to view my clients holistically helped me highlight multiple aspects of their experiences while documenting our progress and pairing down time spent and length of case notes.

Written by Allie Rhinehart and Dareen Basma, 2015. Used with permission.

Lucas

Hello, I hope you are having a great day! Today, I want to talk to you about how I conceptualize my clients. I am sure you are reading how to engage in activities during case conceptualization, so I am going to provide you with a brief example on how I was trained to conceptualize clients at the Tampa Bay Justice Center. First, we normally do an intake to get an understanding of clients' experiences, psychosocial history, and current symptoms. After a couple of sessions obtaining information about the clients' background, current symptoms, and expectations of counseling, then we continue to make sense of our clients by doing one-on-one counseling. This is the basic counseling sessions to get more of a holistic understanding of my clients, develop trust and rapport, and this is the stage I start to develop a treatment plan. This step is important for case conceptualization because this helps bridge the relationship between me and my clients, and setting treatment goals. Once I have an understanding of my clients, we developed trust and rapport, and now we have a framework to follow, based upon their symptoms and diagnoses, then I meet with my site supervisor to determine appropriate interventions. The interventions are usually based upon clients' development, cultural background, and symptoms/diagnosis.

Once I receive supervision and then determine an effective treatment plan for my clients, the next step I have to do is to educate my clients on their case conceptualization, the process of helping, and then I empower them in the helping process. This is an extremely complex process because most of my clients never had counseling before, but I do my best. Case conceptualization, at times, is overwhelming for me, but the more I do it, while receiving supervision, the more confident I am getting, and so will you.

One thing I struggle with at the Tampa Bay Justice Center is documenting the work we do. We currently use an online software to document our notes; however, recently we updated the software, and now I cannot find my notes in the system. I have the IT team teaching me how to use the software and helping me find my notes on the old software. This is frustrating because I rely on notes to remind me of previous sessions, evaluate client progress, and organize sessions. So recently, I have been unprepared. Therefore, if you use software at your internship site, I would recommend documenting on the software, but also have a printed copy as well.

Not only do I have to focus on case conceptualization, I also have to prepare a case study of my cases for internship class. In my opinion, preparing a case study for internship is not difficult because all I do is follow the case conceptualization process, which provides the data. When I conduct case conceptualization at my internship site, I am preparing for the case study assignments for my internship class. Therefore, work smart while you are doing your case conceptualization at your internship site, while adding the objectives for your case study.

I know this was a lot of information, but hopefully this helps clarify case conceptualization and gives you an understanding of my experiences. I know hearing about this information from people in my cohort helped me alleviate my anxieties, and I hope this helps you too!

Written by Jorge Roman, 2015. Used with permission.

Tamika

Case conceptualization is one responsibility that certainly represented a developmental process for me throughout my internship. Although it can seem daunting at first, to make sense of a client's presenting issues, to collaboratively determine how to best prioritize and tackle his/her needs, you'll be happy to know that these skills almost start to become second nature, once you've had ample opportunity to practice. At this point, I feel like I look at my clients in a much more complex manner than I did at the beginning of this experience; I see them as holistic, unique individuals with diverse needs, problems, strengths, and resources, rather than simply as a group of offenders, or people with easily fixed black-and-white issues.

One of my more recently assigned clients is one who's been in and out of the legal system for years, mostly due to his struggle with alcoholism. He presented with what he reported as major depression, a number of legal issues, and issues related to housing, finances, family stressors, and lack of work. I began conceptualizing his case by gathering as much information from him as I could. Although his story was pretty extensive, I felt that it was really important for me to have all of the pieces of the puzzle in front of me before starting to put the whole picture together. Because I use a strengths-based approach to working with my clients, I asked him to collaborate with me in setting priorities and goals for himself. He said that was the first time a counselor had included him in the process. I told him that doing so would help me to design the most effective interventions to help him. He seemed really appreciative of my collaborative approach. At the end of our first couple of sessions together, I felt really confident about understanding his story and his needs, the rapport we had built, and his buy-in related to my plans for treatment.

I decided to use my work with this client for a case study I was assigned to prepare for internship class. When I first looked at the assignment, I was a little intimidated by the sheer amount of information required, but because I had been so thorough in my approach to conceptualizing his case, it really all came together smoothly. I was surprised in the end to see such a comprehensive visual representation of my understanding of his case and our plans for intervention. I was able to review all of the information once the case study was complete and I was able to recognize where there were gaps that I needed to ask my peers and supervisors about helping me to fill. Although the case conceptualization and study preparation processes were time-consuming, I found them really beneficial to laying the puzzle pieces out in front of me and putting it all together, both for myself, for my peers, and for my supervisor when I shared during internship class.

Case documentation is something I honestly still struggle with a bit and I am working slowly to build confidence in this area. My site requires case notes to be written following every individual session and I sometimes struggle with getting them done in between clients; it can be difficult to keep up. I also tend to be too wordy in my case notes, according to my supervisor. The culture at my site is that notes should primarily include just the facts. I am still working on learning how to distinguish what should be included and what shouldn't, as well as when it's appropriate to include my own feelings or impressions. I've learned that this field includes a lot of documentation work and it can be challenging at times to maintain complete files and ensure that I'm documenting everything correctly and accurately. This is something on which I will continue to ask for feedback and a topic I like to bring up during supervision. It's a work in progress.

Written by Brittany Pollard, 2015. Used with permission.

Faculty and Site Supervisor Dialogue: Dr. Bianca and Ms. Bellewa

In addition to hearing from Alicia, Lucas, and Tamika, we asked Dr. Bianca, a human service faculty member, and Ms. Bellewa, a human service site supervisor, to talk about how the internship students grow and develop, especially in their work with clients.

Dr. Claude Bianca

The last third of the semester is usually an incredible time for my internship students. I can see students begin to see more complexities in their own work and in clients' lives. When students first begin to understand complexity, they fear that they cannot help the clients, that somehow they are not good enough. But as they begin to work with the clients, establishing rapport and partnerships with clients, they give both their clients and themselves permission to experience situations in more realistic ways.

I had a student, Juanita, just this last week who presented a case during our internship class. Juanita followed our format and noted that, by the time she completed her case preparations and presentation, she was surprised how much she knew about the client. I remember her first questions to the group early in the semester were about how to greet the client and how to talk about her self-disclosure. A second set of questions related to Juanita's strong feelings about working with specific clients and wondering what to do with those feelings. The focus of her questions at the end of her case presentation reflected how to help the client generate multiple choices for continued intervention and how to develop a supportive social support network. Her peers were able to provide very creative ideas and Juanita stated she would take these ideas back to her client and discuss them with him.

Ms. Zu Bellewa

The process of thoroughly conceptualizing a case can become overwhelming as an individual's complexities begin to unfold. While we try to better understand the individual client and attempt to meet their needs, we also try to understand the client's culture, surrounding system and influencing environmental factors, incorporating those components into our understanding of who they are. When working with immigrants, who come from different cultural backgrounds, conceptualization becomes even trickier. Interns begin to piece together information that was previously unknown to them, and not as readily available as it would be when working with a client from a similar cultural background.

I've found that one of the key factors in encouraging the development of case conceptualization skills is allowing interns a safe space for growth and exploration. As interns progress in their work at the agency, the confidence they have in their abilities very slowly begins to increase. Often times, interns doubt the work that they do and are hesitant about their conceptualizations; as they develop in their practice, their confidence and assuredness in their conceptualization becomes more concrete. Further, they become more comfortable balancing the larger systemic factors that can impact their client's life with the more individualistic issues that need to be met. My role, as their site supervisor, is to ensure that my interns have the space to verbalize and explore their understanding of their clients, their clients' backgrounds, and their clients' stories, piecing them all together to better meet their needs. As they complete their internship, I work on guiding them through their conceptualization, helping them work through the intricate balance of short-term and long-term goals.

Written by Dareen Basma, 2015. Used with permission.

The Professional Voice and Tips for Practice: Gwen

Gwen

I know that you have been thinking about working with clients in more complex ways. Sometimes it is difficult to understand how to move your own thinking to an advanced level. I find that using Bloom's Taxonomy of the Cognitive Domain (Huitt, 2011) provides a concrete way for me to advance the way I am thinking. Bloom presents cognitive activity into six levels; each has its own specific cognitive tasks. I want to explain each of the cognitive levels and present verbs that you can use to guide your thinking about your clients. I will provide an example for each level.

Knowledge—This level of cognitive work means remembering or recalling information. The verbs associated with the knowledge level include listing, memorizing, and recalling. One way you might use this is to identify the information you need from each of your clients during an intake interview. This might include contact information, age, gender, marital status, names of immediate family members, employment, and so on.

Comprehension—At this level of cognitive work, it is possible to explain ideas or concepts. Several verbs associated with comprehension are discussed, explain, or paraphrase. You demonstrate comprehension if you can explain the concept of empathy and why it is important for the helping process.

Application—If application is occurring, then what is known and understood is being used. Verbs such as demonstrate, interpret, and construct illustrate this action. If you are using a specific intervention as you work with a client, you are demonstrating this level of cognition.

Analysis—During analysis, breaking down and distinguishing different parts of a whole illustrates this cognitive level. Verbs associated with analysis are compare, contrast, *and* examine. *If you can distinguish factors such as family structure, meaning of gender, and the nature of helping across three cultures, then you are performing the act of analysis.*

Synthesis—This level of cognitive work occurs when a new product, outcome, or point of view is developed. Construct, create, *and* design *are verbs associated with synthesis. When you develop a case conceptualization or write a case study of a client, you are performing the cognitive task of synthesis.*

Evaluation—In performing evaluation, you will justify or defend a decision or a point of view. Argue, defend, *and* support *are all verbs that denote performing evaluation. When you write a summary of a client conceptualization and then, based upon stated factors, recommend interventions, you are demonstrating the skills of evaluation.*

One way to practice using this information is to look at your assignments outlined in your syllabus. Try to decide what cognitive task each calls for (may be more than one). Explain your choice. List the verbs that describe the cognitive actions you will take.

Good luck with developing your skills.

Written by Gwen Ruttencutter, 2015. Used with permission.

Terms to Remember

Case conceptualization

Case study

Client contact report

Complex ways

Consultation

Continuity of care

Determining interventions

Documentation

Making sense of client needs

Problem-based learning approach

Professional accountability

Recommendations

Representing client needs

Staff observations

Session goals

Summary of client interactions

References

Gallow, D. (2001). *What is problem-based learning? Problem-based learning faculty institute.* Retrieved from University of California, Irvine, Problem-Based Learning Faculty Institute website: http://www.pbl.uci.edu/whatispbl.html

Huitt, W. (2011). Bloom et al.'s taxonomy of the cognitive domain. *Educational Psychology Interactive*. Valdosta, GA: Valdosta State University. Retrieved from http://www.edpsycinteractive.org/topics/cognition/bloom.html

Saleebey, D. (2002). *The strengths perspective in social work practice* (3rd ed.). New York, NY: Allyn & Bacon.

Savery, J. R. (2006). Overview of problem-based learning: Definitions and distinctions. *Interdisciplinary Journal of Problem-based Learning, 1*(1), 9–20.

Seligman, L. (2004). *Diagnosis and treatment planning in counseling*. New York, NY: Springer.

Stoltenberg, C. D., & McNeill, B. W. (2011). *IDM supervision: An integrative developmental model for supervising counselors and therapists*. New York, NY: Routledge.

Tate, K., & Amatea, E. S. (2010). Exploring the process of case conceptualization: A review of the literature. *Wisconsin Counseling Journal, 24*, 10–21. Retrieved from http://www.academia.edu/3576603/Exploring_the_process_of_case_conceptualization_A_review_of_the_literature

Woodside, M., & McClam, T. (2013). *Generalist case management* (4th ed.). Pacific Grove, CA: Brooks Cole/Cengage.

PART IV

Concluding
the Internship

11 Concluding the Internship

Reading this chapter will help you do the following:

- Plan how you will conclude your work at your internship site.
- Describe guidelines for concluding your work with clients.
- Discuss how you will conclude your work with your supervisor and other staff.
- Develop materials to support the search for employment.
- Learn about how peers, a faculty supervisor, a site supervisor, and a human service professional conclude work at an internship site.

This chapter, the final chapter of this text, focuses on concluding your internship. We begin the chapter by describing what you can expect during the **conclusion** of your internship experience and then suggest what you can do to both end your work at your agency site and leave your academic program in a positive way. In the second section of this chapter, we provide some practical tips for making the transition from student to human service professional. We include ideas about developing a professional portfolio and asking for references. In the last section, we return to Alicia, Lucas, and Tamika for a final time to hear about how they are concluding their internships. Dr. Bianca and Ms. Bellewa also share their experiences with interns during this time of transition, and, finally, Gwen provides some ideas about how you might use your experiences in internship to learn what makes a working environment "right" for you.

Box 11.1 describes the organizational framework of the first section of this chapter, that of suggested ways you may conclude your internship. We introduce the reasons for planning the conclusion of internship and then discuss guidelines for ending your work with your clients, site supervisor and other agency staff, faculty supervisor, and other members of your academic program.

Box 11.1 Studying the Text: Leaving Your Internship Site

Studying the text: The following outline will help you read and study the text material in this next section.

Leaving your internship site

1. Planning the conclusion of your internship
2. Concluding your work with your site supervisor
3. Concluding your work with your clients
4. Concluding your work with your academic program

Leaving Your Internship Site

Internship has a temporal dimension. We like to think of it as occurring as **four stages of internship** as shown in Figure 11.1. The first stage is beginning the internship, and we discussed it in the first four chapters of the text. During this early time in internship, you planned and made an initial visit to the internship site. You began your work shadowing your site supervisor and assuming small tasks. During the second stage you increased your participation in the work of the agency. As your work with clients increased, you began to understand and translate the theories you had learned in your human service classes into practice. These theories include relating your experiences to your values and ethics, working through ethical issues and challenges, creating a multicultural awareness, and engaging in supervision. Each of these reflects a growing development of your human service knowledge and skills.

During the third stage of internship, you expanded your skills in working with clients by moving beyond the basic understanding of helping skills and the helping process. You learned how to address pertinent aspects of clients' cultures during service delivery and how to integrate clients' strengths into the helping process. You also began to develop a more complex view of the client that allows you to construct a flexible, yet comprehensive, case conceptualization and case study of the clients you serve.

Finally, in this fourth stage of internship, you begin concluding your work. It is a time to assess your work and your development as a human service professional, to leave your internship site and your academic program in a positive way, and to begin to think about gaining employment.

One feature of the internship that makes it a unique work experience is that it is bound by time. The beginning and the ending dates (or

Figure 11.1   Four Stages of Internship

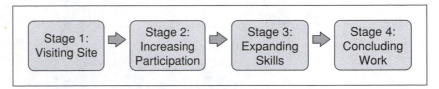

Source: Created by Gwen Ruttencutter, 2015. Used with permission.

approximate dates) are established at the time you make your initial visit. Internship sites and site supervisors begin working with you knowing that you have a required number of hours to work, a set of knowledge and skills to learn, and specific tasks to perform. You have a limited amount of time to accomplish these tasks or assignments. In other words, your placement at an internship site is temporary. Just as we approached the beginning of internship with care (e.g., planning the first visit, understanding expectations for the first week or two, etc.), it is also important to consider how you end it.

Planning the Conclusion of Your Internship

There are several reasons that you will want to carefully plan the conclusion of your internship. First, during your internship, you will likely have become an important part of the agency team, with various individuals depending upon you and your work. Your **leave-taking** will require an orderly transition of the various roles and responsibilities that you have assumed. For work to continue after you leave, you can outline your work, document the status of each facet of the work, and help others plan how they will sustain and move forward with each of your clients. Second, you will have worked with clients and developed relationships with them. For some clients, you may have become an important part of their world. They depend upon your availability for help and your positive support of their growth and change. Even though you have been clear with clients as you began your work with them about the time limitations of your internship, it is critical that you prepare them for your leave taking and help them with the transition to working with another agency staff member.

Another reason to plan how you will conclude your internship relates to the timing of the internship. The work of the internship often occurs during the last term of an academic program. Hence, you will want to decide how you wish to end your work with your faculty supervisor and your academic peers. Over several terms, both faculty and other students will have provided you with valuable guidance, support, and community. You will want to acknowledge the important ways they have influenced your personal and professional development, and you will want to determine how, in the future, you wish to maintain these connections and relationships. Figure 11.2 illustrates the various components of leave-taking.

Leaving Your Internship Site

In some ways, leaving an internship site is comparable to changing jobs. The efforts you make will help those who remain to continue the work you began. Also, leaving in a positive way helps your site supervisor and others think well of you and your internship efforts. We believe that concluding

Figure 11.2   Components of Leave-Taking

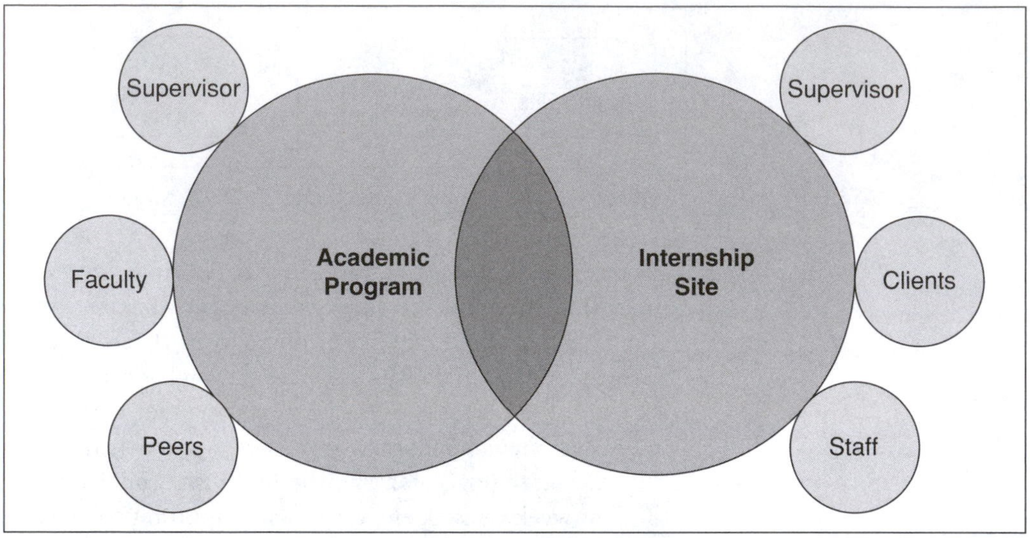

Source: Created by Gwen Ruttencutter, 2015. Used with permission.

your internship is a process that occurs over the last 3 or 4 weeks of the internship. You can begin this process by reminding your site supervisor and your clients about the date you will be leaving. A reminder, about once a week, can help you, your supervisor, members of the agency staff, and your clients adjust and plan for the conclusion of your work.

The following guidelines provide some ideas for planning your departure.

1.   *Make a list of your work projects.* You will want to make a plan about how to complete your projects or find others to continue the work you have begun (Smith & Mind Tools Team, n.d.). Use Table 11.1 to list the projects you are working on. These projects are related to agency-focused work, such as developing materials, planning community programs, and creating electronic forms or databases. We will discuss work with clients in Item 3. This table includes a name of the project or a way to identify the project, the goal of the project, the tasks you have completed to meet the stated goal, and a list of what remains to be accomplished.

2.   *Review the project list with your site supervisor.* Schedule a time to meet with your site supervisor to review the project list and determine what you can complete before you leave and what responsibilities must be assigned to other staff.

Table 11.1   Status of Internship Projects

Name	Goal	Tasks Completed	Tasks Remaining

3. *Make a list of your clients.* It is important to provide a transition plan so that work can continue with the clients with whom you are working. Use Table 11.2 to make this list of clients. This table includes the name of the client, client goals, a summary of your work with the client, and a transition plan.

4. *Review this list of clients with your site supervisor.* You will schedule a time to meet with your site supervisor to review the clients with whom you are working and determine what you and the client can accomplish during your remaining time at the internship site. With your site supervisor you will make a transition plan for each client. (See the section *Concluding Work With Clients* about how to involve clients in the planning.)

5. *Prepare reports for other staff.* Once you determine who will assume the projects you are unable to accomplish and who will work with your clients, meet with each replacement and provide him or her with the information he or she needs to assume the work. Be sure to thank each of these individuals for helping with your transition.

6. *Provide helpful feedback to the agency.* During your internship, it is possible that you have gained some helpful information or insights that you can share with your site supervisor. Examples of insights might include (a) what information and experiences were especially helpful to you during your orientation, (b) what you wished you had known or experienced at an earlier time in the internship, (c) special forms that you developed to help you with your work, (d) supervision that was especially helpful, and (e) ways that you worked with clients that gained positive results.

7. If you have the time, you might prepare a welcome document for the next intern that might ease that intern's transition. If you do prepare such document, let your site supervisor review it and provide suggestions for revision. Your supervisor will be the one to use this document to help orient future interns.

8. *Plan specific ways that you will say good-bye.* Saying good-bye is an important part of concluding an internship. Before you leave, make a list of all of the individuals at your internship site for whom you want to express good wishes and appreciation. Ideas for saying good-bye might include sharing with them what you learned during your time at the internship as well as conveying to them your gratitude for their assistance. You may also want to express your gratitude in writing. Although thank-you notes or cards might seem a little old fashioned, taking the time to share with

Table 11.2   Status of Client Progress

Name of Client	Client Goal(s)	Summary of Work	Transition Plan

individuals how they made a difference for your professional and personal growth is important. Bringing in special snacks such as cookies or cupcakes also provides a concrete way to thank others.

9. *Be positive during your leave-taking.* Focus on the positive, as you conclude your internship (Smith & Mind Tools Team, n.d.). Even if you did not have a very positive experience during your internship, work with your faculty supervisor and your peers to describe what you learned and how others supported your work.

Figure 11.3 provides a visual representation of the considerations for leaving your internship site we described.

Concluding Your Work With Your Site Supervisor

The site supervisor is a key member of your internship team (see Chapter 8 for more details). And the site supervisor is a critical person to help you facilitate the conclusion of your internship experience. Because the internship experience is so complex, there are multiple aspects of the internship that need to be addressed. We have introduced two of them, projects and clients, in the preceding section. We provide a list of specific aspects of internship you will want to discuss with your site supervisor.

1. *Projects*—As we described earlier, review with your site supervisor all of the projects you are working on. As a way to convey information about these projects in writing, create a document similar to Table 11.1 and discuss each project with your supervisor. Together develop a transition plan.

2. *Clients*—Review with your site supervisor all of the clients you are working with. Prepare a document similar to Table 11.2 as a way to record the transition work that needs to occur prior to your departure. Develop a plan for each client.

Figure 11.3   Leaving the Internship Site: Tasks to Complete

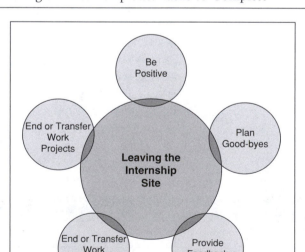

Source: Created by Gwen Ruttencutter, 2015. Used with permission.

3. *Prepare an internship to do list*—Read through your syllabus and check with your faculty supervisor to confirm the final papers, documents, and forms that you need to submit to complete your internship. Several of these may involve your site supervisor. Review these requirements with both your site supervisor and your faculty supervisor and make a plan to complete these in a timely manner (Smith & Mind Tools Team, n.d.).

4. *Be careful beginning new projects*—As you near the conclusion of your internship, you need to keep in mind the amount of time remaining. It may be tempting to begin new projects, but both you and your site supervisor should be realistic about what you can accomplish toward the end of internship.

5. *Evaluation*—Ask your site supervisor to conduct a final evaluation of your work.

Provide your site supervisor with the final evaluation form used by your academic program and faculty supervisor. Share with your site supervisor the deadline for this final evaluation. One aspect of the final evaluation is the development of a professional development plan that will articulate your strengths and next steps for growth. (You will find additional information about the internship evaluation process in Chapters 1, 6, and 8).

6. *Informal feedback to site supervisor*—We think that it is important for you to provide concrete feedback to your site supervisor, particularly with reference to the positive aspects of the internship site and supervision. You will want to take time to prepare this feedback.

We encourage you to note two or three concrete examples that illustrate the feedback you provide. For example, you may have valued the variety of clients with whom you worked, such as stating, "I really learned so much for helping so many different clients. I worked with children, teens, and adults. I also appreciate all of the different cultures my clients represented. I learned that I had to use different language when I talked with children than when I talked with adults. I also learned that many times the children were more open to me than the teens were. Working with the different cultures gave me an opportunity to be sure I asked the client to continually provide feedback about what help looks like in their cultural setting." Even though this may seem to be a lot of information to share, this type of feedback is invaluable as the supervisor prepares to work with other interns. We suggest it is more valuable for supervisors to hear a more in-depth account of one aspect of a positive internship experience, rather than learning about six aspects with little depth in any of them. To help you prepare for sharing feedback, we include Table 11.3 that you can use to prepare.

7. *Plan a farewell event*—Each agency has a culture related to saying good-bye to interns. It is appropriate to ask your site supervisor if there is a traditional way for you to say good-bye to the agency staff as a group. If there is not a tradition of leave-taking, you could bring in cookies or a small cake accompanied by a card that expresses your thanks to everyone in the agency for helping you during your time with them. As we suggested earlier, bringing in special snacks or treats to thank others for their support may be appropriate.

Table 11.3 Feedback to Supervisor: Internship Site and Supervision

Internship Site	Concrete Examples of Professional Growth
Supervision	Concrete Examples of Professional Growth

Exercise 11.1 Leaving Your Internship Site: Concluding Your Work With Your Site Supervisor

Step 1

We indicated that concluding your internship will require planning and a sense of intentionality. Make notes about the several aspects of the conclusion and describe some of your beginning plans of how you will work with your site supervisor on the following aspects of internship.

1. *Projects* _____

   _____

2. *Clients* _____

   _____

3. *Prepare an internship to-do list* _____

   _____

4. *Be careful beginning new projects* _____

   _____

5. *Evaluation* _____

   _____

6. *Informal feedback to site supervisor* _____

   _____

7. *Plan a farewell event* _____

   _____

Step 2

Use Tables 11.1 and 11.2 or a similar planning guide to record projects and clients and the transition plan for each project or client listed.

Step 3

The following three tasks relate to leaving the entire agency. Since you have worked with various staff members across the agency, it is important to think of leave-taking in broad terms.

1. *Be positive during your leave-taking.* _____

_____

_____

2. *Plan specific ways that you will say good-bye.* _____

_____

_____

3. *Provide helpful feedback to the agency.* _____

_____

_____

Now let's think about the ways that you can begin to conclude your work with clients.

Concluding Work With Clients

Traditionally, in the helping professions, we speak of the final stage of the helping process as **termination**. In this text, we refer to the end of the helping process as the **conclusion**. Concluding work with clients often occurs at the end of the internship. However, throughout the helping process there are precursors to the concluding work. There are elements of leave-taking found in the initial visit, 3 or 4 weeks before the internship concludes, and on the final meeting with the client.

The initial visit—Since interns begin their work with clients knowing that their time at their agency is limited, they should be specific about the conditions of their internship, which includes the precise amount of time they will spent working in the agency and timeline (usually related to the academic term). One vehicle for talking about their limited time and how this influences their work with the client occurs while reviewing the professional disclosure statement. In Chapter 4, we described the professional disclosure statement that interns prepare and present to their new clients during the first meeting.

A second way interns discuss the conclusion of their work with clients occurs when they talk to clients about the agency's process of delivering services. Most of the time service delivery constitutes a beginning, middle, and end. Usually service delivery represents the stages of helping introduced in Chapter 9. Clients can begin to understand that help provided by the agency is most often time-limited.

Two or 3 weeks before the internship concludes—A third way interns talk with clients about the conclusion of the helping process or their involvement as helpers begins approximately 3 or 4 weeks before the internship's end. Interns must assume the responsibility to remind their clients of the timeline for their departure and its impact on the helping process. We call this process **counting down,** and it occurs in conversations with the client. We suggest that interns refer to the counting down process at the end of their sessions with clients. This means reminding them of how many more weeks there are to work together or how many more sessions are scheduled. This fits the purpose of the close of a session as professional helper and client summarize their work together, revisit goals, and make plans for the next session. Adding a statement such as the following provides the client with a concrete number to consider: "I wanted to remind you that I will be ending my internship in 4 weeks. We meet twice a week, so that means that you and I have eight more times to work together. I will let you know each week, so we can both keep that in mind."

As interns remind clients of the end of their internships, clients may be surprised. Clients may also feel a sense of loss or feel abandoned. It is important that you share with clients the transition plan that you developed with your site supervisor for the continuity of their care.

The final meeting—During the final meetings with their clients, interns and clients together will focus on their past work together, today's work, and the future. There are several ways to approach this discussion. First, it is important to talk with clients about what they have accomplished together. Interns can help clients summarize achievements in concrete terms. Second, it is also a good time to work with clients to re-articulate client strengths. These strengths can include client beliefs, cultural traditions, positive traits, courage, hope, and positive social roles and relationships (Chan & Chan, 2008). You can revisit Chapter 9 about how to integrate strengths into the helping process.

Third, interns will want to talk with clients about their thoughts and feelings about the transition. In addition, any information interns can provide about the client's future with the agency may help reduce client fears. Fourth, helping clients construct a plan and a list of individuals they can go to if they need help when the intern is no longer available is a concrete way to prepare the client.

The final meeting—The final meeting is a time where the intern's work with the client continues. Taking time to plan the meeting is important. Here is what one plan for the final session might include:

1. Describe intern and client work together by talking about client progress and future goals.

2. Review the transition to help assume client of future help.

3. Encourage client to ask questions.

4. Intern shares with the client what he or she values from their work together.

5. Prepare prior to the meeting or during the meeting something concrete the client can take away as a reminder of the work together or in support of the client's future needs.

6. It is important to be positive throughout this transition.

Exercise 11.2 Concluding Your Work With Clients

Step 1

Concluding your work with clients requires careful planning. For each client document your efforts toward concluding your work with each. Discuss your ideas and efforts with your site supervisor. It is possible that you may use different approaches in your planning and implementation of conclusion of your work for various clients.

The initial visit _____

_____

_____

Two or 3 weeks before the internship concludes _____

_____

_____

The final meeting _____

_____

_____

Leaving the Academic Program

Many times the end of internship also represents the end of the academic program and perhaps graduation. Concluding your work with your faculty supervisor, your peers, and other faculty members is also important. Many of the same guidelines for a positive leave-taking from the internship site also apply for concluding the academic program. The following guidelines may help you conclude your academic work in a positive way.

Concluding Work With Faculty Supervisor

Completing your internship is an important part of your academic program. The following guidelines may help you conclude your academic work in a positive way.

1. *Fulfill the internship responsibilities*—Review your syllabus and make a chart that includes the assignments that you need to complete and their due dates. In Table 11.4 we present an example of what this table might look like. You will want to revise according to the requirements of your own internship class.

2. *Convey to your faculty supervisor your thoughts about internship*— As you conclude internship, you will want to communicate to your faculty supervisor the value of your internship and what you learned from the internship work.

Table 11.4   Internship Assignments and Due Dates

Internship Requirements	Due Dates and Special Instructions	Signatures Needed
Liability insurance		
Professional disclosure statement		
Internship contract		
Midterm evaluation		
Faculty supervisor visit		
Case notes		
Weekly personal reflections or writing your story assignments		
Weekly taping		
Case study presentation		
Written case study		
Final evaluation		
Weekly log		
Term summary of hours		
Evaluation of site and supervision		

Concluding Your Work With the Academic Program

Part of your leave-taking is completing your work in your academic program. During the final term, you will conclude your long-term commitment to your education and preparation as a human service professional. The following guidelines will help you leave the program in a positive way. Some of the actions you take are similar to those suggested for leaving your internship site.

1. *Fulfill the requirements of the academic program*—Many academic programs require students take a comprehensive exam, an oral exam, or write a paper about their professional development in the program. Other programs may require students to participate in an exit interview or a focus group designed to provide the faculty information about how to improve their human service program. In addition, there may be forms that need to be submitted to the undergraduate or graduate school. Make a list of the program requirements and the dates the tasks or written work is due.

2. *Endorsement*—Depending upon your program, you may need to fill out forms or sign up and take examinations for certification or licensure. Gather relevant information for these tasks.

3. *Provide helpful feedback to the program*—If your academic program asks you to provide information about the strengths and the limitations of the program, prepare the feedback you give with care. Be sure to balance positive feedback with the more critical feedback. Be sure to provide concrete examples to support any statements you give.

4. *Plan specific ways that you will say good-bye*—You will use the same process to plan your leave-taking in your academic program as you did in your internship.

5. *Be positive during your leave-taking*—Focus on the positive as you conclude your academic program (Smith & Mind Tools Team, n.d.). Even if your experiences were uneven and include both positive and negative experiences, take time to share what you learned and how aspects of the academic program supported your professional development.

6. *Provide formal feedback about site supervisors*—Some faculty supervisors may ask interns to formally evaluate the quality and characteristics of their internship site and the quality and characteristics of the supervision they received. Many times human service program faculty members use this information to help plan future internship sites. Similar to providing information feedback to site supervisors, the more helpful evaluations provide specific examples related to the site and the supervision. For example, if you as an intern rate the supervision as "excellent," be prepared to provide concrete reasons as to why you rate the supervision as such. Your experience of the supervisor might have been positive because "the supervisor met with me at a regular time every week," "began every morning helping me plan my day," and "listened to my opinions about clients and their issues and possible interventions."

Concluding Your Work With Internship Peers

Very often students in a human service academic program form strong personal and professional bonds. The very nature of human service education and training encourages the development of such relationships. Students enter a human service program with many common values and goals, and then together they experience intense self-reflection and self-disclosure. Also, they support each other during their educational and internship experiences. Students often express excitement as they conclude their academic program, and also express regret to be leaving their fellow students. Here are some ways that you may say good-bye to your peers and plan to keep in touch.

1. *Acknowledge the powerful influence your peers have had on your personal and professional development.* If, in your experience, your peers have played a primary role in your personal and professional development, plan ways to share this with them. You might ask your faculty supervisor to allow time in a final class for peers to share with each other the differences they have made. Written acknowledgement or thank-you notes to peers whose relationship you value help you express your thanks in a meaningful way.

2. *Find ways to celebrate the conclusion of the academic program.* The end of the academic program is a good time to plan a social event to celebrate an end of a program, or perhaps graduation. Finding a time to come together informally marks the end of a meaningful experience.

3. *Establish ways to continue to network and support each other.* In these days of social media and professional use of electronic media, it is easy to plan to stay in touch. Make sure you have contact information

for your peers, especially those with whom you have a special bond. Some peers establish a social media site to share both personal and professional information and ask for support.

In the next exercise, Exercise 11.3, you have the opportunity to plan how you will conclude your work with your academic program.

Exercise 11.3 Concluding Your Work With Your Academic Program, Writing Your Own Story, Entry 31

In this exercise you will plan how you will conclude your academic program. This includes work with your faculty supervisor, your academic program, and your peers. Make notes about your plans about your leave-taking. Use the guidelines we present as a way to begin your planning.

Faculty supervisor _____

_____

_____

Academic program _____

_____

_____

Peers _____

_____

_____

For many interns, the conclusion of internship also marks a final term and graduation. It is a time to seek employment as a human service professional. In the following section, we help you prepare for the job search. Box 11.2 describes the organizational framework of the section focused on preparing for the job search.

Box 11.2 Studying the Text: Preparing for the Job Search

Studying the text: The following outline will help you read and study the text material in this next section.

Preparing for the job search

1. Introduction
2. Developing your professional portfolio
3. Asking for references

Preparing for the Job Search

In most human service academic programs, the internship is one of the culminating experiences in becoming a professional. Once graduated, the next steps are looking for and then finding employment. Although we do not guide you through the entire job search process, in this section, we do help you with two aspects that are directly related to your internship and that are important to searching for and gaining employment. We explain how creating a professional **portfolio** and obtaining **references** will help you in your job search. Before we describe the process of developing your professional portfolio, we ask human service students to talk about how they prepared for searching for jobs in Box 11.3.

Box 11.3 What Students Say: Reflections on Beginning to Search for Employment

Can you describe when you first started thinking about looking for human service positions?

Steve: I have a wife and a son. We are expecting our second baby in 3 months. I guess looking for employment is always on my mind.

Maria: The whole employment thing, well, it caught me by surprise. I was working so hard in my internship and then all of my peers started asking me where I thought I would end up working after graduation. So I am thinking about it now. Maybe I am a little bit late.

Al: I always hoped that I could just stay at my internship. I have told my site supervisor that I would be happy to work with her. She is checking into possibilities. I know that they really like my work in internship.

Shasha: I am in internship now but I don't graduate until next semester. I want to go ahead and get a job and then use that job as an internship. I am going to ask my faculty supervisor if that is a possibility.

What are the steps you are taking to look for employment?

Steve: We are working in my internship class to understand the job seeking process in the human service field. Right now we are writing cover letters and resumes. And we have been developing a portfolio since our first class, so I am adding to it with examples of my work from internship.

Maria: My situation is a little bit different from my peers. I want to move so I can be near my family, and they live in another part of the country. I looked for jobs when I went home for the holidays. It was discouraging. But I also have several people who live in my hometown looking for me. I am working on my list of references right now.

(Continued)

> (Continued)
>
> **Al:**   I have lots of work experience. I called the three supervisors I had before I came back to school. They had asked me to do this. I also went to the career center here at school. I had a meeting and attended a class—both on resume writing. I am taking a class on interviewing next week.
>
> **Shasha:** My site supervisor is helping me think about employment. She asked me if I wanted her to be a reference for me and I said yes. I am so grateful, I almost cried.

Developing Your Professional Portfolio

Constructing a professional **portfolio** is a way to document what you have learned and to describe your actual work. The ultimate goal of the field-based learning is preparation for the world of work in human services. The content of the portfolio reflects the day-to-day activities in internship and its concluding outcomes. These outcomes include (a) describing your professional self and (b) demonstrating the knowledge and skills you use in your work. Let's look at the definition and purpose of the portfolio and how it can help you gain employment as a human service professional.

Simply stated, a portfolio is a documentation of your career accomplishments. In this case, it represents your experiences and accomplishments as a student in human services. This collection of documents allows readers to review examples of your knowledge, interest, skills, and outcomes. In some sense, a portfolio is a window into the type and quality of your work. It may include several papers and projects you prepared for courses and assignments that demonstrate your knowledge and skills. During your internship experience, you will have collected materials related to activities and tasks that you completed for your clients and your agency.

How can a portfolio help you in your search for employment? At the conclusion of your internship, you will be able to use the portfolio to show your readiness to work as a human service professional. Because the portfolio is in a written format, it becomes a way you can share with potential employers some specific examples of your work. While cover letters and resumes provide snapshots of who you are as a professional and as a person, sharing portfolio information with potential employers allows them a more in-depth view of your skills and abilities. For example, in a resume or cover letter you can indicate your experience conducting intake interviews with clients. In a portfolio you can include a mock report of an intake interview or an example of client case conceptualization. Also, if a portfolio is prepared carefully, you can also demonstrate an ability to organize information and to attend to detail.

One use of the portfolio is to distinguish yourself from the other applicants. First, you stand out because of the time you invested to create the portfolio. Second, rather than just presenting yourself as a graduate in human services, you present your unique accomplishments. Employers can more easily see your personal and professional characteristics.

Building Your Portfolio: The Specifics

Building a portfolio is both a personal and a professional activity. In a sense, you are developing illustrations of the various aspects of your professional identity. Perhaps you have already begun to construct your portfolio. If you have, then use the information in this chapter to help you continue your work. If you are just beginning to build a portfolio, you can use this information as a way to make decisions about portfolio format and content. There are excellent resources on the Internet that provide guidelines for portfolio building. We adapted those provided by the Guilford Technical Community College (2014) and UNCF Special Programs Corporation (2015). We list a few key decisions you must make early in the portfolio building and suggest an organizational format.

Key Decisions

1. **Hard copy or electronic?** Determine if you are going to develop a **hard-copy portfolio** or an **electronic portfolio** or both.

There are good reasons to choose either one of these formats (Wise Geek, 2014). The hard-copy portfolio you can share with employers when you visit an agency or interview at the physical site. Also a hard copy is easy to handle, does not require any equipment to access, can be assembled without technology savvy, is less able to be corrupted, and resembles the actual work product. Creating an electronic portfolio also provides benefits. It is easily shared with others online, allows a wide distribution, provides an example of skills using technology, includes creative options such as video, and is easy to revise.

2. **The look?** Once you decide whether to create a hard copy or an electronic portfolio, you can determine the *look* of the work. For a hard-copy portfolio, you make decisions about binder, paper, and cover. You might consider creating a disk for potential employers to review during your interview, or to leave after a job interview. For the electronic portfolio, considerations include website title and background. You want the website to be easy to navigate. If you use visuals, you want to use only a few. You want a portfolio that is simple, clean, and easy to read.

3. **The contents?** Next you want to determine the contents in your portfolio and its organizational structure. We suggest you make an outline of what you wish to include as follows:

- Professional documentation such as cover letter, resume, professional licenses, and professional training
- Evidence of your professional work you already have created (e.g., from former classes, other internships, or work experiences)
- Documents you anticipate you will create or begin to develop (e.g., professional disclosure statement, sample case studies, intake reports, individual or group activities, and presentations)

4. **The organization of materials?** Once you list the materials or documents you want to include in your portfolio, you can begin to organize this information. We suggest a possible format.

- Cover, title page, table of contents (we call this "front matter")
- Cover letter, resume, letters of references
- Documents and samples of internship, work experience, and volunteer experiences
- Documents related to academic work

The following exercise will help you evaluate your current portfolio and/or help you begin to develop one.

Exercise 11.4 Portfolio Building: Writing Your Own Story, Entry 32

In this exercise you will follow the guidelines described in the last section, *Building Your Portfolio: The Specifics*. You will make some key decisions related to the portfolio—either to begin your portfolio work or to evaluate your current portfolio efforts. Just follow the steps that are listed here:

1. **Hard copy or electronic?** Determine if you are going to develop a hard-copy portfolio or an electronic portfolio and describe your reasons for your choice.

    _____

    _____

    _____

2. **The look?** Determine for a hard-copy folder a choice of binder, paper, and cover. For electronic portfolio, include website title and background. Describe how you want to achieve a clear and straightforward look.

    _____

    _____

    _____

3. **The contents?** List what you wish to include. (See earlier description for ideas that reflect your education and internship). Be as specific as you can.

    _____

    _____

    _____

4. **The organization of materials?** Describe the organizational framework. Begin to collect the information and determine where each artifact will be placed. You can use Table 11.5 to help you organize the work.

Once you begin your portfolio planning and development, you will want to share your efforts with others and ask for their feedback. Your site and faculty supervisors and peers can help you from time to time in evaluating your work. It is important to seek continuous feedback about how you present yourself. As you move beyond the first two weeks of internship, the numbers of opportunities you have to develop and demonstrate your

Table 11.5 Organization of Portfolio Materials

Category	Specific Document	Completed

professional skills will increase. One question to keep constantly in mind is "How am I developing my portfolio so that it documents and showcases my experience and work?" Also, be sure to spell-check the portfolio and ask peers to proofread it.

Asking for References

As you think about searching for employment, you will most likely be locating available jobs for which you qualify and are interested in, writing cover letters, constructing resumes, and of course, building your portfolio. One component of the employment process is identifying individuals you believe will be willing to serve as a reference for you. As you consider your possible **references**, let's look at the purpose of identifying references and the function they serve in the employment process.

When employers are hiring professional staff, they gather multiple sources of information about the job applicant they are considering. For instance, employers or human service resource staff review cover letters and resumes, conduct Skype and live interviews, and in many instances, ask candidates to perform tasks that demonstrate the skills needed for the job in question. Another important source of information about a job applicant comes from references. Information gained from a reference, either by phone call, letter, or survey, allows employers to learn more about the job applicant. Employers learn about candidates' past job experiences and responsibilities, strengths and weaknesses, job accomplishments, and expectations from their work and the work environment.

We provide you with descriptions of the types of information that employers might want to gather from a reference, and it may include the following:

- Job applicant's position? Responsibilities?
- Job applicant's attitude about work?
- Job applicant's ability to collaborate?
- Job applicant's strengths and limitations?
- One aspect of job applicant's work that was exceptional?
- Areas where the job applicant might need support?
- Ability of job applicant to work under stress and pressure?
- Willingness of job applicant to demonstrate initiative?
- Job applicant's response to evaluation? Critical feedback?
- Ways that job applicant is a good match for the position? Poor match?
- Would you hire the job applicant for the position?

Since the references you choose can influence the employment process, it is important for you to think carefully about the individuals you will ask to serve as a reference. The following suggestions will help you choose references and prepare them for a reference phone call or survey.

<u>Choose carefully</u>—Because employers will want detailed information about your work experience and your abilities, you need to choose individuals who are familiar with and appreciate your work. In determining a list of five references, you may want to provide a mix of individuals from your academic program, volunteer experiences, work experiences, and internship site. If your references are to support your search for employment, then they must be able to answer most of the questions that employers will ask.

<u>Construct a professional request</u>—Once you have chosen potential references, then you will want to develop a strategy for requesting their help. You can make the initial request in person, by phone, or by e-mail. In the conversation, whatever the medium, you would want to tell potential references you are searching for employment and ask if they would be willing to serve as a reference. Then you want to provide them with the reasons you are asking them to help you. And you want to let them know you understand that serving as a reference represents a considerable amount of their time and effort. You will also plan to confirm with them before you list them as a reference. Additionally, you will provide them with detailed information about your professional knowledge, skill, and experience.

Provide your references background information—There are several ways that you can help prepare the individuals who agree to serve as a reference for you. First, when an individual you identified consents to serve as a reference, it is important to send (a) a follow-up note of thanks for agreeing to serve as a reference and (b) send a copy of a sample cover letter and your resume.

Second, it is a good idea to write a description of yourself that your references can use during a reference interview or in a written letter of reference to talk about your work. The purpose of this description is to provide them with insights about your strengths and concrete ways that your work reflects these strengths. What follows is a two-step process you can use to prepare this information.

Step 1

List three or four strengths that you would like your references to speak about with any potential employers. Next, ask a couple of your peers, who know you well to name three or four strengths they have observed during your time together in the academic program. From your initial list and theirs, choose three strengths.

Step 2

For each of the strengths, provide a set of three concrete examples that demonstrate the strengths. Use examples from your work in class, your volunteer work, and your work in internship. Provide details for each of the examples you choose to describe. To illustrate, one of your strengths might be that you have a strong work ethic. Here is what a description of a strong work ethic might look like.

I have a strong work ethic.

- *During the last 2 years of school, I have attended school full-time, held a 30-hour a week job, and volunteered at the local Boys and Girls Club. I work hard to perform well in each of these sites.*
- *I try to do more than is expected of me. For example, at my internship site, I created a project to collect clothing for the children of our clients. At school, I volunteered to serve as secretary for our honor society. I added to those responsibilities by sending out a monthly newsletter to all members and faculty.*
- *In most classes I wrote my papers early so that I could receive feedback from my professors. Once I received a grade, rather than putting the paper aside, I would make an appointment with my professor to understand the feedback needed for improvement, and then rewrite the paper.*

You can see from this example, this type of information can help those who serve as your references learn even more about you and your work.

Inform references of your employment process—It is good to provide your references a list of agencies where you will seek employment. You could also share with your references a description of each of the agencies and the job descriptions of the positions you are seeking. You will also want to let references know the specific ways each of the agencies will interact with them. Some agencies will follow-up with a phone call, while others may send out electronic surveys.

Some agencies will ask for letters of reference. If this is the case, you will need to provide to each of your references the format requested for the written letter and the submission process. If a hard-copy of a letter is requested, provide your references with a stamped and addressed envelope. If the letter is to be submitted electronically, provide the e-mail address and the point of contact.

As you move through the process of seeking employment, keep your references informed of each application you submit. Finally, many agencies conduct interviews just prior to offering a candidate a job. Once you know a reference call will be made, let your reference know. This allows the individual providing the reference time to prepare for the interview.

Follow-up and provide thanks—Once you receive a job offer and accept it, it is appropriate to thank each of the individuals who served as references. The thank-you can be in many forms: face-to-face communication, personal thank-you note, or e-mail. Individuals who agree to become a reference commit considerable time and effort to help you through the employment process. Choose a way of giving thanks that honors their efforts.

Exercise 11.5 The Job Search and References

Searching for employment and keeping up with the details of the process can be challenging. You might want to use Table 11.6 or develop a spreadsheet to document the details of the process.

Table 11.6 The Job Search Process

Agency	Contact Notes	Materials Sent	Interaction With References	Notes From Interview	Reflections on Job

Our concluding section of Chapter 11 allows us to hear final remarks from Alicia, Lucas, and Tamika, as well as Dr. Bianca, Ms. Bellewa, and Gwen, a human service professional.

Box 11.4 Deepening Your Understanding

1. Peer-to-peer dialogue

   a. Alicia: Concluding the internship

   b. Lucas: Concluding the internship

   c. Tamika: Concluding the internship

2. Faculty and site supervisor dialogue

   a. Dr. Bianca: Helping students conclude the internship

   b. Ms. Bellewa: A special ending

3. The professional voice and tips for practice: Gwen: Finding the right job

4. Terms to remember

5. References

Deepening Your Understanding

We now turn to our peer-to-peer dialogues and see how Alicia, Lucas, Tamika, Dr. Bianca, Ms. Bellewa, and Gwen share their perspectives. Alicia, Lucas, and Tamika describe how they conclude their internships. Dr. Bianca and Ms. Bellewa talk about what it is like to work with interns at the end of their internship and at the conclusion of their academic program. Gwen provides tips about how to know when a job is right for you.

Peer-to-Peer Dialogue: Alicia, Lucas, and Tamika

We asked Alicia, Lucas, and Tamika to talk about their experiences as they conclude their internship. They all end their stories with wishing you well!

Alicia

Greetings for the final time! Congratulations on making it to the end of your internship. This is, certainly, a joyful time. Throughout my internship, I kept a portfolio of my experiences. In class each week, Dr. Lynn focused on a new aspect of the portfolio, including initial contract, goals statements, evaluations, case studies, etc. Upon the conclusion of the semester, we are presenting our portfolios to the entire class. I am looking forward to this, as I am proud of my site and appreciative of the progress I made during this semester of training. I feel the other counselors at the Department of Human Services, along with my peers in class, are part of my academic family. This experience, as outlined by my portfolio, had a significant impact on me, not only as a helping professional, but as a human. We are also finalizing our resumes, building reference lists, and applying for jobs beyond graduation. My references are Dr. Lynn, Dr. Davis, and Dr. Stevens. I feel confident about my ability to secure a human services position in one of the local agencies as a case manager. I must say I am so excited to move forward and begin the next chapter of my life. While it hasn't been easy for me to do this as a single mother, I am thankful for all the support I received from both my own family and my academic family. I can't say I ever found the balance between being a student, having a job and raising my son, but I know I worked hard at it. It won't get easier as I begin a new job, but I am thankful for the opportunity to grow and develop both for myself and my son.

Written by Allie Rhinehart and Dareen Basma, 2015. Used with permission.

Lucas

Well I must say, internship has been an emotional roller coaster for me, but to be honest, I had many positives during internship. After reflecting on my time at the Tampa Bay Justice Center, the most emotional time for me was concluding the internship. Not only did I invest time and energy at my internship site with my site supervisor and the people that work there, I developed positive relationships with my clients. As part of leaving Tampa Bay Justice Center, I had to plan for termination with my clients. Termination consisted of telling my clients and the Tampa Bay Justice Center of my ending date. I told them a month before and then reminded them every week. I could tell my clients were getting emotional each week when I would remind them because they would say things like "Can you please stay longer?" "Can I see you at another facility?" I had to remind them of the importance of termination and then process our time together, from a positive perspective. Most important, what I did with my clients, is help them transition to another counselor, while making it fun and exciting, and discussing the importance of transitions in life. This was not only emotional for my clients, but for me too, so I opened up to them about how I felt, which normalized their feelings.

Another part of concluding the internship, besides terminating with clients, is making sure I have all my notes completed, evaluation forms filled out, and then a final supervision session with my supervisor and full-time counselors. When I completed all my notes and documentation at the Tampa Bay Justice Center, I had my last meeting with my site supervisor and full-time counselors. The meeting consisted of feedback on my development as a counselor, feedback on my experiences at the Tampa Bay Justice Center, and then they asked me how they could help me with my future goals in the helping profession. I really enjoyed the last session because it was a good time to evaluate my progress, but also to talk about my concerns, if I had any, which I did not. After our last meeting, my site supervisor and full-time counselors told me they would serve as references, and they even helped me develop an outline for my portfolio. They told me to add my education, credentials, resume, and work experience at Tampa Bay Justice Center, and recommended to me to provide sample intake documents and treatment plans that I did during internship.

Overall, concluding internship was very emotional for me, and will be for you too. One thing I learned is that termination is not a bad thing, but a normal stage in any relationship. My site supervisor said if you can model healthy termination, then clients will have an easier time transitioning in life due to observing a healthy and positive termination.

Good luck with internship, and enjoy termination, it is a great experience!

Written by Jorge Roman, 2015. Used with permission.

Tamika

Well, here I am at the end of my internship and what a journey it has been! I cannot believe how quickly my time at the justice center has gone, and I am really sad to leave behind the clients and colleagues I've worked with over the past several months. I have grown so much during this experience, both personally and professionally, and really have developed a strong sense of what I want to do with my life. What an exciting thing to be able to say!

I've been terminating with my clients over the past couple of weeks, and I think it's been a difficult process for everyone involved—especially me! Some of my clients' cases are nearing completion, so it's nice to leave knowing that they've worked hard during our time together and will hopefully go on to make healthy choices and live happy, productive lives! These cases feel like they're coming to a more natural end, and although I'm sad to conclude my work with these clients, I feel at peace with it. I do have a couple of clients who are still very much in the midst of their personal struggles, though, and it's these clients I feel most unsettled about leaving. I have worked hard with them to collaboratively develop thorough transition plans, however, and they'll all be placed with really great counselors and case workers at the justice center to help them continue their work. Knowing this makes leaving just a little bit easier.

As I look toward the future, I know that I really want to continue my work within the corrections system and I have decided to apply for a couple of human service positions open at a nearby women's prison. This internship experience has taught me so much about the field of human services and has really solidified my passion for working with this particular population. Also, because of the great supervision I received throughout my time at the justice center, I would love to eventually become a clinical supervisor, once I have the appropriate certification. Overall, I have really enjoyed my internship experience, and, though it's been challenging at times, I wouldn't change any part of it, because I have learned such a tremendous amount. Thanks so much for traveling this journey with me—and best of luck in your own professional endeavors!

Written by Brittany Pollard, 2015. Used with permission.

Faculty and Site Supervisor Dialogue: Dr. Bianca and Ms. Bellewa

Dr. Bianca and Ms. Bellewa share with us their perspectives about how to conclude an internship. Each has good insights for viewing the process.

Dr. Claude Bianca

I have taught the internship in human services for several years. I usually teach the course in the spring. This is also a typical time when students plan to graduate. So, in this spring internship, I have a class full of students who are ending both their internship experience and their academic experience. These interns go about their internship with much seriousness of purpose. Since they can see employment in the near future, they want to learn all that they can before they begin looking for jobs and assuming full-time responsibility for the care of clients. We use the internship contract as a way that students can structure their internships. This helps both them and their supervisors plan internship roles and responsibilities. But we also develop a chart that records each intern's dreams and hopes and strategies they will use to attain these. This is not part of an assignment. Rather it gives interns an opportunity to talk more about their aspirations. They can bring their emotions and creativity as they envision a future. The hopes and dreams also provide for the students an umbrella for the various internship responsibilities they assume. Thinking about hopes and dreams also allows interns to directly connect internship with their transition to work as a human service professional. Here is what the hopes and dreams table looks like in Table 11.7.

We include the hopes and dreams table in our class agenda. This means students are regularly reminded of their aspirations. About every 3 weeks, we spend some time looking at our hopes and dreams and noting progress.

By the middle of the term, most of the students who are enrolled in their final internship experience are performing their work at an advanced level. They have confidence in their abilities, are willing to assume more difficult challenges, and are functioning as one of the staff, rather than just an intern. In addition, their supervisors are indicating the interns' readiness for full-time employment. During the final month of internship, interns assume a dual focus. They are intensely involved at their site. At the same time, they are spending time and energy preparing to search for employment. We spend quite a bit of time during the last half of the term, both developing advanced skills and learning how to conclude their internship and prepare for seeking employment.

I treasure this experience with interns who are concluding their academic program. I believe that it is an honor to observe and support students in the transition from beginning an internship experience to graduating and assuming full-time employment!

Table 11.7   Intern Hopes and Dreams

Student	Supervisor	Hopes and Dreams	Skills
Sharon Brown sbrown@network.com Cell phone number	Justin Santiago JSantiago@agency.com Agency address Phone number	See this experience as a novel experience. See it with fresh eyes—open to anything. Skills: Classroom management. More assertive.	Learn to be more assertive. Take initiative.
Cindy Pulaski pulaski@network.com	Victoria DeMenti DeMenti@agency.com Agency address Phone number	Work with lots of different staff at the agency. Learn to collaborate in the community.	I am quiet. Feel more comfortable getting to know others. Volunteer to take on more responsibility and learn new skills.

Ms. Zu Bellewa

The end of the internship experience is always an emotional time for students as they work through feelings of possible sadness over terminating work with some of their clients, excitement about starting a new chapter in their life, and feelings of anticipation about what's to come. Often times, our work requires us to develop a relationship with others. Even more so, our field demands that we build relationships with individuals who are often times vulnerable and in dire need of our support. As we work towards the growth and development of our clients, we forget that we too grow and develop from that relationship. While much of my role as their site supervisor involves making sure that their clients are transitioned to someone else or are properly terminated, another component of my role involves focusing on the present and allowing the interns to process the loss of the relationship they built with their clients.

Another part of my role as students near the end of their internship experience is to review the contract that we had developed together when they first started. In doing so, we have a chance to address the goals that were initially developed, the progress that was made in achieving those goals, and the work that needs to be continued. I like to end my supervision meetings with the development of new goals for them to have as they move forward with their work. While I won't be there to support them as they work towards these goals, I hope that they will use them to continue their exploration of self and development of the skills they utilize in their work.

Written by Dareen Basma, 2015. Used with permission.

The Professional Voice and Tips for Practice: Gwen

Gwen

Marianne asked me to talk with you about the importance of not only finding a job, but also of finding one that is right for you. There are several questions that you can ask that will help you look for jobs in which you are interested. In addition, these questions may help you decide what information you need from your perspective employer before you interview or accept a job offer. Your past experience may provide some ideas about the kind of work you like and the environment in which you like to work. And your experience in internship may provide you valuable insights into both work responsibility and work environment. We suggest a few things for you to consider as you began your search for employment.

1. *About You—What type of work will bring you satisfaction? Work that encourages*
   - *Creativity*
   - *Initiative*
   - *Variety*
   - *Orientation to detail*
   - *Independence*
   - *Structure*
   - *Collaboration*
   - *Competition*
   - *Hierarchy*

2. *Work Opportunities—Work that offers these professional benefits*
   - *Professional growth*
   - *Advancement*
   - *Leadership*
   - *Career ladder*
   - *Stability*
   - *Time flexibility*
   - *24/7*
   - *Stable work hours*

I suggest that you review these factors in light of your experiences with other jobs and with your internship and consider how important these factors are to you. Although completing this activity is not intended to address all of the many factors involved in making a decision about whether to pursue or accept a job, it will help you begin your thinking about it.

Good luck as you conclude your internship and move into the human service system. I wish you well!

Terms to Remember

Conclusion

Counting down

Electronic portfolio

Four stages of internship

Hard-copy portfolio

Leave-taking

Portfolio

References

Termination

References

Chan, E. Y. K., & Chan, K. (2008). *Strengths-based perspective in working with clients with mental illness: A Chinese cultural articulation.* New York, NY: Nova Science.

Guilford Technical Community College. (2014). *How to make a career portfolio.* Retrieved from https://www.gtcc.edu/media/38323/gtcccareerportfolioguide .pdf

Smith, C., & The Mind Tools Team. (n.d.). A happy ending: Wrapping up your current role before moving on. Retrieved from http://www.mindtools.com/pages/ article/newCDV_43.htm

UNCF Special Programs Corporation. (2015). *Developing your professional portfolio.* Retrieved from https://workspace.imperial.ac.uk/electricalengineering/ Public/Resource_ProfPortfolio_2012.pdf

Wise Geek. (2014). Creating a writing portfolio. Retrieved from http://www .wisegeekedu.com/what-is-a-writing-portfolio.htm

Index